INSTRUCTOR'S RESOURCE MANUAL
(Containing detailed Solutions and Supplementary Tests)

for

STATISTICS AND

PROBABILITY IN

MODERN LIFE

Fifth Edition

BY JOSEPH NEWMARK

The College of Staten Island
of
The City University of New York

SAUNDERS COLLEGE PUBLISHING

Harcourt Brace Jovanovich College Publishers

Fort Worth Philadelphia San Diego New York Orlando Austin

San Antonio Toronto Montreal London Sydney Tokyo

Printed in the United States of America.

Newmark: Instructor's Manual to accompany STATISTICS AND PROBABILITY
IN MODERN LIFE, 5/E

ISBN 0-03-076297-9

234 095 987654321

TABLE OF CONTENTS

ANSWERS TO EXERCISES FOR CHAPTER 1

SECTION 1.5 - (PAGES 12-14)

1. Although it should be descriptive only, in reality it is used as both descriptive and inferential statistics.

2. Choice (d)

3. a) Sex, eye color, etc...
   b) Number of brothers or sisters that each college student has, etc...
   c) Weight or height of each college student, etc...

4. a) Attribute data
   b) Discrete numerical data
   c) Continuous numerical data

5. a) The part that indicates that the number of Americans over 65 years of age increased by 6.3% over last year at this time.
   b) The part that predicts that by the end of the century approximately 25% of the American population will be over 65 years of age.

6. Choice (b) since it involves a prediction about the future.

7. Not necessarily. Other factors have to be considered.

8. No. Ad does not specify "50% closer to what".

9. Not necessarily. The subscribers might have been healthy anyway, without the vitamin C.

10. No

TESTING YOUR UNDERSTANDING OF THIS CHAPTER'S CONCEPTS - (PAGES 15-16)

1. No. The 10% increase represents 10% on a lower base pay.

2. It indicates past performance and possibly represents a prediction of future performance.

3. Not necessarily. Other factors have to be considered.

4. Not necessarily. Other factors have to be considered.

5. No. Sample is likely to be nonrepresentative of the population.

1

ANSWERS TO THINKING CRITICALLY - (PAGES 16-17)

1. No

2. Not necessarily; there may not be many dolphins left.

3. No. Sample is likely to be nonrepresentative of the population.

5. No

6. No

ANSWERS TO REVIEW EXERCISES FOR CHAPTER 1 - (PAGES 17-19)

1. Choice (d). The conclusion involves statistical inference.

2. The part that states that the blood levels at the various hospitals stood at 20% of their normal levels and that 837 pints of blood were donated last week.

3. The part that claims that the drop in blood donations is due to the fear of AIDS and that the findings have far-reaching implications for those individuals needing surgery.

4. Choice (d)

5. No. There are less cars on the road.

6. Statistics seem to indicate that this conclusion may be valid for many illnesses.

7. True

8. True

9. True

10. No

ANSWERS TO CHAPTER TEST - (PAGES 19-22)

1. No

2. Not necessarily; there may be less highway patrol officers.

3. **a)** Statistical inference.
   b) Descriptive statistics
   c) Statistical inference

4. True

5. True

6. Not necessarily; the percentage of the population may not have increased.

7. The part that indicates that 14 of the 527 homes inspected were contaminated with radon gas.

8. The part that estimates that about 15% of the homes in the region are contaminated.

9. Not necessarily; people may be more selective of the foods they eat.

10. Not necessarily.

11. Choice (d)

12. Choice (b)

13. Choice (c)

14. Choice (b)

15. Choice (d)

1. After carefully analyzing tax returns covering the past ten years, an IRS agent claims that 7% of the rejected returns involve mathematical errors. This conclusion involves

   a) foolish statistics
   b) no statistics at all
   c) descriptive statistics
   d) inferential statistics

   Answer _____

2. What type of statistics is presented in the financial section of a newspaper, inferential or descriptive?

   Answer _____

For questions 3 - 5 use the following information which is available from a local video movie rental store.

Year	Price charged to rent movie	Usual number of movies rented daily
1988	$2.00	128
1989	$1.75	212
1990	$1.50	287
1991	$1.00	392

3. The conclusion "The usual number of movies rented daily has been increasing over the years" involves what type of statistics: statistical inference or descriptive statistics?

   Answer _____

4. The conclusion "There is a considerable difference between the number of movies rented daily when the price is $2.00 instead of $1.00" involves what type of statistics: statistical inference or descriptive statistics?

   Answer _____

5. The conclusion "Any future decrease in the price charged to rent a movie will result in an increase in the number of movies rented daily" involves what kind of statistics: statistical inference or descriptive statistics?

   Answer _____

4

1. A television commercial claims that "Our superior laundry detergent leaves laundered material 50% brighter and cleaner." Should we use this detergent on the basis of this claim?

   Answer _____

2. The set of <u>all</u> measurements of interest to the sample collector is referred to as the

   a) sample
   b) population
   c) survey
   d) hypothesis
   e) none of these

   Answer _____

3. A tax agent finds that in the first 100 tax returns reviewed, 8 of them contained mathematical errors. She concludes that the state can expect approximately 8000 of the state's 100,000 tax returns with mathematical errors. This conclusion involves

   a) parametric statistics
   b) descriptive statistics
   c) statistical inference
   d) no statistics at all

   Answer _____

4. After carefully analyzing meteorological data, several scientists have concluded that the Earth has been gradually experiencing warmer temperatures over the past 100 years. This conclusion involves

   a) parametric statistics
   b) inferential statistics
   c) descriptive statistics
   d) no statistics at all

   Answer _____

5. Refer back to the previous question. Several of the scientists have concluded that during the twenty-first century our winters will become milder and milder. This conclusion involves

   a) parametric statistics
   b) inferential statistics
   c) descriptive statistics
   d) no statistics at all

   Answer _____

CHAPTER 1 - THE NATURE OF STATISTICS
SUPPLEMENTARY TEST FORM C

1. An insurance company official claims that 90% of the company's policy holders renew their car insurance with the company when the policy expires. If we select randomly 100 of the company's car insurance policy holders, would we expect exactly 90 of them to renew their car insurance policy with the company when it expires?

   Answer _____

2. An insurance company official is analyzing the following data for a certain city.

Year	Number of reported car thefts
1982	4693
1983	4421
1984	4308
1985	4276
1986	4098

   The conclusion that "the number of reported car thefts has steadily been decreasing over the period 1982 - 1987 involves

   a) descriptive statistics only
   b) inferential statistics only
   c) both descriptive and inferential statistics
   d) neither descriptive nor inferential statistics

   Answer _____

3. A _____ is any small group of individuals or objects selected to represent the entire group.

   Answer _____

4. In 1987, the mathematics department of a mid western university consisted of two unmarried female instructors. Subsequently, one of these instructors married one of her students. Is it mathematically correct to state that 50% of the female mathematics instructors at this school marry their students?

Answer _____

5. The study of statistics was really begun by

    a) John Graunt
    b) Abraham De Moivre
    c) Pierre-Simon Laplace
    d) Carl Friedrich Gauss
    e) Karl Pearson

Answer _____

ANSWERS TO SUPPLEMENTARY TESTS
CHAPTER 1 - THE NATURE OF STATISTICS

Form A	Form B	Form C
1. Choice (c)	1. No	1. No
2. Both	2. Choice (b)	2. Choice (a)
3. Descriptive statistics	3. Choice (c)	3. Sample
4. Descriptive statistics	4. Choice (c)	4. Yes
5. Statistical inference	5. Choice (b)	5. Choice (a)

SECTION 2.2 - (PAGES 35-39)

1.

Number of Parking Tickets Issued	Tally	Frequency
23-28	ⵏ ⵏ ⵏ II	17
29-34	ⵏ ⵏ ⵏ I	16
35-40	ⵏ ⵏ ⵏ III	18
41-46	ⵏ ⵏ	10
47-52	ⵏ ⵏ	10
53-58	ⵏ II	7
59-64	ⵏ	5
65-70	ⵏ	5
71-76	ⵏ ⵏ	10
77-82	II	2
		100

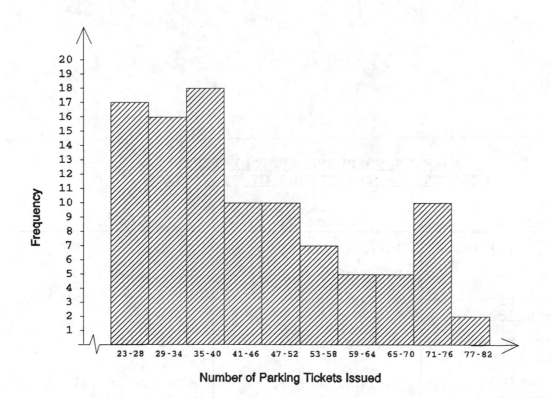

2.

Bids	Tally	Frequency
$2375-$2537	|	1
$2538-$2700		0
$2701-$2863		0
$2864-$3026		0
$3027-$3189		0
$3190-$3352	LHt LHt III	13
$3353-$3515	LHt IIII	8
$3516-$3678	LHt LHt	10
$3679-$3841	LHt IIII	9
$3842-$4004	LHt IIII	9
		50

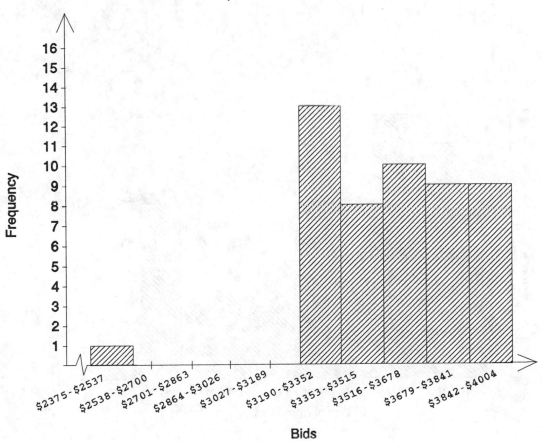

3.

Age of Applicants	Tally	Frequency
17-22	卌 I	6
23-28	卌 III	8
29-34	卌 IIII	9
35-40	III	3
41-46	卌 I	6
47-52	IIII	4
53-58	III	3
59-64	III	3
65-70	卌 I	6
71-76	II	2
		50

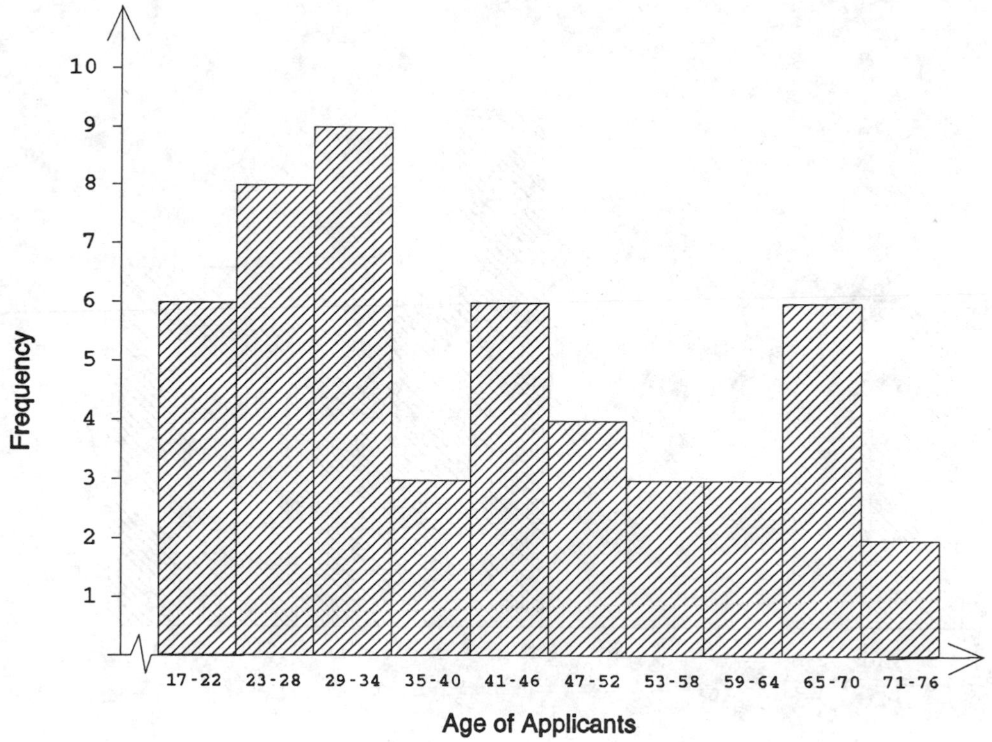

4.

Cost to Customers	Tally	Frequency
$20,000-$33,000	ⅢⅡ	5
$33,001-$46,001	IIII	4
$46,002-$59,002	II	2
$59,003-$72,003	ⅢⅡ III	8
$72,004-$85,004	ⅢⅡ IIII	9
$85,005-$98,005	III	3
$98,006-$111,006	III	3
$111,007-$124,007	III	3
$124,008-$137,008	I	1
$137,009-$151,000	IIII	4
		42

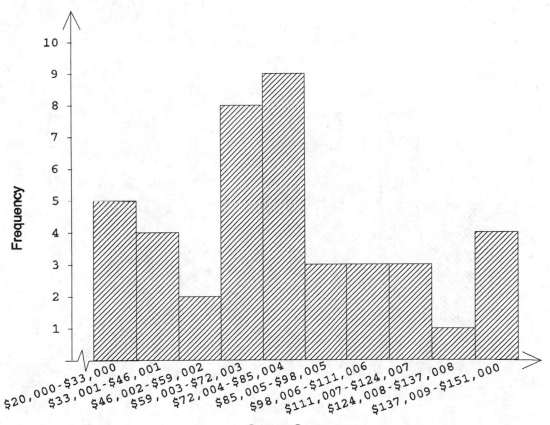

5.

Weight of Luggage	Tally	Frequency
74-80	卌 I	6
81-87	卌	5
88-94	卌 卌	10
95-101	卌	5
102-108	卌 卌	10
109-115	卌 卌 I	11
116-122	卌	5
123-129	II	2
130-136	II	2
137-144	IIII	4
		60

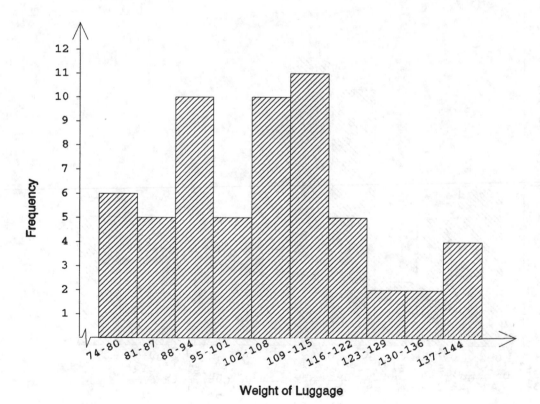

6.

Annual Energy Consumption	Tally	Frequency
114-144	|||	3
145-175		0
176-206	|||	3
207-237	||||		6
238-268	|||| ||||		11
269-299	|||| ||||	9
300-330	||||	5
331-361	||||	5
362-392	||||	5
393-423	|||	3
		50

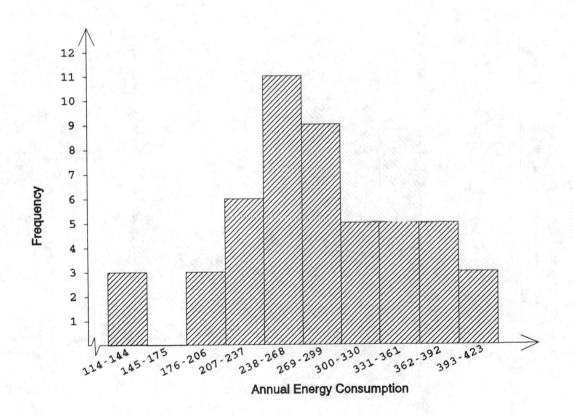

7. a) The frequency distribution using 10 classes.

Number of Pounds Collected	Tally	Frequency
12-31	||||	4
32-51	||||	4
52-71	LHT LHT	10
72-91	LHT LHT |||	13
92-111	LHT LHT |	11
112-131	LHT	5
132-151	LHT |	6
152-171	||||	4
172-191	|	1
192-211	||	2
		60

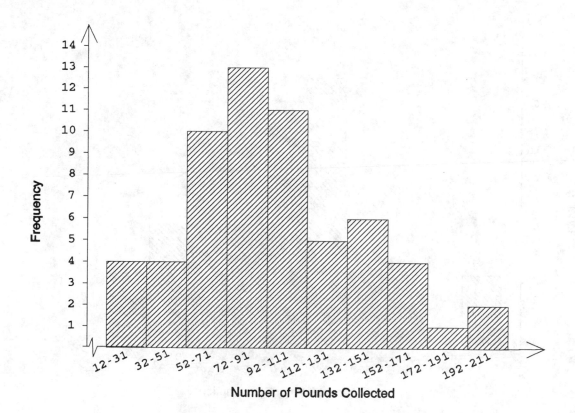

7. **b)** The frequency distribution using 5 classes.

Number of Pounds Collected	Tally	Frequency
12-51	⦀⦀ ⦀⦀⦀	8
52-91	⦀⦀⦀ ⦀⦀⦀ ⦀⦀⦀ ⦀⦀⦀ ⦀⦀⦀	23
92-131	⦀⦀⦀ ⦀⦀⦀ ⦀⦀⦀ ⦀	16
132-171	⦀⦀⦀ ⦀⦀⦀	10
172-211	⦀⦀⦀	3
		60

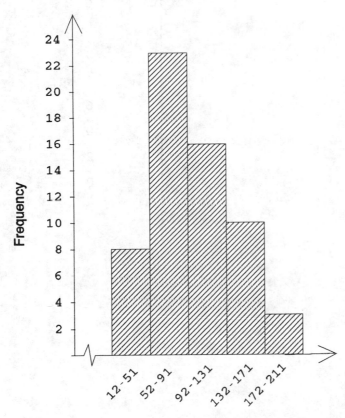

Number of Pounds Collected

7. c) The frequency distribution using 15 classes.

Number of Pounds Collected	Tally	Frequency
12-24	||	2
25-37	|||	3
38-50	|||	3
51-63	卌	5
64-76	卌 ||	7
77-89	卌 卌	10
90-102	卌 |	6
103-115	卌 ||	7
116-128	|||	3
129-141	||||	4
142-154	卌 |	6
155-167		0
168-180	||	2
181-193		0
194-206	||	2
		60

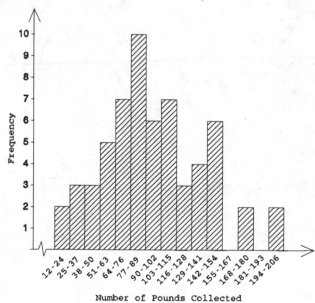

16

8. a)   Factory A

Number of Products Completed	Tally	Frequency
4-7	|||	3
8-11	|||	3
12-15	|	1
16-19	|||	3
20-23	||	2
24-27	|||	3
28-31	||||	4
32-37	|	1
		20

Factory A

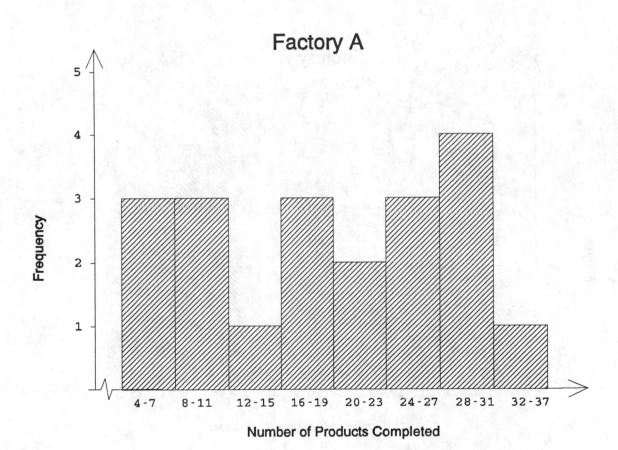

8. a) (Continued)

Factory B

Number of Products Completed	Tally	Frequency
4-7	||	2
8-11	||	2
12-15	||	2
16-19	|||	3
20-23		0
24-27	ⅲ⅟	5
28-31	||||	4
32-37	||	2
		20

Factory B

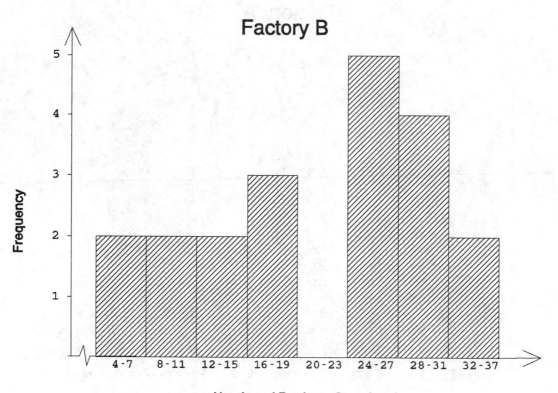

Number of Products Completed

8. b)

Number of Products Completed	Tally	Frequency
4-7	ⅬⱵ	5
8-11	ⅬⱵ	5
12-15	‖‖	3
16-19	ⅬⱵ ‖	6
20-23	‖‖	2
24-27	ⅬⱵ ‖‖‖	8
28-31	ⅬⱵ ‖‖‖	8
32-37	‖‖‖	3
		40

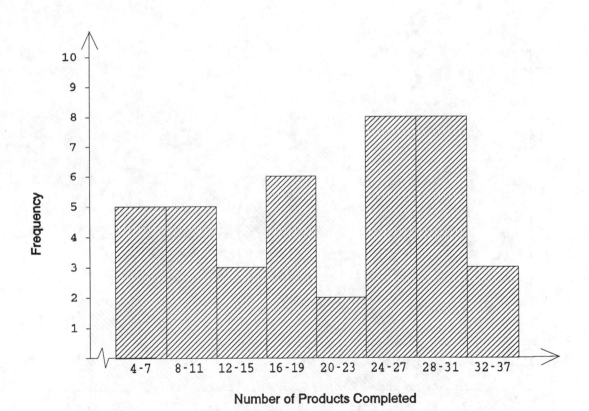

9.   a)

Number of Products Completed	Tally	Frequency
4-7		0
8-11	|	1
12-15	||	2
16-19	⊪|	6
20-23	||||	4
24-27	|	1
28-31	||||	4
32-37	||	2
		20

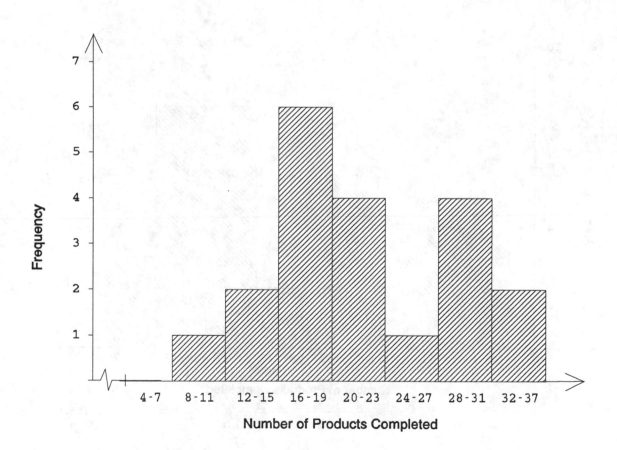

10. a)   Lanceville

Number of Summonses Issued	Tally	Frequency
5	||	2
6	|||	3
7	|||	3
8	|||	3
9	||||	4
10	|||	3
11	|||	3
12	||||	4
13	||	2
14	|||	3
		30

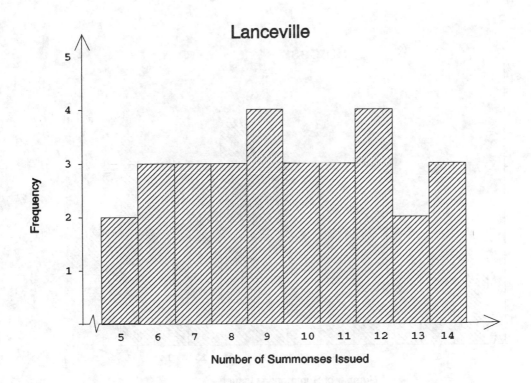

Lanceville

10. a) (Continued)   Burgess

Number of Summonses Issued	Tally	Frequency
5	||	2
6	||	2
7	||	2
8	|||	3
9	||	2
10	||	2
11	||||	4
12	|||||	5
13	|||	3
14	||	2
15	|||	3
		30

Burgess

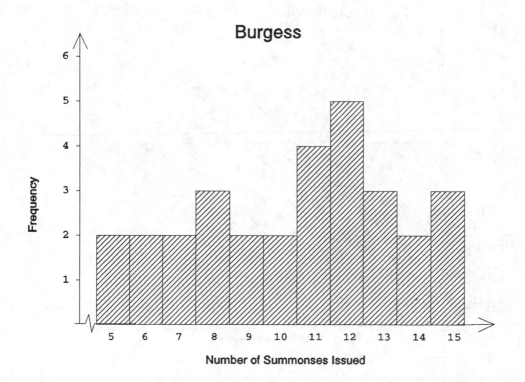

11. To avoid misinterpreting the data.

12. a)   **Jim Harris**

Number of Trees Pruned	Tally	Frequency
26.1 - 30.5	⅃⊞	5
30.6 - 35.0	‖	2
35.1 - 39.5	⅃⊞	5
39.6 - 44.0	⅃⊞	5
44.1 - 48.5	‖	2
48.6 - 53.0	‖‖‖	4
53.1 - 57.5	‖	2
57.6 - 62.0	‖	2
62.1 - 66.5	‖	2
66.6 - 70.0			1
		30

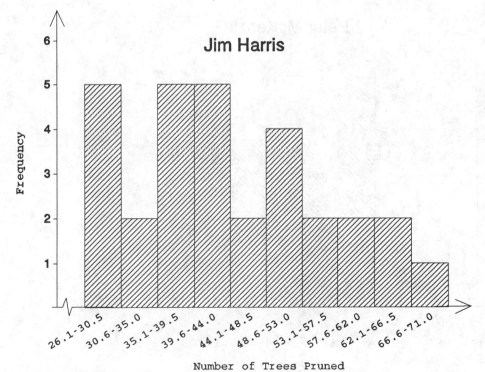

23

12. a) (Continued)

Peter McKenzie

Number of Trees Pruned	Tally	Frequency
26.1 - 30.5	||	2
30.6 - 35.0	||	2
35.1 - 39.5	||||| |||	8
39.6 - 44.0	||||	4
44.1 - 48.5	|||	3
48.6 - 53.0	|||||	5
53.1 - 57.5	||	2
57.6 - 62.0	||||	4
62.1 - 66.5		0
66.6 - 71.0		0
		30

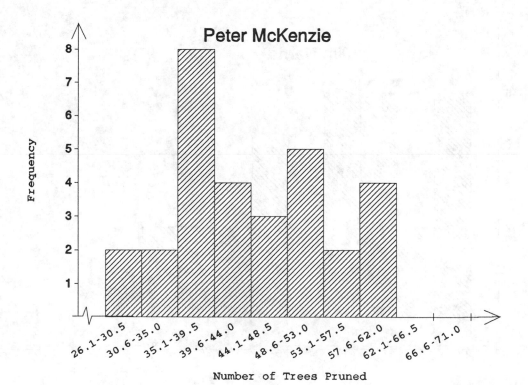

13.

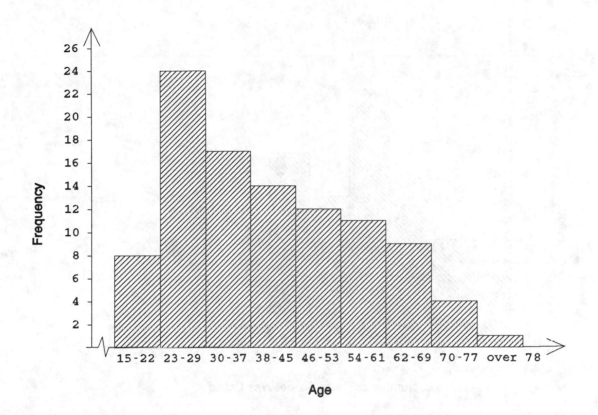

a) $\dfrac{63}{100}$ = 63%   b) $\dfrac{51}{100}$ = 51%   c) $\dfrac{43}{100}$ = 43%   d) $\dfrac{4}{100}$ = 4%

e) $\dfrac{96}{100}$ = 96%

14.

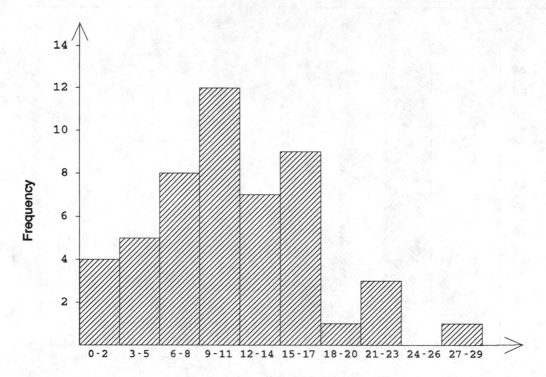

Number of Times School Was Called

a) $\dfrac{29}{50} = 58\%$ **b)** $\dfrac{5}{50} = 10\%$ **c)** $\dfrac{45}{50} = 90\%$ **d)** $\dfrac{5}{50} = 10\%$

e) $\dfrac{33}{50} = 66\%$ **f)** 0

15. a) i)

Number of Stocks	Tally	Frequency
1-6 |卌 |||	8
7-12	卌	5
13-18	卌 卌 |||	13
19-24	卌 卌 卌 ||||	19
25-30	卌	5
		50

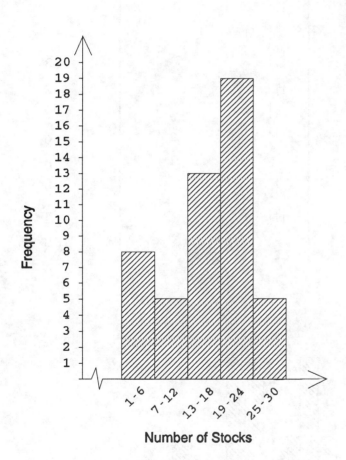

15.   *ii.*

Number of Stocks	Tally	Frequency
1-2	||	2
3-4	|||	3
5-6	|||	3
7-8	|||	3
9-10	||	2
11-12		0
13-14	|||	3
15-16	ⅢⅡ ||	7
17-18	|||	3
19-20	||	2
21-22	ⅢⅡ ||	7
23-24	ⅢⅡ ⅢⅡ	10
25-26		0
27-28	||	2
29-30	|||	3
		50

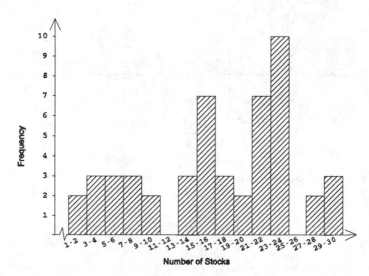

b)   When too few or too many classes are used, much information is lost, or the information that is presented is hard to interpret.

28

16. a)

Number of Minutes Before Scheduled Departure	Tally	Frequency	Relative Frequency
7-15	||	2	$\frac{2}{50}$
16-24	|||	3	$\frac{3}{50}$
25-33	|||	3	$\frac{3}{50}$
34-42	⽶||	7	$\frac{7}{50}$
43-51	⽶|	6	$\frac{6}{50}$
52-60	⽶||||	9	$\frac{9}{50}$
61-69	⽶	5	$\frac{5}{50}$
70-78	⽶|	6	$\frac{6}{50}$
79-87	⽶|||	8	$\frac{8}{50}$
88-97	|	1	$\frac{1}{50}$
		50	$\frac{50}{50} = 1$

b)

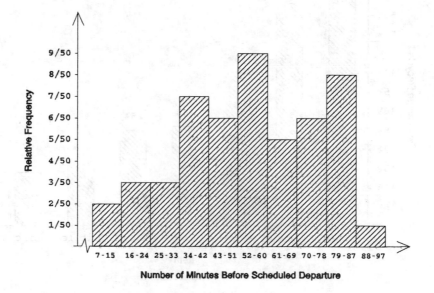

29

1.

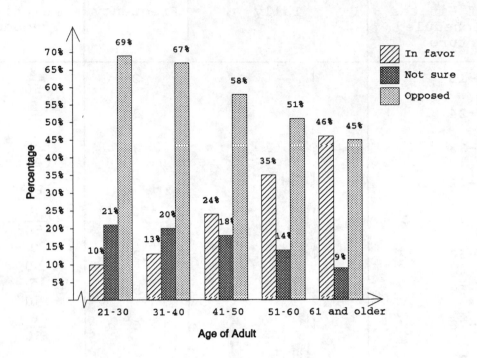

2.

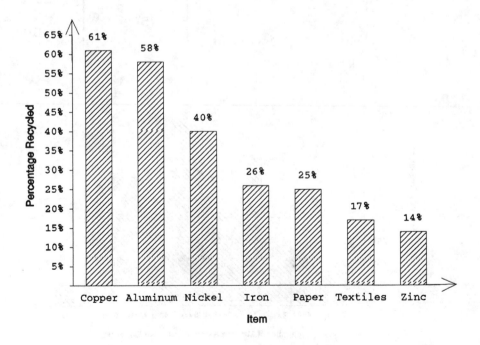

3. a)   Humber Bridge: 1400 meters
        Verrazano Narrows Bridge: 1300 meters
        Golden Gate Bridge: 1200 meters
        Mackinac Straits Bridge: 1100 meters
        Bosporus Bridge: 1100 meters
        George Washington Bridge: 1000 meters
   b)   1420 - 1260 or 160 meters
   c)   1240 - 1070 or 170 meters

4. a)   1974   b)   Between 1971 and 1972
   c)   Between 1973 and 1974
   d)   From 3.1 to 5.0 fatalities per year per 100,000 vehicle
        miles.

5.

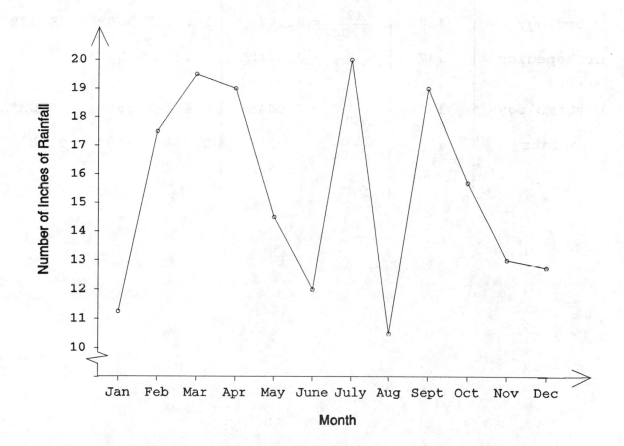

6. a)   196 X 0.547 = $107.212 million
   b)   196 X (0.146 + 0.167) = $61.348 million

7.

Area of Specialization	Number	Percentage of Total	Number of Degrees Assigned
Neurology	775	$\frac{775}{4000}$ = 0.19375	19.375% X 360° = 69.75°
Cardiology	827	$\frac{827}{4000}$ = 0.20675	20.675% X 360° = 74.43°
Pediatrics	769	$\frac{769}{4000}$ = 0.19225	19.225% X 360° = 69.21°
Obstetrics	584	$\frac{584}{4000}$ = 0.146	14.6% X 360° = 52.56°
Urology	428	$\frac{428}{4000}$ = 0.107	10.7% X 360° = 38.52°
Orthopedics	337	$\frac{337}{4000}$ = 0.08425	8.425% X 360° = 30.33°
Opthamology	178	$\frac{178}{4000}$ = 0.0445	4.45% X 360° = 16.02°
Podiatry	102	$\frac{102}{4000}$ = 0.0255	2.55% X 360° = 9.18°
	4000		

32

7. (Continued)

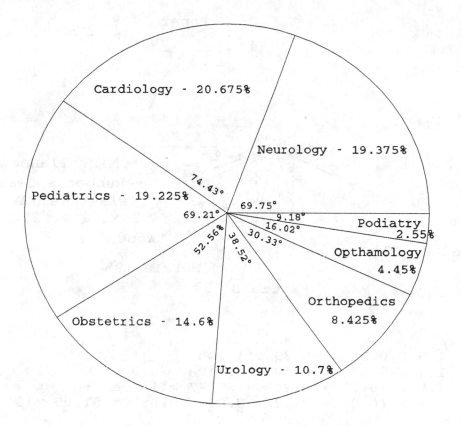

8.

Item	Percentage	Number of Degrees Assigned
Paper	40%	0.40 X 360° = 144°
Food	17%	0.17 X 360° = 61.2°
Yard Waste	13%	0.13 X 360° = 46.8°
Glass	9%	0.09 X 360° = 32.4°
Metals	9%	0.09 X 360° = 32.4°
Wood	3%	0.03 X 360° = 10.8°
Textiles	2%	0.02 X 360° = 7.2°
Plastics	2%	0.02 X 360° = 7.2°
Rubber & Leather	2%	0.02 X 360° = 7.2°
Miscellaneous	3%	0.03 X 360° = 10.8°

8. (Continued)

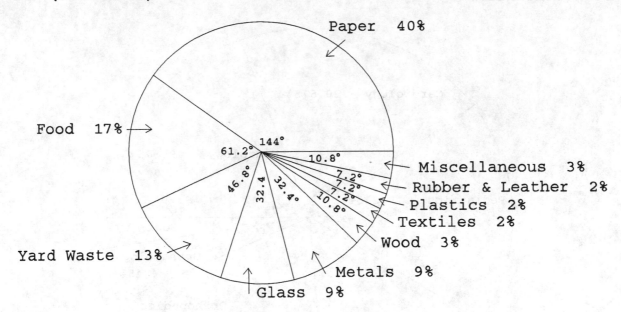

9. **a)** 1.5 X 0.26 = $0.39 million
   b) 1.5 X 0.07 = $0.105 million
   c) 1.5 X (0.32 + 0.26) = $0.87 million
   d) 1.5 X (0.26 + 0.32 + 0.07 + 0.05) = $1.05 million

10. **a)** 1276 X 0.16 = 204.16
    b) 1276 X (0.15 + 0.19) = 433.84
    c) 1276 X (0.15 + 0.16 + 0.29 + 0.19) = 1008.04

11. a)

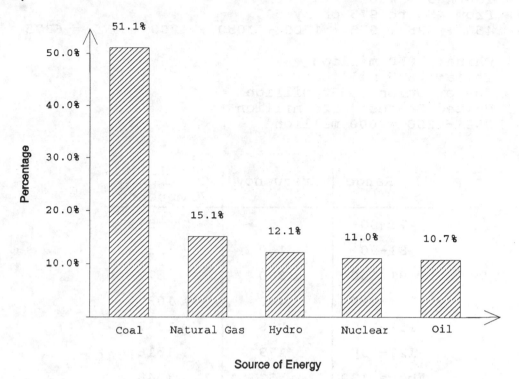

b)

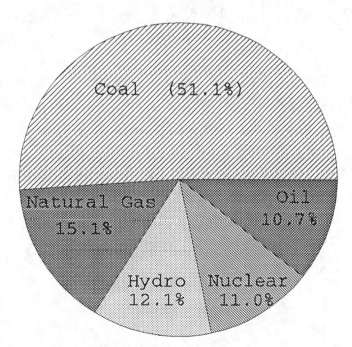

c) They both are useful.

35

12. **a)** 150 X 3 = 450
    b) From 450 to 975 or by 525
    c) 450 + 525 + 975 + 1200 + 1050 + 1200 + 975 = 6375

13. **a)** China: 850 million
        India: 625 million
        Soviet Union: 250 million
        United States: 225 million
    b) 850 - 250 = 600 million

14. **a)**

IQ Range	Frequency	Cumulative Frequency
71-80	57	57
81-90	160	217
91-100	360	577
101-110	462	1039
111-120	298	1337
121-130	179	1516
Above 130	32	1548
	1548	

14. a) (Continued)

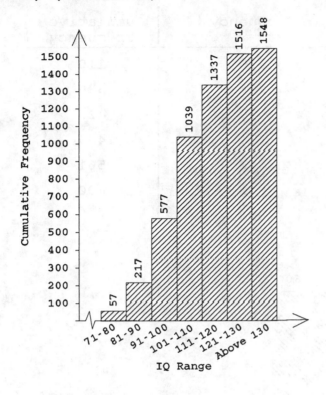

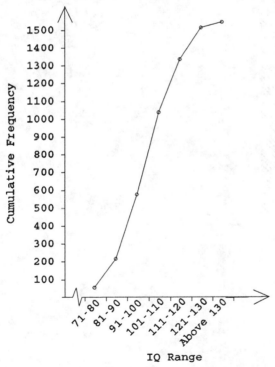

14. b)

Weight	Frequency	Cumulative Frequency
100-110	110	110
111-120	226	336
121-130	89	425
131-140	74	499
141-150	62	561
Over 150	39	600
	600	

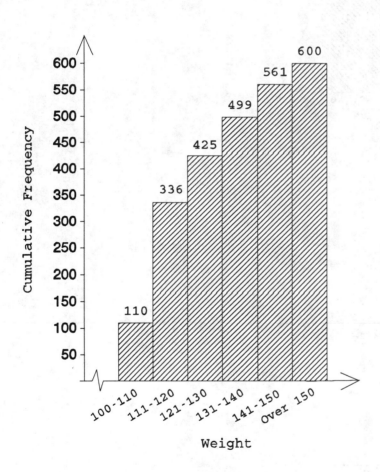

14. b) (Continued)

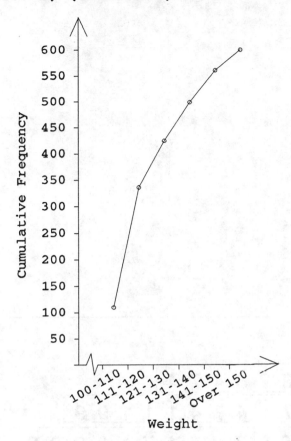

15. **a)** Normally distributed
  b) Normally distributed
  c) Normally distributed
  d) Not normally distributed
  e) Normally distributed
  f) Not normally distributed

1.

STEM	LEAVES
1	9 8 6 6
2	8 5 8 4 8 9 9 8 8
3	6 8 7 9 7 6 3 4 9 1
4	5 3 5 7 9 0
5	1

2.

STEM	LEAVES
7	6 9 6 9 8
8	7 3 7 3 3 3 3 2 5 4 7 4
9	6 3 3 7 1 2 7 1 4 7 4 1 1 1 9 9
10	4 3 1 2 1 4 5 9 7 2 7 1 7 1 3 3 9 8
11	1 5 9 7 8 3 1 6 9 8 0 4 1 1 1 8 5
12	9 2 7 7 1 1 8 9 1 2
13	1 7 9 8 9 9 7 2 4 6
14	1 8 2 4 1 3 9 4
15	3 8 6 3

3.

STEM	LEAVES
18	8 4 9 7 9
19	7 8 9 9 6
20	0 1 4 5 3 1 8 5 8
21	1 8 1 9 6
22	7 1 2 1 3 1 7 7
23	2 8 2 9 8
24	5 1 9 1
25	6 7 1
26	9
27	2
28	3 4 7
29	7

4.

STEM	LEAVES
30	.8 .7 .8
31	.4 .8 .7 .8 .7 .8
32	.4 .9 .8
33	.9 .8 .1 .9
34	.4 .7 .5 .8
35	.3 .6 .8 .7 .9 .5 .7
36	.4 .7 .1 .3 .0 .9
37	.6 .8 .8 .5 .8 .9 .6 .6 .3
38	.3 .8 .6 .1 .8 .4 .1 .2
39	.7 .1 .1 .0 .3 .8 .5
40	.2 .1 .2

41

5.

STEM	LEAVES
(3900-3949) 39	45 01 45 45
(3950-3999) 39	98 89 75 76 84 98 87
(4000-4049) 40	00 00 04 00 49
(4050-4099) 40	50
(4100-4149) 41	49 49 45
(4150-4199) 41	98 50
(4200-4249) 42	49 00 49

6.

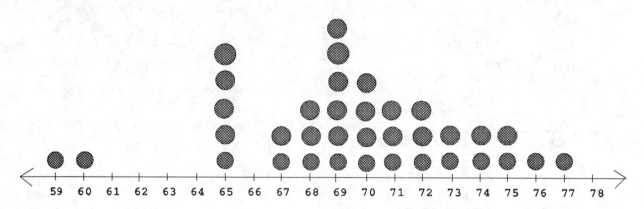

ANSWERS TO EXERCISES FOR SECTION 2.5 - (PAGES 77-78)

1. Both graphs are statistically correct, but because different spacings are used on the vertical scale, the graphs appear different.

2. When you double the diameter of a swimming pool, its area becomes four times as great.

3. The graph is truncated. Also the scale is misleading.

4. Both graphs are statistically correct, but because different spacings are used on the vertical scale, the graphs appear different.

ANSWERS TO EXERCISES FOR SECTION 2.6 - (PAGES 81-83)

1. $\dfrac{0.75}{0.43}$ X 100 = 174.42 or an increase of approximately 74.42% when compared to 1986.

2. $\dfrac{0.65}{0.43}$ X 100 = 151.16 or an increase of approximately 51.16% when compared to 1986.

3. $\dfrac{0.43}{0.75}$ X 100 = 57.33 or that prices were approximately 57.33 - 100 or 42.67% cheaper in 1986 when compared to 1991.

4. $\dfrac{0.65}{0.75}$ X 100 = 86.67 or that prices were approximately 86.67 - 100 = 13.33% cheaper in 1989 when compared to 1991

5.

Year	Cost Index	Interpretation
1985	$\frac{2.75}{2.75}$ X 100 = 100	Base year price
1986	$\frac{3.25}{2.75}$ X 100 = 118.18	Price increased by approximately 18.18% when compared to 1985
1987	$\frac{4.00}{2.75}$ X 100 = 145.45	Price increased by approximately 45.45% when compared to 1985
1988	$\frac{4.25}{2.75}$ X 100 = 154.55	Price increased by approximately 54.55% when compared to 1985
1989	$\frac{5.00}{2.75}$ X 100 = 181.82	Price increased by approximately 81.82% when compared to 1985
1990	$\frac{6.00}{2.75}$ x 100 = 218.18	Price increased by approximately 118.18% when compared to 1985

6.

Year	Cost Index	
1984	$\frac{1420}{1420}$ x 100 = 100	⟵ Base year price
1985	$\frac{1605}{1420}$ x 100 = 113.028	
1986	$\frac{1840}{1420}$ x 100 = 129.577	
1987	$\frac{1992}{1420}$ X 100 = 140.282	
1988	$\frac{2079}{1420}$ X 100 = 146.408	
1989	$\frac{2250}{1420}$ X 100 = 158.451	
1990	$\frac{2408}{1420}$ X 100 = 169.577	

7.

Year	Cost Index
1984	$\frac{1420}{1992}$ X 100 = 71.285
1985	$\frac{1605}{1992}$ X 100 = 80.572
1986	$\frac{1840}{1992}$ X 100 = 92.369
1987	$\frac{1992}{1992}$ X 100 = 100 ⟸ Base year price
1988	$\frac{2079}{1992}$ X 100 = 104.367
1989	$\frac{2250}{1992}$ X 100 = 112.952
1990	$\frac{2408}{1992}$ X 100 = 120.884

8. **a)** Vegetables. It decreased.

  b) Eggs

9. The cost of paper supplies decreased by 1% in February 1989 when compared to January 1988.

10. Index for salary = $\frac{56,000}{55,000}$ X 100 = 101.818. Increase is

1.818% when compared to 1988. CPI = 108.1 - 106.7 = 1.4. Increase in CPI is 1.4% when compared to 1988. Purchasing power increased.

ANSWERS TO TESTING YOUR UNDERSTANDING OF THIS CHAPTER'S CONCEPTS - (PAGES 88-89)

1. The interval endpoints are overlapping. In which category should we put a monthly bill of $15? Also, the interval lengths are not the same.

2. Yes

3. True

ANSWERS TO TESTING YOUR UNDERSTANDING OF THIS CHAPTER'S CONCEPTS (CONTINUED) - (PAGES 88-89)

4. $\dfrac{112 - 0}{12} = 9.33$.   Use 10 as the class width.

ANSWERS TO THINKING CRITICALLY - (PAGES 89-90)

1. Yes. The next interval is supposed to begin where the previous interval ends. No gaps. Also, the interval lengths are not the same.

2. **a)** $4 + 6 + 9 + 8 + 4 + 3 + 7 + 5 + 1 = 47$
   b) Frequency histogram

3. Nothing is wrong mathematically, although it is misleading because of the small sample size.

4. **a)** No. Vertical scale is inaccurate
   b) Should not be twice as tall.
   c) Although the conclusion may be true, the graph presenting this information is inaccurate.

ANSWERS TO REVIEW EXERCISES FOR CHAPTER 2 - (PAGES 90-93)

1.

Class No.	Interval	Midpoint	Tally	Frequency
1	2-16	9	|||	3
2	17-31	24	|||| ||||	9
3	32-46	39	||||	4
4	47-61	54	|||	3
5	62-76	69	||||	5
6	77-91	84	||||		6
				30

1.   (Continued)

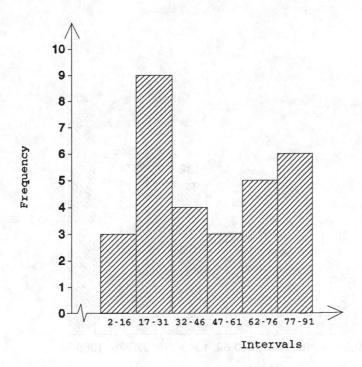

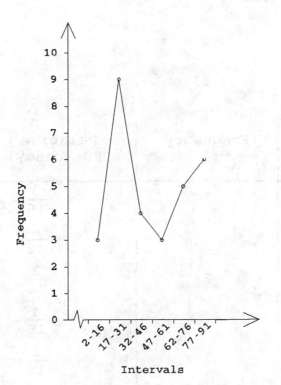

2.

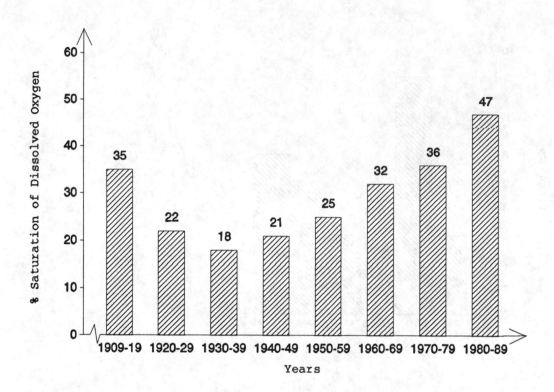

3. **a)** 8 X 0.31 = 2.48 million
    b) 8 X 0.23 = 1.84 million
    c) 8(0.23 + 0.01 + 0.08) = 2.56 million

4.

Mileage	Tally	Frequency	Relative Frequency
36-37	|||	3	$\frac{3}{16}$
38-39	||||	4	$\frac{4}{16}$
40-41	|||	3	$\frac{3}{16}$
42-43	||||	4	$\frac{4}{16}$
44-45	||	2	$\frac{2}{16}$

5.

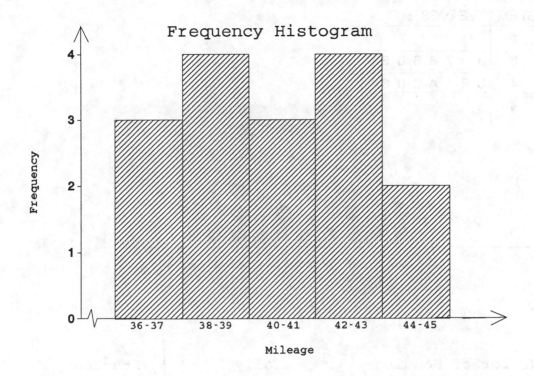

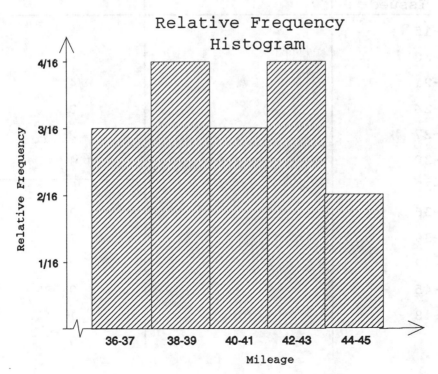

6.

STEM	LEAVES
3	
3	8 9 7 8 8 6 6
4	3 2 1 4 3 0 3 1
4	5

7.

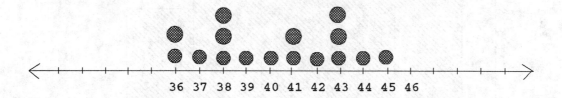

8.

Number of Housing Permits Issued	Tally	Frequency
13-15	|	1
16-18	⊞ |	6
19-21	||||	4
22-24	||	2
25-27	||	2
28-30	||||	4
31-33	⊞	5
34-36	||	2
37-39	||	2
40-42		0
43-45		0
46-48	|	_1_
		29

8. (Continued)

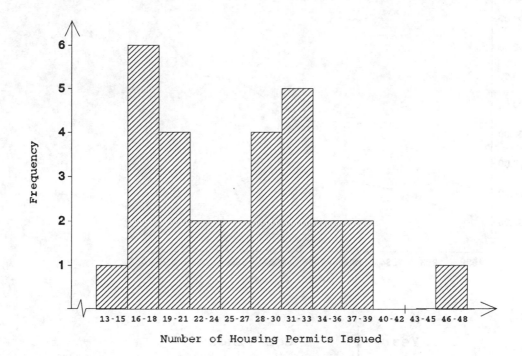

Number of Housing Permits Issued

9. a)

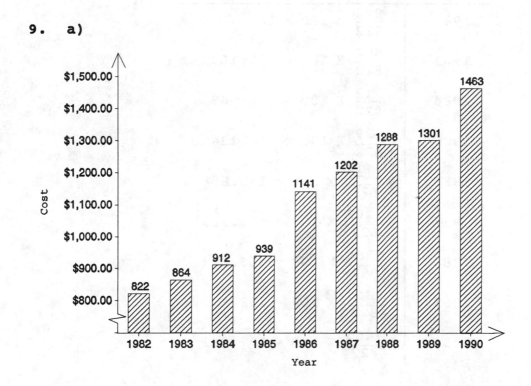

9. b)

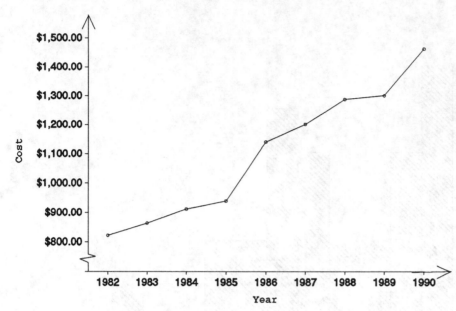

10.

Year	Cost Index
1982	$\frac{822}{822}$ X 100 = 100
1983	$\frac{864}{822}$ X 100 = 105.109
1984	$\frac{912}{822}$ X 100 = 110.949
1985	$\frac{939}{822}$ X 100 = 114.234
1986	$\frac{1141}{822}$ X 100 = 138.808
1987	$\frac{1202}{822}$ X 100 = 146.229
1988	$\frac{1288}{822}$ X 100 = 156.691
1989	$\frac{1301}{822}$ X 100 = 158.273
1990	$\frac{1463}{822}$ X 100 = 177.981

1.

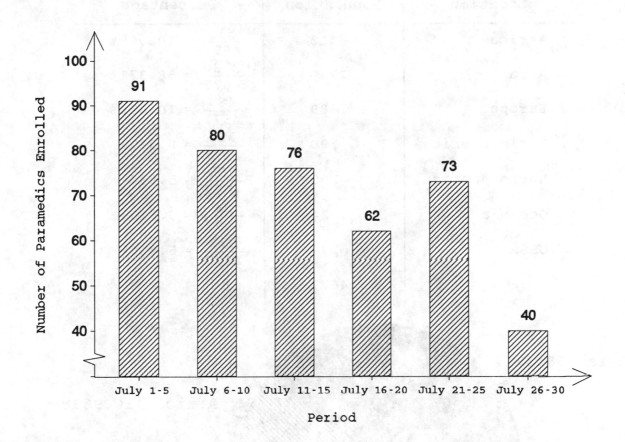

2.

Location	Population	Percentage
Africa	513	$\frac{513}{4677}$ = 10.969%
Asia	2730	$\frac{2730}{4677}$ = 58.371%
Europe	489	$\frac{489}{4677}$ = 10.455%
Latin America	390	$\frac{390}{4677}$ = 8.339%
North America	259	$\frac{259}{4677}$ = 5.538%
Oceania	24	$\frac{24}{4677}$ = 0.513%
USSR	272	$\frac{272}{4677}$ = 5.816%
	4677	

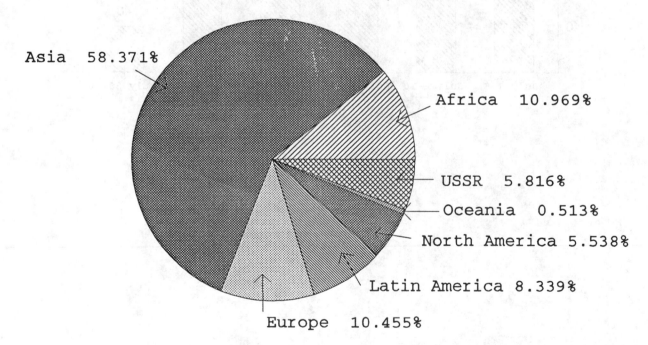

3.

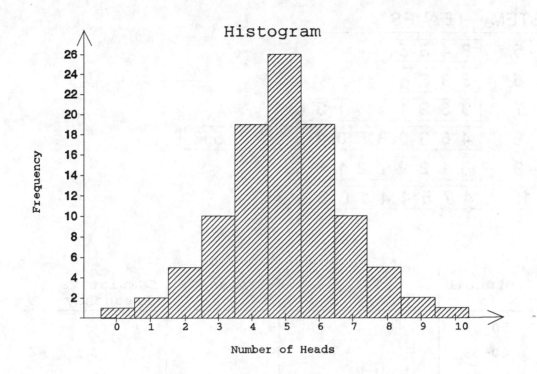

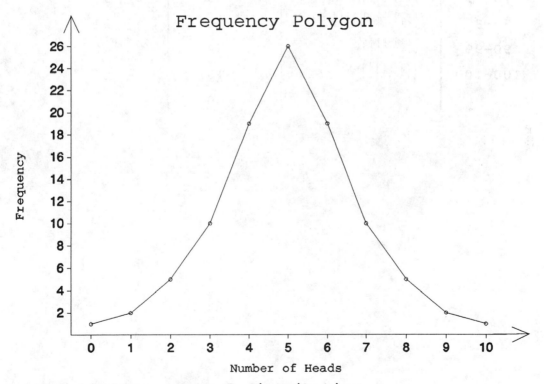

It resembles a normal distribution.

4. a)

STEM	LEAVES
5	8 4 3 5
6	3 9 3 4
7	3 6 9 1 4 4 1 3 6
8	4 6 3 0 8 5 0 9 5 8 2 3 5 6
9	8 1 2 2 7 3 1 6 8
10	4 7 5 4 4 1 6 2 5 9

b)

Interval	Tally	Frequency	Cumulative Frequency
50-59	||||	4	4
60-69	||||	4	8
70-79	⊮ ||||	9	17
80-89	⊮ ⊮ ||||	14	31
90-99	⊮ ||||	9	40
100-109	⊮ ⊮	10	50
		50	

4. b)   (Continued)

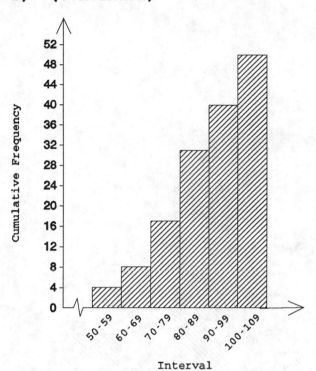

5.

Year	Cost Index
1984	$\frac{341}{341}$ X 100 = 100
1985	$\frac{363}{341}$ X 100 = 106.452
1986	$\frac{387}{341}$ X 100 = 113.4897
1987	$\frac{399}{341}$ X 100 = 117.009
1988	$\frac{407}{341}$ X 100 = 119.355
1989	$\frac{419}{341}$ X 100 = 122.874
1990	$\frac{439}{341}$ X 100 = 128.739

6. a)   130 - 50 = 80 million (approximately)
    b)   205 - 150 = 55 million (approximately)

7.

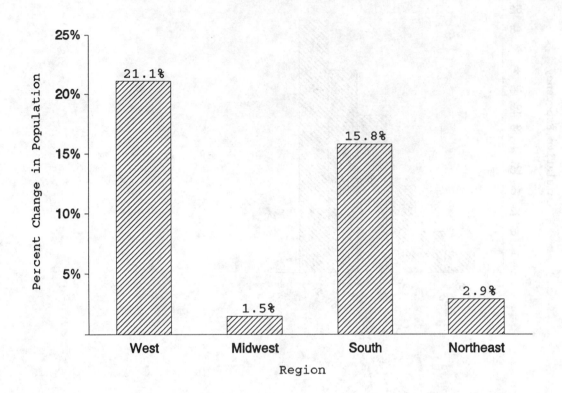

8. The number of people per family living in the same household has been decreasing. The number of housing units has been increasing. Thus there may be more housing units but there are less people per household.

9. The coins should be of the same size, and there should be twice as many coins stacked vertically for 1989 as compared to the number of coins stacked vertically for 1980.

10. Probably all are.

11. Choice (c)

12. Choice (a)

13. Choice (b)

14. Choice (e)

15. Choice (c)

For questions 1 - 3 refer to the circle graph below which gives the place of origin of the 150,000 immigrants living in one section of a large city in the Northeast.

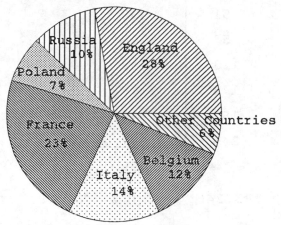

1. How many of the immigrants originated in Italy?

   a) 21,028   b) 28,000   c) 2100   d) 21,000
   e) none of these

   Answer _____

2. How many of these immigrants originated in France or Poland?

   a) 34,500   b) 10,500   c) 45,000   d) 4500
   e) none of these

   Answer _____

3. How many of the immigrants did not originate in Russia, England or Belgium?

   a) 72,000   b) 78,000   c) 42,000   d) 135,000
   e) none of these

   Answer _____

4. When constructing frequency polygons, the point which is midway between the limits of a class is called the

   a) class number
   b) class mark
   c) frequency
   d) boundary
   e) none of these

   Answer _____

5. Consider the following frequency distribution. What is the relative frequency of the score of 183?

Score	Frequency
36	33
51	30
57	48
123	42
174	93
183	246
246	207
	699

a) 183/699   b) 183/246   c) 246/123   d) 246/699
e) 246

Answer _____

6. Refer to question 5. What is the relative frequency of the score of 81?

a) 699/174   b) 699/93   c) 93/699   d) 0
e) 174/699

Answer _____

7. Consider the following frequency distribution. Find the class mark for interval 5.

Interval	Score	Frequency
1	70 - 89	36
2	90 - 109	48
3	110 - 129	84
4	130 - 149	39
5	150 - 169	33
6	170 - 189	18
		258

a) 150   b) 169   c) 159.5   d) 33   e) 33/258

Answer _____

8. Refer back to the previous question. What is the relative frequency of a score of 178?

a) 18   b) 18/258   c) 0   d) 258/18
e) none of these

Answer _____

9. The cost of a 3 minute telephone call between 2 cities dialed at the same time on Thanksgiving Day each year over the past few years was as follows:

Year	Price
1982	$0.85
1983	$0.96
1984	$1.03
1985	$0.89
1986	$0.99
1987	$1.03

Using 1983 as a base year, compute the price index for 1987.

Answer _____

10. Draw a stem-and-leaf diagram for the following data: 58, 37, 69, 46, 89, 53, 75, 37, 58, 39, 64, 78, 56, 82, 76, 58, 78, 98, 46, 57

1. The graph below shows the distribution of the ages of the
    workers in a large office building. How many people work in
    the building?

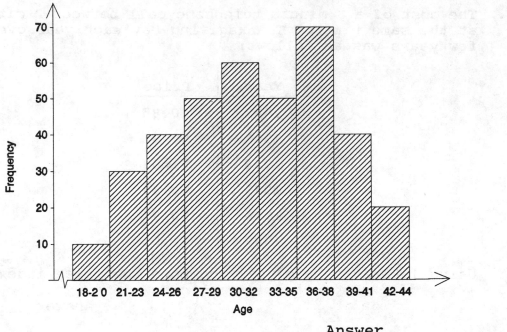

Answer _____

Use the following information to answer questions 2 and 3. The graph below shows how many applications for admission were received by a particular medical school over the period 1960 - 1985.

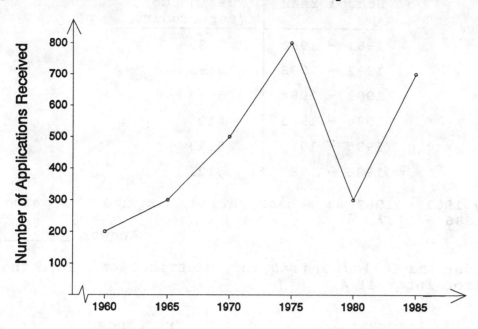

2. In which time period did the number of applications received increase the most?

   a) 1960 - 1965   b) 1965 - 1970   c) 1970 - 1975
   d) 1975 - 1980   e) 1980 - 1985

   Answer _____

3. In which time period did the number of applications received increase the least?

   a) 1960 - 1965   b) 1965 - 1970   c) 1970 - 1975
   d) 1975 - 1980   e) 1980 - 1985

   Answer _____

4. Based upon your own experience, which of the following do you think is (are) likely to be normally distributed?

   a. The number of daily traffic accidents reported over a year period
   b. The time needed by many students to complete this exam
   c. The ages of fellow students at your college
   d. The number of children that each of the 10,000 families in a particular city has
   e. The height of spectators at a football game

   Answer _____

63

5. The cost of tuition at a particular college over the years was as follows:

School Year	Tuition Cost (per credit)
1981 - 1982	$ 85
1982 - 1983	$ 93
1983 - 1984	$ 99
1984 - 1985	$104
1985 - 1986	$113
1986 - 1987	$121

Using 1981 - 1982 as a base period, compute the price index for 1986 - 1987.

Answer _____

6. Consider the following frequency distribution. Find the class mark for interval 4.

Interval	Score	Frequency
1	140 - 153	27
2	154 - 166	33
3	167 - 179	28
4	180 - 199	43
5	200 - 213	16
		147

a) 180   b) 199   c) 43   d) 189.5   e) 190

Answer _____

7. Refer back to question 6. What is the relative frequency of a score of 202.5?

a) 16   b) 16/147   c) 146/16   d) none of these

Answer _____

For questions 8 - 10 refer to the circle graph below which shows the student body make-up of a large university which has an enrollment of 22,000 students.

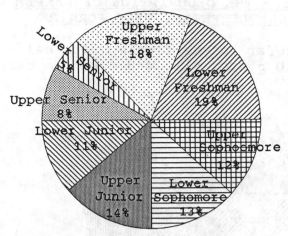

8. How many students are upper seniors?

 a) 1760   b) 1188   c) 17,600   d) 1100   e) none of these

Answer _____

9. How many students are juniors or seniors?

 a) 8360   b) 3080   c) 2860   d) 5500   e) none of these

Answer _____

10. How many students are <u>not</u> freshmen, sophomores or juniors?

 a) 8140   b) 13,860   c) 3960   d) 4180   e) none of these

Answer _____

CHAPTER 2 - THE DESCRIPTION OF SAMPLE DATA
SUPPLEMENTARY TEST FORM C

For questions 1 - 3 refer to the circle graph below which shows the blood type of the 9800 pints collected during a recent blood drive.

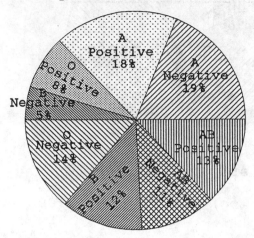

1. How many pints of blood were type AB positive?

    a) 1764   b) 1176   c) 2940   d) 1274   e) none of these

    Answer _____

2. How many pints of blood were type A or B?

    a) 3626   b) 1666   c) 2352   d) 7056   e) none of these

    Answer _____

3. How many pints of blood were <u>not</u> type A, nor type B, nor type AB?

    a) 3626   b) 2156   c) 2352   d) 7056   e) none of these

    Answer _____

4. Consider the following frequency distribution. What is the relative frequency of the score of 87?

Score	Frequency
57	89
62	71
78	64
82	53
87	29
90	12
95	6
	324

a) 29   b) 29/324   c) 29/87   d) 87/324
e) none of these

Answer _____

5. Refer back to question 4. What is the relative frequency of the score of 12?

a) 90/324   b) 12/324   c) 324/12   d) 0   e) none of these

Answer _____

6. Consider the following frequency distribution. Find the class mark for interval 4.

Interval	Score	Frequency
1	115 - 124	18
2	125 - 134	16
3	135 - 144	13
4	145 - 154	11
5	155 - 164	9
6	165 - 174	6
		73

a) 149.5   b) 145   c) 154   d) 11   e) none of these

Answer _____

7. Refer back to the previous question. What is the relative frequency of a score of 159.5?

   a) 9   b) 9/73   c) 0   d) 5/73   e) none of these

   Answer _____

8. The average cost of a cab ride from the airport to the center of a large city over the years has changed as follows:

Year	Cost
1982	$12.45
1983	$13.16
1984	$15.67
1985	$16.49
1986	$18.11
1987	$19.95

   Using 1982 as a base year, compute the cost index for 1987.

   Answer _____

9. Each of 20 students was asked to select one number from the following choices: 6, 7, 8, 9, 10. The table below gives the distribution of these selections.

Number	Frequency
6	3
7	10
8	1
9	4
10	2

   Draw a frequency histogram for the data.

10. Draw a stem-and-leaf diagram for the following grades received by 24 students on a math test. 73, 83, 14, 80, 67, 80, 68, 97, 68, 85, 75, 82, 82, 80, 66, 89, 86, 97, 91, 89, 92, 82, 94, 99

Form A	Form B	Form C
1. Choice (d)	1. 370	1. Choice (d)
2. Choice (c)	2. Choice (e)	2. Choice (e)
3. Choice (e)	3. Choice (d)	3. Choice (b)
4. Choice (b)	4. All choices	4. Choice (b)
5. Choice (d)	5. 1.42	5. Choice (d)
6. Choice (d)	6. Choice (d)	6. Choice (a)
7. Choice (c)	7. Choice (b)	7. Choice (b)
8. Choice (b)	8. Choice (a)	8. 1.60
9. 1.07	9. Choice (a)	9. See below
10. See below	10. Choice (e)	10. See below

Form A - Question 10

STEM	LEAVES
3	7 7 9
4	6 6
5	8 3 8 6 8 7
6	9 4
7	5 8 6 8
8	9 2
9	8

Form C - Question 9

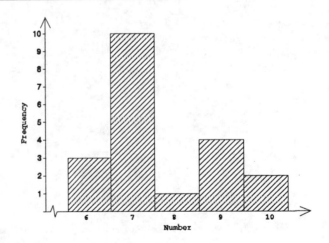

STEM	LEAVES
1	4
2	
3	
4	
5	
6	7 8 8 6
7	3 5
8	3 0 0 5 2 2 0 9 6 9 2
9	7 7 1 2 4 9

SECTION 3.2 – (PAGES 106 – 107)

1. **a)** $\displaystyle\sum_{i=1}^{8} y_i$

    b) $\displaystyle\sum_{i=1}^{8} y_i^2$

    c) $\displaystyle\sum_{i=1}^{8} y_i f_i$

    d) $\displaystyle\sum_{i=1}^{7} 19 y_i$

    e) $\displaystyle\sum_{i=1}^{n} (3y_i + x_i)$

2. **a)** $y_1 + y_2 + y_3 + y_4 + y_5 + y_6 + y_7$

    b) $x_4 y_4 + x_5 y_5 + x_6 y_6 + x_7 y_7 + x_8 y_8 + x_9 y_9$

    c) $(5x_4 + 2) + (5x_5 + 2) + (5x_6 + 2) + (5x_7 + 2) + (5x_8 + 2) +$

    $(5x_9 + 2) + (5x_{10} + 2) + (5x_{11} + 2)$

    d) $2x_1^2 + 2x_2^2 + 2x_3^2 + 2x_4^2 + 2x_5^2 + 2x_6^2 + 2x_7^2$

    e) $y_1^2 f_1 + y_2^2 f_2 + y_3^2 f_3 + y_4^2 f_4 + y_5^2 f_5 + y_6^2 f_6 + y_7^2 f_7$

    f) $y_4^2 + y_5^2 + y_6^2 + y_7^2 + y_8^2$

3. **a)** $\sum x = 5 + 19 + 8 + 29 + 25 = 86$

b) $\left(\sum x\right)^2 = 86^2 = 7396$

c) $\sum x^2 = 5^2 + 19^2 + 8^2 + 29^2 + 25^2 = 1916$

d) $\sum (x + 1) = (5 + 1) + (19 + 1) + (8 + 1) + (29 + 1) +$
$(25 + 1) = 91$

e) $\sum (x + 1)^2 = (5 + 1)^2 + (19 + 1)^2 + (8 + 1)^2 + (29 + 1)^2 +$
$(25 + 1)^2 = 2093$

f) $\sum (2x + 3) = (2 \cdot 5 + 3) + (2 \cdot 19 + 3) + (2 \cdot 8 + 3) +$
$(2 \cdot 29 + 3) + (2 \cdot 25 + 3) = 187$

g) $\sum (2x + 3)^2 = (2 \cdot 5 + 3)^2 + (2 \cdot 19 + 3)^2 + (2 \cdot 8 + 3)^2 +$
$(2 \cdot 29 + 3)^2 + (2 \cdot 25 + 3)^2 = 8741$

4. **a)** $\sum x^2 = 5^2 + 8^2 + 14^2 + 34^2 = 1441$

b) $\sum x \cdot f = 5 \cdot 3 + 8 \cdot 7 + 14 \cdot 9 + 34 \cdot 12 = 605$

c) $\left(\sum x\right)\left(\sum y\right) = (5 + 8 + 14 + 34)(2 + 4 - 3 - 6) = -183$

d) $\sum xy = 5 \cdot 2 + 8 \cdot 4 + 14(-3) + 34(-6) = -204$

e) $\sum x \cdot y \cdot f = 5 \cdot 3 \cdot 2 + 8 \cdot 7 \cdot 4 + 14(9)(-3) + 34(12)(-6) = -2572$

f) $\sum (x - y)f = (5 - 2)3 + (8 - 4)7 + (14 + 3)9 + (34 + 6)12$
$= 670$

5. **a)** $\displaystyle\sum_{i=1}^{10} (x_1 + 9) = \sum_{i=1}^{10} x_1 + \sum_{i=1}^{10} 9 = 27 + 10 \cdot 9 = 117$

b) $\displaystyle\sum_{i=1}^{10} (x_1 + 9)^2 = \sum_{i=1}^{10} (x_1^2 + 18x_1 + 81) \quad = \sum_{i=1}^{10} x_1^2 + 18\sum_{i=1}^{10} x_1 + \sum_{i=1}^{10} 81$

$$= 50 + 18(27) + 10 \cdot 81$$
$$= 1346$$

6. a) $\displaystyle\sum_{i=1}^{n}(x_1 - y_1)$ $= (x_1 - y_1) + (x_2 - y_2) + (x_3 - y_3) + \ldots$

$+ (x_n - y_n)$

$= x_1 + x_2 + x_3 + \ldots + x_n - y_1 - y_2 - y_3 - \ldots - y_n$

$= (x_1 + x_2 + x_3 + \ldots + x_n) - (y_1 + y_2 + y_3 + \ldots + y_n)$

$= \displaystyle\sum_{i=1}^{n} x_1 - \sum_{i=1}^{n} y_1$

b) $\displaystyle\sum_{i=1}^{n}(x_1 + k)$ $= (x_1 + k) + (x_2 + k) + (x_3 + k) + \ldots$

$+ (x_n + k)$

$= x_1 + x_2 + x_3 + \ldots + x_n + k + k + k + \ldots + k$

$= \displaystyle\sum_{i=1}^{n} x_1 + nk$

7. a) The total number of students submitting essays.
b) The total number of essays (of all types) that she has received.

ANSWERS TO EXERCISES FOR SECTION 3.3 – (PAGES 118 – 124)

1. Mean $= \dfrac{39 + 42 + 38 + \ldots + 35}{12} = \dfrac{379}{12} = 31.58$ inches

Median = 19, 23, 25, 25, 27, 31, 35, 36, 38, 39, 39, 42
Between 31 and 35 or 33
Mode = 25 and 39

2. Mean $= \dfrac{68,000 + 58,000 + \ldots + 69,500}{21} = \dfrac{1,386,500}{21} = \$66,024$

Median = $60,000
Mode = $61,000

3. Mean = $\dfrac{68{,}000 + 58{,}000 + \ldots + 69{,}500}{20} = \dfrac{1{,}147{,}500}{20} = \$57{,}375$

   Median = $59,000
   Mode = $61,000
   Extreme scores have a significant effect on the mean.

4. Mean = $\dfrac{41.12 + 48.58 + \ldots + 48.58}{9} = \dfrac{407.67}{9} = \$45.30$

   Median = $46.19
   Mode = $48.58 and $41.12
   Probably the mean is more useful.

5. Mean = $\dfrac{6800 + 5700 + 6300 + 5995 + 6100 + 5850}{6} = \dfrac{36745}{6}$

   $= \$6124.17$
   Median = Between 5995 and 6100 or $6047.50
   Mode = None

6. Mean = 6140.83 + 400 = $6524.17
   Median = 6047.50 + 400 = $6447.50
   Mode = None

7.

Size, x	Tally	Frequency, f	x·f
6					3	18
8	LHI LHI	10	80
10	LHI LHI LHI		16	160
12	LHI LHI LHI ||	17	204
14	LHI		6	84
16	LHI	5	80
18						4	72
20				2	40
24			1	24
		64	762

Mean = $\dfrac{\Sigma xf}{\Sigma f}$ = $\dfrac{762}{64}$ = 11.906

Median = 12
Mode = 12
The mode is more important to the management of the store.

8.

IQ Score Class Mark, x	Frequency, f	x·f
75.5	3	226.5
85.5	6	513.0
95.5	12	1146.0
105.5	14	1477.0
115.5	8	924.0
125.5	5	627.5
135.5	2	271.0
	50	5185

$$\text{Mean} = \frac{\Sigma xf}{\Sigma f} = \frac{5185}{50} = 103.7$$

Median = 105.5 using the class mark or $101 + \frac{4.5}{14}(10) = 104.2$

   assuming entries are evenly distributed in each class.
Mode = in the 101-110 interval

9.

Price, x	Frequency, f	x·f
$1.70	38	64.60
1.75	64	112.00
1.80	7	12.60
1.85	3	5.55
	112	194.75

$$\text{Mean} = \frac{\Sigma xf}{\Sigma f}$$

$$= \frac{194.75}{112} \quad \$1.74$$

Median = $1.75
Mode = $1.75

10.

Price, x	Frequency, f	x·f
30	36	1080
35	28	980
40	19	760
45	17	765
	100	3585

$$\text{Mean} = \frac{\Sigma xf}{\Sigma f} = \frac{3585}{100}$$

$$= \$35.85$$

11.

Salary, Class Mark, x	Frequency, f	x·f
$27,499.50	3	82,498.50
32,499.50	6	194,997.00
37,499.50	12	449,994.00
42,499.50	14	594,993.00
47,499.50	8	379,996.00
52,499.50	5	262,497.50
57,499.50	2	114,999.00
	50	2,079,975.00

$$\text{Mean} = \frac{\Sigma xf}{\Sigma f} = \frac{2079975}{50} = \$41,599.50$$

Median = $42,499.50 using the class mark or 40000

$$+ \frac{4.5}{14}(5000) = \$41,607.14 \text{ assuming entries are evenly}$$

distributed in each class.

Mode = In the $40,000 - $44,999 interval

12.

Class Mark, x	Frequency, f	x·f
3	6	18
8	13	104
13	14	182
18	17	306
23	19	437
28	15	420
33	8	264
38	6	228
43	3	129
	101	2088

Mean $= \dfrac{\Sigma xf}{\Sigma f} = \dfrac{2088}{101} = 20.67$

Median = 23 using the class mark or $21 + \dfrac{1}{19}(5) = 21.26$ assuming entries are evenly distributed in each class.

Mode = In the 21 to 25 interval

13. No. Both classes may not have the same number of students.

14. Average $= \dfrac{68,000}{12} = 5666.67$ pounds

15. Mean $= \dfrac{7 + 3 + 5 + 4 + 8 + 4 + 3 + 3 + 6}{9} = \dfrac{43}{9} = 4.78$

Median = 4
Mode = 3
Probably the mode

16. Company A: Mean $= \dfrac{40}{8} = 5$ Median = 4.5   Mode = None

Company B: Mean $= \dfrac{98}{11} = 8.91$ Median = 6   Mode = 5

Company C: Mean $= \dfrac{61}{8} = 7.63$ Median = 5   Mode = 4

a)   Company A is using the mean.
Company B is using the mode.
Company C is using the median.

16. b) Probably Company B. Others might pick Company A since both the mean and median are both smaller, as is the maximum processing time.

17. Harmonic mean $= \dfrac{4}{\frac{1}{8} + \frac{1}{5} + \frac{1}{9} + \frac{1}{6}} = \dfrac{4}{\frac{651}{1080}} = \dfrac{4320}{651} = 6.6359$

Geometric mean $= \sqrt[4]{8 \cdot 5 \cdot 9 \cdot 6} = \sqrt[4]{2160}$

18. a) Arithmetic mean $= \dfrac{560 + 539 + \ldots + 543}{20} = \dfrac{11278}{20} = 563.9$

b) To calculate the 5% trimmed mean, we exclude the top 5% (the number 623) and the bottom 5% (the number 482). The mean of the remaining numbers is

5% trimmed mean $= \dfrac{560 + 539 + 553 + \ldots + 599 + 601}{18} = \dfrac{10173}{18}$

$= 565.17$

c) To calculate the 10% trimmed mean, we exclude the top 10% (the numbers 601 and 623) and the bottom 10% (the numbers 482 and 528). The mean of the remaining numbers is

10% trimmed mean $= \dfrac{560 + 539 + \ldots + 592 + 599}{16} = \dfrac{9044}{16}$

$= 565.25$

d) Since all three means are pretty close to each other, probably the arithmetic mean should be used. It is the easiest to calculate.

19. a) Midrange of bank failures $= \dfrac{2 + 14}{2} = 8$

b) Midrange of scholastic aptitude test scores

$= \dfrac{482 + 623}{2} = 552.5$

1. a) Range = 69 - 31 = 38

b)

x	x^2
41	1681
38	1444
44	1936
49	2401
52	2704
58	3364
63	3969
39	1521
31	961
69	4761
484	24742

$n = 10$

$\Sigma x = 484$

$\Sigma x^2 = 24742$

Sample variance = s^2

$$= \frac{10(24742) - 484^2}{10(10 - 1)}$$

$$= \frac{13164}{90} = 146.26667$$

Sample standard deviation = $\sqrt{146.26667}$

$$\approx 12.094$$

2. Range: 145,000 - 58,000 = $87,000

3.

x	$x - \bar{x}$	$(x - \bar{x})^2$	$|x - \bar{x}|$
2578	42	1764	42
1800	-736	541696	736
1579	-957	915849	957
2500	-36	1296	36
1210	-1326	1758276	1326
2650	114	12996	114
2398	-138	19044	138
3600	1064	1132096	1064
4100	1564	2446096	1564
2900	364	132496	364
3100	564	318096	564
3055	519	269361	519
1995	-541	292681	541
3175	639	408321	639
1400	-1136	1290496	1136
38040	0	9540564	9740

Mean $= \bar{x} = \dfrac{38040}{15}$

$= 2536$

Sample variance $= \dfrac{9540564}{14}$

$= 681468.857$

Sample standard deviation $=$

$\sqrt{681468.857} \approx 825.51$

Average deviation $= \dfrac{9740}{15}$

$= 649.33$

81

4.

x	x – $\bar{x}$	$(x – \bar{x})^2$	|x – $\bar{x}$|
13	-2	4	2
19	4	16	4
10	-5	25	5
8	-7	49	7
26	11	121	11
17	2	4	2
19	4	16	4
7	-8	64	8
12	-3	9	3
13	-2	4	2
5	-10	100	10
31	16	256	16
180	0	668	74

$\bar{x} = \dfrac{180}{12} = 15$

Sample variance $= \dfrac{668}{11}$

$= 60.7273$

Sample standard deviation

$= \sqrt{60.7273}$

≈ 7.7928

Average deviation $= \dfrac{74}{12}$

$= 6.167$

5.

x	$x - \mu$	$(x - \mu)^2$	$|x - \mu|$
28	-24	576	24
48	-4	16	4
56	4	16	4
63	11	121	11
49	-3	9	3
55	3	9	3
42	-10	100	10
60	8	64	8
40	-12	144	12
57	5	25	5
52	0	0	0
64	12	144	12
53	1	1	1
61	9	81	9
728	0	1306	106

$\mu = \dfrac{728}{14} = 52$

Population variance

$\quad = \dfrac{1306}{14} = 93.2857$

Population standard
deviation

$\quad = \sqrt{93.2857}$

$\quad \approx 9.658$

Average deviation $= \dfrac{106}{14}$

$\quad = 7.571$

6.

x	$x - \bar{x}$	$(x - \bar{x})^2$	$|x - \bar{x}|$
5	1	1	1
6	2	4	2
4	0	0	0
3	-1	1	1
1	-3	9	3
6	2	4	2
4	0	0	0
3	-1	1	1
4	0	0	0
36	0	20	10

Range = 6 - 1 = 5

Sample mean = $\bar{x} = \dfrac{36}{9} = 4$

Sample variance = $\dfrac{20}{8} = 2.5$

Sample standard deviation
$$= \sqrt{2.5}$$
$$\approx 1.5811$$

Average deviation = $\dfrac{10}{9}$
$$= 1.111$$

7. New range = 15
New sample mean = 12
New sample variance = 22.5

New standard deviation = $\sqrt{22.5}$
$$\approx 4.743$$
New average deviation = 3.333
The range, sample mean, sample standard deviation, and average deviation are 3 times as great as they were originally. The sample variance is 9 times as great as it was originally.

8.

x (men)	x^2	y (women)	y^2
31	961	26	676
37	1369	21	441
36	1296	23	529
41	1681	22	484
33	1089	35	1225
37	1369	39	1521
38	1444	43	1849
253	9209	209	6725

a) Population standard deviation

$$= \sqrt{\frac{9209}{7} - \frac{253^2}{49}}$$

$$= \sqrt{9.2653} \approx 3.044$$

b) Population standard deviation

$$= \sqrt{\frac{6725}{7} - \frac{209^2}{49}}$$

$$= \sqrt{69.2653} \approx 8.323$$

9. New mean will be 3400 + 500 or $3900. New standard deviation will remain at $375.

10. Assuming each customer's cost for insurance is increased by 20%, the new mean will also be increased by 20%. It will now be 3400 + (0.20)(3400) = $4080. The new standard deviation will be 1.20 times as great as it was before or (1.20)(375) = $450.

11.

x - 1.29	(x - 1.29)²	x - 1.36	(x - 1.36)²
0.12	0.0144	0.05	0.0025
0.09	0.0081	0.02	0.0004
0.16	0.0256	0.09	0.0081
0.07	0.0049	0	0
0	0.0000	−0.07	0.0049
0.44	0.0530	0.09	0.0159

a) Mean $= \dfrac{0.44}{5} + 1.29 = \$1.378$

Population standard deviation $= \sqrt{\dfrac{0.0530}{5} - \dfrac{(0.44)^2}{5^2}} \approx 0.053$

b) Mean $= \dfrac{0.09}{5} + 1.36 = \$1.378$

Population standard deviation $= \sqrt{\dfrac{0.0159}{5} - \dfrac{(0.09)^2}{25}} \approx 0.053$

c) In either case, the population mean and standard deviation turn out to be the same.

12. Probably battery B as the standard deviation is smaller.

13. We will use the class mark for each interval.

x	f	x·f	x^2	x^2·f
35	2	70	1225	2450
45	4	180	2025	8100
55	16	880	3025	48400
65	14	910	4225	59150
75	9	675	5625	50625
85	5	425	7225	36125
360	50	3140	23,350	204,850

$$\text{Mean} = \frac{\Sigma xf}{\Sigma f} = \frac{3140}{50} = 62.8$$

$$\text{Sample variance} = \frac{50(204,850) - (3140)^2}{50(49)}$$

$$= \frac{382900}{2450} = 156.2857$$

$$\text{Sample standard deviation} = \sqrt{156.2857}$$

$$\approx 12.501$$

14.

Class Mark, x	f	x·f	x^2	x^2·f
100	6	600	10,000	60,000
300	7	2100	90,000	630,000
500	16	8000	250,000	4,000,000
700	32	22400	490,000	15,680,000
900	21	18900	810,000	17,010,000
1100	15	16500	1,210,000	18,150,000
1300	3	3900	1,690,000	5,070,000
4900	100	72400	4,550,000	60,600,000

$$\text{Mean} = \frac{72400}{100} = 724$$

$$\text{Sample variance} = \frac{100(60,600,000) - (72400)^2}{100(99)}$$

$$= \frac{818,240,000}{9900} = 82650.505$$

Sample standard deviation $\approx$ 287.49

15. Although the average cost per gallon of gas in both neighborhoods is the same, the standard deviation is smaller in the poorer neighborhoods.

1. We must first calculate the sample standard deviation. We have

x	x^2
69	4761
58	3364
68	4624
37	1369
76	5776
53	2809
41	1681
38	1444
39	1521
37	1369
516	28,718

Sample mean = $\dfrac{516}{10}$ = 51.6

Sample standard deviation

$$= \sqrt{\frac{10(28,718) - (516)^2}{10(9)}}$$

s ≈ 15.25

When k = 2, Chebyshev's Theorem says that at least $\dfrac{3}{4}$ of the

sample measurements will fall within 51.6 ± 2(15.25) or

between 21.1 and 82.1. Since n = 10, $\dfrac{3}{4}$ of the sample is 7.5

Actually all 10 of the numbers are between 21.1 and 82.1,

which is greater than 7.5. Thus, Chebyshev's Theorem is

true. When k = 3, Ckebyshev's Theorem says that at least $\dfrac{8}{9}$

of the sample measurements will fall within 51.6 ± 3(15.25)

or between 5.85 and 97.35. Since n = 10, $\dfrac{8}{9}$ of the sample is

8.89. In our case, all 10 of the numbers are between 5.85 and

97.35, which is greater than 8.89. Thus, Chebyshev's Theorem

is again true.

2. We must first calculate the sample standard deviation.

x	x^2
8.3	68.89
8.1	65.61
5.1	26.01
5.5	30.25
6.9	47.61
4.3	18.49
2.7	7.29
3.5	12.25
5.1	26.01
2.9	8.41
3.8	14.44
2.2	4.84
58.4	330.1

Sample mean = $\dfrac{58.4}{12}$ = 4.8667

Sample standard deviation

$= \sqrt{\dfrac{12(330.1) - (58.4)^2}{12(11)}}$

$= 2.042$

When k = 2, at least $\dfrac{3}{4}$ of the measurements will fall within 4.8667 ± 2(2.042) or between 0.7827 and 8.9507.

When k = 3, at least $\dfrac{8}{9}$ of the measurements will fall within 4.8667 ± 3(2.042) or between -1.2593 and 10.9927.

3.   66 - 54 = 54 - 42 = 12
          8k = 12
           k = 1.5

$1 - \dfrac{1}{k^2} = 1 - \dfrac{1}{(1.5)^2} = 0.5556$ At least 55.56%

90

ANSWERS TO EXERCISES FOR SECTION 3.6 (CONTINUED) - (PAGES 139 - 140)

4. $1035 - 985 = 985 - 935 = 50$

$$25k = 50$$
$$k = 2$$

$$1 - \frac{1}{2^2} = 1 - \frac{1}{4} = \frac{3}{4}$$

At least 75%

5.

x	x^2
85	7225
87	7569
74	5476
64	4096
66	4356
56	3136
53	2809
72	5184
90	8100
62	3844
92	8464
50	2500
84	7056
82	6724
71	5041
68	4624
68	4624
78	6084
87	7569
59	3481
1448	107962

a) Sample mean $= \dfrac{1448}{20} = 72.4$

Sample standard deviation

$$= \sqrt{\frac{20(107,962) - 1448^2}{20(19)}}$$

$$= 12.828$$

b) $1 - \dfrac{1}{(2.5)^2} = 1 - 0.16$

$= 0.84$
At least 84%

$1 - \dfrac{1}{4^2} = 1 - 0.0625$

$= 0.9375$
At least 93.75%

c) When k = 2.5, at least 84% of the measurements will fall within 72.4 ± 2.5(12.828) or between 40.33 and 104.47. In our case, 100% of the observations fall in this interval.

When k = 4, at least 93.75% of the measurements will fall within 72.4 ± 4(12.828) or between 21.088 and 123.712. The percentage of measurements falling within these intervals is indeed true. In our case, 100% of the observations fall in this interval.

d) Chebyshev's theorem is valid.

1. Percentile rank of Alfred = $\dfrac{6 + \frac{1}{2}(2)}{24} \cdot 100 = 29.16$ percentile

   Percentile rank of Bruce = $\dfrac{1 + \frac{1}{2}(2)}{24} \cdot 100 = 8.33$ percentile

2. **a)** $\dfrac{88 + \frac{1}{2}(9)}{100} \cdot 100 = 92.5$ percentile

   b) $\dfrac{46 + \frac{1}{2}(24)}{100} \cdot 100 = 58$ percentile

3. $\dfrac{59 + \frac{1}{2}(6)}{84} \cdot 100 = 73.81$ percentile

4. **a)** 25% **b)** 15% **c)** 50% **d)** 85% − 25% = 60%

5. $\dfrac{18 + \frac{1}{2}(2)}{25} \cdot 100 = 76$ percentile

6. **a)**

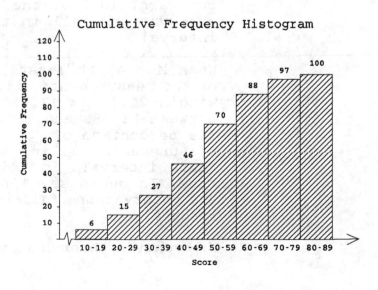

92

6. b)

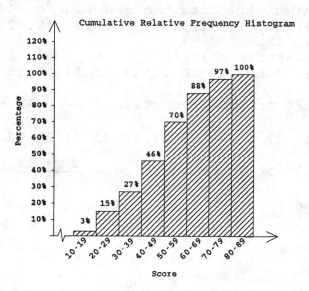

Cumulative Relative Frequency Histogram

7. a) smallest value = 50   largest value = 98
When arranged in order, the data becomes 50, 55, 59, 65,
68, 69, 73, 76, 78, 80, 80, 80, 80, 83, 84, 85, 85, 86,
90, 90, 93, 95, 96, 97, 98.
Median or middle quartile = 80
Lower half of data: 50 55 59 65 68 69 73 76 78 80 80 80

Median of lower half or lower quartile = $\dfrac{69 + 73}{2}$ = 71

b) Upper half of data: 83 84 85 85 86 90 90 93 95 96 97 98
Median of upper half or upper quartile = 90

c)

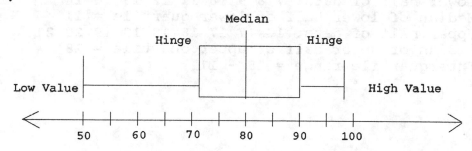

8. **a)** smallest value = 3   largest value = 32
When arranged in order, the data becomes 3, 8, 9, 10, 10,
11, 12, 13, 14, 15, 15, 16, 17, 17, 18, 19, 19, 21, 22,
23, 24, 25, 28, 31, 32.
Median or middle quartile = 17
Lower half of data: 3 8 9 10 10 11 12 13 14 15 15 16

Median of lower half or lower quartile = $\dfrac{11 + 12}{2}$ = 11.5

b) Upper half of data: 17 18 19 19 21 22 23 24 25 28 31 32

Median of upper half or upper quartile = $\dfrac{22 + 23}{2}$ = 22.5

c) Interquartile range = 22.5 - 11.5 = 11
d)

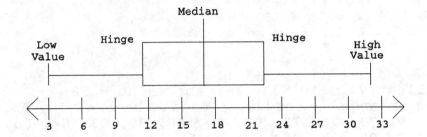

9. **a)** smallest value = 7   largest value = 21
When arranged in order, the data becomes 7, 8, 9, 10, 11,
12, 13, 14, 14, 15, 16, 17, 17, 17, 18, 18, 19, 19, 20,
21

Median or middle quartile = $\dfrac{15 + 16}{2}$ = 15.5

Lower half of data: 7 8 9 10 11 12 13 14 14
Median of lower half or lower quartile = 11
b) Upper half of data: 17 17 17 18 18 19 19 20 21
Median of upper half or upper quartile = 18
c) Interquartile range = 18 - 11 = 7

9. d)

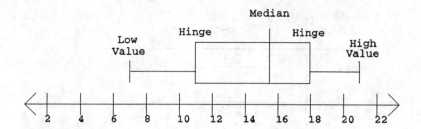

10. a) 0.01 + 0.02 + 0.06 + 0.10 + 0.17 + 0.19 + 0.15 = 0.70
70th percentile falls in the 100-109 category. Using class mark of this category 70th percentile = 104.5

    b) 0.01 + 0.02 + 0.06 + 0.10 + 0.17 + 0.19 + 0.18 + 0.15 + 0.02 = 0.90   90th percentile falls in the 120-129 category. Using class mark of this category 90th percentile = 124.5

ANSWERS TO EXERCISES FOR SECTION 3.8 – (PAGES 156 – 159)

1. a) $z = \dfrac{200 - 185}{15} = 1$ **b)** $z = \dfrac{120 - 185}{15} = -4.33$

   c) $z = \dfrac{185 - 185}{15} = 0$ **d)** $z = \dfrac{240 - 185}{15} = 3.67$

2. a) Hilda, Ike, Sherry, Susan, Marilyn
   b) Susan, Marilyn
   c) Hilda, Ike, and Sherry

3. New York Lakes ($\mu = 23.33$, $\sigma = 6.289$)

Lake	z-value
A	$\dfrac{22 - 23.33}{6.289} = -0.21$
B	$\dfrac{15 - 23.33}{6.289} = -1.32$
C	$\dfrac{29 - 23.33}{6.289} = 0.90$
D	$\dfrac{33 - 23.33}{6.289} = 1.54$
E	$\dfrac{24 - 23.33}{6.289} = 0.11$
F	$\dfrac{17 - 23.33}{6.289} = -1.01$

New Jersey Lakes ($\mu = 68.8$, $\sigma = 4.534$)

Lake	z-value
Q	$\dfrac{68 - 68.8}{4.534} = -0.18$
R	$\dfrac{75 - 68.8}{4.534} = 1.37$
S	$\dfrac{61 - 68.8}{4.534} = -1.72$
T	$\dfrac{70 - 68.8}{4.534} = 0.26$
U	$\dfrac{70 - 68.8}{4.534} = 0.26$

a) Lake D since it has the highest z-value ($z = 1.54$).
b) Lake S since it has the lowest z-value ($z = -1.72$).

4. We use formula $x = \mu + z\sigma$ with $\mu = 36$ and $\sigma = 2.4$
Joe's age $= 36 + (-1.6)(2.4) = 32.16$ years
Drew's age $= 36 + (2.1)(2.4) = 41.04$ years
Derek's age $= 36 + (-0.12)(2.4) = 35.712$ years

5. Alan's z-score = $\dfrac{75 - 82}{4}$ = -1.75

   Derek's z-score = $\dfrac{120 - 137}{12}$ = -1.42

   Since Derek's z-score is better, he has a higher math aptitude.

6. **a)** $60 as the z-score is 0.
   b) Between a percentile rank of 16 and 50 or 34%
   c) $x = \mu + z\sigma$
   $= 60 + (-1.38)10 = \$46.20$

7. **a)** Accounting: $z = \dfrac{49 - 45}{4.7} = 0.85$

   Finance: $z = \dfrac{81 - 80}{8.3} = 0.12$

   Marketing/Management: $z = \dfrac{62 - 79}{11.2} = -1.52$

   Real Estate/Insurance: $z = \dfrac{19 - 20}{3.1} = -0.32$

   Retailing/Sales: $z = \dfrac{40 - 41}{2.6} = -0.38$

   b) Accounting since it has the highest z-score.
   c) Marketing/Management since it has the lowest z-score.

8. For Table 3.2   For Table 3.3

z	$z - \mu$	$(z - \mu)^2$
-1.52	-1.52	2.3104
-0.54	-0.54	0.2916
0	0	0
0.65	0.65	0.4225
1.41	1.41	<u>1.9881</u>
		5.0126

$\mu = 0$

z	$z - \mu$	$(z - \mu)^2$
-1.32	-1.32	1.7424
-0.66	-0.66	0.4356
0	0	0
0.33	0.33	0.1089
1.65	1.65	<u>2.7225</u>
		5.0094

$\mu = 0$

$$\text{Standard deviation} = \sqrt{\frac{5.0126}{5}}$$
$$= 1.001$$
$$\text{or approximately 1}$$

$$\text{Standard deviation} = \sqrt{\frac{5.0094}{5}}$$
$$= 1.0009$$
$$\text{or approximately 1}$$

9. **a)** 84.13%   **b)** 100 - 15.87 = 84.13%   **c)** 84.13%

ANSWERS TO TESTING YOUR UNDERSTANDING OF THIS CHAPTER'S CONCEPTS – (PAGES 165 – 166)

1. He may not necessarily be accepted to college. The high school average has nothing to do with percentile rank.

2. Yes. Especially when you have extreme scores.

3. $\Sigma(x - \mu) = \Sigma x - \Sigma \mu$
$$= \Sigma x - n\mu$$
$$= \Sigma x - n\left(\frac{\Sigma x}{n}\right) \quad \text{since } \mu = \frac{\Sigma x}{n}$$
$$= \Sigma x - \Sigma x = 0$$

4. $$\sqrt{\frac{\sum(x - \overline{x})^2}{n - 1}} = \sqrt{\frac{\sum(x^2 - 2x\overline{x} + \overline{x}^2)}{n - 1}}$$

$$= \sqrt{\frac{\sum x^2 - \sum 2x\overline{x} + \sum(\overline{x}^2)}{n - 1}}$$

$$= \sqrt{\frac{\sum x^2}{n - 1} - \frac{2\overline{x}\sum x}{n - 1} + \frac{n(\overline{x}^2)}{n - 1}} \qquad \text{Note} \quad \overline{x} = \frac{\sum x}{n}$$

$$= \sqrt{\frac{\sum x^2}{n - 1} - \frac{2n(\overline{x}^2)}{n - 1} + \frac{n(\overline{x}^2)}{n - 1}}$$

$$= \sqrt{\frac{\sum x^2}{n - 1} - \frac{n(\overline{x}^2)}{n - 1}}$$

$$= \sqrt{\frac{\sum x^2}{n - 1} - \frac{(\sum x)(\sum x)}{n(n - 1)}}$$

$$= \sqrt{\frac{n\sum x^2 - (\sum x)^2}{n(n - 1)}}$$

5. b)   c)

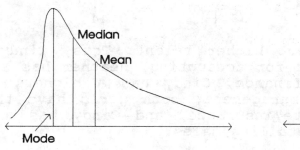

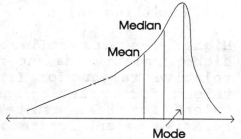

6. You will have 99.7% of the terms of the distribution falling
    between z = -3 and z = +3.

1. a) $\quad \mu = \dfrac{\Sigma x}{n} \qquad\qquad 75 = \dfrac{\Sigma x}{10} \qquad\qquad \Sigma x = 750$

   b) $\quad \sigma^2 = \dfrac{\Sigma x^2}{n} - \dfrac{(\Sigma x)^2}{n^2}$

   $\qquad\qquad 64 = \dfrac{\Sigma x^2}{10} - \dfrac{750^2}{100}$

   $\qquad\qquad 64 = \dfrac{\Sigma x^2}{10} - 5625$

   $\qquad\quad 5689 = \dfrac{\Sigma x^2}{10}$

   $\qquad 56{,}890 = \Sigma x^2$

2. Using the results of the graphs given in Exercise 9 of Section 3.8, we convert each of Cindy's percentile ranks into z-scores.

	Percentile rank	Approximate z-score
Accounting	99	+2.33
Finance	72	+0.58
Marketing/Management	87	+1.13
Real Estate/Insurance	50	0
Retailing/Sales	33	-0.44

   Higher z-scores reflect higher talent: Thus, Cindy has a higher relative talent for accounting, Heather has a higher relative talent for finance, Cindy has a higher relative talent for marketing/management, both girls have the same talent for real estate/insurance, and Cindy has a higher relative talent for retailing/sales.

3. Yes, if all the terms of the distribution are the same.

4. Zero

5. Not necessarily true. See the data given in Exercise 4 of Section 3.7.

6. False. Positive z-scores will occur for any terms (positive or negative) that are above the mean.

ANSWERS TO THINKING CRITICALLY (CONTINUED) - (PAGE 166)

7. Since $\sigma = 0$, all the terms are the same.

8. No. Both teams may have different numbers of members. A weighted average is needed.

ANSWERS TO REVIEW EXERCISES FOR CHAPTER 3 - (PAGES 167 - 168)

1. Probably brand A because of its smaller standard deviation. Others may disagree.

2. **a)** $\Sigma x = 19 + 23 + 11 + 16 + 13 = 82$

   b) $\Sigma x^2 = 19^2 + 23^2 + 11^2 + 16^2 + 13^2 = 1436$

3. The standard deviation for the number of windows on Trafalagar Ave is less than the standard deviation for the number of windows on Billings Lane.

4. No. If the average depth is 3 feet, there can be parts of the pool that are more than 6 feet in depth.

5. $\dfrac{4(750) + 7(650)}{11} = \$686.36$

6. Yes, although both dating services have the same average age of 20 years, the standard deviation for dating service A is considerably larger.

7. We use the class mark.

x	f	x·f	x^2	x^2·f
149.5	12	1794	22350.25	268203.00
249.5	28	6986	62250.25	1743007.00
349.5	20	6990	122150.25	2443005.00
449.5	18	8091	202050.25	3636904.50
549.5	14	7693	301950.25	4227303.50
649.5	8	5196	421850.25	3374802.00
2397	100	36750	1132601.50	15693225

$$\text{Sample mean} = \frac{\Sigma xf}{\Sigma f} = \frac{36750}{100} = 367.5$$

$$\text{Sample standard deviation} = \sqrt{\frac{n(\Sigma x^2 \cdot f) - (\Sigma x \cdot f)^2}{n(n-1)}}$$

$$= \sqrt{\frac{100(15693225) - (36750)^2}{100(99)}}$$

$$\approx 148.65$$

8. P_{55} = In the 300-399 category as 12 + 28 + 15 = 55. Thus P_{55} = 349.5 (using the class mark).

9. $z = \dfrac{6200 - 6000}{185} = 1.08$

10. Using the class marks, **a)** P_{70} = 524.5 as 0.01 + 0.02 + 0.06 + 0.10 + 0.17 + 0.19 + 0.15 = 0.70
    b) P_{90} = 624.5 as 0.01 + 0.02 + 0.06 + 0.10 + 0.17 + 0.19 + 0.18 + 0.15 + 0.02 = 0.90

11. 25% as the third quartile is the same as the upper quartile and thus that 75% of the scores are below 83.

1. **a)** The mode is 15

    b) The median is between 24 and 35 or $\dfrac{24 + 35}{2} = 29.5$

    c) The mean is $\dfrac{9 + 13 + 15 + \ldots + 96}{12} = \dfrac{485}{12} = 40.417$

    d) The lower quartile or P_{25} is median of lower half of numbers 9, 13, 15, 15, 15, 24. Thus lower quartile is 15.

    e) The upper quartile or P_{75} is median of upper half of numbers 35, 42, 64, 75, 82, 96. Thus upper quartile is 69.5.

2. Midterm z-score $\dfrac{80 - 85}{8} = -0.625$. Final z-score $\dfrac{60 - 68}{12} =$

    -0.666. When compared to the rest of the class, she did better on the midterm as it has a higher z-score.

3. Using Chebyshev's theorem, at least $1 - \dfrac{1}{(1.5)^2}$ of the terms

    will lie within 1.5 standard deviation units of the mean so at least 55.56% of the terms will fall in this category.

4. We use the class mark.

x	f	x·f	x^2	x^2·f
7	2	14	49	98
12	16	192	144	2304
17	55	935	289	15895
22	111	2442	484	53724
27	65	1755	729	47385
32	9	288	1024	9216
117	258	5626	2719	128622

$$\text{Sample mean} = \frac{\Sigma xf}{\Sigma f} = \frac{5626}{258} = 21.8062$$

$$\text{Sample standard deviation} = \sqrt{\frac{n(\Sigma x^2 \cdot f) - (\Sigma x \cdot f)^2}{n(n-1)}}$$

$$= \sqrt{\frac{258(128,622) - (5626)^2}{258(257)}}$$

$$\approx 4.8077$$

5. **a)** $Q_1 = 3$
   b) $Q_3 = 4$
   c) $P_{80} = 5$
   d) $P_{95} = 6$

6. **a)** 29
   b) lower quartile = 23 and upper quartile = 31
   c) Interquartile range = 31 - 23 = 8

7. We will group the data

Interval	Frequency	Relative Frequency
28-29	6	0.20
30-31	3	0.10
32-33	4	0.13
34-35	4	0.13
36-37	1	0.03
38-39	4	0.13
40-41	3	0.10
42-43	3	0.10
44-45	2	0.07
	30	≈1.00

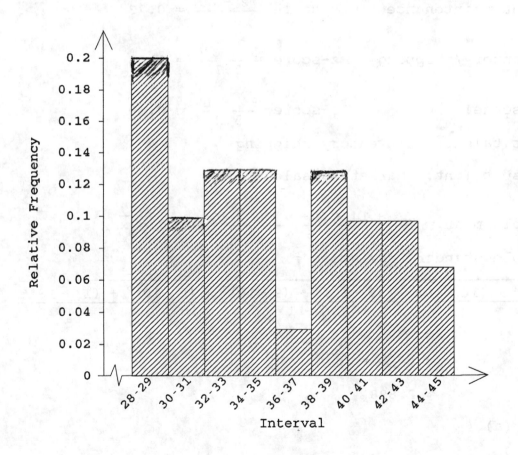

8. $\mu = 48$ and $\sigma = 9.1$. Using formula $x = \mu + z\sigma$
   Bob: $48 + (3.3)(9.1) = 78.03$ seconds
   Mark: $48 + (-0.45)(9.1) = 43.905$ seconds
   Chris: $48 + (1.43)(9.1) = 61.013$ seconds

9. Average age $= \dfrac{25(28) + 36(32)}{25 + 36} = 30.36$ years

10. $\overline{x} = 19.2$ and $\Sigma(x - \overline{x}) = 0$

11. Maureen's percentile rank $= \dfrac{32 + \frac{1}{2}(7)}{50} \cdot 100 = 71$

12. **a)** Marketing/sales   z-score $\dfrac{59 - 58}{6.8} = 0.15$

    Plant maintenance   z-score $\dfrac{72 - 69}{4.1} = 0.73$

    Inventory/shipping   z-score $\dfrac{31 - 27}{3.7} = 1.08$

    Personnel   z-score $\dfrac{84 - 83}{5.2} = 0.19$

    b) Most talent: Inventory/shipping

    c) Least talent: Marketing/sales

13.   Sample mean $= \dfrac{12 + 14 + 6 + 9 + 8 + 11}{6} = 10 = \overline{x}$

    Sample standard deviation =

$$\sqrt{\dfrac{(12-10)^2 + (14-10)^2 + (6-10)^2 + (9-10)^2 + (8-10)^2 + (11-10)^2}{6 - 1}}$$

$$= \sqrt{\dfrac{42}{5}} = \sqrt{8.4}$$

$$\approx 2.898$$

14. Choice (a)

15. Choice (a)

16. Choice (d)

17. Choice (c)

18. Choice (c)

19. Choice (d)

20. Choice (b)

1. If $x_1 = 5$, $x_2 = 8$, $x_3 = 9$, $x_4 = 10$, and $x_5 = 13$, find Σx^2.

    a) 2025   b) 439   c) 45   d) 25   e) none of these

    Answer _____

For question 2 - 7 use the following information which gives the weights (in pounds) of some of the people who joined the Brighton Health Club on January 17.

    George 153   Heather 123   Peter 165   Tom 147
    Martha 102   Gail 119   Priscilla 123
    Bill 137   Jim 145   Robert 156

2. Find the (sample) mean weight of these people.

    a) 137   b) 123   c) 141   d) 145   e) none of these

    Answer _____

3. Find the median weight for these people.

    a) 137   b) 123   c) 141   d) 145   e) none of these

    Answer _____

4. Find the modal weight for these people.

    a) 137   b) 123   c) 141   d) 145   e) none of these

    Answer _____

5. Find Heather's percentile rank

    a) 20th percentile   b) 25th percentile
    c) 80th percentile   d) 75th percentile
    e) none of these

    Answer _____

6. Find Heather's z-score.

    a) -0.709   b) +0.709   c) -0.7477   d) +0.7477
    e) none of these

    Answer _____

7. Find the sample standard deviation for this data.

a) 350.6   b) 18.724   c) 389.556   d) 19.737
e) none of these

Answer _____

8. All applicants for a prestigious office managerial job are required to take four different exams. Arlene's results, as well as the results of the other applicants for the job, are shown below.

Type of Exam	Arlene's score	Average Score	Standard Deviation
Personality	89	76	14.7
Business skills	74	67	7.3
Medical	56	49	9.6
Computer skills	107	95	11.2

By transforming each of Arlene's results into z-scores, determine in which test Arlene performed the best (on a comparative basis).

a) Personality   b) Business skills   c) Medical
d) Computer skills

Answer _____

9. If the variance of a set of numbers is 0.81, find the standard deviation.

a) 0.9   b) 9   c) 0.81   d) 0.09   e) none of these

Answer _____

10. On February 14, the 10 busses on the Rawley route carried an average of 40 riders whereas the 16 busses on the Piedro route carried an average of 46 riders. Find the average number of riders carried by the busses on both of these routes on February 14.

a) 13   b) 43   c) 40   d) 43.692   e) none of these

Answer _____

CHAPTER 3 - NUMERICAL METHODS FOR ANALYZING DATA
SUPPLEMENTARY TEST FORM B

1. If $x_1 = 17$, $x_2 = 19$, $x_3 = 16$, $x_4 = 5$, $x_5 = 11$, find $(\Sigma x)^2$.

    a) 68   b) 4624   c) 1052   d) 25   e) none of these

    Answer _____

For questions 2 - 7 use the following formation: On January 11, a newspaper reporter surveyed ten hospitals in a city to determine the number of vacant beds available on that day and obtained the results shown below.

Mercy Hospital 22   Arverne Hospital 18   Marrow Hospital 23
Lincoln Hospital 14   Pylor Hospital 17   Arcadia Hospital 8
Washington Hospital 16   Bellton Hospital 37   Stately Hospital 19
Vernon Hospital 16

2. Find the (sample) mean number of beds available at these hospitals.

    a) 19   b) 16   c) 17.5   d) 17   e) none of these

    Answer _____

3. Find the median number of beds available at these hospitals.

    a) 19   b) 16   c) 17.5   d) 17   e) none of these

    Answer _____

4. Find the modal number of beds available at these hospitals.

    a) 19   b) 16   c) 17.5   d) 17   e) none of these

    Answer _____

5. Find the percentile rank for Bellton Hospital.

    a) 90th percentile   b) 95th percentile
    c) 80th percentile   d) 5th percentile
    e) none of these

    Answer _____

6. Find the z-score for Washington Hospital.
    a) -0.395   b) +0.395   c) -0.4168   d) +0.4168
    e) none of these

    Answer _____

7. Find the (sample) standard deviation.

    a) 57.556   b) 7.587   c) 51.8   d) 7.197
    e) none of these

                                        Answer _____

8. For the set of numbers 3, 5, 8, 14, 17, and 23, find $\Sigma(x - \mu)$.

    a) 70   b) 11.667   c) 58.333   d) 0   e) none of these

                                        Answer _____

9. Refer back to question 8. If 16 is added to each term, what happens to the standard deviation?

    a) It remains the same
    b) It becomes 16 times as great as it was before
    c) It becomes 4 times as great as it was before
    d) It is increased by 16
    e) none of these

                                        Answer _____

10. Gwendolyn had a z-score of -2.34 on an aptitude test where the average score was 58 with a standard deviation of 2.61. What was Gwendolyn's actual score?

    a) 58   b) 64.1074   c) 6.1074   d) 51.8926
    e) none of these

                                        Answer _____

111

1. Consider the distribution 21, 14, 16, 20, and 19. The population standard deviation of this distribution is

    a) 34   b) $\sqrt{34}$ c) 6.8   d) $\sqrt{6.8}$ e) none of these

    Answer _____

2. The median of the distribution 130, 70, 190, 90, and 70 is

    a) 190   b) 70   c) 130   d) 90   e) none of these

    Answer _____

3. In the array of scores 8, 20, 48, 60, 68, 92, 128, 164, 164, the score of 68 is

    a) the mean
    b) the median
    c) the mode
    d) all of the above
    e) none of these

    Answer _____

4. If $x_1 = 4$, $x_2 = 7$, $x_3 = 9$, $x_4 = 10$, and $x_5 = 14$, then $\Sigma x - \mu$ equals

    a) 44   b) 0   c) 35.2   d) 8.8   e) none of these

    Answer _____

5. If the mean of a distribution is 15 and if we add 5 to each score, the new mean is
    a) 20   b) 5   c) 15
    d) insufficient information given to answer   e) none of these

    Answer _____

6. Consider the following set of numbers which represents the number of mislabelled items that the ten labelling machines of the Apex Packaging Company produced during the first week of June.

    14, 30, 8, 18, 6, 28, 24, 42, 28, 20

    The percentile rank of 28 is
    a) 80th percentile   b) 65th percentile   c) 75th percentile
    d) 70th percentile   e) none of these

    Answer _____

7. At Pete's fruitstand, plums cost 39 cents/lb, potatoes cost 28 cents/lb, and cherries cost 98 cents/lb. Sherman purchases 7 pounds of plums, 8 pounds of potatoes, and 3 pounds of cherries. Find the average cost per pound of these items.

a) 53 cents   b) $7.91   c) $1.65   d) 18 cents   e) 44 cents

Answer _____

8. What is the average deviation of the following set of numbers?

8, 5, 6, 2, 4

a) 1.6   b) $\sqrt{5}$ c) 8   d) 5   e) none of these

Answer _____

9. The following is the grade distribution on a statistics midterm examination:

Interval	Frequency
90 - 100	5
80 - 89	17
70 - 79	11
60 - 69	9
0 - 59	4
	46

In which interval is the median located?

a) 90 - 100   b) 80 - 89   c) 70 - 79   d) 60 - 69   e) 0 - 59

Answer _____

10. Refer back to the previous question. In which interval is the mean located?

a) 90 - 100   b) 80 - 89   c) 70 - 79   d) 60 - 69   e) 0 - 59

Answer _____

Form A	Form B	Form C
1. Choice (b)	1. Choice (b)	1. Choice (d)
2. Choice (a)	2. Choice (a)	2. Choice (d)
3. Choice (c)	3. Choice (c)	3. Choice (b)
4. Choice (b)	4. Choice (b)	4. Choice (c)
5. Choice (e)	5. Choice (b)	5. Choice (a)
6. Choice (a)	6. Choice (a)	6. Choice (d)
7. Choice (d)	7. Choice (b)	7. Choice (e)
8. Choice (d)	8. Choice (d)	8. Choice (a)
9. Choice (a)	9. Choice (a)	9. Choice (c)
10. Choice (d)	10. Choice (d)	10. Choice (c)

Answers to Exercises for Chapter 4

1. a) $\dfrac{2619}{10,672}$

   b) $\dfrac{1424 + 2619 + 3227}{10,672} = \dfrac{7270}{10,672} = \dfrac{3635}{5336}$

   c) 0

   d) 1

2. a) $\dfrac{70000 + 5000}{702000} = \dfrac{75000}{702000} = \dfrac{75}{702}$

   b) $\dfrac{157000 + 5000}{702,000} = \dfrac{162,000}{702000} = \dfrac{81}{351}$

   c) $\dfrac{470000}{702,000} = \dfrac{235}{351}$

3. a) $\dfrac{12}{274} = \dfrac{6}{137}$

   b) $\dfrac{55 + 42}{274} = \dfrac{97}{274}$

   c) $\dfrac{31 + 29}{274} = \dfrac{60}{274} = \dfrac{30}{137}$

   d) $\dfrac{12 + 40 + 42 + 29}{274} = \dfrac{123}{274}$

4. a) $\dfrac{1}{4}$ b) No

5. a) $\dfrac{4}{20} = \dfrac{1}{5}$ b) $\dfrac{7}{20}$

   c) $\dfrac{3 + 6}{20} = \dfrac{9}{20}$ d) $\dfrac{7 + 3 + 6}{20} = \dfrac{16}{20} = \dfrac{4}{5}$

6. Choices (b), (d) and (e).

7. By listing the elements of the sample space, one finds that there are 10 possible combinations of 3 winners from the 5 nominated. Thus the probability that the winners are Jeremy,

   Mary and Ahamad is $\frac{1}{10}$.

8. $\frac{1}{7}$

9. There are 16 elements in the sample space: BBBB, BBBG, BBGB, BGBB, GBBB, BBGG, BGBG, BGGB, GBBG, GBGB, GGBB, BGGG, GBGG, GGBG, GGGB, AND GGGG. Six of these are favorable. Thus

$$p(2 \text{ boys and 2 girls}) = \frac{6}{16} = \frac{3}{8}$$

10. **a)** CCC, CCW, CWC, WCC, CWW, WCW, WWC, WWW

    b) $\frac{1}{8}$

    c) $\frac{7}{8}$

    d) $\frac{1}{8}$

11. **a)** $\frac{226 + 307}{1000} = \frac{533}{1000}$

    b) $\frac{17}{1000}$

    c) $\frac{307 + 112 + 97 + 9}{1000} = \frac{525}{1000} = \frac{21}{40}$

    d) $\frac{97}{1000}$

12. $\frac{197}{200}$

13. **a)** $\dfrac{88 + 65 + 39}{656} = \dfrac{192}{656}$

    b) $\dfrac{88 + 95 + 31 + 56}{656} = \dfrac{270}{656}$

    c) $\dfrac{65}{256}$

14. $\dfrac{2000}{10000} = \dfrac{1}{5}$

15.

Disc 1	Disc 2	Disc 3
Label 1	Label 2	Label 3
Label 1	Label 3	Label 2
Label 2	Label 1	Label 3
Label 2	Label 3	Label 1
Label 3	Label 2	Label 1
Label 3	Label 1	Label 2

Probability is $\dfrac{1}{6}$.

16. List the sample space as in previous problem. Probability is $\dfrac{1}{24}$.

17. **a)** Let L = lemon, C = cherry and A = apple. The sample space is LLL, LLC, LCL, LCC, LCA, LLA, LAA, LAC, LAL, CLL, CLC, CCL, CCC, CCA, CLA, CAA, CAC, CAL, ALL, ALC, ACL, ACC, ACA, ALA, AAA, AAC, AAL. There are 27 possible outcomes.

    b) $\dfrac{3}{27} = \dfrac{1}{9}$

1. 3 X 2 X 2 = 12 different ways

2. 9 X 8 = 72 different ways

3. 4 X 3 X 5 = 60 possible meals

4. 6 X 4 X 3 = 72 possible ways

5. **a)** $5 \cdot 4 \cdot 3 \cdot 2 \cdot 1 = 120$ possible ways
   b) $5 \cdot 5 \cdot 5 \cdot 5 \cdot 5 = 3125$ possible ways

6. $1 \cdot 26 \cdot 26 \cdot 10 \cdot 10 = 67,600$ possible tags

7. $10 \cdot 10 \cdot 10 \cdot 10 \cdot 10 \cdot 10 = 1,000,000$ possible combinations

8. $7 \cdot 6 \cdot 5 \cdot 4 \cdot 3 \cdot 2 \cdot 1 = 5040$ different ways.

9. $3 \cdot 3 \cdot 2 \cdot 1 = 18$ possible numbers. Note: There are only 3 choices for the first digit since the number must be greater than 3000.

10. There are 70 possible outcomes: 2 ways to end in four games, 8 ways to end in five games, 20 ways to end in six games and 40 ways to end in seven games.

11.

Child 1 Child 2 Child 3 Child 4 Child 5 Family Consists of

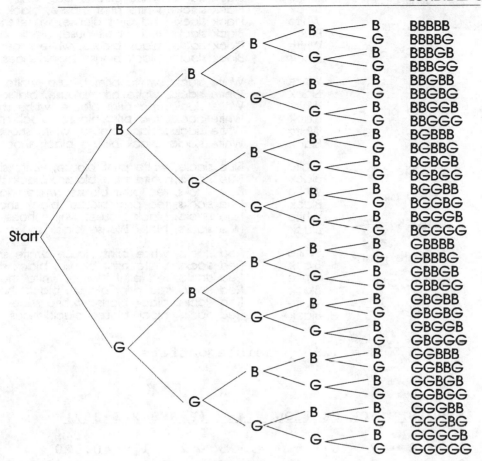

12. $10 \cdot 10 \cdot 10 \cdot 10 \cdot 10 \cdot 10 \cdot 10 \cdot 10 \cdot 10 = 10^9$ possible zip codes.

13. **a)** $10 \cdot 9 \cdot 8 \cdot 26 \cdot 26 \cdot 26 = 12,654,720$ possible plates.
b) $10 \cdot 10 \cdot 10 \cdot 26 \cdot 26 \cdot 26 = 17,576,000$ possible plates.

14. $3 \cdot 2 \cdot 1 = 6$ different ways

15. **a)** $7 \cdot 6 \cdot 5 \cdot 4 \cdot 3 \cdot 2 \cdot 1 = 5040$ possible ways
b) 3600

c) $\dfrac{1440}{5040} = \dfrac{2}{7}$

16. $26 \cdot 26 \cdot 26 = 17,576$ possible pairs

119

17.

Slacks	Blouses	Shoes	Outfit consists of
Black	White print	White	Black slacks, white print blouse, white shoes
		Black	Black slacks, white print blouse, black shoes
	Red print	White	Black slacks, red print blouse, white shoes
		Black	Black slacks, red print blouse, black shoes
	Black	White	Black slacks, black blouse, white shoes
		Black	Black slacks, black blouse black shoes
White	White print	White	White slacks, white print blouse, white shoes
		Black	White slacks, white print blouse, black shoes
	Red print	White	White slacks, red print blouse, white shoes
		Black	White slacks, red print blouse, black shoes
	Black	White	White slacks, black blouse, white shoes
		Black	White slacks, black blouse black shoes
Blue	White print	White	Blue slacks, white print blouse, white shoes
		Black	Blue slacks, white print blouse, black shoes
	Red print	White	Blue slacks, red print blouse, white shoes
		Black	Blue slacks, red print blouse, black shoes
	Black	White	Blue slacks, black blouse, white shoes
		Black	Blue slacks, black blouse black shoes
Red	White print	White	Red slacks, white print blouse, white shoes
		Black	Red slacks, white print blouse, black shoes
	Red print	White	Red slacks, red print blouse, white shoes
		Black	Red slacks, red print blouse, black shoes
	Black	White	Red slacks, black blouse, white shoes
		Black	Red slacks, black blouse black shoes

Start

18. 6 X 4 X 3 X 6 X 3 = 1296 possible outfits

1. a) $8! = 8 \cdot 7 \cdot 6 \cdot 5 \cdot 4 \cdot 3 \cdot 2 \cdot 1 = 40,320$

b) $9! = 9 \cdot 8 \cdot 7 \cdot 6 \cdot 5 \cdot 4 \cdot 3 \cdot 2 \cdot 1 = 362,880$

c) $3! = 3 \cdot 2 \cdot 1 = 6$

d) $\dfrac{6!}{5!} = \dfrac{6 \cdot 5 \cdot 4 \cdot 3 \cdot 2 \cdot 1}{5 \cdot 4 \cdot 3 \cdot 2 \cdot 1} = 6$

e) $\dfrac{0!}{4} = \dfrac{1}{4}$

f) $\dfrac{5!}{3!2!} = \dfrac{5 \cdot 4 \cdot 3 \cdot 2 \cdot 1}{3 \cdot 2 \cdot 1 \cdot 2 \cdot 1} = 10$

g) $\dfrac{6!}{4!2!} = \dfrac{6 \cdot 5 \cdot 4 \cdot 3 \cdot 2 \cdot 1}{4 \cdot 3 \cdot 2 \cdot 1 \cdot 2 \cdot 1} = 15$

h) $\dfrac{7!}{5!2!} = \dfrac{7 \cdot 6 \cdot 5 \cdot 4 \cdot 3 \cdot 2 \cdot 1}{5 \cdot 4 \cdot 3 \cdot 2 \cdot 1 \cdot 2 \cdot 1} = 21$

1. i) $\quad _8P_5 = \dfrac{8!}{(8-5)!} = \dfrac{8!}{3!} = 6720$

j) $\quad _7P_4 = \dfrac{7!}{(7-4)!} = \dfrac{7!}{3!} = 840$

k) $\quad _9P_5 = \dfrac{9!}{(9-5)!} = \dfrac{9!}{4!} = 15,120$

l) $\quad _0P_0 = \dfrac{0!}{(0-0)!} = \dfrac{0!}{0!} = 1$

m) $\quad _7P_0 = \dfrac{7!}{(7-0)!} = \dfrac{7!}{7!} = 1$

n) $\quad _7P_7 = 7! = 5040$

o) $\quad _6P_4 = \dfrac{6!}{(6-4)!} = \dfrac{6!}{2!} = 360$

p) $\quad _3P_2 = \dfrac{3!}{(3-2)!} = \dfrac{3!}{1!} = 6$

2. $\quad _7P_7 = 7! = 5040$

3. $\quad _8P_5 = \dfrac{8!}{(8-5)!} = \dfrac{8!}{3!} = 6720$

4. $\quad _{14}P_5 = \dfrac{14!}{(14-5)!} = \dfrac{14!}{9!} = 240,240$

5. a) $\quad _8P_4 = \dfrac{8!}{(8-4)!} = \dfrac{8!}{4!} = 1680$

b) $\quad \dfrac{1}{8}$

c) $\quad \dfrac{1}{2}$

6. $\quad _9P_3 = \dfrac{9!}{(9-3)!} = \dfrac{9!}{6!} = 504$

7. The letter C is repeated twice. If the first letter is an E, there are $\frac{8!}{2!2!}$ = 10,080 possible ways.

   If the first letter is an O, there are $\frac{2 \cdot 8!}{2!}$ = 40,320 possible ways.

   If the first letter is an I, there are $\frac{8!}{2!2!}$ = 10,080 possible ways.

   Thus, there are 10,080 + 40,320 + 10,080 = 60,480 possible ways.

8. a) $\frac{10!}{3!}$ = 604,800 possible permutations

   b) $\frac{8!}{2!2!}$ = 10,080 possible permutations

   c) $\frac{10!}{2!2!2!2!}$ = 226,800 possible permutations

   d) $\frac{12!}{2!2!2!2!}$ = 29,937,600 possible permutations

9. $\frac{10!}{2!2!}$ = 907,200

10. a) $_{12}P_{12}$ = 12! = 479,001,600
    b) $_5P_5 \cdot {_4}P_4 \cdot {_3}P_3$ = 120 · 24 · 6 = 17,280. However, since books on the same subject matter can be permuted as a group, we must multiply this by $_3P_3$ or 6. Thus we have 6(17280) = 103,680 possible permutations.

11.   **a)** $_{10}P_{10} = 10! = 3,628,800$

      b)   The men can be seated in $_5P_5 = 120$ possible ways and the women can also be seated in $_5P_5$ or 120 possible ways. However, the men can be seated on either the left side or right side, so that there are 120 x 120 x 2 = 28,800 possible ways to seat the guests.

      c)   The couples can be seated in $_5P_5 = 5!$ ways. However, each man can sit on the left or right side of his wife. Thus, there are $2^5 \cdot 120 = 3840$ possible ways.

12. $_4P_4 = 4! = 24$

13.   **a)** $1 \cdot 10 \cdot 10 \cdot 10 \cdot 10 = 10,000$

      b) $10 \cdot 9 \cdot 8 \cdot 7 \cdot 6 = 30,240$

      c) $10 \cdot 10 \cdot 10 \cdot 10 \cdot 10 = 100,000$

14.   **a)** $10 \cdot 10 \cdot 10 \cdot 10 \cdot 10 \cdot 10 \cdot 10 \cdot 10 \cdot 10 \cdot 10$
$= 10,000,000,000$

      b) $\dfrac{1}{10,000,000,000}$

15.   **a)**   Assuming there is no "head" of the circle we can think of any one as being arbitrarily designated as the "head" and the other n - 1 people then can be arranged in (n - 1)! ways.

      b) $5! = 120$

16. $(6 - 1)! = 5! = 120$

17. $_{10}P_4 = \dfrac{10!}{(10 - 4)!} = \dfrac{10!}{6!} = 5040$

18.   **a)** $_9P_9 = 9! = 362,880$

      b) $\dfrac{1}{9}$

      c)   No

19. $_7P_7 = 7! = 5040$ assuming that order counts.

20. $\dfrac{7!}{3!2!2!} = 210$

1. a) $_7C_3 = \dfrac{7!}{3!\,4!} = 35$

    b) $_6C_5 = \dfrac{6!}{5!\,1!} = 6$

    c) $_8C_5 = \dfrac{8!}{5!\,3!} = 56$

    d) $_7C_0 = \dfrac{7!}{0!\,7!} = 1$

    e) $_7C_1 = \dfrac{7!}{1!\,6!} = 7$

    f) $_8C_4 = \dfrac{8!}{4!\,4!} = 70$

    g) $_7C_4 = \dfrac{7!}{4!\,3!} = 35$

    h) $\dbinom{9}{5} = {}_9C_5 = \dfrac{9!}{5!\,4!} = 126$

    i) $\dbinom{5}{5} = {}_5C_5 = \dfrac{5!}{5!\,0!} = 1$

    j) $\dbinom{8}{9} = {}_8C_9 = $ Impossible

2. $_{12}C_9 = \dfrac{12!}{9!\,3!} = 220$

3. $_{18}C_8 = \dfrac{18!}{8!\,10!} = 43,758$

4. $_{12}C_7 = \dfrac{12!}{7!\,5!} = 792$

5. $_{10}C_4 = \dfrac{10!}{4!\,6!} = 210$

6. $_{15}C_7 \cdot _{13}C_9 = \dfrac{15!}{7!8!} \cdot \dfrac{13!}{9!4!} = (6435)(715) = 4,601,025$

7. $_{20}C_5 = \dfrac{20!}{5!15!} = 15,504$

8. **a)** $\dfrac{_{11}C_2}{_{24}C_2} = \dfrac{\dfrac{11!}{2!9!}}{\dfrac{24!}{2!22!}} = \dfrac{55}{276}$

b) $\dfrac{_{13}C_2}{_{24}C_2} = \dfrac{\dfrac{13!}{2!11!}}{276} = \dfrac{78}{276} = \dfrac{39}{138}$

c) $\dfrac{_{11}C_1 \cdot _{13}C_1}{_{24}C_2} = \dfrac{\dfrac{11!}{1!10!} \cdot \dfrac{13!}{1!12!}}{\dfrac{24!}{2!22!}} = \dfrac{143}{276}$

9. **a)** $_8C_3 \cdot _9C_3 = \dfrac{8!}{3!5!} \cdot \dfrac{9!}{3!6!} = 56 \cdot 84 = 4704$

b)

$$\begin{array}{cccccc} \dfrac{1 \text{ woman}}{5 \text{ men}} & + \dfrac{2 \text{ women}}{4 \text{ men}} & + \dfrac{3 \text{ women}}{3 \text{ men}} & + \dfrac{4 \text{ women}}{2 \text{ men}} & + \dfrac{5 \text{ women}}{1 \text{ man}} & + \dfrac{6 \text{ women}}{0 \text{ men}} \end{array}$$

$$_9C_1 \cdot _8C_5 + _9C_2 \cdot _8C_4 + _9C_3 \cdot _8C_3 + _9C_4 \cdot _8C_2 + _9C_5 \cdot _8C_1 + _9C_6 \cdot _8C_0$$

$$= \dfrac{9!}{1!8!} \cdot \dfrac{8!}{5!3!} + \dfrac{9!}{2!7!} \cdot \dfrac{8!}{4!4!} + \dfrac{9!}{3!6!} \cdot \dfrac{8!}{3!5!} + \dfrac{9!}{4!5!} \cdot \dfrac{8!}{2!6!}$$

$$+ \dfrac{9!}{5!4!} \cdot \dfrac{8!}{1!7!} + \dfrac{9!}{6!3!} \cdot \dfrac{8!}{0!8!}$$

$$= 9 \cdot 56 + 36 \cdot 70 + 84 \cdot 56 + 126 \cdot 28 + 126 \cdot 8 + 84 \cdot 1$$
$$= 504 + 2520 + 4704 + 3528 + 1008 + 84$$
$$= 12,348$$

9. **c)**

$$\begin{array}{ccccccccc} \text{1 man} & + & \text{2 men} & + & \text{3 men} & + & \text{4 men} & + & \text{5 men} \\ \text{5 women} & & \text{4 women} & & \text{3 women} & & \text{2 women} & & \text{1 woman} \end{array}$$

$$_8C_1 \cdot {_9C_5} + {_8C_2} \cdot {_9C_4} + {_8C_3} \cdot {_9C_3} + {_8C_4} \cdot {_9C_2} + {_8C_5} \cdot {_9C_1}$$

$$= \frac{8!}{1!7!} \cdot \frac{9!}{5!4!} + \frac{8!}{2!6!} \cdot \frac{9!}{4!5!} + \frac{8!}{3!5!} \cdot \frac{9!}{3!6!}$$

$$+ \frac{8!}{4!4!} \cdot \frac{9!}{2!7!} + \frac{8!}{5!3!} \cdot \frac{9!}{1!8!}$$

$$= 8 \cdot 126 + 28 \cdot 126 + 56 \cdot 84 + 36 \cdot 70 + 56 \cdot 9$$
$$= 1008 + 3528 + 4704 + 2520 + 504$$
$$= 12,264$$

d)

$$\begin{array}{ccccc} \text{0 men} & + & \text{1 man} & + & \text{2 men} \\ \text{6 women} & & \text{5 women} & & \text{4 women} \end{array}$$

$$= {_8C_0} \cdot {_9C_6} + {_8C_1} \cdot {_9C_5} + {_8C_2} \cdot {_9C_4}$$

$$= \frac{8!}{0!8!} \cdot \frac{9!}{6!3!} + \frac{8!}{1!7!} \cdot \frac{9!}{5!4!} + \frac{8!}{2!6!} \cdot \frac{9!}{4!5!}$$

$$= 1 \cdot 84 + 8 \cdot 126 + 28 \cdot 126$$
$$= 84 + 1008 + 3528$$
$$= 4620$$

10. $_{15}C_5 = \dfrac{15!}{5!10!} = 3003$

11. **a)** $_{11}C_4 = \dfrac{11!}{4!7!} = 330$

  b) $_{11}C_7 = \dfrac{11!}{7!4!} = 330$

  c) They are equal.

13. **a)** $_8C_1 \cdot {_5C_1} \cdot {_4C_1} \cdot {_2C_1}$

  $$\frac{8!}{1!7!} \cdot \frac{5!}{1!4!} \cdot \frac{4!}{1!3!} \cdot \frac{2!}{1!1!} = 8 \cdot 5 \cdot 4 \cdot 2 = 320$$

126

13. b)

$$\begin{pmatrix} 1 \text{ Cardiologist} \\ 1 \text{ Surgeon} \\ 1 \text{ Anesthesiologist} \\ 1 \text{ Obstetrician} \end{pmatrix} + \begin{pmatrix} 1 \text{ Cardiologist} \\ 2 \text{ Surgeons} \\ 1 \text{ Anestesiologist} \end{pmatrix} +$$

$$\begin{pmatrix} 1 \text{ Cardiologist} \\ 2 \text{ Surgeons} \\ 1 \text{ Obstetrician} \end{pmatrix} + \begin{pmatrix} 1 \text{ Cardiologist} \\ 3 \text{ Surgeons} \end{pmatrix} + \begin{pmatrix} 2 \text{ Cardiologists} \\ 1 \text{ Surgeon} \\ 1 \text{ Anestesiologist} \end{pmatrix} +$$

$$\begin{pmatrix} 2 \text{ Cardiologists} \\ 1 \text{ Surgeon} \\ 1 \text{ Obstetrician} \end{pmatrix} + \begin{pmatrix} 2 \text{ Cardiologists} \\ 2 \text{ Surgeons} \end{pmatrix} + \begin{pmatrix} 3 \text{ Cardiologists} \\ 1 \text{ Surgeon} \end{pmatrix} +$$

$$\begin{pmatrix} 1 \text{ Cardioligist} \\ 1 \text{ Surgeons} \\ 2 \text{ Anesthesiologist} \end{pmatrix} + \begin{pmatrix} 1 \text{ Cardioligist} \\ 1 \text{ Surgeon} \\ 2 \text{ Obstetrician} \end{pmatrix}$$

$$= {}_8C_1 \cdot {}_5C_1 \cdot {}_4C_1 \cdot {}_2C_1 + {}_8C_1 \cdot {}_5C_2 \cdot {}_4C_1 + {}_8C_1 \cdot {}_5C_2 \cdot {}_2C_1$$
$$+ {}_8C_1 \cdot {}_5C_3 + {}_8C_2 \cdot {}_5C_1 \cdot {}_4C_1 + {}_8C_2 \cdot {}_5C_1 \cdot {}_2C_1 + {}_8C_2 \cdot {}_5C_2$$
$$+ {}_8C_3 \cdot {}_5C_1 + {}_8C_1 \cdot {}_5C_1 \cdot {}_4C_2 + {}_8C_1 \cdot {}_5C_1 \cdot {}_2C_2$$
$$= 320 + 320 + 160 + 80 + 560 + 280 + 280 + 280 + 240 + 40$$
$$= 2560$$

14.

$$\begin{pmatrix} n+1 \\ r \end{pmatrix} = \begin{pmatrix} n \\ r \end{pmatrix} + \begin{pmatrix} n \\ r-1 \end{pmatrix}$$

$$\frac{(n+1)!}{r!(n+1-r)!} = \frac{n!}{r!(n-r)!} + \frac{n!}{(r-1)!(n-r+1)!}$$

$$= \frac{(n-r+1)n! + n!(r-1)}{r!(n-r+1)!} = \frac{(n+1)!}{r!(n+1-r)!}$$

15.

$$\begin{pmatrix} n \\ r \end{pmatrix} = \begin{pmatrix} n \\ n-r \end{pmatrix}$$

$$\frac{n!}{r!(n-r)!} = \frac{n!}{(n-r)![n-(n-r)]!}$$

$$= \frac{n!}{(n-r)!r!}$$

$$= \frac{n!}{r!(n-r)!}$$

16. For row 0, the only entry is 1. Sum is $2^0 = 1$.
    For row 1, the entries are 1 and 1. Sum is $2^1 = 2$.
    For row 2, the entries are 1, 2, and 1. Sum is $2^2 = 4$.
    For row 3, the entries are 1, 3, 3, and 1. Sum is $2^3 = 8$.
    For row 4, the entries are 1, 4, 6, 4, and 1. Sum is $2^4 = 16$.
    For row 5, the entries are 1, 5, 10, 10, 5, and 1.
        Sum is $2^5 = 32$.
    etc.

ANSWERS TO EXERCISES FOR SECTION 4.6 – (PAGES 224 – 226)

1. $(300,000)\left(\dfrac{3}{5}\right) + (-50,000)\left(\dfrac{2}{5}\right) = \$160,000$

2. $(5800)\left(\dfrac{2}{5}\right) + (2000)\left(\dfrac{3}{5}\right) = \$3520$

3. $2\left(\dfrac{1}{8}\right) + 16\left(\dfrac{3}{8}\right) + (-8)\left(\dfrac{4}{8}\right) = \dfrac{18}{8} = \$2.25$

4. $10\left(\dfrac{5}{20}\right) + (-3)\left(\dfrac{8}{20}\right) + (-5)\left(\dfrac{7}{20}\right) = -\$0.45$

5. $1\left(\dfrac{9}{60}\right) + 5\left(\dfrac{8}{60}\right) + 10\left(\dfrac{12}{60}\right) + 25\left(\dfrac{16}{60}\right) + 50\left(\dfrac{11}{60}\right) + 100\left(\dfrac{4}{60}\right) = 25.32$ cents

6. $6\left(\dfrac{14}{36}\right) + (-4)\left(\dfrac{8}{36}\right) + 7\left(\dfrac{3}{36}\right) + 5\left(\dfrac{3}{36}\right) + (-1)\left(\dfrac{8}{36}\right) = \dfrac{80}{36} = \$2.22$

7. 372:628 or 93:157

8. 5:4

9. 5:95 or 1:19

10. 15:85 or 3:17

11. Account I: (3975)(0.61) = $2424.75
        Account II: (3300)(0.82) = $2706.00
       Account III: (4100)(0.59) = $2419.00
        Account IV: (4880)(0.51) = $2488.80
        Account V: (5705)(0.46) = $2624.30

12. Visit accounts II and V since they have the highest mathematical expectation.

13. **a)** 7(0.85) + (-2.5)(0.15) = $5.575 million
         b) 85:15 or 17:3

ANSWERS TO TESTING YOUR UNDERSTANDING OF THIS CHAPTER'S CONCEPTS -
(PAGES 228 - 229)

1.

Toss 1	Toss 2	Toss 3	Toss 4	Toss 5	Possible Outcome
			H	H	HHHHH
		H		T	HHHHT
			T	H	HHHTH
	H			T	HHHTT
		T	H	H	HHTHH
H				T	HHTHT
			T	H	HHTTH
			H	H	HTHHH
	T	H		T	HTHHT
			T	H	HTHTH

Start

2. **a)** There are 10 · 10 · 10 = 1000 possible identification tags. This is not sufficient for 17,225 students.
        b) There are 26 · 26 · 26 = 17,576 possible identification tags. This is sufficient for 17,225 students.

3. **a)** Assuming no restrictions 10 · 10 · 10 · 10 · 10 · 10 · 10 · 10 · 10 = 1,000,000,000 possible numbers
        b) 10 · 10 · 10 · 10 · 10 · 10 · 10 · 10 · 10 · 10 = 10,000,000,000 possible numbers
        c) 10 · 10 · 10 · 10 · 10 · 10 · 10 · 10 · 10 · 26 = 26,000,000,000 possible numbers

ANSWERS TO TESTING YOUR UNDERSTANDING OF THIS CHAPTER'S CONCEPTS (CONTINUED) - (PAGES 228 - 229)

4. $9 \cdot 8 \cdot 12 \cdot 6 = 5184$ possible cases.

ANSWERS TO THINKING CRITICALLY - (PAGES 229 - 230)

1. No, the events do not have the same probability.

2. Yes, the sample space has been reduced.

3. No, the events do not have the same probability.

ANSWERS TO REVIEW EXERCISES FOR CHAPTER 4 - (PAGES 230 - 231)

1. $\dfrac{3}{5}$

2. $\dfrac{7!}{4!3!} = 35$

3. $\text{p(at least 4 X's)} = \text{p(4 X's)} + \text{p(5 X's)}$

    $$= 5\left(\frac{1}{26}\right)\left(\frac{1}{26}\right)\left(\frac{1}{26}\right)\left(\frac{1}{26}\right)\left(\frac{25}{26}\right) + \left(\frac{1}{26}\right)\left(\frac{1}{26}\right)\left(\frac{1}{26}\right)\left(\frac{1}{26}\right)\left(\frac{1}{26}\right)$$

    $$= \frac{126}{26^5}$$

    $$= \frac{126}{11,881,376}$$

4. The sample space consists of 16 possible outcomes. Of these, the outcomes GBBG, GGBG, GBGG and GGGG are favorable. Thus, probability is $\dfrac{4}{16} = \dfrac{1}{4}$.

5. $_8P_8 = 8! = 40,320$

6. $2 \cdot 3 \cdot 2 = 12$

7. $_7P_3 = \dfrac{7!}{4!} = 210$

8. $4 \cdot 6 \cdot 2 = 48$

9. $3:4$

10. $\dfrac{1}{2^6} = \dfrac{1}{64}$

11. $4\left(\dfrac{6}{36}\right) + (-1)\left(\dfrac{30}{36}\right) = \dfrac{-6}{36} = \$-0.17$

ANSWERS TO CHAPTER TEST – (PAGES 231 – 232)

1. Choice (b). Probability cannot be negative.

2. $_7P_7 = 7! = 5040$ assuming order counts.

3. $_6C_4 \cdot _5C_3 = 15 \cdot 10 = 150$

4. $4 \cdot 5 \cdot 4 \cdot 3 = 240$

5. $\dfrac{10!}{3!} = 604{,}800$

6. a) $\dfrac{_{12}C_4 \cdot _{38}C_0}{_{50}C_4} = \dfrac{495}{230{,}300}$

   b) $\dfrac{_{12}C_4 \cdot _{38}C_0 + _{12}C_3 \cdot _{38}C_1 + _{12}C_2 \cdot _{38}C_2}{_{50}C_4}$

   $= \dfrac{495 + 8360 + 46398}{230{,}300} = \dfrac{55253}{230{,}300}$

   c) $\dfrac{_{12}C_0 \cdot _{38}C_4}{_{50}C_4} = \dfrac{73815}{230{,}300}$

7. Four letters followed by three numbers yields
   $26 \cdot 26 \cdot 26 \cdot 26 \cdot 10 \cdot 10 \cdot 10 = 456{,}976{,}000$ codes
   Three letters followed by four numbers yields
   $26 \cdot 26 \cdot 26 \cdot 10 \cdot 10 \cdot 10 \cdot 10 = 175{,}760{,}000$ codes
   Use the code of four letters followed by three numbers.

8.

Corn Label 1	Carrots Label 2	Peas Label 3
Corn	Carrots	Peas
Corn	Peas	Carrots
Carrots	Peas	Corn
Carrots	Corn	Peas
Peas	Corn	Carrots
Peas	Carrots	Corn

The probability that cans are labeled correctly is $\frac{1}{6}$.

9.

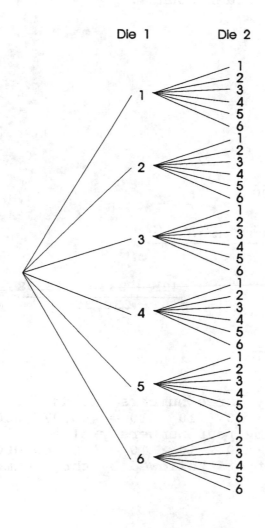

132

10. $_{11}C_5 = \dfrac{11!}{5!6!} = 462$ assuming order does not count.

11. $_{11}C_6 \cdot \, _{13}C_7 = 462 \cdot 1716 = 792{,}792$

12. $_4P_4 \cdot \, _3P_3 \cdot \, _2P_2 \cdot \, _3P_3 = 24 \cdot 6 \cdot 2 \cdot 6 = 1728$. The groups of soda can be arranged in 4! ways so that there are 24 · 1728 or 41,472 possible ways of arranging these cans if the cans of the same brand are to stay together.

13. **a)** 3:3 or 1:1

    b) $9\left(\dfrac{2}{6}\right) + 7\left(\dfrac{1}{6}\right) + (-2)\left(\dfrac{2}{6}\right) + 0\left(\dfrac{1}{6}\right) = \dfrac{21}{6} = \$3.50$

14. 2.3:97.7 or 23:977

15. $_7P_3 = \dfrac{7!}{(7 - 3)!} = 210$

16. Choice (b)

17. Choice (d)

18. Choice (b)

19. Choice (b)

20. Choice (a) as 26 · 26 · 10 · 10 · 10 = 676,000

1. A pair of dice is rolled. Find the probability that the sum of the number of dots appearing is larger than 9.

   a) 3/36   b) 6/36   c) 10/36   d) 5/36   e) none of these

   Answer _____

2. A family is known to have four children. Find the probability that the family consists of at least 2 boys.

   a) 6/16   b) 4/16   c) 1/16   d) 11/16   e) none of these

   Answer _____

3. Which of the events shown below has the greatest likelihood of occurring?

Event	Probability that this event will occur
A	0.18
B	0.81
C	0.97
D	0.097

   a) event A   b) event B   c) event C   d) event D
   e) none of these

   Answer _____

4. Each license plate in a certain state consists of 3 letters followed by 2 numbers with repetition allowed. How many different license plates are possible in this state?

   a) 1,757,600   b) 328,536   c) 1,404,000   d) 365,040
   e) none of these

   Answer _____

5. Assuming no restrictions, how many different eight digit identification numbers are possible?

   a) 40,320   b) 10,000,000   c) 100,000,000
   d) 16,777,216   e) none of these

   Answer _____

6. How many different male-female committees can be formed from among 9 males and 10 females to investigate discrimination charges if each committee is to consist of 5 males and 6 females?

   a) 39,916,800   b) 126   c) 210   d) 26,460
   e) none of these

                                    Answer _____

7. These is a 90% chance that a certain active volcano will erupt this year. What are the odds in favor that the volcano will erupt this year?

   a) 9 to 10   b) 9 to 1   c) 1 to 9   d) 10 to 9
   e) none of these

                                    Answer _____

8. In how many different ways can the letters of the word RESEARCH be arranged?

   a) 40,320   b) 20,160   c) 10,080   d) 24
   e) none of these

                                    Answer _____

9. At a local fund-raising drive, tickets numbered consecutively from 1 to 100 sold. One winning ticket will be selected. What is the probability that the winning number is a multiple of 9?

   a) 11/100   b) 10/100   c)9/100   d) 1/9
   e) none of these

                                    Answer _____

10. The probability that Nicole will go on to medical school after graduating college is 0.89. What is the probability that she will not go on to medical school?

    a) 0.011   b) 0.11   c) 1.1   d) 0.089   e) none of these

                                    Answer _____

CHAPTER 4 - PROBABILITY
SUPPLEMENTARY TEST FORM B

1. Which of the events shown below has the least likelihood of occurring?

Event	Probability that this event will occur
A	0.13
B	0.087
C	0.93
D	0.57

   a) event A   b) event B   c) event C   d) event D
   e) none of these

   Answer _____

2. A family is known to have 5 children. Find the probability that the family consists of 3 boys and 2 girls.

   a) 10/32   b) 5/32   c) 10/16   d) 10/64
   e) none of these

   Answer _____

3. A card is drawn from an ordinary deck of cards. Find the probability that it is a red ace.

   a) 1/52   b) 2/13   c) 2/52   d) 4/52   e) none of these

   Answer _____

4. In how many different ways can the letters of the word EXPECTATION be arranged?

   a) 907,200   b) 3,628,800   c) 1,814,400   d) 151,200
   e) none of these

   Answer _____

5. A high school student must write a report on 4 novels and 5 biographies from a possible 11 novels and 8 biographies. In how many different ways can this be done?

   a) 362,880   b) 330   c) 56   d) 18,480
   e) none of these

   Answer _____

6. Each radio manufactured by a large electronics company is labelled with a serial number which consists of 2 letters followed by 4 numbers. How many different serial identification numbers are possible?

a) 6,760,000   b) 6,473,376   c) 3,276,000   d) 4,435,236
e) none of these

Answer _____

7. Given the numbers 4, 5, 6, 8, and 9. How many different three-digit numbers larger than 700 can be formed from these numbers if repetition is not allowed?

a) 36   b) 18   c) 40   d) 24   e) none of these

Answer _____

8. The probability that Gina's new VCR will function properly after installation is 8/9. What are the odds against it functioning properly?

a) 8 to 1   b) 1 to 8   c) 1 to 9   d) 8 to 9
e) none of these

Answer _____

9. In how many different ways can a publisher select 4 math books from a possible 9 math books to be used in a sales advertisement campaign?

a) 15,120   b) 3024   c) 126   d) 24   e) none of these

Answer _____

10. A teacher receives 3 test papers from 3 students. Unfortunately, the 3 students forgot to write their names on the papers. The teacher decides to randomly assign each of the test papers to one of these students. Find the probability that each student receives his or her own test paper.

a) 1/6   b) 1/3   c) 2/3   d) 1/2   e) none of these

Answer _____

1. In how many different ways can the letters of the word POLLUTION be arranged?

    a) 362,880   b) 181,440   c) 90,720   d) 15,120
    e) none of these

    Answer _____

2. Steve and Joan (who do not know each other) are each registering for next semester's courses at their college. Each student must register for one of four different courses. Assuming that there is only one open section of each of these courses and that they are all offered at the same time, what is the probability that Steve and Joan both register for the same course?

    a) 1/4   b) 1/2   c) 3/4   d) 1/16   e) none of these

    Answer _____

3. How many different four-digit numbers larger than 800 can be formed from the digits 4, 5, 6, 7, 8, and 9 if repetition is allowed?

    a) 24   b) 432   c) 120   d) 72   e) none of these

    Answer _____

4. How many different three-person paramedic crews can be formed to drive a special ambulance if 10 equally qualified paramedics are available for the job?

    a) 3,628,800   b) 604,800   c) 120   d) 720
    e) none of these

    Answer _____

5. A baseball scout is ranking the top four promising baseball prospects from a possible list of 11 candidates. In how many different ways can this be done?

    a) 24   b) 39,916,800   c) 1,663,200   d) 7920
    e) none of these

    Answer _____

6. A nurse can select any one of 5 skirts, 4 blouses, and 3 hats to wear for work. How many different outfits are possible?

    a) 12   b) 60   c) 17,280   d) 32   e) none of these

    Answer _____

7. There is a 5/9 probability that Brian will arrive on time for his scheduled dental appointment. What are the odds that he is late for the appointment?

a) 5 to 9   b) 4 to 9   c) 4 to 5   d) 5 to 4
e) none of these

Answer _____

8. Government investigators have determined that there is a 98% chance that a nurse at Brooks Hospital will administer the appropriate quantity of medication on time. What is the probability that the nurse will <u>not</u> administer the appropriate quantity of medication on time?

a) 0.098   b) 0.02   c) 0.2   d) 0.002
e) none of these

Answer _____

9. How many different identification tags can be made if each tag is to consist of four letters followed by two numbers with no repetition allowed?

a) 45,697,600   b) 10,545,600   c) 41,127,840
d) 32,292,000   e) none of these

Answer _____

10. There are 8 maintenance workers on the night shift and 9 maintenance workers on the day shift of an office building. Due to changing economic conditions, management has decided to dismiss 3 workers from the night shift and 4 workers from the day shift. Neglecting seniority and any other factors, in how many ways can the workers to be dismissed be selected?

a) 7056   b) 56   c) 126   d) 5040   e) none of these

Answer _____

ANSWERS TO SUPPLEMENTARY TESTS
CHAPTER 4 - PROBABILITY

Form A		Form B		Form C	
1.	Choice (b)	1.	Choice (b)	1.	Choice (c)
2.	Choice (d)	2.	Choice (a)	2.	Choice (a)
3.	Choice (c)	3.	Choice (c)	3.	Choice (b)
4.	Choice (a)	4.	Choice (e)	4.	Choice (c)
5.	Choice (c)	5.	Choice (d)	5.	Choice (d)
6.	Choice (d)	6.	Choice (a)	6.	Choice (b)
7.	Choice (b)	7.	Choice (d)	7.	Choice (c)
8.	Choice (c)	8.	Choice (b)	8.	Choice (b)
9.	Choice (a)	9.	Choice (c)	9.	Choice (d)
10.	Choice (b)	10.	Choice (a)	10.	Choice (a)

ANSWERS TO EXERCISES FOR CHAPTER 5

SECTION 5.2 - (PAGES 247 - 250)

1. a) Mutually exclusive
    b) Not mutually exclusive
    c) Mutually exclusive
    d) Not mutually exclusive
    e) Not mutually exclusive
    f) Not mutually exclusive
    g) Not mutually exclusive
    h) Mutually exclusive

2. p(high blood pressure or overweight) = 0.31 + 0.40 - 0.16
    = 0.55

3. p(mugged or house burglarized) = 0.19 + 0.24 - 0.02 = 0.41

4. p(owns VCR or a car) = 0.65 + 0.76 - 0.50 = 0.91

5. p(needs remediation or has collegebound brother or sister)
    = 0.36 + 0.57 - 0.10 = 0.83

6. p(either smokes) $= \frac{15}{28} + \frac{2}{7} - \frac{1}{7} = \frac{15}{28} + \frac{8}{28} - \frac{4}{28} = \frac{19}{28}$

    p(exactly one of the two smokes) $= \frac{19}{28}$ - p(both smokes)

    $$= \frac{19}{28} - \frac{1}{7} = \frac{19}{28} - \frac{4}{28} = \frac{15}{28}$$

7. p(has pet dog or pet cat) = p(pet dog) + p(pet cat)
        - p(has both pet dog and pet cat)
    0.86 = 0.64 + 0.33 - p(has both pet dog and pet cat)
    p(has both pet dog and pet cat) = 0.64 + 0.33 - 0.86 = 0.11

8. p(paid by card or check) = p(paid by card) + p(paid by check)
        - p(paid by both)
    0.88 = p(paid by card) + 0.47 - 0
    0.41 = p(paid by credit card)

9. p(either unsafe tires or defective brakes) = p(unsafe tires)
        + p(defective brakes) - p(both defects)
    0.36 = 0.29 + 0.15 - p(both defects)
    p(both defects) = 0.29 + 0.15 - 0.36 = 0.08

10. p(single or home run) = p(single) + p(home run)

   p(single or home run) = $\frac{1}{3} + \frac{1}{9} = \frac{3}{9} + \frac{1}{9} = \frac{4}{9}$

11. p(either wrong form used or not filled out completely)

   $= \frac{1}{9} + \frac{1}{8} - \frac{1}{16}$

   $= \frac{16}{144} + \frac{18}{144} - \frac{9}{144} = \frac{25}{144}$

12. p(either division)

   $= \frac{63}{120} + \frac{70}{120} + \frac{64}{120} - \frac{34}{120} - \frac{30}{120} - \frac{38}{120} + \frac{8}{120} = \frac{103}{120}$

13. $1 = \frac{2}{3} + \frac{74}{120} + \frac{26}{60} - \frac{38}{120} - \frac{6}{20} - \frac{2}{6} +$ p(all three courses)

   $1 - \frac{2}{3} - \frac{74}{120} - \frac{26}{60} + \frac{38}{120} + \frac{6}{20} + \frac{2}{6} =$ p(all three courses)

   $\frac{120}{120} - \frac{80}{120} - \frac{74}{120} - \frac{52}{120} + \frac{38}{120} + \frac{36}{120} + \frac{40}{120}$

   $=$ p(all three courses)

   $\frac{28}{120} =$ p(all three courses)

14. $1 = \frac{290}{470} + \frac{250}{470} + \frac{170}{470} - \frac{110}{470} - \frac{80}{470} - \frac{70}{470}$

   $+$ p(all three violations)

   $1 - \frac{290}{470} - \frac{250}{470} - \frac{170}{470} + \frac{110}{470} + \frac{80}{470} + \frac{70}{470}$

   $=$ p(all three violations)

   $\frac{470}{470} - \frac{290}{470} - \frac{250}{470} - \frac{170}{470} + \frac{110}{470} + \frac{80}{470} + \frac{70}{470}$

   $=$ p(all three violations)

   $\frac{20}{470} =$ p(all three violations)

1. a) $\dfrac{66 + 54}{200} = \dfrac{120}{200} = \dfrac{3}{5}$

    b) $\dfrac{54 + 41}{200} = \dfrac{95}{200} = \dfrac{19}{40}$

    c) $\dfrac{54}{200} = \dfrac{27}{100}$

    d) $\dfrac{39}{200}$

    e) $\dfrac{39 + 54}{200} = \dfrac{93}{200}$

2. p(female | receiving supplemental insurance)

    $= \dfrac{\text{p(female and receiving supplemental insurance)}}{\text{p(receiving supplemental insurance)}}$

    $= \dfrac{0.32}{0.72} = \dfrac{4}{9}$

3. p(develops reaction | takes medication)

    $= \dfrac{\text{p(takes medication and develops reaction)}}{\text{p(takes medication)}}$

    $= \dfrac{0.09}{0.14} = \dfrac{9}{14}$

4. p(exercises | jogs) $= \dfrac{\text{p(jogs and exercises)}}{\text{p(jogs)}} = \dfrac{0.12}{0.22} = \dfrac{6}{11}$

5. p(hunter | mountain climber)

    $= \dfrac{\text{p(hunter and mountain climber)}}{\text{p(mountain climber)}} = \dfrac{0.23}{0.92} = \dfrac{23}{92}$

6. p(buys software in a computer store | bought computer in

    computer store) $= \dfrac{\text{p(buys both in computer store)}}{\text{p(buys computer in computer store)}}$

    $= \dfrac{0.41}{0.77} = \dfrac{41}{77}$

7. p(accepts Discover Card | accepts Master Card)

$$= \frac{p(\text{accepts both})}{p(\text{accepts Master Card})}$$

$$= \frac{0.53}{0.74} = \frac{53}{74}$$

8. p(hospitalized | no insurance)

$$= \frac{p(\text{hospitalized and no insurance})}{p(\text{no insurance})} = \frac{0.13}{0.35} = \frac{13}{35}$$

9. a) $\dfrac{221}{1000}$

    b) $\dfrac{221}{31 + 62 + 147 + 221} = \dfrac{221}{461}$

    c) $\dfrac{62 + 94}{1000} = \dfrac{156}{1000}$

10. a) $\dfrac{120 + 29 + 10 + 310}{1000} = \dfrac{469}{1000}$

    b) $\dfrac{29}{29 + 360 + 11} = \dfrac{29}{400}$

    c) $\dfrac{120 + 69 + 8}{1000} = \dfrac{197}{1000}$

    d) $\dfrac{310}{120 + 29 + 10 + 310} = \dfrac{310}{469}$

    e) $\dfrac{310}{310 + 6 + 4} = \dfrac{310}{320}$

11. a) $\dfrac{79 + 297 + 188}{1412} = \dfrac{564}{1412} = \dfrac{141}{353}$

b) $\dfrac{188}{423 + 188} = \dfrac{188}{611}$

c) $\dfrac{188}{79 + 297 + 188} = \dfrac{188}{564} = \dfrac{47}{141} = \dfrac{1}{3}$

12.

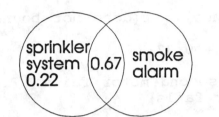

0.22

ANSWERS TO EXERCISES FOR SECTION 5.4 - (PAGES 264 - 266)

1. p(both have policies) = p(wife has policy | husband has policy) · p(husband has policy)
    = (0.54)(0.89) = 0.4806

2. p(registers for both semesters) = p(registers in spring | registered in fall) · p(registers in fall)
    = (0.86)(0.47) = 0.4042

3. p(both ring) = p(phone 1 rings) · p(phone 2 rings)
    = (0.89)(0.64) = 0.5696

4. p(increases prices and ridership drops) = p(ridership drops | prices increased) · p(prices increase)
    = (0.97)(0.85) = 0.8245

5. p(gets BA degree and MBA degree) = p(gets MBA degree | got BA degree) · p(gets BA degree)
    = (0.76)(0.53) = 0.4028

6. p(all 3 are approved) = (0.85)(0.92)(0.79) = 0.61778

7. p(only Janet's application is approved) = p(Philip's is not approved) · (Janet's is approved) · p(Fredric's is not approved) = (1 - 0.85)(0.92)(1 - 0.79)
    = (0.15)(0.92)(0.21) = 0.02898

8. p(neither has functioning pump) = p(station 1 does not have
    pump) · p(station 2 does not have pump)
    = (1 - 0.57)(1 - 0.42) = (0.43)(0.58) = 0.2494

9. p(stopped by neither) = p(not stopped by guard) · p(not
    stopped by metal detector)
    = (1 - 0.74)(1 - 0.99) = (0.26)(0.01) = 0.0026

10. p(demands are met and price goes up) = p(price goes up |
    demands met) · p(demands are met)
    = (0.89)(0.19) = 0.1691

11. p(pays by check and does not bounce) = p(does not bounce |
    paid by check) · p(pays by check)
    = (1 - 0.37)(0.59) = (0.63)(0.59) = 0.3717

12. **a)** p(both fail to operate) = p(second motor fails | first
         motor failed) · p(first motor fails)
         = (0.35)(0.20) = 0.07

    b) 1 - 0.07 = 0.93

13. p(all are not functioning) = p(alarm 1 is not functioning) ·
    p(alarm 2 is not functioning) · p(alarm 3 is not functioning)
    = (1 - 0.92)(1 - 0.86)(1 - 0.89) = (0.08)(0.14)(0.11)
    = 0.001232

14. The probability that family 1 has a computer and the others
    don't = (0.47)(0.53)(0.53)(0.53)(0.53)(0.53)(0.53). Since any
    1 of the 7 families can have the computer, the probability is
    $7(0.47)(0.53)^6$ or 0.0729

ANSWERS TO EXERCISES FOR SECTION 5.5 – (PAGES 275 – 277)

1. p(came from truckload II | defective)

    $$= \frac{p(\text{defective} \mid \text{truckload II}) \cdot p(\text{truckload II})}{p(\text{defective}\mid\text{truckload I}) \cdot p(\text{truckload I}) + p(\text{defective}\mid\text{truckload II}) \cdot p(\text{truckload II})}$$

    $$= \frac{\left(\frac{5}{21}\right)\left(\frac{1}{2}\right)}{\left(\frac{6}{38}\right)\left(\frac{1}{2}\right) + \left(\frac{5}{21}\right)\left(\frac{1}{2}\right)} = \frac{\frac{5}{42}}{\frac{3}{38} + \frac{5}{42}} = \frac{190}{316} = \frac{95}{158}$$

2. p(drawer D_2 | counterfeit)

$$= \frac{\left(\frac{5}{17}\right)\left(\frac{1}{2}\right)}{\left(\frac{4}{29}\right)\left(\frac{1}{2}\right) + \left(\frac{5}{17}\right)\left(\frac{1}{2}\right)} = \frac{\frac{5}{34}}{\frac{2}{29} + \frac{5}{34}} = \frac{145}{213}$$

3. p(came from blood bank B | contaminated)

$$= \frac{(0.09)(0.25)}{(0.11)(0.25) + (0.09)(0.25) + (0.13)(0.5) + (0.10)(0.25)}$$

$$= \frac{0.0225}{0.1075} = \frac{45}{215} = \frac{9}{43}$$

4. p(came from blood bank C | not contaminated)

$$= \frac{(0.87)(0.25)}{(0.89)(0.25) + (0.91)(0.25) + (0.87)(0.25) + (0.90)(0.25)}$$

$$= \frac{0.2175}{0.8925} = \frac{87}{357}$$

5. p(came from distributor B | defective)

$$= \frac{(0.09)(0.25)}{(0.08)(0.75) + (0.09)(0.25)}$$

$$= \frac{0.0225}{0.0825} = \frac{225}{825} = \frac{3}{11}$$

6. p(used method B | successful) $= \dfrac{\left(\frac{10}{18}\right)\left(\frac{1}{3}\right)}{\left(\frac{12}{16}\right)\left(\frac{1}{3}\right) + \left(\frac{10}{18}\right)\left(\frac{1}{3}\right) + \left(\frac{7}{13}\right)\left(\frac{1}{3}\right)}$

$$= \frac{\frac{10}{54}}{\frac{1}{4} + \frac{10}{54} + \frac{7}{39}} = \frac{780}{2589} = \frac{260}{863}$$

7. p(guilty | polygraph test says innocent)=

$$\frac{\text{p(says innocent|guilty)} \cdot \text{p(guilty)}}{\text{p(says innocent|guilty)} \cdot \text{p(guilty)} + \text{p(says innocent|innocent)} \cdot \text{p(innocent)}}$$

$$= \frac{(0.15)\left(\frac{25}{250}\right)}{(0.15)\left(\frac{25}{250}\right) + (0.98)\left(\frac{225}{250}\right)} = 0.0167$$

8. p(attempting to steal car | alarm ringing)

$$= \frac{(0.96)\left(\frac{1}{4}\right)}{(0.96)\left(\frac{1}{4}\right) + \left(\frac{7}{35}\right)\left(\frac{3}{4}\right)}$$

$$= \frac{0.24}{0.24 + 0.15} = \frac{24}{39} = \frac{8}{13}$$

9. p(no cancer | results positive)

$$= \frac{(0.08)(0.93)}{(0.08)(0.93) + (0.97)(0.07)} = \frac{0.0744}{0.1423} = 0.5228$$

10. p(greater than permissible levels | tests indicate that it is within permissible levels)

$$= \frac{(0.01)(0.30)}{(0.01)(0.30) + (0.96)(0.70)}$$

$$= \frac{0.003}{0.675} = \frac{3}{675} = \frac{1}{225}$$

ANSWERS TO TESTING YOUR UNDERSTANDING OF THIS CHAPTER'S CONCEPTS –
(PAGES 278 – 279)

1. Two events A and B are mutually exclusive if they both cannot occur at the same time. The events A and B are independent if the likelihood of the occurrence of event B is in no way affected by the occurrence or non-occurrence of event A.

2. **a)** Not mutually exclusive   **b)** Not mutually exclusive

3. **a)** Not independent   **b)** Not independent

4. False. The probability of selecting the ace of spades plus the probability of selecting the queen of spades does not add up to 1.

5. No. Events are not necessarily independent. (One could be present while the other is absent.)

6. No. The number of names listed in the phone directory under each letter is not the same.

ANSWERS TO THINKING CRITICALLY - (PAGES 279 - 280)

1. No. Probability is 1/2.

2. p(second different from first) = $\frac{364}{365}$ Assuming no leap year

3. p(all different) = p(second different from first) · p(third different than first 2 | first and second are different)

$$= \left(\frac{364}{365}\right)\left(\frac{363}{365}\right) = 0.9918 \qquad \text{Assuming no leap year}$$

4. p(only one delivered) = p(machine delivered in morning and carpet in afternoon) + p(machine delivered in afternoon and carpet in morning)
   = (0.57)(0.32) + (0.43)(0.68) = 0.4748

5. **a)**   p(at least one subscribes)
   = 1 - p(no one subscribes to closed circuit TV)
   = 1 - $(0.83)^6$ = 0.6731
   b)   p(at most one subscribes)
   = p(0 subscribes) + p(1 subscribes)
   = $(0.83)^6 + 6(0.17)(0.83)^5$
   = 0.3269 + 0.4018 = 0.7287

6. No, they are dependent since p(B|A) = 0 and is not equal to p(B)

ANSWERS TO REVIEW EXERCISES FOR CHAPTER 5 - (PAGES 280 - 282)

1. **a)** (0.4)(0.5)(0.35) = 0.07
   b) (0.6)(0.5)(0.65) = 0.195
   c) p(at least one succeeds) = 1 - p(none succeed)
                                     = 1 - 0.195 = 0.805

2. 1/5

3. (0.45)(0.35) = 0.1575

4. (0.45)(0.45) + (0.15)(0.15) + (0.05)(0.05) + (0.35)(0.35)
    = 0.35

5. **a)** 1/13   **b)** 1/4   **c)** $\dfrac{4}{40} = \dfrac{1}{10}$

6. $\dfrac{3}{15} = \dfrac{1}{5}$

7. p(Paul contacted and Juliana not contacted) + p(Paul
    not contacted and Juliana contacted) + p(both contacted)
    = (0.75)(0.45) + (0.25)(0.55) + (0.75)(0.55) = 0.8875

8. p(at least one will default) = 1 – p(none will default)
    $$= 1 - (0.6)(0.4)(0.25)$$
    $$= 0.94$$

9. $\left(\dfrac{2}{9}\right)\left(\dfrac{1}{8}\right) = \dfrac{1}{36}$

10. **a)** $\dfrac{336 + 72 + 386}{3200} = \dfrac{794}{3200} = \dfrac{397}{1600}$

    b) $\dfrac{72}{794} = \dfrac{36}{397}$

    c) $\dfrac{72}{862} = \dfrac{36}{431}$

11. p(all different) = p(second different than first) · p(third
    different from first 2 | first and second are different)

    $$= \left(\dfrac{364}{365}\right)\left(\dfrac{363}{365}\right) = 0.9918 \qquad \text{Assuming no leap year.}$$

12. Similar to last problem:

    $$p(\text{all different}) = \left(\dfrac{364}{365}\right)\left(\dfrac{363}{365}\right)\left(\dfrac{362}{365}\right) = 0.9836$$

1. $\frac{1}{7}$

2. a) $\left(\frac{42}{50}\right)\left(\frac{41}{49}\right) = \frac{1722}{2450}$

    b) $\left(\frac{8}{50}\right)\left(\frac{7}{49}\right) = \frac{56}{2450}$

    c) $2\left(\frac{8}{50}\right)\left(\frac{42}{49}\right) = \frac{672}{2450}$

3. p(at least two have same birthday)
    = 1 - p(all birthdays are different)
    = 1 - 0.9918
    = 0.0082
    See question 11 in Review Exercises for this chapter.

4. $(0.78)(0.65)(0.57) = 0.28899$

5. $(0.78)(0.35)(0.43) = 0.11739$

6. p(caused by either) = p(caused by patient) + p(caused by doctor) - p(caused by both)

    $= \frac{1}{8} + \frac{1}{9} - \frac{1}{15} = \frac{135}{1080} + \frac{120}{1080} - \frac{72}{1080} = \frac{183}{1080}$

7. p(selected nearer machine | wins)

    $= \dfrac{\left(\frac{1}{9}\right)\left(\frac{3}{5}\right)}{\left(\frac{1}{9}\right)\left(\frac{3}{5}\right) + \left(\frac{1}{15}\right)\left(\frac{2}{5}\right)} = \dfrac{\frac{1}{15}}{\frac{1}{15} + \frac{2}{75}} = \frac{5}{7}$

8. a) $\frac{59 + 122}{871} = \frac{181}{871}$

    b) $\frac{59}{181}$

    c) $\frac{59}{334}$

9. p(orders either)

$$= \frac{4}{7} + \frac{1}{2} + \frac{5}{11} - \frac{2}{9} - \frac{1}{7} - \frac{1}{4} + \frac{1}{44}$$

$$= \frac{1584}{2772} + \frac{1386}{2772} + \frac{1260}{2772} - \frac{616}{2772} - \frac{396}{2772} - \frac{693}{2772} + \frac{63}{2772}$$

$$= \frac{2588}{2772} = \frac{647}{693}$$

10. p(either) = 0.27 + 0.22 + 0.42 - 0.17 - 0.09 - 0.16 + 0.07
    = 0.56

11. p(both same color) = p(both white) + p(both red) + p(both

black) $= \left(\frac{4}{12}\right)\left(\frac{3}{11}\right) + \left(\frac{3}{12}\right)\left(\frac{2}{11}\right) + \left(\frac{5}{12}\right)\left(\frac{4}{11}\right) = \frac{38}{132} = \frac{19}{66}$

12. p(neither speaks foreign language) = (0.17)(0.34) = 0.0578

13. a) $p(B|A) = \dfrac{(0.15)(0.20)}{(0.15)(0.20) + (0.12)(0.40) + (0.09)(0.40)}$

$$= \frac{0.030}{0.114} = \frac{15}{57} = \frac{5}{19}$$

b) $p(C|A) = \dfrac{(0.12)(0.40)}{(0.15)(0.20) + (0.12)(0.40) + (0.09)(0.40)}$

$$= \frac{0.048}{0.114} = \frac{24}{57} = \frac{8}{19}$$

c) $p(D|A) = \dfrac{(0.09)(0.40)}{(0.15)(0.20) + (0.12)(0.40) + (0.09)(0.40)}$

$$= \frac{0.036}{0.114} = \frac{18}{57} = \frac{6}{19}$$

14. Choice (c)

15. Choice (b)

16. Choice (c)

17. Choice (d)

18. Choice (d)

For question 1 - 4 use the following information. Two hundred seventy people were asked to comment on the assembly instructions supplied with a particular computer. The results are shown below:

	Very easy to follow	Average difficulty to follow	Very difficult to follow	Impossible to follow
Male	51	39	27	19
Female	47	45	22	20

1. One of these people is randomly selected. Find the probability that this individual is <u>not</u> a male.

   a) 136/270   b) 134/270   c) 134/136   d) 47/270
   e) none of these

   Answer _____

2. One of these people is randomly selected. If it is known that this person found the instructions very difficult to follow, find the probability that this individual is a male.

   a) 27/136   b) 22/134   c) 27/270   d) 27/49
   e) none of these

   Answer _____

3. One of these people is randomly selected. If it is known that this person is a male, find the probability that this person found the instructions very difficult to follow.

   a) 27/136   b) 22/134   c) 27/270   d) 27/49
   e) none of these

   Answer _____

4. Find the probability of selecting an individual from this group who is a male and who found the instructions very difficult to follow.

   a) 27/136   b) 22/134   c) 27/270   d) 27/49
   e) none of these

   Answer _____

5. Samantha has just received a tip about a particular stock. The probability that Samantha will buy 100 shares of this stock is 20/27. The probability that Samantha will be unable to travel overseas next year given that she buys the shares of stock is 1/3. Find the probability that Samantha buys the shares of stock <u>and</u> that she is unable to travel overseas next summer.

Answer _____

6. A card is randomly selected from an ordinary deck of cards. Find the probability that it is a jack or a club.

   a) 13/52   b) 4/52   c) 17/52   d) 16/52   e) none of these

Answer _____

7. Two students at a college are randomly selected. The probability that the first student is majoring in mathematics is 0.72. The probability that the second student is majoring in art is 0.51. Assuming independence, find the probability that the first student is a math major and that the second student is an art major.

Answer _____

8. In a particular unit of a girls scout group, the probability that a girl scout is a good mountain climber is 0.83, and the probability that a girl scout is a good mountain climber as well as a good hunter is 0.52. If a girl scout that is a good mountain climber is randomly selected, what is the probability that she is also a good hunter?

Answer _____

9. Refer back to the previous question. The probability that a girl scout in this group knows how to treat a snake bite is 0.67. Find the probability that 3 independently selected and totally unrelated girl scouts in this group do <u>not</u> know how to treat a snake bite.

Answer _____

10. If $p(A|B) = 0.2$, $p(A|C) = 0.4$, $p(A|D) = 0.3$, $p(B) = 0.31$, $p(C) = 0.48$, and $p(D) = 0.21$, find $p(C|A)$.

Answer _____

For question 1 - 4 use the following information. Four hundred eighteen junior or senior college students were asked to rate a particular teacher. Their comments are shown below:

	Explains well; easy tests	Explains well; hard tests	Explains poorly; easy tests	Explains poorly; hard tests
Junior	59	63	52	31
Senior	61	47	79	26

1. One of these students is randomly selected. Find the probability that the student is a junior.

   a) 213/418 b) 205/213 c) 205/418 d) 59/418
   e) none of these

   Answer _____

2. One of these students is randomly selected. If it is known that the student is a junior, find the probability that the student rated the teacher as "explains well, easy tests".

   a) 59/120 b) 59/205 c) 59/418 d) 59/61
   e) none of these

   Answer _____

3. One of these students is randomly selected. If it is known that the student rated the teacher as "explains well, easy test", find that probability that the student is a junior.

   a) 59/120 b) 59/205 c) 59/418 d) 59/61
   e) none of these

   Answer _____

4. Find the probability that a randomly selected individual from this group is a junior who rated the teacher as "explains well, easy tests."

   a) 59/120 b) 59/205 c) 59/418 d) 59/61
   e) none of these

   Answer _____

5. A card is randomly selected from an ordinary deck of cards. Find the probability that it is a picture card or a red card.

    a) 12/52   b) 26/52   c) 38/52   d) 36/52   e) none of these

    Answer _____

6. The probability that the Johnson family will buy a new car next year is 9/11. The probability that they trade in their old car given that they buy a new car is 16/17. Find the probability that the Johnson family buys a new car next year and that they trade in their old car.

    Answer _____

7. A tax agent randomly selects two tax returns. The probability that the first tax return contains mathematical errors is 0.76, and the probability that the second tax return contains a questionable deduction is 0.51. Assuming independence, find the probability that the first return contains a mathematical error and that the second return contains a questionable deduction.

    Answer _____

8. A stock broker makes three telephone calls to three prospective customers detailing a particular stock. The probabilities that these three customers buy the particular stock are 0.81, 0.71, and 0.69 respectively. Find the probability that none of the customers buy the particular stock.

    Answer _____

9. A pair of dice is rolled. Find the probability that the sum of the number of dots showing on both dice is 10 or 12.

    Answer _____

10. If $p(A|B) = 0.3$, $p(A|C) = 0.5$, $p(A|D) = 0.2$, $p(B) = 0.27$, $p(C) = 0.57$, and $p(D) = 0.16$, find $p(C|A)$.

    Answer _____

CHAPTER 5 - RULES OF PROBABILITY
SUPPLEMENTARY TEST FORM C

For question 1 - 4 use the following information. An airport official interviewed 491 returning travellers as they departed from both charter and non-charter flights to obtain information on the kind of service each carrier provided.

	Very good service	Average service	Very poor service	No service at all
Charter flight	138	55	16	42
Non-charter flight	162	42	22	14

1. One of these travellers is randomly selected. Find the probability that this traveller did not travel on a charter flight.
   a) 55/97   b) 240/251   c) 240/491   d) 162/491
   e) none of these

   Answer _____

2. One of these travellers is randomly selected. If it is known that this traveller was on a charter flight, find the probability that the traveller rated the service provided as average.

   a) 55/97   b) 55/251   c) 55/491   d) 42/491
   e) none of these

   Answer _____

3. One of these travellers is randomly selected. If it is known that this traveller rated the service provided as average, find the probability that this traveller was on a charter flight.

   a) 55/97   b) 55/251   c) 55/491   d) 42/491
   e) none of these

   Answer _____

4. Find the probability of selecting a traveller from this group who travelled on a charter flight and who rated the service provided as average.

   a) 55/97   b) 55/251   c) 55/491   d) 42/291
   e) none of these

   Answer _____

5. A pair of dice is rolled. Find the probability that the sum of the number of dots appearing is 5 or less.

Answer _____

6. A fish tank contains 7 guppies, 6 algae-eaters and 4 cat fish. A store keeper randomly selects 2 fish (one after another without replacement) from the tank for a customer. Find the probability that both fish selected are catfish.

Answer _____

7. A restaurant owner receives food supplies from one of four different vendors, A, B, C, or D, which the owner selects on a random basis. The probabilities that the food received from these vendors is fresh are 0.93, 0.90, 0.89, and 0.87 respectively. The restaurant owner randomly selects a food supply received from one of these vendors. If the food is fresh, what is the probability that it was supplied by vendor C?

Answer _____

8. Refer back to the previous question. If the food selected is not fresh, what is the probability that it was supplied by vendor B?

Answer _____

9. The Marleton Elementary School uses school busses supplied by companies A, B, and C. The probability that the busses supplied by company A arrive on time is 0.95, the probability that the busses supplied by company B arrive on time is 0.93, and the probability that the busses supplied by company C arrive on time is 0.97. If a day is randomly selected, find the probability that the busses supplied by all three companies to the school will be late. (Assume independence.)

Answer _____

10. A gas station attendant finds that the probability that a customer will ask to have the oil checked is 0.7. Furthermore, the attendant finds that the probability is 0.51 that a customer will ask to have the oil checked and also to clean the windows. If a customer is observed asking the attendant to check the oil, find the probability that the customer will also ask the attendant to clean the windows.

Answer _____

ANSWERS TO SUPPLEMENTARY TESTS
CHAPTER 5 - RULES OF PROBABILITY

Form A	Form B	Form C
1. Choice (b)	1. Choice (c)	1. Choice (c)
2. Choice (d)	2. Choice (b)	2. Choice (b)
3. Choice (a)	3. Choice (a)	3. Choice (a)
4. Choice (c)	4. Choice (c)	4. Choice (c)
5. 20/81	5. Choice (e)	5. 5/18
6. Choice (d)	6. 144/187	6. 3/68
7. 0.3672	7. 0.3876	7. 2225/8975 or 89/359
8. 52/83	8. 0.0171	8. 250/1025 or 10/41
9. 0.0359	9. 1/9	9. 0.000105
10. 192/317	10. 285/398	10. 51/70

SECTION 6.2 (PAGES 295 - 298)

1. Any positive number greater than 0.

2. **a)** 0, 1, 2, ... , 227
    b) 0, 1, 2, ... , 26
    c) 0, 1, 2, 3, 4, or 5
    d) 0, 1, 2, ... , 28 assuming no leap year
    e) 0, 1, 2, 3, or 4
    f) 0, 1, 2, ... , 22
    g) 1, 2, ...

3. No. The sum of all the probabilities is not 1.

4. 0.16 since all the probabilities must sum to 1.

5.

Number of girls, x	p(x)
0	$\frac{1}{8}$
1	$\frac{3}{8}$
2	$\frac{3}{8}$
3	$\frac{1}{8}$
	$\frac{8}{8} = 1$

6.

Number of heads, x	p(x)
0	$\frac{1}{4}$
1	$\frac{1}{2}$
2	$\frac{1}{4}$
	$\frac{4}{4} = 1$

7.

Number of 1's, x	p(x)
0	$\frac{25}{36}$
1	$\frac{10}{36}$
2	$\frac{1}{36}$
	$\frac{36}{36} = 1$

8.

Sum (in cents), x	p(x)
2	$\frac{1}{36}$
6	$\frac{2}{36}$
10	$\frac{1}{36}$
11	$\frac{2}{36}$
15	$\frac{2}{36}$
20	$\frac{1}{36}$
26	$\frac{2}{36}$
30	$\frac{2}{36}$
35	$\frac{2}{36}$
50	$\frac{1}{36}$
51	$\frac{2}{36}$
55	$\frac{2}{36}$
60	$\frac{2}{36}$
75	$\frac{2}{36}$
100	$\frac{1}{36}$
101	$\frac{2}{36}$
105	$\frac{2}{36}$
110	$\frac{2}{36}$
125	$\frac{2}{36}$
150	$\frac{2}{36}$
200	$\frac{1}{36}$
	$\frac{36}{36} = 1$

9.

Number of heads, x	p(x)
0	$\frac{1}{8}$
1	$\frac{3}{8}$
2	$\frac{3}{8}$
3	$\frac{1}{8}$
	$\frac{8}{8} = 1$

10.

Number of seedlings that sprout, x	p(x)
0	$\frac{1}{16}$
1	$\frac{4}{16}$
2	$\frac{6}{16}$
3	$\frac{4}{16}$
4	$\frac{1}{16}$
	$\frac{16}{16} = 1$

11.

Number of yellow balls, x	p(x)
0	$\left(\frac{14}{19}\right)\left(\frac{14}{19}\right)\left(\frac{14}{19}\right) = \frac{2744}{6859}$
1	$3\left(\frac{5}{19}\right)\left(\frac{14}{19}\right)\left(\frac{14}{19}\right) = \frac{2940}{6859}$
2	$3\left(\frac{5}{19}\right)\left(\frac{5}{19}\right)\left(\frac{14}{19}\right) = \frac{1050}{6859}$
3	$\left(\frac{5}{19}\right)\left(\frac{5}{19}\right)\left(\frac{5}{19}\right) = \frac{125}{6859}$
	$\frac{6859}{6859} = 1$

12.

Number of games won, x	p(x)
0	$\frac{1}{32}$
1	$5\left(\frac{1}{32}\right) = \frac{5}{32}$
2	$10\left(\frac{1}{32}\right) = \frac{10}{32}$
3	$10\left(\frac{1}{32}\right) = \frac{10}{32}$
4	$5\left(\frac{1}{32}\right) = \frac{5}{32}$
5	$\frac{1}{32}$
	$\frac{32}{32} = 1$

13.

Number of defective spark plugs, x	p(x)
0	$\left(\frac{6}{8}\right)\left(\frac{6}{8}\right) = \frac{36}{64}$
1	$2\left(\frac{2}{8}\right)\left(\frac{6}{8}\right) = \frac{24}{64}$
2	$\left(\frac{2}{8}\right)\left(\frac{2}{8}\right) = \frac{4}{64}$
	$\frac{64}{64} = 1$

164

14.

x	p(x)
1	$\frac{5}{15}$
2	$\frac{4}{15}$
3	$\frac{3}{15}$
4	$\frac{2}{15}$
5	$\frac{1}{15}$
	$\frac{15}{15} = 1$

Yes, as the sum of the probabilities is 1.

15.

x	p(x)
0	$\frac{5}{9}$
1	$\frac{4}{9}$
2	$\frac{3}{9}$
3	$\frac{2}{9}$
4	$\frac{1}{9}$
	$\frac{15}{9}$

No, as the sum of the probabilities is not 1.

16.
a) 0.40 + 0.05 = 0.45
b) 0.29 + 0.08 = 0.37
c) 0
d) 0.40 + 0.05 + 0.29 + 0.08 = 0.82

17.
a) 0.106   **b)** 0.106 + 0.098 + 0.088 + 0.039 + 0.029 = 0.360
c) 1   **d)** 0.243 + 0.252 + 0.106 + 0.098 = 0.699

ANSWERS TO EXERCISES FOR SECTION 6.2 (CONTINUED) – (PAGES 295 – 298)

18. **a)** 0. 03 + 0.05 + 0.08 + 0.15 = 0.31
    b) 0.24 + 0.22 = 0.46
    c) 1
    d) 0.05 + 0.08 + 0.15 + 0.23 + 0.24 + 0.22 = 0.97

ANSWERS TO EXERCISES FOR SECTION 6.4 – (PAGES 306 – 310)

1. $\mu = \Sigma x \cdot p(x) = 0(0.02) + 1(0.03) + 2(0.25) + 3(0.19)$
   $+ 4(0.16) + 5(0.14) + 6(0.12) + 7(0.08) + 8(0.01) = 3.8$

2.

x	p(x)	$x \cdot p(x)$	x^2	$x^2 \cdot p(x)$
1	0.01	0.01	1	0.01
2	0.02	0.04	4	0.08
3	0.01	0.03	9	0.09
4	0.20	0.80	16	3.20
5	0.10	0.50	25	2.50
6	0.18	1.08	36	6.48
7	0.07	0.49	49	3.43
8	0.14	1.12	64	8.96
9	0.12	1.08	81	9.72
10	0.09	0.90	100	9.00
11	0.05	0.55	121	6.05
12	0.01	0.12	144	1.44
		6.72		50.96

Mean $= \mu = \Sigma x \cdot p(x) = 6.72$
Variance $= \sigma^2 = 50.96 - (6.72)^2 = 5.8016$

Standard deviation $= \sigma = \sqrt{5.8016} \approx 2.40865$

3.

x	p(x)	x · p(x)	x^2	x^2 · p(x)
0	0.08	0	0	0
1	0.09	0.09	1	0.09
2	0.13	0.26	4	0.52
3	0.07	0.21	9	0.63
4	0.14	0.56	16	2.24
5	0.23	1.15	25	5.75
6	0.19	1.14	36	6.84
7	0.07	0.49	49	3.43
		3.90		19.50

Mean = μ = Σx · p(x) = 3.90
Variance = σ^2 = 19.50 $-(3.90)^2$ = 4.29

Standard deviation = σ = $\sqrt{4.29}$ $\approx$ 2.0712

4.

x	p(x)	x · p(x)	x^2	x^2 · p(x)
5	0.07	0.35	25	1.75
6	0.14	0.84	36	5.04
7	0.17	1.19	49	8.33
8	0.21	1.68	64	13.44
9	0.18	1.62	81	14.58
10	0.19	1.90	100	19.00
11	0.03	0.33	121	3.63
12	0.01	0.12	144	1.44
		8.03		67.21

Mean = μ = Σx · p(x) = 8.03
Variance = σ^2 = 67.21 $-$ $(8.03)^2$ = 2.7291

Standard deviation = $\sqrt{2.7291}$ $\approx$ 1.652

5.

x	p(x)	x · p(x)	x^2	x^2 · p(x)
0	0.05	0	0	0
1	0.09	0.09	1	0.09
2	0.13	0.26	4	0.52
3	0.15	0.45	9	1.35
4	0.16	0.64	16	2.56
5	0.29	1.45	25	7.25
6	0.06	0.36	36	2.16
7	0.05	0.35	49	2.45
8	0.02	<u>0.16</u>	64	<u>1.28</u>
		3.76		17.66

Mean = μ = Σx · p(x) = 3.76
Variance = σ^2 = 17.66 - $(3.76)^2$ = 3.5224

Standard deviation = σ = $\sqrt{3.5224}$ ≈ 1.8768

6.

x	p(x)	x · p(x)	x^2	x^2 · p(x)
0	0.04	0	0	0
1	0.05	0.05	1	0.05
2	0.33	0.66	4	1.32
3	0.27	0.81	9	2.43
4	0.10	0.40	16	1.60
5	0.08	0.40	25	2.00
6	0.06	0.36	36	2.16
7	0.07	<u>0.49</u>	49	<u>3.43</u>
		3.17		12.99

Mean = μ = Σx · p(x) = 3.17
Variance = σ^2 = 12.99 - $(3.17)^2$ = 2.9411
Standard deviation = σ ≈ 1.71496

7.

x	p(x)	x · p(x)	x^2	x^2 · p(x)
0	0.08	0	0	0
1	0.14	0.14	1	0.14
2	0.16	0.32	4	0.64
3	0.18	0.54	9	1.62
4	0.21	0.84	16	3.36
5	0.17	0.85	25	4.25
6	0.03	0.18	36	1.08
7	0.02	0.14	49	0.98
8	0.01	0.08	64	0.64
		3.09		12.71

Mean = μ = $\Sigma x \cdot p(x)$ = 3.09
Variance = σ^2 = 12.71 - $(3.09)^2$ = 3.1619

Standard deviation = $\sqrt{3.1619} \approx 1.7782$

8.

x	$p(x)$	$x \cdot p(x)$	x^2	$x^2 \cdot p(x)$
1	$\frac{1}{6}$	$\frac{1}{6}$	1	$\frac{1}{6}$
2	$\frac{1}{6}$	$\frac{2}{6}$	4	$\frac{4}{6}$
3	$\frac{1}{6}$	$\frac{3}{6}$	9	$\frac{9}{6}$
4	$\frac{1}{6}$	$\frac{4}{6}$	16	$\frac{16}{6}$
5	$\frac{1}{6}$	$\frac{5}{6}$	25	$\frac{25}{6}$
6	$\frac{1}{6}$	$\frac{6}{6}$	36	$\frac{36}{6}$
		$\frac{21}{6}$		$\frac{91}{6}$

Mean $= \mu = \Sigma x \cdot p(x) = \dfrac{21}{6} = 3.5$

Variance $= \sigma^2 = \dfrac{91}{6} - \left(\dfrac{21}{6}\right)^2 = \dfrac{35}{12} \approx 2.9167$

Standard deviation $= \sigma = \sqrt{2.9167} \approx 1.7078$

9. a)

x	p(x)	x · p(x)	x^2	x^2 · p(x)
2	$\frac{1}{36}$	$\frac{2}{36}$	4	$\frac{4}{36}$
3	$\frac{2}{36}$	$\frac{6}{36}$	9	$\frac{18}{36}$
4	$\frac{3}{36}$	$\frac{12}{36}$	16	$\frac{48}{36}$
5	$\frac{4}{36}$	$\frac{20}{36}$	25	$\frac{100}{36}$
6	$\frac{5}{36}$	$\frac{30}{36}$	36	$\frac{180}{36}$
7	$\frac{6}{36}$	$\frac{42}{36}$	49	$\frac{294}{36}$
8	$\frac{5}{36}$	$\frac{40}{36}$	64	$\frac{320}{36}$
9	$\frac{4}{36}$	$\frac{36}{36}$	81	$\frac{324}{36}$
10	$\frac{3}{36}$	$\frac{30}{36}$	100	$\frac{300}{36}$
11	$\frac{2}{36}$	$\frac{22}{36}$	121	$\frac{242}{36}$
12	$\frac{1}{36}$	$\frac{12}{36}$	144	$\frac{144}{36}$
		$\frac{252}{36} = 7$		$\frac{1974}{36}$

b) $\text{Mean} = \mu = \Sigma x \cdot p(x) = \frac{252}{36} = 7$

c) $\text{Variance} = \sigma^2 = \frac{1974}{36} - 7^2 \approx 5.8333$

10. a)

x	p(x)	x · p(x)	x^2	x^2 · p(x)
2	$\frac{2}{6}$	$\frac{4}{6}$	4	$\frac{8}{6}$
3	$\frac{1}{6}$	$\frac{3}{6}$	9	$\frac{9}{6}$
4	$\frac{1}{6}$	$\frac{4}{6}$	16	$\frac{16}{6}$
5	$\frac{1}{6}$	$\frac{5}{6}$	25	$\frac{25}{6}$
6	$\frac{1}{6}$	$\frac{6}{6}$	36	$\frac{36}{6}$
		$\frac{22}{6}$		$\frac{94}{6}$

b)   Mean = $\mu = \dfrac{22}{6} = \dfrac{11}{3}$

Variance = $\sigma^2 = \dfrac{94}{6} - \left(\dfrac{11}{3}\right)^2 = \dfrac{40}{18} \approx 2.2222$

Standard deviation = $\sigma = \sqrt{2.2222} \approx 1.4907$

172

11.

x	p(x)	x · p(x)	x^2	x^2 · p(x)
0	0.02	0	0	0
1	0.06	0.06	1	0.06
2	0.19	0.38	4	0.76
3	0.33	0.99	9	2.97
4	0.23	0.92	16	3.68
5	0.13	0.65	25	3.25
6	0.03	0.18	36	1.08
7	0.01	<u>0.07</u>	49	<u>0.49</u>
		3.25		12.29

a) $\mu = \Sigma x \cdot p(x) = 3.25$

b) $\sigma^2 = 12.29 - (3.25)^2 = 1.7275$

$\sigma = \sqrt{1.7275} \approx 1.3143$

12.

x	p(x)	x · p(x)	x^2	x^2 · p(x)
0	0.02	0	0	0
1	0.08	0.08	1	0.08
2	0.12	0.24	4	0.48
3	0.14	0.42	9	1.26
4	0.22	0.88	16	3.52
5	0.20	1.00	25	5.00
6	0.15	0.90	36	5.40
7	0.04	0.28	49	1.96
8	0.03	<u>0.24</u>	64	<u>1.92</u>
		4.04		19.62

a) $\mu = \Sigma x \cdot p(x) = 4.04$

b) $\sigma^2 = 19.62 - (4.04)^2 = 3.2984$

$\sigma = \sqrt{3.2984} \approx 1.8161$

13.

x	p(x)	x · p(x)	x^2	x^2 · p(x)
0	0.04	0	0	0
1	0.05	0.05	1	0.05
2	0.09	0.18	4	0.36
3	0.17	0.51	9	1.53
4	0.22	0.88	16	3.52
5	0.14	0.70	25	3.50
6	0.12	0.72	36	4.32
7	0.11	0.77	49	5.39
8	0.06	0.48	64	3.84
		4.29		22.51

a) $\mu = \Sigma x \cdot p(x) = 4.29$

b) $\sigma^2 = 22.51 - (4.29)^2 = 4.1059$

$\sigma = \sqrt{4.1059} \approx 2.0263$

14. a)

Advertising Medium	Expected Sales, x · p(x)
Television	(70,000)(0.37) = $25,900
Radio	(37,000)(0.56) = $20,720
Magazines	(45,000)(0.49) = $22,050
Distributing Free Samples	(50,000)(0.42) = $21,000

b) Select television since it has the highest expected sales.

ANSWERS TO EXERCISES FOR SECTION 6.5 - (PAGES 324 - 327)

1. p(exactly 4 work) = $\dfrac{7!}{4! \, 3!} (0.70)^4 (0.30)^3 = 0.2269$

2. p(all six have VCR) = $\dfrac{6!}{6! \, 0!} (0.80)^6 (0.20)^0 = 0.2621$

3. $p = \dfrac{1}{8} = 0.125$ $q = \dfrac{7}{8} = 0.875$ $n = 10$

   p(at most 2 women) = p(0 women) + p(1 woman) + p(2 women)

$$= \frac{10!}{0!10!}(0.125)^0(0.875)^{10}$$

$$+ \frac{10!}{1!9!}(0.125)^1(0.875)^9$$

$$+ \frac{10!}{2!8!}(0.125)^2(0.875)^8$$

$$= 0.2631 + 0.3758 + 0.2416 = 0.8805$$

4. **a)** $\dfrac{6!}{3!3!}(0.32)^3(0.68)^3 = 0.2061$

   b)   p(at most 3) = p(0) + p(1) + p(2) + p(3)

$$= \frac{6!}{0!6!}(0.32)^0(0.68)^6 + \frac{6!}{1!5!}(0.32)^1(0.68)^5$$

$$+ \frac{6!}{2!4!}(0.32)^2(0.68)^4 + \frac{6!}{3!3!}(0.32)^3(0.68)^3$$

$$= 0.0989 + 0.2792 + 0.3284 + 0.2061 = 0.9126$$

   c)   p(at least 3) = 1 - p(0) - p(1) - p(2)
   $= 1 - 0.0989 - 0.2792 - 0.3284 = 0.2935$

5. **a)** p(at most half will be audited)
             = p(0) + p(1) + p(2) + p(3)

$$= \frac{6!}{0!6!}(0.08)^0(0.92)^6 + \frac{6!}{1!5!}(0.08)^1(0.92)^5$$

$$+ \frac{6!}{2!4!}(0.08)^2(0.92)^4 + \frac{6!}{3!3!}(0.08)^3(0.92)^3$$

$$= 0.6064 + 0.3164 + 0.0688 + 0.0080 = 0.9996$$

   b) $p(0) = \dfrac{6!}{0!6!}(0.03)^0(0.97)^6 = 0.8330$

6. a) $\dfrac{7!}{3!4!} (0.6)^3 (0.4)^4 = 0.1935$

   b) $\dfrac{7!}{7!0!} (0.6)^7 (0.4)^0 = 0.0280$

   c) $\dfrac{7!}{0!7!} (0.6)^0 (0.4)^7 = 0.0016$

7. $\dfrac{9!}{3!6!} (0.28)^3 (0.72)^6 = 0.2569$

8. $p(\text{at most } 3) = p(0) + p(1) + p(2) + p(3)$

$= \dfrac{7!}{0!7!} (0.52)^0 (0.48)^7 \quad + \dfrac{7!}{1!6!} (0.52)^1 (0.48)^6$

$+ \dfrac{7!}{2!5!} (0.52)^2 (0.48)^5 + \dfrac{7!}{3!4!} (0.52)^3 (0.48)^4$

$= 0.0059 + 0.0445 + 0.1447 + 0.2612 = 0.4563$

9. $p(\text{at least } 4) = 1 - p(0) - p(1) - p(2) - p(3)$
$= 1 - 0.349 - 0.387 - 0.194 - 0.057 = 0.013$

10. $\dfrac{5!}{2!3!} (0.25)^2 (0.75)^3 = 0.2637$

11. $\dfrac{6!}{4!2!} \left(\dfrac{3}{5}\right)^4 \left(\dfrac{2}{5}\right)^2 = 0.3110$

12. a) $\dfrac{4!}{4!0!} \left(\dfrac{1}{4}\right)^0 \left(\dfrac{3}{4}\right)^4 = 0.3164$

   b) $\dfrac{4!}{2!2!} \left(\dfrac{1}{4}\right)^2 \left(\dfrac{3}{4}\right)^2 = 0.2109$

   c) $\dfrac{4!}{0!4!} \left(\dfrac{1}{4}\right)^4 \left(\dfrac{3}{4}\right)^0 = 0.0039$

13. **a)** $\dfrac{9!}{9!\,0!} (0.93)^9(0.07)^0 = 0.5204$

   b) $\dfrac{9!}{5!\,4!} (0.93)^5(0.07)^4 = 0.0021$

14. p(at most two) = p(0) + p(1) + p(2)

$$= \dfrac{8!}{0!\,8!} (0.096)^0(0.904)^8 + \dfrac{8!}{1!\,7!} (0.096)^1(0.904)^7$$

$$+ \dfrac{8!}{2!\,6!} (0.096)^2(0.904)^6$$

$$= 0.4460 + 0.3789 + 0.1408 = 0.9657$$

15. **a)** $\dfrac{8!}{2!\,6!} (0.31)^2(0.69)^6 = 0.2904$

   b) p(at most 2) = p(0) + p(1) + p(2)

$$= \dfrac{8!}{0!\,8!} (0.31)^0(0.69)^8 + \dfrac{8!}{1!\,7!} (0.31)^1(0.69)^7$$

$$+ \dfrac{8!}{2!\,6!} (0.31)^2(0.69)^6$$

$$= 0.0514 + 0.1847 + 0.2904 = 0.5265$$

   c) p(at least 2) = 1 - p(0) - p(1)
   = 1 - 0.0514 - 0.1847 = 0.7639

16. **a)**

$$p(\text{at least } 4) = 1 - p(0) - p(1) - p(2) - p(3)$$

$$= 1 - \frac{12!}{0!12!} (0.44)^0 (0.56)^{12}$$

$$- \frac{12!}{1!11!} (0.44)^1 (0.56)^{11}$$

$$- \frac{12!}{2!10!} (0.44)^2 (0.56)^{10} - \frac{12!}{3!9!} (0.44)^3 (0.56)^9$$

$$= 1 - 0.00095 - 0.00897 - 0.03876 - 0.10150$$
$$= 0.84982$$

b)

$$p(\text{at most } 2) = p(0) + p(1) + p(2)$$
$$= 0.00095 + 0.00897 + 0.03876 = 0.04868$$

c)

$$p(\text{none}) = 0.00095$$

1. $\mu = np$
$= 600(0.38)$
$= 228$

$\sigma = \sqrt{npq}$

$= \sqrt{600(0.38)(0.62)}$

≈ 11.889

2. $\mu = 14,278(0.02) = 285.56$. Yes, since this exceeds 280.

3. $\mu = 965,425(0.18) = 173,776.5$

$\sigma = \sqrt{(965,425)(0.18)(0.82)} \approx 377.487$

4. $\mu = 375(0.43) = 161.25$

5. $\mu = (495)\left(\frac{2}{3}\right) = 330$

$\sigma = \sqrt{495\left(\frac{2}{3}\right)\left(\frac{1}{3}\right)} \approx 10.488$

6. $\mu = (60,000)(0.08) = 4800$

$\sigma = \sqrt{(60,000)(0.08)(0.92)} \approx 66.453$

7. $\mu = (2000)(0.85) = 1700$

$\sigma = \sqrt{(2000)(0.85)(0.15)} \approx 15.9687$

8. $\mu = 75\left(\frac{1}{4}\right) = 18.75$

$\sigma = \sqrt{75\left(\frac{1}{4}\right)\left(\frac{3}{4}\right)} = 3.75$

9. $\mu = (1450)(0.53) = 768.5$

$\sigma = \sqrt{(1450)(0.53)(0.47)} \approx 19.005$

10. $\mu = (500)(0.22) = 110$

$\sigma = \sqrt{(500)(0.22)(0.78)} \approx 9.2628$

11. $\mu = 2000(0.85) = 1700$

$\sigma = \sqrt{(2000)(0.85)(0.15)} \approx 15.9687$

12. $1500 = n(0.85)$ 1765 letters

          $1764.71 = n$

13. $\mu = 240(0.88) = 211.2$.   Since the airline only has 210 available seats, it will not have a seat for everyone, if the average or more show up.

14. By definition

$\mu = \sum x \cdot p(x)$

$= \sum x \dfrac{n!}{x!(n-x)!} p^x q^{n-x}$

$= np \sum \dfrac{(n-x)!}{(x-1)![(n-x)-(x-1)!]} p^{x-1} q^{n-1-(x-1)}$

$= np$ as the expression to be summed represents a binomial distribution whose sum is 1.

ANSWERS TO EXERCISES FOR SECTION 6.7 - (PAGES 334 - 336)

1. a)   p(at most 2 customers) $= p(0) + p(1) + p(2)$

$= \dfrac{e^{-5}5^0}{0!} + \dfrac{e^{-5}5^1}{1!} + \dfrac{e^{-5}5^2}{2!}$

$= 0.00674 + 0.03369 + 0.08422$

$= 0.12465$

b)   p(at least 2 customers) $= 1 - p(0) - p(1)$

$= 1 - 0.00674 - 0.03369$

$= 0.95957$

c)   p(exactly 2 customers) $= \dfrac{e^{-5}5^2}{2!} = 0.08422$

2. $\left[\dfrac{e^{-3}3^0}{0!}\right]^2 = 0.00248$

3. p(less than or equal to 4)

$$= p(0) + p(1) + p(2) + p(3) + p(4)$$

$$= \frac{e^{-7}7^0}{0!} + \frac{e^{-7}7^1}{1!} + \frac{e^{-7}7^2}{2!} + \frac{e^{-7}7^3}{3!} + \frac{e^{-7}7^4}{4!}$$

$$= 0.0009 + 0.0064 + 0.0223 + 0.0521 + 0.0912$$

$$= 0.1729$$

4. a) $\frac{e^{-1.8}(1.8)^0}{0!} = 0.1653$

b) $\frac{e^{-1.8}(1.8)^2}{2!} + \frac{e^{-1.8}(1.8)^3}{3!} = 0.26778 + 0.16067 = 0.42845$

5. a) p(at least 3) $= 1 - p(0) - p(1) - p(2)$

$$= 1 - \frac{e^{-8}8^0}{0!} - \frac{e^{-8}8^1}{1!} - \frac{e^{-8}8^2}{2!}$$

$$= 1 - 0.00034 - 0.00268 - 0.01073$$

$$= 0.98625$$

b) p(at most 3) $= p(0) + p(1) + p(2) + p(3)$

$$= 0.00034 + 0.00268 + 0.01073 + \frac{e^{-8}8^3}{3!}$$

$$= 0.04238$$

c) p(exactly 3) $= \frac{e^{-8}8^3}{3!} = 0.028626$

d) p(between two and four) $= 0.028626$

6. a) p(at least one) $= 1 - p(0) = 1 - 0.00674 = 0.99326$

b) p(at most one) $= p(0) + p(1)$

$$= \frac{e^{-5}5^0}{0!} + \frac{e^{-5}5^1}{1!}$$

$$= 0.00674 + 0.03369 = 0.04043$$

c) p(exactly one) $= \frac{e^{-5}5^1}{1!} = 0.03369$

7. $\frac{e^{-4}4^4}{4!} = 0.1954$

8. a) $p(4 \text{ or more}) = 1 - p(0) - p(1) - p(2) - p(3)$

$$= 1 - \frac{e^{-3}3^0}{0!} - \frac{e^{-3}3^1}{1!} - \frac{e^{-3}3^2}{2!} - \frac{e^{-3}3^3}{3!}$$

$$= 1 - 0.04979 - 0.14936 - 0.22404$$
$$- 0.22404 = 0.35277$$

b) $p(0) = \dfrac{e^{-3}3^0}{0!} = 0.04979$

9. a) $p(\text{at least two}) = 1 - p(0) - p(1)$

$$= 1 - \frac{e^{-4}4^0}{0!} - \frac{e^{-4}4^1}{1!}$$

$$= 1 - 0.018316 - 0.07326 = 0.90842$$

b) $p(\text{no errors}) = \dfrac{e^{-4}4^0}{0!} = 0.018316$

10. $p(\text{at most 3}) = p(0) + p(1) + p(2) + p(3)$

$$= \frac{e^{-4}4^0}{0!} + \frac{e^{-4}4^1}{1!} + \frac{e^{-4}4^2}{2!} + \frac{e^{-4}4^3}{3!}$$

$$= 0.018316 + 0.07326 + 0.14653 + 0.19537$$
$$= 0.43348$$

11. $p(\text{at most 3}) = p(0) + p(1) + p(2) + p(3)$

$$= \frac{e^{-5}5^0}{0!} + \frac{e^{-5}5^1}{1!} + \frac{e^{-5}5^2}{2!} + \frac{e^{-5}5^3}{3!}$$

$$= 0.00674 + 0.03369 + 0.08422 + 0.14037$$
$$= 0.26502$$

12. $\displaystyle\sum \frac{e^{-6}6^x}{x!} \geq 0.90$ By trial and error, the grocer should have 9 or

more on hand.

1. a) $\dfrac{\binom{10}{2}\binom{90}{8}}{\binom{100}{10}} = \dfrac{(45)\,(77,515,521,435)}{17,310,309,456,440} = 0.2015$

   b) $\dfrac{\binom{10}{0}\binom{90}{10} + \binom{10}{1}\binom{90}{9} + \binom{10}{2}\binom{90}{8}}{\binom{100}{10}} =$

   $\dfrac{5,720,645,481,903 + 7,062,525,286,300 + 3,488,198,464,575}{17,310,309,456,440}$

   $= 0.93998142$

2. $\dfrac{\binom{39}{3}\binom{61}{4}}{\binom{100}{7}} = \dfrac{(9139)\,(521,855)}{16,007,560,800} = 0.2979$

3. $\dfrac{\binom{48}{0}\binom{21}{6} + \binom{48}{1}\binom{21}{5} + \binom{48}{2}\binom{21}{4} + \binom{48}{3}\binom{21}{3}}{\binom{69}{6}}$

   $\dfrac{1,330 + 10,080 + 23,688 + 17,296}{119,877,472} = 0.00044$

4. $\dfrac{\binom{11}{2}\binom{14}{2}}{\binom{25}{4}} = \dfrac{(55)\,(91)}{12650} = 0.3957$

5. $\dfrac{\binom{5}{0}\binom{7}{3}}{\binom{12}{3}} = \dfrac{35}{220} = \dfrac{7}{44}$

6.
$$\frac{\binom{26}{0}\binom{24}{9} + \binom{26}{1}\binom{24}{8} + \binom{26}{2}\binom{24}{7} + \binom{26}{3}\binom{24}{6}}{\binom{50}{9}}$$

$$\frac{1,307,504 + 7,873,866 + 112,483,800 + 349,949,600}{2,505,433,700} = 0.1882$$

7. a)
$$\frac{\binom{9}{0}\binom{6}{4}}{\binom{15}{4}} = \frac{15}{1365}$$

b)
$$\frac{\binom{9}{1}\binom{6}{3}}{\binom{15}{4}} = \frac{180}{1365}$$

c)
$$\frac{\binom{9}{2}\binom{6}{2}}{\binom{15}{4}} = \frac{540}{1365}$$

d)
$$\frac{\binom{9}{3}\binom{6}{1}}{\binom{15}{4}} = \frac{504}{1365}$$

e)
$$\frac{\binom{9}{4}\binom{6}{0}}{\binom{15}{4}} = \frac{126}{1365}$$

8.
$$\frac{\binom{18}{0}\binom{54}{8}}{\binom{72}{8}} = \frac{1,040,465,790}{11,969,016,345} = 0.08693$$

184

9. $\dfrac{\dbinom{18}{0}\dbinom{9}{3}}{\dbinom{27}{3}} = \dfrac{84}{2925}$

10. $\dfrac{\dbinom{10}{0}\dbinom{90}{5}}{\dbinom{100}{5}} = \dfrac{43,949,268}{75,287,520}$

ANSWERS TO TESTING YOUR UNDERSTANDING OF THIS CHAPTER'S CONCEPTS –
(PAGES 345 – 346)

1. a)

x	p(x)	x · p(x)	x^2	x^2 · p(x)
4	$\dfrac{4}{36}$	$\dfrac{16}{36}$	16	$\dfrac{64}{36}$
5	$\dfrac{4}{36}$	$\dfrac{20}{36}$	25	$\dfrac{100}{36}$
6	$\dfrac{5}{36}$	$\dfrac{30}{36}$	36	$\dfrac{180}{36}$
7	$\dfrac{6}{36}$	$\dfrac{42}{36}$	49	$\dfrac{294}{36}$
8	$\dfrac{7}{36}$	$\dfrac{56}{36}$	64	$\dfrac{448}{36}$
9	$\dfrac{4}{36}$	$\dfrac{36}{36}$	81	$\dfrac{324}{36}$
10	$\dfrac{3}{36}$	$\dfrac{30}{36}$	100	$\dfrac{300}{36}$
11	$\dfrac{2}{36}$	$\dfrac{22}{36}$	121	$\dfrac{242}{36}$
12	$\dfrac{1}{36}$	$\dfrac{12}{36}$	144	$\dfrac{144}{36}$
		$\dfrac{264}{36}$		$\dfrac{2096}{36}$

1. b) Mean $= \dfrac{264}{36} = \dfrac{22}{3}$

Variance $= \sigma^2 = \dfrac{2096}{36} - \left(\dfrac{22}{3}\right)^2 \approx 4.4444$

Standard deviation $= \sigma = \sqrt{4.4444} \approx 2.108$

2. No.

3. $\dfrac{6!}{0!6!}(0.70)^0(0.30)^6 = 0.000729$

4. a) $p(x) = \dfrac{\binom{6}{x}\binom{3}{5-x}}{\binom{9}{5}}$

x	p(x)	x · p(x)	x^2	x^2 · p(x)
2	$\dfrac{15}{126}$	$\dfrac{30}{126}$	4	$\dfrac{60}{126}$
3	$\dfrac{60}{126}$	$\dfrac{180}{126}$	9	$\dfrac{540}{126}$
4	$\dfrac{45}{126}$	$\dfrac{180}{126}$	16	$\dfrac{720}{126}$
5	$\dfrac{6}{126}$	$\dfrac{30}{126}$	25	$\dfrac{150}{126}$
		$\dfrac{420}{126}$		$\dfrac{1470}{126}$

b) Mean $= \mu = \dfrac{420}{126} \approx 3.3333$

Variance $= \sigma^2 = \dfrac{1470}{126} - \left(\dfrac{420}{126}\right)^2 \approx 0.5556$

Standard deviation $= \sigma = \sqrt{0.5556} \approx 0.7454$

186

4. c) Using Chebyshev's theorem, the probability that x will fall within k = 2 standard deviations of the mean is at

least $1 - \dfrac{1}{2^2} = 0.75$

5.

	Outcome 1	Outcome 2	Possible Outcomes (Number of branches)
		Success	Success Success
Start Success		Failure	Success Failure
		Success	Failure Success
Failure		Failure	Failure Failure

ANSWERS TO THINKING CRITICALLY - (PAGES 346 - 347)

1.

x	p(x)	x · p(x)	x^2	x^2 · p(x)
1	$\dfrac{7}{28}$	$\dfrac{7}{28}$	1	$\dfrac{7}{28}$
2	$\dfrac{6}{28}$	$\dfrac{12}{28}$	4	$\dfrac{24}{28}$
3	$\dfrac{5}{28}$	$\dfrac{15}{28}$	9	$\dfrac{45}{28}$
4	$\dfrac{4}{28}$	$\dfrac{16}{28}$	16	$\dfrac{64}{28}$
5	$\dfrac{3}{28}$	$\dfrac{15}{28}$	25	$\dfrac{75}{28}$
6	$\dfrac{2}{28}$	$\dfrac{12}{28}$	36	$\dfrac{72}{28}$
7	$\dfrac{1}{28}$	$\dfrac{7}{28}$	49	$\dfrac{49}{28}$
		$\dfrac{84}{28} = 3$		$\dfrac{336}{28} = 12$

Mean = $\dfrac{84}{28} = 3$

Variance = $12 - 3^2 = 3$

Standard deviation = $\sqrt{3} \approx 1.7321$

2. a)

x	p(x)	x · p(x)	x^2	x^2 · p(x)
1	0.05	0.05	1	0.05
2	0.43	0.86	4	1.72
3	0.17	0.51	9	1.53
4	0.25	1.00	16	4.00
5	0.06	0.30	25	1.50
6	0.03	0.18	36	1.08
7	0.01	<u>0.07</u>	49	<u>0.49</u>
		2.97		10.37

$\mu = \sum x \cdot p(x) = 2.97$
$\sigma^2 = 10.37 - (2.97)^2 = 1.5491$

$\sigma = \sqrt{1.5491} \approx 1.2446$

b)   Using Chebyshev's theorem, the probability that x will
fall within k = 2 standard deviations of the mean is at

least $1 - \dfrac{1}{2^2} = 0.75$

3. $\sigma^2 = \sum (x - \mu)^2 \cdot p(x)$
$= \sum (x^2 - 2\mu x + \mu^2) \cdot p(x)$
$= \sum x^2 \cdot p(x) - 2\mu \sum x \cdot p(x) + \mu^2 \sum p(x)$ Note: $\mu = \sum x \cdot p(x)$
$= \sum x^2 \cdot p(x) - 2\mu\mu + \mu^2$ and $\sum p(x) = 1$
$= \sum x^2 \cdot p(x) - \mu^2$

$= \sum x^2 \cdot p(x) - \left[\sum x \cdot p(x)\right]^2$

4. $(p + q)^3 = p^3 + 3p^2 q + 3pq^2 + q^3$
The first term p^3 is the probability of successes on all 3
trials when a binomial experiment is performed 3 times. The
second term $3p^2 q$ is the probability of two successes in the
three trials. The third term $3pq^2$ is the probability of one
success in the three trials and the last term q^3 is the
probability of no successes in the three trials.

188

5. a)

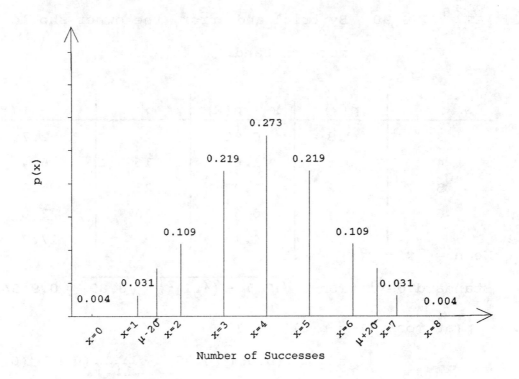

b) $\mu = np = 8\left(\dfrac{1}{2}\right) = 4$

$\sigma = \sqrt{npq} = \sqrt{8\left(\dfrac{1}{2}\right)\left(\dfrac{1}{2}\right)} = \sqrt{2} \approx 1.4141$

ANSWERS TO REVIEW EXERCISES FOR CHAPTER 6 - (PAGES 347 - 348)

1.   0.03   Since the sum of all the probabilities must be 1.

2. a)   p(at least 5) = p(5) + p(6) + p(7) + p(8) + p(9)
        Using Table III in Appendix, we get
                = 0.066 + 0.176 + 0.302 + 0.302 + 0.134
                = 0.98
b)   p(at most 3) = p(0) + p(1) + p(2) + p(3) = 0.003

3. $\mu = (400)(0.23) = 92$

$\sigma = \sqrt{(400)(0.23)(0.77)} \approx 8.4167$

189

4. $\sum \dfrac{e^{-5} 5^x}{x!} \geq 0.90$ By trial and error, the owner should have 8 or
more on hand.

5.

x	p(x)	x · p(x)	x^2	x^2 · p(x)
3	0.3	0.90	9	2.7
4	0.4	1.6	16	6.4
5	0.2	1.0	25	5.0
6	0.1	0.6	36	3.6
		4.1		17.7

Mean = $\sum x \cdot p(x) = 4.1$

Standard deviation = $\sqrt{17.7 - (4.1)^2} = \sqrt{0.89} \approx 0.9434$

6. $p(\text{at most } 1) = p(0) + p(1)$

$= \dfrac{8!}{0!8!}(0.95)^8(0.05)^0 + \dfrac{8!}{1!7!}(0.95)^7(0.05)^1$

$= 0.6634 + 0.2793 = 0.9427$

7. $p(\text{at most } 3) = p(0) + p(1) + p(2) + p(3)$

$= \dfrac{e^{-4}4^0}{0!} + \dfrac{e^{-4}4^1}{1!} + \dfrac{e^{-4}4^2}{2!} + \dfrac{e^{-4}4^3}{3!}$

$= 0.0183 + 0.0733 + 0.1465 + 0.1954 = 0.4335$

8. $\mu = (320)(0.88) = 281.6$

$\sigma = \sqrt{(320)(0.88)(0.12)} \approx 5.8131$

9. $310 = n(0.88)$
$352.27 = n$
Accept 353 reservations

10. $\dfrac{4!}{0!4!}\left(\dfrac{15}{25}\right)^0\left(\dfrac{10}{25}\right)^4 = 0.0256$

11.   p(at most 3) = p(0) + p(1) + p(2) + p(3)

$$= \frac{12!}{0!12!}(0.20)^0(0.80)^{12} + \frac{12!}{1!11!}(0.20)^1(0.80)^{11}$$

$$+ \frac{12!}{2!10!}(0.20)^2(0.80)^{10} + \frac{12!}{3!9!}(0.20)^3(0.80)^9$$

$$= 0.0687 + 0.2062 + 0.2835 + 0.2362 = 0.7946$$

ANSWERS TO CHAPTER TEST - (PAGES 348 - 350)

1.

x	p(x)
0	$\left(\frac{3}{8}\right)\left(\frac{3}{8}\right) = \frac{9}{64}$
1	$2\left(\frac{5}{8}\right)\left(\frac{3}{8}\right) = \frac{30}{64}$
2	$\left(\frac{5}{8}\right)\left(\frac{5}{8}\right) = \frac{25}{64}$

2. a)   p(at most 4) = p(0) + p(1) + p(2) + p(3) + p(4)

$$= \frac{e^{-6}6^0}{0!} + \frac{e^{-6}6^1}{1!} + \frac{e^{-6}6^2}{2!} + \frac{e^{-6}6^3}{3!} + \frac{e^{-6}6^4}{4!}$$

$$= 0.0025 + 0.0149 + 0.0446 + 0.0892$$
$$+ 0.1339$$
$$= 0.2851$$

b)   p(at least 2) = 1 - p(0) - p(1)
$$= 1 - 0.0025 - 0.0149 = 0.9826$$

3.   p(at least 1) = 1 - p(0)

$$= 1 - \frac{10!}{0!10!}(0.004)^0(0.996)^{10} = 0.0393$$

4. a)

x	p(x)
0	$\left(\frac{40}{52}\right)\left(\frac{40}{52}\right)\left(\frac{40}{52}\right) = \frac{64000}{140608}$
1	$3\left(\frac{40}{52}\right)\left(\frac{40}{52}\right)\left(\frac{12}{52}\right) = \frac{57600}{140608}$
2	$3\left(\frac{40}{52}\right)\left(\frac{12}{52}\right)\left(\frac{12}{52}\right) = \frac{17280}{140608}$
3	$\left(\frac{12}{52}\right)\left(\frac{12}{52}\right)\left(\frac{12}{52}\right) = \frac{1728}{140608}$

b)

x	p(x)
0	$\left(\frac{40}{52}\right)\left(\frac{39}{51}\right)\left(\frac{38}{50}\right) = \frac{59,280}{132,600}$
1	$3\left(\frac{40}{52}\right)\left(\frac{39}{51}\right)\left(\frac{12}{50}\right) = \frac{56,160}{132,600}$
2	$3\left(\frac{40}{52}\right)\left(\frac{12}{51}\right)\left(\frac{11}{50}\right) = \frac{15,840}{132,600}$
3	$\left(\frac{12}{52}\right)\left(\frac{11}{51}\right)\left(\frac{10}{50}\right) = \frac{1320}{132,600}$

5. $\mu = 400(0.85) = 340$

$\sigma = \sqrt{400(0.85)(0.15)} \approx 7.1414$

6. p(more than 5) = $1 - p(0) - p(1) - p(2) - p(3) - p(4) - p(5)$

$= 1 - \frac{12!}{0!12!}(0.12)^0(0.88)^{12} - \frac{12!}{1!11!}(0.12)^1(0.88)^{11}$

$- \frac{12!}{2!10!}(0.12)^2(0.88)^{10} - \frac{12!}{3!9!}(0.12)^3(0.88)^9$

$- \frac{12!}{4!8!}(0.12)^4(0.88)^8 - \frac{12!}{5!7!}(0.12)^5(0.88)^7$

$= 1 - 0.2157 - 0.3529 - 0.2647 - 0.1203$
$\quad - 0.0369 - 0.0081$
$= 0.0014$

7. **a)**

x	p(x)	x · p(x)	x^2	x^2 · p(x)
1	0.001	0.001	1	0.001
2	0.028	0.056	4	0.112
3	0.134	0.402	9	1.206
4	0.312	1.248	16	4.992
5	0.356	1.780	25	8.900
6	0.169	1.014	36	6.084
		4.501		21.295

$\mu = \sum x \cdot p(x) = 4.501$

b) $\sigma = \sqrt{21.295 - (4.501)^2} \approx 1.0178$

c) Using Chebyshev's theorem, the probability that x will fall within k = 2 standard deviations of the mean is at

least $1 - \dfrac{1}{2^2} = 0.75$

8. **a)** $\dfrac{\binom{8}{5}\binom{7}{0}}{\binom{15}{5}} = \dfrac{56 \cdot 1}{3003} = \dfrac{56}{3003}$

b) $\dfrac{\binom{8}{0}\binom{7}{5}}{\binom{15}{5}} = \dfrac{1 \cdot 21}{3003} = \dfrac{21}{3003}$

c) $\dfrac{\binom{8}{3}\binom{7}{2} + \binom{8}{4}\binom{7}{1} + \binom{8}{5}\binom{7}{0}}{\binom{15}{5}} = \dfrac{56 \cdot 21 + 70 \cdot 7 + 56 \cdot 1}{3003} = \dfrac{1722}{3003}$

9. p(at most 2) = p(0) + p(1) + p(2)

$= \dfrac{10!}{0!10!}(0.4)^0(0.6)^{10} + \dfrac{10!}{1!9!}(0.4)^1(0.6)^9$

$+ \dfrac{10!}{2!8!}(0.4)^2(0.6)^8$

$= 0.0060 + 0.0403 + 0.1209 = 0.1672$

193

10. $\dfrac{\dbinom{11}{0}\dbinom{34}{8} + \dbinom{11}{1}\dbinom{34}{7} + \dbinom{11}{2}\dbinom{34}{6} + \dbinom{11}{3}\dbinom{34}{5}}{\dbinom{45}{8}} = \dfrac{197,213,940}{215,553,195} = 0.9149$

11. 0.238   Since the sum of all the probabilities must be 1.

12. Choice (c)

13. Choice (d)

14. Choice (c)

15. Choice (b)

16. Choice (d)

1. The following represents a probability distribution for a random variable x. Find the probability that x = 7.

x	6	7	8	9	10
p(x)	0.18	?	0.32	0.25	0.17

   a) 0   b) 0.92   c) 0.8   d) 0.08   e) none of these

   Answer _____

2. Is the following a probability distribution for some random variable x?

x	5	6	7	10	14
p(x)	0.23	0.27	0.29	0.12	0.09

   a) yes   b) no   c) not enough information given
   d) none of these

   Answer _____

3. An auto mechanic installs 8 automatic transmissions in 8 cars. If the probability that any one of the transmissions will not need any adjustments is 1/5, what is the probability that exactly 3 of the transmissions will not need any adjustments?

   a) $\dfrac{8!}{3!}\left(\dfrac{1}{5}\right)^3\left(\dfrac{4}{5}\right)^5$ b) $\dfrac{8!}{3!5!}\left(\dfrac{1}{5}\right)^3\left(\dfrac{4}{5}\right)^5$ c) $\dfrac{8!}{5!}\left(\dfrac{1}{5}\right)^3\left(\dfrac{4}{5}\right)^5$

   d) $\dfrac{8!}{3!5!}\left(\dfrac{1}{5}\right)^5\left(\dfrac{4}{5}\right)^3$ e) none of these

   Answer _____

4. Consider the following probability distribution. Find its mean.

x	0	2	4	7	8	9
p(x)	0.13	0.36	0.23	0.19	0.05	0.04

   a) 3.73   b) 3.86   c) 5   d) 3.92   e) none of these

   Answer _____

5. Refer back to the previous question. Find the variance.

a) 20.87   b) 13.9129   c) 6.9571   d) 2.6376
e) none of these

Answer _____

6. It is estimated that 20% of the members of a health club have high blood pressure. If 300 members of the club are randomly selected, about how many of them can be expected to have high blood pressure?

a) 240   b) 60   c) 300   d) 20   e) none of these

Answer _____

7. Refer back to the previous question. Find the standard deviation.

a) 48   b) 6.9282   c) 0.2   d) 0.16   e) none of these

Answer _____

8. Assume that the daily number of train cancellations on a particular railroad follows a Poisson distribution with $\mu = 7$. What is the probability that on any given day there will be 5 cancellations.

Answer _____

9. Six cards are randomly selected from a standard deck of cards. Find the probability that 3 of them are aces.

Answer _____

10. A fair die is rolled once. Find the expected number of dots showing.

a) 3   b) 3.5   c) 4   d) 21   e) none of these

Answer _____

CHAPTER 6 - SOME DISCRETE PROBABILITY DISTRIBUTIONS
SUPPLEMENTARY TEST FORM B

1. The following represents a probability distribution for a random variable x. Find the probability that x = 0.

x	0	1	2	3	4	5
p(x)	?	0.25	0.18	0.23	0.14	0.11

   a) 0.91   b) 0.09   c) 0   d) 0.9   e) none of these

   Answer _____

2. Is the following a probability distribution for some random variable x?

x	5	7	11	13	15	17	21
p(x)	0.04	0.09	0.15	0.19	0.23	0.27	0.03

   a) yes   b) no   c) not enough information given
   d) none of these

   Answer _____

3. An inspector from the state's Clean Air Pollution Department claims that 8% of the cars on the state's highways cannot pass the emission control test. If 10 cars are randomly selected, what is the probability that exactly 3 of them cannot pass the emission control test?

   a) $\frac{10!}{3!}(0.08)^3(0.92)^7$ b) $\frac{10!}{3!7!}(0.08)^7(0.92)^3$

   c) $\frac{10!}{7!}(0.08)^3(0.92)^7$ d) $\frac{10!}{3!7!}(0.08)^3(0.92)^7$

   e) none of these

   Answer _____

4. Refer back to the previous question. If 200 cars are randomly selected, about how many of them can be expected not to be able to pass the emission control test?

   a) 200   b) 8 c) 16   d) 184   e) none of these

   Answer _____

5. Refer back to the previous question. Find the standard deviation.

   a) 16   b) 14.72   c) 4   d) 3.8367   e) none of these

   Answer _____

6. Consider the following probability distribution. Find its mean.

x	0	3	4	5	6
p(x)	0.11	0.19	0.21	0.29	0.20

   a) 4   b) 4.06   c) 4.17   d) 4.10   e) none of these

   Answer _____

7. In the previous question what is the standard deviation?

   a) 19.52   b) 16.4836   c) 3.0364   d) 1.7425
   e) none of these

   Answer _____

8. A washing machine manufacturer claims that daily service calls for the company's washing machines follow a Poisson distribution with $\mu = 5$. What is the probability that on any given day there will be 3 calls for service?

   Answer _____

9. An urn contains 9 red balls and 15 green balls. Five balls are randomly selected from the urn without replacement. Find the probability that 3 of the balls are red.

   Answer _____

10. In a certain region, the probability that a house contains a dangerous accumulation of radon gas is 1/5. If six houses in the region are randomly selected, what is the probability that exactly four of these houses contain dangerous accumulations of radon gas?

    Answer _____

1. A coin is tossed in such a way that the probability of it coming up heads is 0.3. The coin is tossed five times. What is the probability of getting exactly three heads?

   a) $\frac{5!}{3!}(0.3)^3(0.7)^2$ b) $\frac{5!}{2!}(0.3)^3(0.7)^2$ c) $\frac{5!}{3!2!}(0.3)^3(0.7)^2$

   d) $\frac{5!}{3!2!}(0.3)^2(0.7)^3$ e) none of these

   Answer _____

2. A camp has found that about 3% of its campers become seriously ill during the season. If 600 campers have registered for the summer season, about how many can be expected to become seriously ill?

   a) 18   b) 582   c) 600   d) 3   e) none of these

   Answer _____

3. Refer back to the previous question. Find the standard deviation.

   a) 17.46   b) 4.1785   c) 0.03   d) 3.738   e) none of these

   Answer _____

4. A cook randomly selects 10 eggs without replacement from a case of eggs which contains 15 dozen (360) eggs. If it is known that 15 of the eggs in the case are broken, what is the probability that the cook will select 5 broken eggs?

   Answer _____

5. The following table gives the probabilities of the number of police officers who will call in sick (daily) for a large police force.

Number of police officers, x	5	6	7	8	9	10	11
Probability, p(x)	0.07	0.14	0.17	0.21	0.18	0.19	0.04

   Find the mean of this distribution.

   a) 8   b) 7.82   c) 8.13   d) 8.02   e) none of these

   Answer _____

6. Refer back to the previous question. Find the standard deviation.

   a) 66.98 b) 64.3204 c) 2.6596 d) 1.6308
   e) none of these

   Answer _____

7. Can the following be a probability distribution for a random variable x?

Random variable, x	1	2	3	4	5
Probability, p(x)	1/3	1/7	1/21	4/21	3/7

   a) yes   b) no   c) not enough information given
   e) none of these

   Answer _____

8. Given the following probability distribution for the random variable x. What is the probability that x = 0?

x	0	1	2	3	4
p(x)	?	1/5	3/10	2/20	9/30

   a) 0   b) 1/5   c) 1/10   d) 1/20   e) none of these

   Answer _____

9. A die is altered by painting an additional dot on the face that originally had one dot. Let x be the number of dots that appears when this die is rolled. Find the probability distribution of x.

   Answer _____

10. A research organization decides to mail out ten questionnaires to people selected at random. If the probability of any one person answering the questionnaire is 1/7, find the probability that exactly six people will answer the questionnaire.

   Answer _____

Form A	Form B	Form C
1. Choice (d)	1. Choice (b)	1. Choice (c)
2. Choice (a)	2. Choice (a)	2. Choice (a)
3. Choice (b)	3. Choice (d)	3. Choice (b)
4. Choice (a)	4. Choice (c)	4. $\dfrac{\binom{15}{5}\binom{345}{5}}{\binom{360}{10}}$
5. Choice (c)	5. Choice (d)	5. Choice (d)
6. Choice (b)	6. Choice (b)	6. Choice (d)
7. Choice (b)	7. Choice (d)	7. Choice (b)
8. 0.1277	8. 0.1404	8. Choice (c)
9. $\dfrac{\binom{4}{3}\binom{48}{3}}{\binom{52}{6}}$	9. $\dfrac{\binom{9}{3}\binom{15}{2}}{\binom{24}{5}}$	9.
10. Choice (b)	10. 0.0154	10. $\dfrac{10!}{6!\,4!}\left(\dfrac{1}{7}\right)^{6}\left(\dfrac{6}{7}\right)^{4}$

Form C, 9.

2	3	4	5	6
2/6	1/6	1/6	1/6	1/6

Section 7.3 - (PAGES 370 - 372)

1. **a)**   0.4292

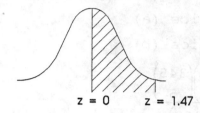

b)   0.2123

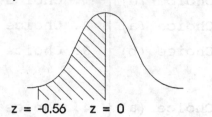

c)

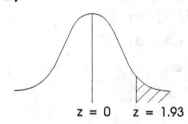

0.5000
−0.4732
0.0268

d)

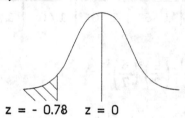

0.5000
−0.2823
0.2177

e)

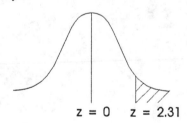

0.5000
−0.4896
0.0104

f)

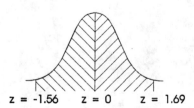

0.4406
+ 0.4545
0.8951

202

1. g)

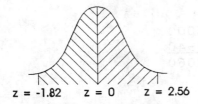

```
  0.4656
+ 0.4948
  0.9604
```

h)

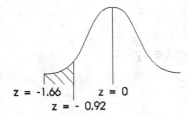

```
  0.4515
- 0.3212
  0.1303
```

2. a)

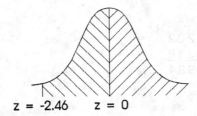

```
  0.5000
+ 0.4931
  0.9931
```

b)

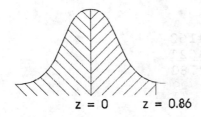

```
  0.5000
+ 0.3051
  0.8051
```

c)

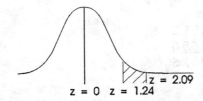

```
  0.4817
- 0.3925
  0.0892
```

2. d)

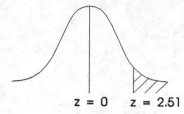

z = 0   z = 2.51

```
  0.5000
- 0.4940
  0.0060
```

e)

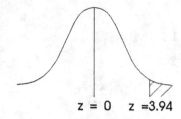

z = 0   z = 3.94

Approximately 0

f)

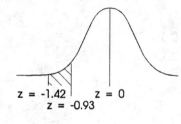

z = -1.42   z = 0
     z = -0.93

```
  0.4222
- 0.3238
  0.0984
```

g)

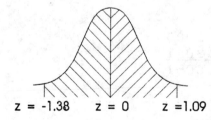

z = -1.38   z = 0   z = 1.09

```
  0.4162
+ 0.3621
  0.7783
```

h)

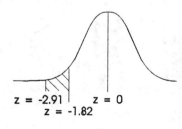

z = -2.91   z = 0
     z = -1.82

```
  0.4982
- 0.4656
  0.0326
```

204

3. a)   0.5000
          - 0.1500   z = -1.04
           0.3500

    b)   0.5000
          - 0.2000   z = -0.84
           0.3000

3. c)   0.5000
          - 0.2500   z = -0.67
           0.2500

    d)   0.5000
          - 0.3000   z = -0.52
           0.2000

4. a)   10% on each side of the mean.
          Between $z = -0.25$ and $z = 0.25$
    b)   15% on each side of the mean.
          Between $z = -0.39$ and $z = 0.39$
    c)   20% on each side of the mean.
          Between $z = -0.52$ and $z = 0.52$

5. a)

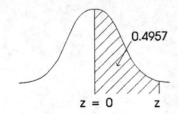

                       $z = 2.63$

    b)

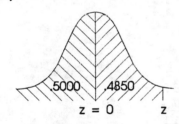

                       $z = 2.17$

    c)

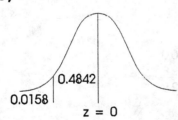

                       $z = -2.15$

5. d)

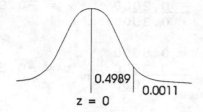

$z = 3.05$ or
$z = 3.06$ or
$z = 3.07$

e)

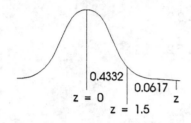

$$\begin{array}{r} 0.4332 \\ + 0.0617 \\ \hline 0.4949 \end{array}$$

$z = 2.57$

f)

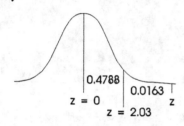

$$\begin{array}{r} 0.4788 \\ + 0.0163 \\ \hline 0.4951 \end{array}$$

$z = 2.58$

6. a) $z = \dfrac{88 - 80}{12} = 0.67$

$$\begin{array}{r} 0.2486 \\ - 0.0675 \\ \hline 0.1811 \end{array}$$

  $z = \dfrac{82 - 80}{12} = 0.17$

b) $z = \dfrac{75 - 80}{12} = -0.42$

$$\begin{array}{r} 0.5000 \\ + 0.1628 \\ \hline 0.6628 \end{array}$$

c) $z = \dfrac{69 - 80}{12} = -0.92$

$$\begin{array}{r} 0.5000 \\ - 0.3212 \\ \hline 0.1788 \end{array}$$

6. **d)** $z = \dfrac{85 - 80}{12} = 0.42$

$z = \dfrac{71 - 80}{12} = -0.75$

$$\begin{array}{r} 0.1628 \\ +\; 0.2734 \\ \hline 0.4362 \end{array}$$

e) $z = \dfrac{74 - 80}{12} = -0.50$

$z = \dfrac{67 - 80}{12} = -1.08$

$$\begin{array}{r} 0.3599 \\ -\; 0.1915 \\ \hline 0.1684 \end{array}$$

7. **a)** $z = \dfrac{40 - 47}{3} = -2.33$

$$\begin{array}{r} 0.5000 \\ -0.4901 \\ \hline 0.0099 \end{array}$$ 0.99 percentile

b) $z = \dfrac{52 - 47}{3} = 1.67$

$$\begin{array}{r} 0.5000 \\ +\; 0.4525 \\ \hline 0.9525 \end{array}$$ 95.25 percentile

c) $z = \dfrac{39 - 47}{3} = -2.67$

$$\begin{array}{r} 0.5000 \\ -\; 0.4962 \\ \hline 0.0038 \end{array}$$ 0.38 percentile

8. **a)** 45th percentile corresponds to $z = -0.13$.
$x = \mu + z\sigma$
$\;\;\; = 180 + (-0.13)9 = 178.83$

b) 79th percentile corresponds to $z = 0.81$.
$x = 180 + (0.81)9 = 187.29$

c) 95th percentile corresponds to $z = 1.64$ or 1.65.
Using $z = 1.64$ gives $x = 180 + (1.64)9 = 194.76$
Using $z = 1.65$ gives $x = 180 + (1.65)9 = 194.85$

9.

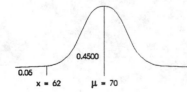

We can use either $z = -1.64$ or $z = -1.65$.
Using $z = -1.64$, we have $62 = 70 + (-1.64)\sigma$
and $\sigma = 4.878$. Using $z = -1.65$, we have
$62 = 70 + (-1.65)\sigma$ and $\sigma = 4.848$.

10. $z = -2.0$ so that $45 = \mu + (-2)(15.3)$ and $\mu = 75.6$

11.

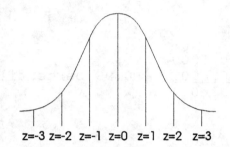

$\left.\begin{array}{l} 9.63 = \mu - 1.82\sigma \\ 12.19 = \mu + 1.02\sigma \end{array}\right\}$ Solving Simultaneously

gives $\mu = 11.2706$ and
$\sigma = 0.9014$

12.

$z = 0$ becomes 24
    as $x = \mu + z\sigma$
    and $24 = 24 + \sigma(5)$
$z = 1$ becomes 29
$z = 2$ becomes 34
$z = 3$ becomes 39
$z = -1$ becomes 19
$z = -2$ becomes 14
$z = -3$ becomes 9

z=-3 z=-2 z=-1 z=0 z=1 z=2 z=3

13. **a)** $1 - 0.4649 - 0.4649 = 0.0702$

b) $1 - 0.4931 - 0.4931 = 0.0138$

c) $1 - 0.4738 - 0.4788 = 0.0474$

d) $1 - 0.3508 - 0.3106 = 0.3386$

e) $1 - 0.4788 - 0.4306 = 0.0906$

f) $0.4699 - 0.3051 = 0.1648$

14. $x = 4$ gives $z = \dfrac{4 - 10}{2} = -3$

  $x = 6$ gives $z = \dfrac{6 - 10}{2} = -2$

  $x = 8$ gives $z = \dfrac{8 - 10}{2} = -1$

  $x = 10$ gives $z = \dfrac{10 - 10}{2} = 0$

  $x = 12$ gives $z = \dfrac{12 - 10}{2} = 1$

  $x = 14$ gives $z = \dfrac{14 - 10}{2} = 2$

  $x = 16$ gives $z = \dfrac{16 - 10}{2} = 3$

The area of region I is between $z = -3$ and $z = -2$.
    Area is $0.4987 - 0.4772 = 0.0215$.
The area of region II is between $z = -2$ and $z = -1$.
    Area is $0.4772 - 0.3413 = 0.1359$.
The area of region IV is between $z = 1$ and $z = 0$.
    Area is 0.3413.
The area of region V is between $z = 1$ and $z = 2$.
    Area is $0.4772 - 0.3413 = 0.1359$.
The area of region VI is between $z = 2$ and $z = 3$.
    Area is $0.4987 - 0.4772 = 0.0215$.

ANSWERS TO EXERCISES FOR SECTION 7.4 – (PAGES 376 – 378)

1. $z = \dfrac{15 - 11}{2.9} = 1.38$

$\begin{array}{r} 0.4162 \\ +\ 0.1331 \\ \hline 0.5493 \end{array}$

  $z = \dfrac{10 - 11}{2.9} = -0.34$

2. $z = \dfrac{55 - 45}{6} = 1.67$

$\begin{array}{r} 0.5000 \\ +\ 0.4525 \\ \hline 0.9525 \end{array}$

3. $z = \dfrac{6 - 9}{2.3} = -1.30$

$$\begin{array}{r} 0.5000 \\ -\ 0.4032 \\ \hline 0.0968 \end{array}$$

4. a) $z = \dfrac{2 - 4.3}{1.8} = -1.28$

$$\begin{array}{r} 0.5000 \\ -\ 0.3997 \\ \hline 0.1003 \end{array}$$

b) $z = \dfrac{5.0 - 4.3}{1.8} = 0.39$

$$\begin{array}{r} 0.1517 \\ +0.3413 \\ \hline 0.4930 \end{array}$$

$z = \dfrac{2.5 - 4.3}{1.8} = -1.00$

5. $z = \dfrac{450 - 520}{100} = -0.7$

$$\begin{array}{r} 0.5000 \\ -\ 0.2580 \\ \hline 0.2420 \end{array}$$

6. $z = \dfrac{6 - 5.3}{1.93} = 0.36$

$$\begin{array}{r} 0.5000 \\ -\ 0.1406 \\ \hline 0.3594 \end{array}$$

7. $z = \dfrac{25000 - 22000}{3500} = 0.86$

$$\begin{array}{r} 0.3051 \\ +\ 0.4772 \\ \hline 0.7823 \end{array}$$

$z = \dfrac{15000 - 22000}{3500} = -2.00$

8. $z = \dfrac{3 - 6.3}{2.31} = -1.43$

$$\begin{array}{r} 0.5000 \\ +\ 0.4236 \\ \hline 0.9236 \end{array}$$

9. a) $z = \dfrac{52 - 62}{12} = -0.83$

$$\begin{array}{r} 0.5000 \\ -\ 0.2967 \\ \hline 0.2033 \end{array}$$

b) $x = 62 + (-0.84)12 = 51.92$

c) $x = 62 + (1.41)12 = 78.92$

10. $x = 50 + (1.04)17 = 67.68$ minutes

11. $z = \dfrac{102 - 109}{11} = -0.64$

 $\begin{array}{r} 0.2389 \\ +\ 0.3980 \\ \hline 0.6369 \end{array}$

$ z = \dfrac{123 - 109}{11} = 1.27$

12. $x = 4.7 + (-1.645)(0.9) = 3.2195$ years

13. $z = \dfrac{18 - 25}{5.3} = -1.32$

 $\begin{array}{r} 0.5000 \\ +\ 0.4066 \\ \hline 0.9066 \end{array}$

14. $z = \dfrac{4000 - 3900}{400} = 0.25$

 $\begin{array}{r} 0.5000 \\ +\ 0.0987 \\ \hline 0.5987 \end{array}$

15.

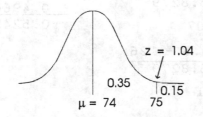

$1.04 = \dfrac{75 - 74}{\sigma}$

$\sigma = \dfrac{1}{1.04} = 0.9615$

16. $x = 25 + (1.645)6$
$ = 34.87$ minutes

Mary should leave 34.87 minutes or 35 minutes before her 8:00 AM appointment. She should leave at 7:25 AM.

17. **a)** $7 = \mu + (-1.645)(0.3)$ $\qquad \mu = 7.4935$
 **b)** $7.5 = \mu + (1.645)(0.3)$ $\qquad \mu = 7.0065$

18.

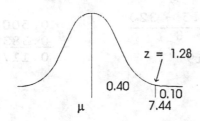

$7.44 = \mu + (1.28)(0.21)$
$ \mu = 7.1712$

1. $\mu = 500(0.63) = 315$

   $\sigma = \sqrt{500(0.63)(0.37)}$

   ≈ 10.7958

   $z = \dfrac{320.5 - 315}{10.7958}$

   $= 0.51$

   $\begin{array}{r} 0.5000 \\ +\ 0.1950 \\ \hline 0.6950 \end{array}$

2. $\mu = 700(0.68) = 476$

   $\sigma = \sqrt{700(0.68)(0.32)}$

   ≈ 12.3418

   $z = \dfrac{509.5 - 476}{12.3418}$

   $= 2.71$

   $\begin{array}{r} 0.5000 \\ -\ 0.4966 \\ \hline 0.0034 \end{array}$

3. $\mu = 80(0.55) = 44$

   $\sigma = \sqrt{80(0.55)(0.45)}$

   ≈ 4.4497

   $z = \dfrac{46.5 - 44}{4.4497}$

   $= 0.56$

   $\begin{array}{r} 0.5000 \\ +\ 0.2123 \\ \hline 0.7123 \end{array}$

4. $\mu = 200(0.63) = 126$

   $\sigma = \sqrt{200(0.63)(0.37)}$

   ≈ 6.8279

   $z = \dfrac{125.5 - 126}{6.8279}$

   $= -0.07$

   $z = \dfrac{144.5 - 126}{6.8279}$

   $= 2.71$

   $\begin{array}{r} 0.0279 \\ +\ 0.4966 \\ \hline 0.5245 \end{array}$

5. $\mu = 5000\left(\dfrac{1}{5}\right) = 1000$

   $\sigma = \sqrt{5000\left(\dfrac{1}{5}\right)\left(\dfrac{4}{5}\right)}$

   ≈ 28.2843

   $z = \dfrac{960.5 - 1000}{28.2843}$

   $= -1.40$

   $\begin{array}{r} 0.5000 \\ -\ 0.4192 \\ \hline 0.0808 \end{array}$

6. $\mu = 400(0.80) = 320$

   $\sigma = \sqrt{400(0.80)(0.20)}$

   $= 8$

   $z = \dfrac{310.5 - 320}{8}$

   $= -1.19$

   $\begin{array}{r} 0.5000 \\ -\ 0.3830 \\ \hline 0.1170 \end{array}$

7. $\mu = 50(0.95) = 47.5$

$\sigma = \sqrt{50(0.95)(0.05)}$

≈ 1.5411

$z = \dfrac{48.5 - 47.5}{1.5411}$

$= 0.65$

$z = \dfrac{49.5 - 47.5}{1.5411}$

$= 1.30$

$$\begin{array}{r} 0.4032 \\ -\ 0.2422 \\ \hline 0.1610 \end{array}$$

8. $\mu = 90(0.92) = 82.8$

$\sigma = \sqrt{90(0.92)(0.08)}$

≈ 2.5737

$z = \dfrac{81.5 - 82.8}{2.5737}$

$= -0.51$

$$\begin{array}{r} 0.5000 \\ -\ 0.1950 \\ \hline 0.3050 \end{array}$$

9. $\mu = 80\left(\dfrac{1}{2}\right) = 40$

$\sigma = \sqrt{80\left(\dfrac{1}{2}\right)\left(\dfrac{1}{2}\right)}$

≈ 4.4721

$z = \dfrac{49.5 - 40}{4.4721}$

$= 2.12$

$$\begin{array}{r} 0.5000 \\ -\ 0.4830 \\ \hline 0.0170 \end{array}$$

10. $\mu = 450(0.08) = 36$

$\sigma = \sqrt{450(0.08)(0.92)}$

≈ 5.7550

$z = \dfrac{27.5 - 36}{5.7550}$

$= -1.48$

$z = \dfrac{28.5 - 36}{5.7550}$

$= -1.30$

$$\begin{array}{r} 0.4306 \\ -\ 0.4032 \\ \hline 0.0274 \end{array}$$

11. $\mu = 1000(0.12) = 120$

$\sigma = \sqrt{1000(0.12)(0.88)}$

≈ 10.2762

$z = \dfrac{110.5 - 120}{10.2762}$

$= -0.92$

$$\begin{array}{r} 0.5000 \\ -\ 0.3212 \\ \hline 0.1788 \end{array}$$

12.
a) $\mu = 400(0.55) = 220$

$\sigma = \sqrt{400(0.55)(0.45)}$

≈ 9.9499

$z = \dfrac{239.5 - 220}{9.9499}$

$= 1.96$

$$\begin{array}{r} 0.5000 \\ +\ 0.4750 \\ \hline 0.9750 \end{array}$$

12.

b) $\mu = 220$

$\sigma = 9.9499$

$z = \dfrac{210.5 - 220}{9.9499}$

$= -0.95$

$\begin{array}{r} 0.5000 \\ + \underline{0.3289} \\ 0.8289 \end{array}$

13.

a) $\mu = 100(0.90) = 90$

$\sigma = \sqrt{100(0.90)(0.10)}$

$= 3$

$z = \dfrac{89.5 - 90}{3}$

$= -0.17$

$\begin{array}{r} 0.5000 \\ - \underline{0.0675} \\ 0.4325 \end{array}$

b) $\mu = 90$

$\sigma = 3$

$z = \dfrac{89.5 - 90}{3}$

$= -0.17$

$z = \dfrac{90.5 - 90}{3}$

$= 0.17$

$\begin{array}{r} 0.0675 \\ + \underline{0.0675} \\ 0.1350 \end{array}$

14. $\mu = 150(0.87) = 130.5$

$\sigma = \sqrt{150(0.87)(0.13)}$

≈ 4.1189

$z = \dfrac{140.5 - 130.5}{4.1189}$

$= 2.43$

$\begin{array}{r} 0.5000 \\ + \underline{0.4925} \\ 0.9925 \end{array}$

15. $\mu = 300(0.95) = 285$

$\sigma = \sqrt{300(0.95)(0.05)}$

≈ 3.7749

$z = \dfrac{284.5 - 285}{3.7749}$

$= -0.13$

$\begin{array}{r} 0.5000 \\ + \underline{0.0517} \\ 0.5517 \end{array}$

16. $\mu = 500(0.55) = 275$

$\sigma = \sqrt{500(0.55)(0.45)}$

≈ 11.1243

$z = \dfrac{274.5 - 275}{11.1243}$

$= -0.04$

$\begin{array}{r} 0.5000 \\ + \underline{0.0160} \\ 0.5160 \end{array}$

17. $\mu = 2000(0.29) = 580$

$\sigma = \sqrt{2000(0.29)(0.71)}$

≈ 20.2929

$z = \dfrac{549.5 - 580}{20.2929}$

$= -1.50$

$\begin{array}{r} 0.5000 \\ - \underline{0.4332} \\ 0.0668 \end{array}$

18. $\mu = 300(0.60) = 180$

  $\sigma = \sqrt{300(0.60)(0.40)}$

  ≈ 8.4853

  $z = \dfrac{159.5 - 180}{8.4853}$

  $= -2.42$

  0.5000
  $- \underline{0.4922}$
  0.0078

19. $\mu = 60\left(\dfrac{1}{5}\right) = 12$

  $\sigma = \sqrt{60\left(\dfrac{1}{5}\right)\left(\dfrac{4}{5}\right)}$

  ≈ 3.0984

  $z = \dfrac{18.5 - 12}{3.0984}$

  $= 2.10$

  0.5000
  $- \underline{0.4821}$
  0.0179

20. $\mu = 75(0.75) = 56.25$

  $\sigma = \sqrt{75(0.75)(0.25)}$

  $= 3.75$

  $z = \dfrac{47.5 - 56.25}{3.75}$

  $= -2.33$

  0.5000
  $- \underline{0.4901}$
  0.0099

ANSWERS TO TESTING YOUR UNDERSTANDING OF THIS CHAPTER'S CONCEPTS –
(PAGE 392)

1. One with a standard deviation of 5.

2. a)

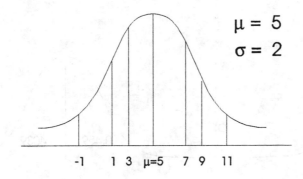

$\mu = 5$
$\sigma = 2$

-1   1 3 μ=5   7 9   11

215

2. **b)**

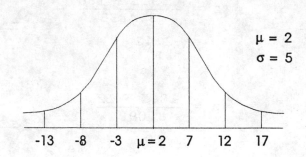

$\mu = 2$
$\sigma = 5$

-13 -8 -3 $\mu=2$ 7 12 17

c)

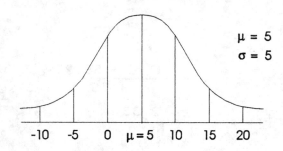

$\mu = 5$
$\sigma = 5$

-10 -5 0 $\mu=5$ 10 15 20

3. $102 = \mu + (-1.28)6$
    $109.68 = \mu$

4. Not really, as $np = 8\left(\dfrac{1}{2}\right)$ is not greater than 5.

5.

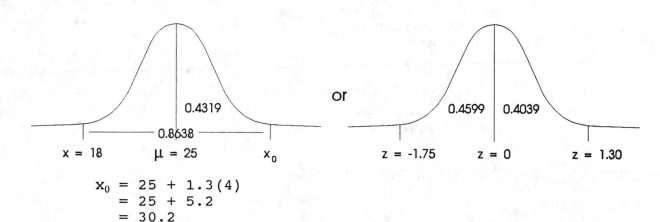

0.4319

0.8638

x = 18 $\mu = 25$ x_0

or

0.4599 0.4039

z = -1.75   z = 0   z = 1.30

$x_0 = 25 + 1.3(4)$
$\quad = 25 + 5.2$
$\quad = 30.2$

1.

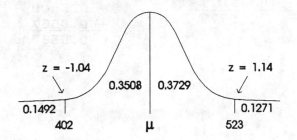

$402 = \mu - 1.04\sigma$
$523 = \mu + 1.14\sigma$

Solving simultaneously gives $\mu = 459.7249$, and $\sigma = 55.5046$

2.

$$1 - \frac{1}{k^2} \geq 0.997$$

$$-\frac{1}{k^2} \geq -0.003$$

$$\frac{1}{k^2} \leq 0.003$$

$$k^2 \geq \frac{1}{0.003}$$

$$k \geq 18.2574$$

3.
$$8.9 = 10 + (-1.645)\sigma$$
$$-1.1 = -1.645\sigma$$
$$0.6687 = \sigma$$

4. No. Different values of σ will make the curve wider or narrower. μ locates the center of the distribution.

5. $\frac{42 - 38}{3} = \frac{4}{3}$. It is $1\frac{1}{3}$ standard deviations away from the mean of x.

ANSWERS TO REVIEW EXERCISES FOR CHAPTER 7 - (PAGES 393 - 395)

1. Choice (b)

2. $0.5000 + 0.4306 = 0.9306$

3. $0.5000 - 0.4484 = 0.0516$

4. $\mu = 80\left(\dfrac{4}{5}\right) = 64$

$\sigma = \sqrt{80\left(\dfrac{4}{5}\right)\left(\dfrac{1}{5}\right)}$

$= \sqrt{12.8} \approx 3.5777$

$z = \dfrac{63.5 - 64}{3.5777}$

$= -0.14$

$\begin{array}{r} 0.5000 \\ + 0.0557 \\ \hline 0.5557 \end{array}$

5. $\mu = 600(0.15) = 90$

$\sigma = \sqrt{600(0.15)(0.85)}$

≈ 8.7464

$z = \dfrac{79.5 - 90}{8.7464}$

$= -1.20$

$\begin{array}{r} 0.5000 \\ + 0.3849 \\ \hline 0.8849 \end{array}$

6. $\mu = 100(0.95) = 95$

$\sigma = \sqrt{100(0.95)(0.05)}$

≈ 2.1794

$z = \dfrac{95.5 - 95}{2.1794}$

$= 0.23$

$z = \dfrac{94.5 - 95}{2.1794}$

$= -0.23$

$\begin{array}{r} 0.0910 \\ + 0.0910 \\ \hline 0.1820 \end{array}$

7. $\mu = 50(0.12) = 6$

$\sigma = \sqrt{50(0.12)(0.88)}$

≈ 2.2978

$z = \dfrac{3.5 - 6}{2.2978}$

$= -1.09$

$\begin{array}{r} 0.5000 \\ - 0.3621 \\ \hline 0.1379 \end{array}$

8.

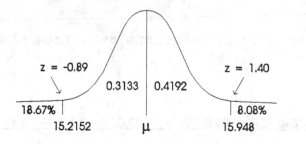

z = -0.89   z = 1.40
        0.3133 0.4192
18.67%   8.08%
    15.2152   μ   15.948

$15.948 = \mu + 1.40\sigma$
$15.2152 = \mu - 0.89\sigma$

Solving simultaneously
gives $\sigma = 0.32$ and
$\mu = 15.5$

9. a) $z = \dfrac{750,000 - 580,000}{150,000}$

$= 1.13$

$$\begin{array}{r} 0.5000 \\ -\ 0.3708 \\ \hline 0.1292 \end{array}$$

b) $z = \dfrac{400,000 - 580,000}{150,000}$

$= -1.2$

$$\begin{array}{r} 0.5000 \\ +\ 0.3849 \\ \hline 0.8849 \end{array}$$

10. $\mu = 1400(0.30) = 420$

$\sigma = \sqrt{1400(0.30(0.70)}$

≈ 17.1464

$z = \dfrac{400.5 - 420}{17.1464}$

$= -1.14$

$$\begin{array}{r} 0.5000 \\ -\ 0.3729 \\ \hline 0.1271 \end{array}$$

11. $x = \mu + z\sigma$

$= 1200 + (-1.41)(85)$

$= 1080.15 \text{ hours}$

After 1080.15 hours

12. $x = 210 + (1.175)38 = 254.65$ Allow 254.65 minutes

13. $x = 2000 + (1.41)(175)$

$= 2246.75$ When production exceeds 2246.75 sweaters

14. $\mu = 500(0.236) = 118$

$\sigma = \sqrt{500(0.236)(0.764)}$

≈ 9.4948

$z = \dfrac{100.5 - 118}{9.4948}$

$= -1.84$

$$\begin{array}{r} 0.5000 \\ -\ 0.4671 \\ \hline 0.0329 \end{array}$$

15. $\mu = 200(0.092) = 18.4$

$\sigma = \sqrt{200(0.092)(0.908)} \approx 4.0874$

a) $z = \dfrac{19.5 - 18.4}{4.0874} = 0.27$

$$\begin{array}{r} 0.5000 \\ -\ 0.1064 \\ \hline 0.3936 \end{array}$$

b) $z = \dfrac{16.5 - 18.4}{4.0874}$

$= -0.46$

$$\begin{array}{r} 0.5000 \\ -\ 0.1772 \\ \hline 0.3228 \end{array}$$

15. c) $z = \dfrac{18.5 - 18.4}{4.0874} = 0.02$ 0.0871
                                                              + 0.0080
                                                                0.0951

            $z = \dfrac{17.5 - 18.4}{4.0874}$

              $= -0.22$

16. $z = \dfrac{2000 - 2100}{60} = -1.67$ 0.5000
                                                        – 0.4525
                                                          0.0475

ANSWERS TO CHAPTER TEST – (PAGES 395 – 397)

1.

                                        $z = -0.77$

2. $z = -1.08$

3. $x = 63 + (1.28)(2.1) = 65.688$ inches

4. $x = 82 + (1.28)(3) = 85.84$

5. $\mu = 1000(0.92) = 920$
      $\sigma = \sqrt{1000(0.92)(0.08)}$ $z = \dfrac{919.5 - 920}{8.5790}$ 0.0239
        ≈ 8.5790 $= -0.06$ + 0.0239
                                                                                  0.0478
                                          $z = \dfrac{920.5 - 920}{8.5790}$

                                            $= 0.06$

6. $\mu = 200(0.30) = 60$
      $\sigma = \sqrt{200(0.30)(0.70)} \approx 6.4807$

   a) $z = \dfrac{49.5 - 60}{6.4807} = -1.62$ 0.5000
                                                              – 0.4474
                                                                0.0526

220

6. **b)** $\quad z = \dfrac{65.5 - 60}{6.4807} = 0.85$

$$\begin{array}{r} 0.5000 \\ - \ 0.3023 \\ \hline 0.1977 \end{array}$$

c) $\quad z = \dfrac{55.5 - 60}{6.4807} = -0.69$

$$\begin{array}{r} 0.5000 \\ -0.2549 \\ \hline 0.2451 \end{array}$$

d) $\quad z = \dfrac{60.5 - 60}{6.4807} = 0.08$

$$\begin{array}{r} 0.0319 \\ + \ 0.0319 \\ \hline 0.0638 \end{array}$$

$\quad\quad z = \dfrac{59.5 - 60}{6.4807} = -0.08$

7. $\quad z = \dfrac{57 - 54}{5} = 0.6$

$$\begin{array}{r} 0.2257 \\ + \ 0.3413 \\ \hline 0.5670 \end{array}$$

$\quad\quad z = \dfrac{49 - 54}{5} = -1$

8. $\quad \mu = 75\left(\dfrac{2}{3}\right) = 50$

$\quad z = \dfrac{48.5 - 50}{4.0825}$

$$\begin{array}{r} 0.5000 \\ - \ 0.1443 \\ \hline 0.3557 \end{array}$$

$\quad\quad \sigma = \sqrt{75\left(\dfrac{2}{3}\right)\left(\dfrac{1}{3}\right)} \approx 4.0825$

$\quad\quad\quad = -0.37$

9. $\quad 120 = \mu + (-1.645)(1.88)$
$\quad\quad \mu = 123.0926$

10. $\quad z = \dfrac{5700 - 6000}{310} = -0.97$

$$\begin{array}{r} 0.3340 \\ + \ 0.2422 \\ \hline 0.5762 \end{array}$$

$\quad\quad z = \dfrac{6200 - 6000}{310} = 0.65$

11. $\quad \mu = 300(0.38) = 114$

$\quad z = \dfrac{99.5 - 114}{8.4071}$

$$\begin{array}{r} 0.5000 \\ + \ 0.4573 \\ \hline 0.9573 \end{array}$$

$\quad\quad \sigma = \sqrt{300(0.38)(0.62)}$

$\quad\quad\quad = 8.4071$

$\quad\quad\quad = -1.72$

12. $\quad 278 = 250 + 1.28\sigma$
$\quad\quad 21.875 = \sigma$

13. $\mu = 75\left(\dfrac{2}{7}\right) = 21.4286$

$\sigma = \sqrt{75\left(\dfrac{2}{7}\right)\left(\dfrac{5}{7}\right)} \approx 3.9123$

$z = \dfrac{20.5 - 21.4286}{3.9123}$

$\quad = -0.24$

$\begin{array}{r} 0.5000 \\ -\ 0.0948 \\ \hline 0.4052 \end{array}$

14. **a)** $4 = \mu + (-1.645)(0.33)$
$4.54285 = \mu$

b) $4.25 = \mu + (1.645)(0.33)$
$3.70715 = \mu$

15. $4.47 = \mu + (1.28)(0.29)$
$4.0988 = \mu$

16. Choice (a)

17. Choice (a)

18. Choice (c)

19. Choice (b)

20. Choice (a)

1. In a standard normal distribution, find the closet z-score corresponding to the 39th percentile.

   a) 0.1517   b) 1.23   c) -1.23   d) 0.39   e) none of these

   Answer _____

2. It is claimed that 45% of all students at Bork College smoke. What is the probability that a survey of 700 randomly selected students at this school will contain at most 300 smokers?

   a) 0.1271   b) 0.1335   c) 0.1357   d) 0.1314
   e) none of these

   Answer _____

3. In a standard normal distribution, find the area that lies to the right of z = 1.68.

   a) 0.0465   b) 0.4535   c) 0.9535   d) 0.9625
   e) none of these

   Answer _____

4. Find the percentage of z-scores in a standard normal distribution that are between z = -1.48 and z = 2.03.

   a) 0.4306   b) 0.4788   c) 0.0482   d) 0.9094
   e) none of these

   Answer _____

5. A gas station attendant claims that 65% of all cars in the city are equipped with studded tires. If 200 cars in the city are randomly selected, what is the probability that at least 130 of them will be equipped with studded tires?

   a) 0.5000   b) 0.5279   c) 0.4721   d) 0.0596
   e) none of these

   Answer _____

6. The time needed to process a mortgage application at one particular commercial bank is approximately normally distributed with a mean of 15 days and a standard deviation of 2 days. If one mortgage application is randomly selected, what is the probability that the bank will need more than 10 days to process it?

   a) 0.9878   b) 0.0062   c) 0.4938   d) 0.9938
   e) none of these

   Answer _____

7. Refer back to the previous question. What is the probability that the bank will need at most 19 days to process a randomly selected mortgage application?

    a) 0.9772   b) 0.4772   c) 0.0228   d) 0.9878
    e) none of these

    Answer _____

8. Melissa owns a fish hatchery. She finds that the lengths of the fish in the hatchery are normally distributed with μ = 8 cm and σ = 1.2 cm. Approximately what percentage of the fish in the hatchery are more than 8.5 cm in length?

    a) 41.67%   b) 16.28%   c) 33.72%   d) 33.16%
    e) none of these

    Answer _____

9. The life of a certain flashlight battery is normally distributed with a mean of 87 hours and a standard deviation of 5.1 hours. Find the probability that a randomly selected battery from this group will last at most 76 hours.

    a) 0.4846   b) 0.0154   c) 0.5014   d) 0.9846
    e) none of these

    Answer _____

10. The life of a certain air conditioner compressor is normally distributed with a mean of 5 years and a standard deviation of 1.1 years. The manufacturer will replace any defective air conditioner compressor free of charge while under the guarantee. If the manufacturer does not wish to replace more than 6% of the air conditioner compressors, for how many years should they be guaranteed?

    a) 4.934 yrs   b) 4.85 yrs   c) 3.2895 yrs   d) 4.835 yrs
    e) none of these

    Answer _____

CHAPTER 7 - THE NORMAL DISTRIBUTION
SUPPLEMENTARY TEST FORM B

1. In a standard normal distribution, find the closest z-score corresponding to the 21st percentile.

   a) 0.0832   b) -0.81   c) -0.55   d) -0.0832
   e) none of these

   Answer _____

2. It is claimed that 40% of all women at The Baxt Corporation use roll-on deodorant. A survey of 160 randomly selected women from The Baxt Corp. is taken. What is the probability that at most 70 of these women will be found to use roll-on deodorant?

   a) 0.3531   b) 0.8531   c) 0.8340   d) 0.8133
   e) none of these

   Answer _____

3. Find the percentage of z-scores in a standard normal distribution that are between z = -1.86 and z = 1.37.

   a) 0.4686   b) 0.4147   c) 0.0539   d) 0.8833
   e) none of these

   Answer _____

4. In a standard normal distribution, find the area that lies above z = -1.39?

   a) 0.9177   b) 0.4177   c) 0.0823   d) 0.5823
   e) none of these

   Answer _____

5. A cookie baking company claims that 5% of each day's production contains boxes with broken cookies. If 300 boxes in a day's production are randomly selected, what is the probability that at least 18 of the boxes will contain broken cookies?

   a) 0.0256   b) 0.2148   c) 0.2454   d) 0.2546
   e) none of these

   Answer _____

6. The amount of time required to install a special gas burner is approximately normally distributed with a mean of 95 minutes and a standard deviation of 7 minutes. What is the probability that a randomly selected gas burner of the type described required between 90 and 103 minutes to install?

a) 0.2611   b) 0.3729   c) 0.6340   d) 0.1118
e) none of these

Answer _____

7. The heights of the players on a certain college basketball team are normally distributed with a mean of 74 inches and a standard deviation of 2.1 inches. What is Dave's percentile rank if he is 76 inches tall?

a) 95th percentile   b) 33rd percentile   c) 85th percentile
d) 83rd percentile   e) none of these

Answer _____

8. Refer back to the previous question. If John Brown is in the 90th percentile, what is his actual height?

a) 76.688 inches   b) 76.923 inches   c) 77.321 inches
d) 77.014 inches   e) none of these

Answer _____

9. It is claimed that 35% of all students at Dorx College have a credit card issued in their name. What is the probability that a survey of 100 randomly selected students at this college will contain at least 40 students who have a credit card issued in their name?

a) 0.1469   b) 0.1736   c) 0.1251   d) 0.3531
e) none of these

Answer _____

10. The drying time for a certain paint is approximately normally distributed with a mean of 4 hours and a standard deviation of 0.23 hours. What percentage of the time will this paint dry in less than 3.6 hours?

a) 0.4591   b) 0.0409   c) 0.1554   d) 0.3446
e) none of these

Answer _____

CHAPTER 7 - THE NORMAL DISTRIBUTION
SUPPLEMENTARY TEST FORM C

1. In a standard normal distribution, find the closest z-score corresponding to the 37th percentile.

   a) 0.1443   b) 1.13   c) -1.13   d) -0.33
   e) none of these

   Answer _____

2. In a standard normal distribution, find the area that lies below z = 1.07.

   a) 0.3577   b) 0.8577   c) 0.1423   d) 0.3599
   e) none of these

   Answer _____

3. In a standard normal distribution, find the area that lies to the right of z = -0.58.

   a) 0.2224   b) 0.2810   c) 0.2190   d) 0.7190
   e) none of these

   Answer _____

4. Find the percentage of z-scores in a standard normal distribution that are between z = -0.82 and z = -0.39.

   a) 0.1422   b) 0.2939   c) 0.1517   d) 0.4456
   e) none of these

   Answer _____

5. A tire manufacturer claims that the life of the company's steel belted tire is normally distributed with an average of 35,000 miles and a standard deviation of 2200 miles. What is the probability that a randomly selected steel belted tire manufactured by this company will last at most 30,000 miles?

   a) 0.4884   b) 0.0116   c) 0.9884   d) 0.4887
   e) none of these

   Answer _____

6. It is claimed that 70% of the people in a certain town eat at a fast-food restaurant several times during the month. If 300 people in this town are randomly selected, what is the probability that at least 205 of these people eat at a fast-food restaurant several times during the month?

   a) 0.7549   b) 0.2549   c) 0.7357   d) 0.7157
   e) none of these

   Answer _____

7. A statistician for a police department finds that the number of parking tickets issued daily by the city's police officers is normally distributed with a mean of 270 and a standard deviation of 11. If a day is randomly selected, what is the probability that the number of parking tickets issued will be between 250 and 280?

    a) 0.4656   b) 0.3186   c) 0.7842   d) 0.1470
    e) none of these

                                    Answer _____

8. The traffic department of a certain city has found that the probability that the lampposts on the city's highways are functioning properly is 0.93. If 400 lampposts on the city's highways are randomly selected, what is the probability that at least 375 of them will be functioning properly?

    a) 0.2776   b) 0.2451   c) 0.2549   d) 0.3121
    e) none of these

                                    Answer _____

9. A fund raiser has found that the amount of money that can be raised through a telephone solicitation is normally distributed with a mean of $36 and a standard deviation of $4. If a telephone solicitation is randomly selected, what is the probability that the amount of money pledged is at least $30?

    a) 0.4332   b) 0.9332   c) 0.0668   d) 0.4452
    e) none of these

                                    Answer _____

10. It is alleged that about 65% of all households in Bergenville have a VCR.   If 600 households in this city are randomly selected, what is the probability that at least 380 of them have a VCR?

    a) 0.8159   b) 0.8051   c) 0.3159   d) 0.1841
    e) none of these

                                    Answer _____

ANSWERS TO SUPPLEMENTARY EXERCISES
CHAPTER 7 - THE NORMAL DISTRIBUTION

Form A	Form B	Form C
1. Choice (e)	1. Choice (b)	1. Choice (d)
2. Choice (b)	2. Choice (b)	2. Choice (b)
3. Choice (a)	3. Choice (d)	3. Choice (d)
4. Choice (d)	4. Choice (a)	4. Choice (a)
5. Choice (b)	5. Choice (d)	5. Choice (b)
6. Choice (d)	6. Choice (c)	6. Choice (a)
7. Choice (a)	7. Choice (d)	7. Choice (c)
8. Choice (c)	8. Choice (a)	8. Choice (d)
9. Choice (b)	9. Choice (b)	9. Choice (b)
10. Choice (c)	10. Choice (b)	10. Choice (a)

ANSWERS TO EXERCISES FOR CHAPTER 8

SECTION 8.2 - (PAGES 405 - 406)

1. Pages 104, 223, 241, 421, 375, 289, 94, 103, 71, 510, 23, 10, 521, 70, 486, 541, 326, 293, 24, 296, 7, 53, 5, 259, and 97.

2. Those prisoners whose numbers are 816, 309, 763, 78, 61, 277, 188, 174, 530, 709, 496, 889, 482, 772, 774, 893, 312, and 232.

3. Those officers whose numbers are 191, 196, 749, 69, 818, 210, 849, 449, 114, 855, 271, 202, 744, 639, 19, 177, 195, 616, 152, 641, 76, 866, 571, 645, 665, 424, 766, 658, 801, 542, 378, 92, 835, 533, and 212.

4. Those recipients whose case numbers are 0126, 1063, 0558, 1859, 2997, 2855, 0594, 2562, 1829, 0784, 1277, 2056, 0010, 0654, 2372, 1637, 1295, 2285, 1851, and 2528.

5. Those refrigerators whose serial numbers are 36207, 34095, 32081, 57004, 60672, 48840, 60045, 31595, 53900, 65255, 64350, 46104, 41135, 67658, 66134, 64568, 42607, 59920, 69774, 41688, 48413, 49518, 45585, 70002, 69352, 48223, 52666, 30680, 63213, 58678, 70960, 64835, 51132, 30421, 32586, 64760, 43808, 33611, 34952, and 56942.

6. Those whose numbers are 36207, 34095, 32081, 57004, 60672, 15053, 48840, 60045, 12566, 17983, 31595, 20847, 08272, 26358, 85977, 53900, 65255, 85030, 64350, 46104, 22178, 06646, 06912, 41135, 67658, 14780, 12659, 66134, 64568, and 42607.

7. Those whose numbers are 015, 255, 225, 062, 110, 054, 333, 463, 337, 224, 055, 288, 048, 390, 256, 298, 279, and 188.

8. Those bonds whose numbers are 02011, 07972, 03427, 08178, 09998, 07351, 07391, 07856, 06121, 09172, 04024, 02304, 01638, 04146, 06691, and 00256.

9. Those containers whose numbers are 4934, 4968, 4401, 2533, 0815, 5218, 3001, 0151, 4944, 0118, 2349, 5185, 3580, 4655, 5000, 4576, 4080, 0599, 1805, and 2816.

10. Those whose numbers are 3099, 0785, 0612, 2775, 1887, 1745, 3127, 2321, 4269, 0917, 4707, 1336, 1973, 2487, 4690, 4440, 2676, 4220, 1898, and 3088.

1.

Number of babies, x	Sample mean, $\overline{x}$	$\overline{x} - \mu_{\overline{x}}$	$(\overline{x} - \mu_{\overline{x}})^2$
9 and 10	9.5	9.5 - 7.5 = 2.0	4.00
9 and 5	7.0	7.0 - 7.5 = -0.5	0.25
9 and 8	8.5	8.5 - 7.5 = 1.0	1.00
9 and 7	8.0	8.0 - 7.5 = 0.5	0.25
9 and 6	7.5	7.5 - 7.5 = 0	0.00
10 and 5	7.5	7.5 - 7.5 = 0	0.00
10 and 8	9.0	9.0 - 7.5 = 1.5	2.25
10 and 7	8.5	8.5 - 7.5 = 1.0	1.00
10 and 6	8.0	8.0 - 7.5 = 0.5	0.25
5 and 8	6.5	6.5 - 7.5 = -1.0	1.00
5 and 7	6.0	6.0 - 7.5 = -1.5	2.25
5 and 6	5.5	5.5 - 7.5 = -2.0	4.00
8 and 7	7.5	7.5 - 7.5 = 0	0.00
8 and 6	7.0	7.0 - 7.5 = -0.5	0.25
7 and 6	6.5	6.5 - 7.5 = -1.0	1.00
	112.5		17.50

$$\mu_{\overline{x}} = \frac{112.5}{15} = 7.5$$

$$\sigma_{\overline{x}} = \sqrt{\frac{17.50}{15}} = \sqrt{1.66667} \approx 1.0801$$

231

2.

Number of claimants, x	Sample mean, $\bar{x}$	$\bar{x} - \mu_{\bar{x}}$	$(\bar{x} - \mu_{\bar{x}})^2$
54 and 118	86	86 − 81 = 5	25
54 and 62	58	58 − 81 = −23	529
54 and 79	66.5	66.5 − 81 = −14.5	210.25
54 and 92	73	73 − 81 = − 8	64
118 and 62	90	90 − 81 = 9	81
118 and 79	98.5	98.5 − 81 = 17.5	306.25
118 and 92	105	105 − 81 = 24	576
62 and 79	70.5	70.5 − 81 = −10.5	110.25
62 and 92	77	77 − 81 = − 4	16
79 and 92	85.5	85.5 − 81 = 4.5	20.25
	810		1938

$$\mu_{\bar{x}} = \frac{810}{10} = 81$$

$$\sigma_{\bar{x}} = \sqrt{\frac{1938}{10}} = \sqrt{193.8} \approx 13.9212$$

3.

Number of responses, x	Sample mean, $\overline{x}$	$\overline{x} - \mu_{\overline{x}}$	$(\overline{x} - \mu_{\overline{x}})^2$
45, 48, and 39	44	-0.17	0.0289
45, 48, and 52	48.33	4.16	17.3056
45, 48, and 37	43.33	-0.84	0.7056
45, 48, and 44	45.67	1.5	2.2500
48, 39, and 52	46.33	2.16	4.6656
48, 39, and 37	41.33	-2.84	8.0656
48, 39, and 44	43.67	-0.5	0.2500
39, 52, and 37	42.67	-1.5	2.2500
39, 52, and 44	45	0.83	0.6889
39, 37, and 44	40	-4.17	17.3889
45, 39, and 52	45.33	1.16	1.3456
45, 39, and 37	40.33	-3.84	14.7456
45, 39, and 44	42.67	-1.5	2.2500
45, 52, and 37	44.67	0.5	0.2500
45, 52, and 44	47	2.83	8.0089
48, 52, and 37	45.67	1.50	2.2500
48, 52, and 44	48	3.83	14.6689
48, 37, and 44	43	-1.17	1.3689
45, 37, and 44	42	-2.17	4.7089
52, 37, and 44	<u>44.33</u>	0.16	<u>0.0256</u>
	883.33		103.2215

$$\mu_{\overline{x}} = \frac{883.33}{20} = 44.17$$

$$\sigma_{\overline{x}} = \sqrt{\frac{103.2215}{20}} = \sqrt{5.161075} \approx 2.2718$$

233

4.

$\overline{x}$	$\overline{x} - \mu_{\overline{x}}$	$(\overline{x} - \mu_{\overline{x}})^2$
14	−1.6667	2.7779
28	12.3333	152.1103
11	−4.6667	21.7781
13	−2.6667	7.1113
9	−6.6667	44.4449
19	3.3333	11.1109
94		239.3334

$$\mu_{\overline{x}} = \frac{94}{6} = 15.6667$$

$$\sigma_{\overline{x}} = \sqrt{\frac{239.3334}{6}} = \sqrt{39.8889} \approx 6.3158$$

5.   a)

x	x − μ	$(x - \mu)^2$
9	−6	36
18	3	9
13	−2	4
12	−3	9
23	8	64
75		122

$$\mu = \frac{75}{5} = 15$$

$$\sigma = \sqrt{\frac{122}{5}} = \sqrt{24.4} \approx 4.9396$$

5. b) **Size 2**

Number of arrests, x	Sample mean, $\overline{x}$	$\overline{x} - \mu_{\overline{x}}$	$(\overline{x} - \mu_{\overline{x}})^2$
9 and 18	13.5	-1.5	2.25
9 and 13	11	-4	16.00
9 and 12	10.5	-4.5	20.25
9 and 23	16	1	1.00
18 and 13	15.5	0.5	0.25
18 and 12	15	0	0.00
18 and 23	20.5	5.5	30.25
13 and 12	12.5	-2.5	6.25
13 and 23	18	3	9.00
12 and 23	17.5	2.5	6.25
	150		91.50

Size 3

Number of arrests, x	Sample mean, $\overline{x}$	$\overline{x} - \mu_{\overline{x}}$	$(\overline{x} - \mu_{\overline{x}})^2$
9, 18, and 13	13.3333	-1.6667	2.7779
9, 18, and 12	13	-2	4.0000
9, 18, and 23	16.6667	1.6667	2.7779
9, 13, and 12	11.3333	-3.6667	13.4447
9, 13, and 23	15	0	0.0000
9, 12, and 23	14.6667	-0.3333	0.1111
18, 13, and 12	14.3333	-0.6667	0.4445
18, 13, and 23	18	3	9.0000
18, 12, and 23	17.6667	2.6667	7.1113
13, 12, and 23	16	1	1.0000
	150		40.6674

5. c) **Size 2**

$$\mu_{\overline{x}} = \frac{150}{10} = 15$$

$$\sigma_{\overline{x}} = \sqrt{\frac{91.50}{10}} = \sqrt{9.15} \approx 3.0249$$

Size 3

$$\mu_{\overline{x}} = \frac{150}{10} = 15$$

$$\sigma_{\overline{x}} = \sqrt{\frac{40.6674}{10}} = \sqrt{4.06674} \approx 2.0166$$

d) We use $\sigma_{\overline{x}} = \dfrac{\sigma}{\sqrt{n}}\sqrt{\dfrac{N-n}{N-1}}$ In both cases N = 5

$$\sigma_{\overline{x}} = \frac{4.9396}{\sqrt{2}}\sqrt{\frac{5-2}{5-1}} \qquad \sigma_{\overline{x}} = \frac{4.9396}{\sqrt{3}}\sqrt{\frac{5-3}{5-1}}$$

$$\approx 3.0249 \qquad\qquad\qquad \approx 2.0166$$

6. $\mu_{\overline{x}} = 6428$

$$\sigma_{\overline{x}} = \frac{\sigma}{\sqrt{n}} = \frac{461}{\sqrt{100}} = 46.1$$

7. a) $\mu_{\overline{x}} = 6428$

$$\sigma_{\overline{x}} = \frac{461}{\sqrt{144}} \approx 38.4167$$

b) $\mu_{\overline{x}} = 6428$

$$\sigma_{\overline{x}} = \frac{461}{\sqrt{64}} \approx 57.625$$

1. $z = \dfrac{10,500 - 10,200}{860/\sqrt{49}} = 2.44$

$$\begin{array}{r} 0.4927 \\ + \ 0.4994 \\ \hline 0.9921 \end{array}$$

 $z = \dfrac{9800 - 10,200}{860/\sqrt{49}} = -3.26$

2. $z = \dfrac{22 - 23}{2.9/\sqrt{36}} = -2.07$

$$\begin{array}{r} 0.5000 \\ - \ 0.4808 \\ \hline 0.0192 \end{array}$$

3. $z = \dfrac{4100 - 3900}{525/\sqrt{36}} = 2.29$

$$\begin{array}{r} 0.5000 \\ - \ 0.4890 \\ \hline 0.0110 \end{array}$$

4. $z = \dfrac{3100 - 3000}{640/\sqrt{64}} = 1.25$

$$\begin{array}{r} 0.5000 \\ - \ 0.3944 \\ \hline 0.1056 \end{array}$$

5. $z = \dfrac{88 - 86.40}{7.95/\sqrt{81}} = 1.81$

$$\begin{array}{r} 0.5000 \\ - \ 0.4649 \\ \hline 0.0351 \end{array}$$

6. $z = \dfrac{24 - 26}{5.6/\sqrt{49}} = -2.5$

$$\begin{array}{r} 0.4938 \\ - \ 0.3944 \\ \hline 0.0994 \end{array}$$

 $z = \dfrac{25 - 26}{5.6/\sqrt{49}} = -1.25$

7. $z = \pm 1.96$ Between 4.9371 and 5.0629 ounces.

 $x = \mu \pm z\sigma$

 $x = 5 \pm (1.96)\dfrac{(0.19)}{\sqrt{35}}$

 $x = 5 \pm 0.0629$

8. $z = \pm 1.96$ Between 78.6748 and 81.3252 ounces.
      $x = \mu + z\sigma$

      $= 80 \pm (1.96)\left(\dfrac{4}{\sqrt{35}}\right)$

      $= 80 \pm 1.3252$

9. $z = \dfrac{45 - 43.3}{8.2/\sqrt{100}} = 2.07$

                                                    0.4808
                                                    + 0.4441
      $z = \dfrac{42 - 43.3}{8.2/\sqrt{100}} = -1.59$ 0.9249

10. $z = \dfrac{900 - 921}{102/\sqrt{49}} = -1.44$

                                                    0.5000
                                                    - 0.4251
                                                    0.0749

11. $z = \dfrac{450 - 438}{87/\sqrt{100}} = 1.38$

                                                    0.4162
                                                    + 0.5000
      $z = \dfrac{400 - 438}{87/\sqrt{100}} = -4.37$ 0.9162

__ANSWERS TO TESTING YOUR UNDERSTANDING OF THIS CHAPTER'S CONCEPTS -__
__(PAGE 430)__

1.   The relationship is expressed in the formula $\sigma_{\bar{x}} = \dfrac{\sigma}{\sqrt{n}}$ when the

      sample size is less than 5% of the population size.

2.   Yes

3. a)

Number of stores, x	$x - \mu$	$(x - \mu)^2$
17	3	9
12	-2	4
22	8	64
8	-6	36
11	-3	9
70		122

$$\mu = \frac{70}{5} = 14$$

$$\sigma = \sqrt{\frac{122}{5}} = \sqrt{24.4} \approx 4.9396$$

3. b)   Size 2

Number of stores, x	Sample mean, $\bar{x}$	$\bar{x} - \mu_{\bar{x}}$	$(\bar{x} - \mu_{\bar{x}})^2$
17 and 12	14.5	0.5	0.25
17 and 22	19.5	5.5	30.25
17 and 8	12.5	-1.5	2.25
17 and 11	14	0	0.00
12 and 22	17	3	9.00
12 and 8	10	-4	16.00
12 and 11	11.5	-2.5	6.25
22 and 8	15	1	1.00
22 and 11	16.5	2.5	6.25
8 and 11	9.5	-4.5	20.25
	140		91.50

239

3. b)   Size 3

Number of stores, x	Sample mean, $\overline{x}$	$\overline{x} - \mu_{\overline{x}}$	$(\overline{x} - \mu_{\overline{x}})^2$
17, 12, and 22	17	3	9.0000
17, 12, and 8	12.3333	-1.6667	2.7779
17, 12, and 11	13.3333	-0.6667	0.4449
12, 22, and 8	14	0	0.0000
12, 22, and 11	15	1	1.0000
12, 8, and 11	10.3333	-3.6667	13.4447
17, 22, and 8	15.6667	1.6667	2.7779
17, 22, and 11	16.6667	2.6667	7.1113
22, 8, and 11	13.6667	-0.3333	0.1111
17, 8, and 11	12	2	4.0000
	140		40.6678

3. c)   Size 2 $\mu_{\overline{x}} = \dfrac{140}{10} = 14$

$$\sigma_{\overline{x}} = \sqrt{\dfrac{91.5}{10}} = \sqrt{9.15} \approx 3.0249$$

Size 3 $\mu_{\overline{x}} = \dfrac{140}{10} = 14$

$$\sigma_{\overline{x}} = \sqrt{\dfrac{40.6678}{10}} = \sqrt{4.06678} \approx 2.0166$$

d)   Size 2 $\sigma_{\overline{x}} = \dfrac{4.9396}{\sqrt{2}} \sqrt{\dfrac{5 - 2}{5 - 1}} \approx 3.0249$

Size 3 $\sigma_{\overline{x}} = \dfrac{4.9396}{\sqrt{3}} \sqrt{\dfrac{5 - 3}{5 - 1}} \approx 2.0166$

240

3. e)

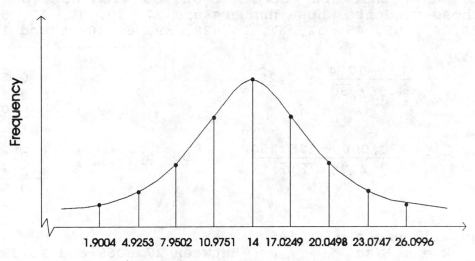

ANSWERS TO THINKING CRITICALLY - (PAGE 430)

1. a)

$$z = \frac{16 - 14}{2.63} = 0.76$$

$$\begin{array}{r} 0.5000 \\ - \ 0.2764 \\ \hline 0.2236 \end{array}$$

b)

$$z = \frac{16 - 14}{2.63/\sqrt{36}} = 4.56$$

$$\begin{array}{r} 0.5000 \\ - \ 0.4999999 \\ \hline \approx 0 \end{array}$$

Approximately 0

2. The larger the sample size the better the estimate of the population mean since it is based on more data which encompass more of the population.

3. σ_x represents the standard deviation of the x's, whereas $\sigma_{\bar{x}}$ represents the standard deviation of the sampling distribution of the mean. It is the standard error of the mean. Generally, $\sigma_{\bar{x}}$ will be smaller than σ.

1. The students selected are the first 20 2-digit numbers in column 7 that are between 1 and 58 with no repeats. Select those students whose numbers are 27, 15, 39, 18, 57, 38, 56, 36, 47, 55, 45, 32, 37, 26, 28, 29, 6, 20, 9 and 11.

2. $z = \dfrac{19 - 17.4}{4.96/\sqrt{50}} = 2.28$

$$\begin{array}{r} 0.5000 \\ -\ 0.4887 \\ \hline 0.0113 \end{array}$$

3. $z = \dfrac{270{,}000 - 275{,}000}{14275/\sqrt{100}} = -3.50$

$$\begin{array}{r} 0.5000 \\ +\ 0.4998 \\ \hline 0.9998 \end{array}$$

4. We will use $z = \pm 1.645$

$x = \mu + z\sigma$ Between 27.6068 and 28.3932 ounces

$= 28 \pm (1.645)\left(\dfrac{1.69}{\sqrt{50}}\right)$

$= 28 \pm 2.78005$

5. $z = \dfrac{8700 - 8900}{987/\sqrt{75}} = -1.75$

$$\begin{array}{r} 0.5000 \\ +\ 0.4599 \\ \hline 0.9599 \end{array}$$

6. $z = \dfrac{3500 - 3200}{862/\sqrt{30}} = 1.91$

$$\begin{array}{r} 0.5000 \\ +\ 0.4719 \\ \hline 0.9719 \end{array}$$

7. $z = -1.28$ Above 523

$x = 529 + (-1.28)\left(\dfrac{27}{\sqrt{35}}\right) \approx 523.158$

8. Those doctors whose numbers are 06907, 12765, 04213, 04711, 07523, 00358, 10493, 01536, 06243, 11008, 05463, 05597, 04839, 06990, 02011, 07972, 10281, 03427, 08178, 09998, 07351, 12908, 07391, 07856, and 06121.

9.

Sample mean, $\bar{x}$	$\bar{x} - \mu$	$(\bar{x} - \mu)^2$
49,000	13000	169,000,000
38,000	2000	4,000,000
31,000	– 5000	25,000,000
33,000	– 3000	9,000,000
29,000	– 7000	49,000,000
180,000		256,000,000

$$\mu_{\bar{x}} = \frac{180,000}{5} = 36,000$$

$$\sigma_{\bar{x}} = \sqrt{\frac{256,000,000}{5}} = \sqrt{51,200,000} \approx 7155.4175$$

10. $z = \dfrac{70000 - 68500}{8750/\sqrt{64}} = 1.37$

$$\begin{array}{r} 0.5000 \\ - \ 0.4147 \\ \hline 0.0853 \end{array}$$

ANSWERS TO CHAPTER TEST – (PAGES 432 – 434)

1.   We will use $z = \pm 1.645$
$x = \mu + z\sigma$ Between \$404.67 and \$441.33

$$= 423 \pm (1.645)\left(\frac{78}{\sqrt{49}}\right)$$

$$= 423 \pm 18.33$$

2. $z = \dfrac{38 - 36}{3.61/\sqrt{40}} = 3.50$

$$\begin{array}{r} 0.5000 \\ - \ 0.4998 \\ \hline 0.0002 \end{array}$$

3. $z = \dfrac{5 - 4.87}{2.69/\sqrt{64}} = 0.39$

$$\begin{array}{r} 0.5000 \\ - \ 0.1517 \\ \hline 0.3483 \end{array}$$

4. $z = \dfrac{165,000 - 170,000}{12,000/\sqrt{40}} = -2.64$

$$\begin{array}{r} 0.5000 \\ + \ 0.4959 \\ \hline 0.9959 \end{array}$$

5. $z = \dfrac{2300 - 2175}{182/\sqrt{30}} = 3.76$

$$\begin{array}{r} 0.4999 \\ - \ 0.2734 \\ \hline 0.2265 \end{array}$$

$z = \dfrac{2200 - 2175}{182/\sqrt{30}} = 0.75$

6. a)

Number of children, x	Sample mean, $\overline{x}$	$\overline{x} - \mu_{\overline{x}}$	$(\overline{x} - \mu_{\overline{x}})^2$
4 and 3	3.5	-0.5	0.25
4 and 6	5	1	1.00
4 and 5	4.5	0.5	0.25
4 and 2	3	-1	1.00
3 and 6	4.5	0.5	0.25
3 and 5	4	0	0
3 and 2	2.5	-1.5	2.25
6 and 5	5.5	1.5	2.25
6 and 2	4	0	0.00
5 and 2	3.5	-0.5	0.25
	40		7.50

c) $\mu_{\overline{x}} = \dfrac{40}{10} = 4$

d) $\sigma_{\overline{x}} = \sqrt{\dfrac{7.5}{10}} = \sqrt{0.75} \approx 0.866$

7. Those cars whose serial numbers are 64809, 53498, 31016, 59533, 69445, 33488, 52267, 30168, 38005, 40027, 44048, 35126, 48708, 59931, 51038, 47358, 53416, 38857, 34072, 69179, 39440, 60468, 57740, 38867, 56865, 36320, 67869, 47564, 60756, 55322, 45834, 60952, 66556, 32832, and 37937.

244

8. $$z = \frac{190 - 188.72}{12.41/\sqrt{49}} = 0.72$$

$$\begin{array}{r} 0.5000 \\ + \ 0.2642 \\ \hline 0.7642 \end{array}$$

9. We will use $z = \pm 1.645$

$$x = \mu + z\sigma$$

$$= 35000 \pm 1.645 \frac{(5600)}{\sqrt{100}}$$

$$= 35000 \pm 921.2$$

Between 34,078.8 and

35,921.2 miles

10. $\mu_{\bar{x}} = 168$

$$\sigma_{\bar{x}} = \frac{53}{\sqrt{64}} = 6.625$$

11. a)

Number of years, x	$x - \mu$	$(x - \mu)^2$
5	-3	9
10	2	4
4	-4	16
8	0	0
13	5	25
40		54

$$\mu = \frac{40}{5} = 8$$

$$\sigma = \sqrt{\frac{54}{5}} = \sqrt{10.8} \approx 3.2863$$

11. b)   Size 2

Number of years, x	Sample mean, $\overline{x}$	$\overline{x} - \mu_{\overline{x}}$	$(\overline{x} - \mu_{\overline{x}})^2$
5 and 10	7.5	-0.5	0.25
5 and 4	4.5	-3.5	12.25
5 and 8	6.5	-1.5	2.25
5 and 13	9	1	1.00
10 and 4	7	-1	1.00
10 and 8	9	1	1.00
10 and 13	11.5	3.5	12.25
4 and 8	6	-2	4.00
4 and 13	8.5	0.5	0.25
8 and 13	10.5	2.5	6.25
	80		40.5

11. b)
     Size 3

Number of years,x	Sample mean, $\overline{x}$	$\overline{x} - \mu_{\overline{x}}$	$(\overline{x} - \mu_{\overline{x}})^2$
5, 10, and 4	6.3333	-1.6667	2.7779
5, 10, and 8	7.6667	-0.3333	0.1111
5, 10, and 13	9.3333	1.3333	1.7777
5, 4, and 8	5.6667	-2.3333	5.4443
5, 4, and 13	7.3333	-0.6667	0.4445
5, 8, and 13	8.6667	0.6667	0.4445
10, 4, and 8	7.3333	-0.6667	0.4445
10, 4, and 13	9	1	1.0000
10, 8, and 13	10.3333	2.3333	5.4443
4, 8, and 13	8.3333	0.3333	0.1111
	80		17.9999

246

11. c) $\mu_{\bar{x}} = \dfrac{80}{10} = 8$

$$\sigma_{\bar{x}} = \sqrt{\dfrac{40.5}{10}} = \sqrt{4.05} \approx 2.0125$$

and $\mu_{\bar{x}} = \dfrac{80}{10} = 8$

$$\sigma_{\bar{x}} = \sqrt{\dfrac{17.9999}{10}} = \sqrt{1.79999} \approx 1.3416$$

d) We use $\sigma_{\bar{x}} = \dfrac{\sigma}{\sqrt{n}} \sqrt{\dfrac{N-n}{N-1}}$ In both cases N = 5

$$\sigma_{\bar{x}} = \dfrac{3.2863}{\sqrt{2}} \sqrt{\dfrac{5-2}{5-1}} \approx 2.0125$$

and $\sigma_{\bar{x}} = \dfrac{3.2863}{\sqrt{3}} \sqrt{\dfrac{5-3}{5-1}} \approx 1.3416$

12. Choice (e)

13. Choice (c)

14. Choice (a)

15. Choice (b)

16. Choice (a)

17. Choice (d)

CHAPTER 8 - SAMPLING
SUPPLEMENTARY TEST FORM A

1. The average number of pages in a certain type of book is 488 pages with a standard deviation of 18.3 pages. What is the probability that the average number of pages in 49 randomly selected books of the type described will be greater than 495 pages?

Answer _____

2. Five schools have each been testing 100 bulbs of a particular brand. The average life of the bulbs at each of these schools was 2100, 3200, 2600, 2800, and 2900 hours. Find the overall average of these sample means.

Answer _____

3. In the previous exercise, find the standard deviation of these samples.

Answer _____

4. The average life of a washing machine produced by the Bob Corp. is 8.3 years with a standard deviation of 2.13 years. If a random sample of 36 washing machines produced by this company is selected, what is the probability that the average life of these machines will be between 7.3 and 9 years?

Answer _____

5. Refer back to the previous questions. If a random survey of 36 washing machines produced by this company is selected, within what limits should the weights of 95 percent of these machines lie?

Answer _____

6. The average weight of an employee at the Bork Corp. is 135 pounds with a standard deviation of 11 pounds. Within what limits should the average weights of 95 percent of 50 randomly selected employees of this company lie?

Answer _____

7. There are 817 nurses on the staff of a hospital, each of whom has been assigned a number from 1 to 817. A committee of 10 nurses is to be randomly selected from among them to discuss changing the shift patterns. By using Column V of Table VII, which nurses should be selected?

Answer _____

8. The average cost for replacing an automatic transmission of a certain model car is $575 with a standard deviation of $28. A sample of the repair bills for replacing 45 automatic transmissions of the type mentioned is taken. What is the probability that the average replacement cost is between $565 and $580?

Answer _____

9. The average gas purchase at Pete's service station is $15 with a standard deviation of $2.25. If 39 gas purchases are selected at random, what is the probability that the average purchases will be less than $14?

Answer _____

10. The average amount of money that the teachers of the Armington School District have accumulated in the tax-deferred annuity program is $2250 with a standard deviation of $117. If a sample of 45 participating teachers is randomly selected, what is the probability that these teachers will have accumulated an average of at least $2300?

Answer _____

249

1. The average weight of a certain size of grapefruit is 10 ounces with a standard deviation of 1.92 ounces. What is the probability that the average weight of 64 randomly selected grapefruits of the size described will be greater than 10.5 ounces?

    Answer _____

2. Five supermarkets have been testing 100 special shopping carts produced by a particular company. The average life of the carts at each of these supermarkets was 410, 510, 480, 500, and 490 days. Find the overall average of these sample means.

    Answer _____

3. In the previous exercise, find the standard deviation of these samples.

    Answer _____

4. The average life of a refrigerator produced by the West Corp. is 11.5 years with a standard deviation of 1.47 years. If a random sample of 81 refrigerators produced by this company is selected, what is the probability that the average life of these refrigerators will be between 11.2 and 11.9 years?

    Answer _____

5. Refer back to the previous question. If a random sample of 81 refrigerators is selected, within what limits should the life of 95 percent of these refrigerators lie?

    Answer _____

6. The average height of an employee of the Gant Corp. is 65 inches with a standard deviation of 3 inches. Within what limits should the average heights of 95 percent of 60 randomly selected employees lie?

    Answer _____

7. There are 768 police officers in a large city assigned to traffic patrol, each of whom has been assigned a number from 1 to 768. A committee of 10 police officers is to be randomly selected from among them to discuss reassignment problems. By using column VI of Table VII, which police officers should be selected?

    Answer _____

8. The average cost of replacing the loading mechanism on a particular VCR is $84 with a standard deviation of $9. A sample of the repair bills for replacing 40 loading mechanisms of the type mentioned is taken. What is the probability that the average replacement cost is between $80 and $87.

                                        Answer _____

9. The average bill at Maggie's Restaurant is $21 with a standard deviation of $2.85. If 43 bills are selected at random, what is the probability that the average of these bills will be less than $20

                                        Answer _____

10. The pilots of a particular airline have accumulated an average of 5000 flying hours with a standard deviation of 175 hours. If a sample of 47 pilots of this airline is randomly selected, what is the probability that these pilots will have accumulated an average of at least 4975 hours of flying time?

                                        Answer _____

1. The average weight of a certain type of bird is 12 ounces with a standard deviation of 1.86 ounces. What is the probability that the average weight of 81 randomly selected birds of the type described will be greater than 12.3 ounces?

    Answer _____

2. Five companies have each been field testing 100 beepers manufactured by the Caldwell Corp. The average life of these beepers for each of these companies was 710, 800, 740, 760, and 780 days. Find the overall average of these sample means.

    Answer _____

3. In the previous exercise, find the standard deviation of these sample means.

    Answer _____

4. The average life of a microwave oven produced by the West Corp. is 9.7 years with a standard deviation of 1.23 years. If a random sample of 64 microwave ovens produced by this company is selected, what is the probability that the average life of these microwave ovens will be between 9.5 and 10 years?

    Answer _____

5. Refer back to the previous question. If a random survey of 64 microwave ovens produced by this company is selected, within what limits should the lives of 95 percent of these microwave ovens lie?

    Answer _____

6. The average age of a doctor at Washington Hospital is 43 years with a standard deviation of 3.2 years. Within what limits should the average age of 95 percent of 40 randomly selected doctors from this hospital lie?

    Answer _____

7. There are 812 doctors at Washington Hospital, each of whom has been assigned a number from 1 to 812. A committee of 10 doctors is randomly selected from among them to discuss the rising malpractice insurance costs. By using Column VII of Table VII, which doctors should be selected?

    Answer _____

8. The average cost for replacing a disk drive of a particular model computer is $95 with a standard deviation of $10.50. A sample of the repair bills for replacing 37 disk drives of the type mentioned is taken. What is the probability that the average replacement cost is between $90 and $100?

Answer _____

9. The average monthly electric bill in a certain city is $28 with a standard deviation of $4.75. If 52 electric bills are randomly selected, what is the probability that the average of these bills will be less than $26?

Answer _____

10. The drivers of a particular overnight delivery service have been with the company an average of 8.6 years with a standard deviation of 1.46 years. If a sample of 39 drivers of this company is randomly selected, what is the probability that these drivers will have been with the company an average of at least 8 years?

Answer _____

Form A

1. 0.0037   2. 2720   3. 408.656   4. 0.9732   5. Between 7.6042 and 8.9958 years   6. Between 131.951 and 138.049 pounds   7. Those whose numbers are 816, 309, 763, 78, 61, 277, 188, 174, 530, and 709   8. 0.8767   9. 0.0027   10. 0.0021

Form B

1. 0.0188   2. 478   3. 39.6232   4. 0.9600   5. Between 11.1799 and 11.8201 years   6. Between 64.2409 and 65.7591 inches   7. Those whose numbers are 648, 163, 534, 310, 209, 181, 595, 694, 334, and 522   8. 0.9801   9. 0.0107   10. 0.8365

Form C

1. 0.0735   2. 758   3. 34.928   4. 0.8776   5. Between 9.399 and 10.001 years   6. Between 42.01 and 43.99 years   7. Those whose numbers are 691, 279, 151, 394, 604, 186, 711, 577, 388, and 568   8. 0.9962   9. 0.0012   10. 0.9949

ANSWERS TO EXERCISES FOR CHAPTER 9

SECTION 9.3 - (PAGES 445 - 447)

1. Lower boundary: $2.75 - 1.645\left(\dfrac{0.25}{\sqrt{49}}\right) = 2.69$

   Upper boundary: $2.75 + 1.645\left(\dfrac{0.25}{\sqrt{49}}\right) = 2.81$

   90% confidence interval: $2.69 to $2.81

2. Lower boundary: $0.35 - 2.58\left(\dfrac{0.05}{\sqrt{64}}\right) = 0.334$ or 33.4%

   Upper boundary: $0.35 + 2.58\left(\dfrac{0.05}{\sqrt{64}}\right) = 0.366$ or 36.6%

   99% confidence interval: 33.4% to 36.6%

3. Lower boundary: $10 - 1.96\left(\dfrac{1.23}{\sqrt{500}}\right) = 9.89$

   Upper boundary: $10 + 1.96\left(\dfrac{1.23}{\sqrt{500}}\right) = 10.11$

   95% confidence interval: 9.89 to 10.11 days

4. Lower boundary: $30,000 - 1.645\left(\dfrac{7000}{\sqrt{100}}\right) = 28848.50$

   Upper boundary: $30,000 + 1.645\left(\dfrac{7000}{\sqrt{100}}\right) = 31151.50$

   90% confidence interval: $28,848.50 to $31,151.50

5. Lower boundary: $15 - 1.96\left(\dfrac{2.98}{\sqrt{36}}\right) = 14.03$

   Upper boundary: $15 + 1.96\left(\dfrac{2.98}{\sqrt{36}}\right) = 15.97$

   95% confidence interval: $14.03 to $15.97

6. Lower boundary: $627 - 2.58\left(\dfrac{83}{\sqrt{64}}\right) = 600.23$

Upper boundary: $627 + 2.58\left(\dfrac{83}{\sqrt{64}}\right) = 653.77$

99% confidence interval: \$600.23 to \$653.77

7. Lower boundary: $522.85 - 1.96\left(\dfrac{29.55}{\sqrt{49}}\right) = 514.58$

Upper boundary: $522.85 + 1.96\left(\dfrac{29.55}{\sqrt{49}}\right) = 531.12$

95% confidence interval: Between \$514.58 and \$531.12

8. Lower boundary: $16 - 2.58\left(\dfrac{2.13}{\sqrt{64}}\right) = 15.31$

Upper boundary: $16 + 2.58\left(\dfrac{2.13}{\sqrt{64}}\right) = 16.69$

99% confidence interval: Between 15.31 and 16.69 days

9. Lower boundary: $1375 - 1.44\left(\dfrac{178}{\sqrt{36}}\right) = 1332.28$

Upper boundary: $1375 + 1.44\left(\dfrac{178}{\sqrt{36}}\right) = 1417.72$

85% confidence interval: Between \$1332.28 and \$1417.72

10. Lower boundary: $425 - 1.645\left(\dfrac{51}{\sqrt{75}}\right) = 415.31$

Upper boundary: $425 + 1.645\left(\dfrac{51}{\sqrt{75}}\right) = 434.69$

90% confidence interval: Between \$415.31 and \$434.69

11. We must first find $\bar{x}$ and s. We have

$$\bar{x} = \frac{\sum x}{n} = \frac{850}{40} = 21.25 \text{ and}$$

$$s = \sqrt{\frac{n(\sum x^2) - (\sum x)^2}{n(n-1)}} = \sqrt{\frac{40(18,400) - 850^2}{40(40-1)}} \approx 2.9417$$

a) Lower boundary: $21.25 - 1.96\left(\dfrac{2.9417}{\sqrt{40}}\right) = 20.34$

Upper boundary: $21.25 + 1.96\left(\dfrac{2.9417}{\sqrt{40}}\right) = 22.16$

95% confidence interval: Between 20.34 and 22.16

b) Lower boundary: $21.25 - 2.58\left(\dfrac{2.9417}{\sqrt{40}}\right) = 20.05$

Upper boundary: $21.25 + 2.58\left(\dfrac{2.9417}{\sqrt{40}}\right) = 22.45$

99% confidence interval: Between 20.05 and 22.45

ANSWERS TO EXERCISES FOR SECTION 9.4 - (PAGES 451 - 454)

1. Lower boundary: $7200 - 3.355\left(\dfrac{812}{\sqrt{9}}\right) = 6291.91$

Upper boundary: $7200 + 3.355\left(\dfrac{812}{\sqrt{9}}\right) = 8108.09$

99% confidence interval: Between $6291.91 and $8108.09

2. Lower boundary: $61 - 1.796\left(\dfrac{8.3}{\sqrt{12}}\right) = 56.7$

Upper boundary: $61 + 1.796\left(\dfrac{8.3}{\sqrt{12}}\right) = 65.3$

90% confidence interval: Between 56.7 and 65.3 gallons.

3. Lower boundary: $2371 - 2.145\left(\dfrac{278}{\sqrt{15}}\right) = 2217.03$

   Upper boundary: $2371 + 2.145\left(\dfrac{278}{\sqrt{15}}\right) = 2524.97$

   95% confidence interval: Between \$2217.03 and \$2524.97

4. We must first find $\overline{x}$ and s. We have $\overline{x} = \dfrac{\Sigma x}{n} = \dfrac{227,394}{9}$

   $= 25,266$

x	$x - \overline{x}$	$(x - \overline{x})^2$
25,000	-266	70756
25,280	14	196
25,300	34	1156
25,200	- 66	4356
25,400	134	17956
25,250	- 16	256
25,600	334	111556
25,014	-252	63504
25,350	84	7056
227,394		276792

   $s = \sqrt{\dfrac{276792}{9 - 1}} = \sqrt{34599} \approx 186.008$

   Lower boundary: $25266 - 1.860\left(\dfrac{186.008}{\sqrt{9}}\right) = 25150.68$

   Upper boundary: $25266 + 1.860\left(\dfrac{186.008}{\sqrt{9}}\right) = 25381.32$

   90% confidence interval: Between 25,150.68 and 25,381.32

258

5. Lower boundary: $29.9 - 2.145\left(\dfrac{7.4}{\sqrt{15}}\right) = 25.802$

    Upper boundary: $29.9 + 2.145\left(\dfrac{7.4}{\sqrt{15}}\right) = 33.998$

    95% confidence interval: Between 25.802 and 33.998 years.

6. Lower boundary: $28 - 1.86\left(\dfrac{2.82}{\sqrt{9}}\right) = 26.2516$

    Upper boundary: $28 + 1.86\left(\dfrac{2.82}{\sqrt{9}}\right) = 29.7484$

    90% confidence interval: Between 26.2516 and 29.7484 patients.

    We are assuming that previous experience indicates that the

    number treated is approximately normally distributed.

7. We must first find $\overline{x}$ and s. We have $\overline{x} = \dfrac{\Sigma x}{n} = \dfrac{44.8}{8} = 5.6$

x	$x - \overline{x}$	$(x - \overline{x})^2$
5.8	0.2	0.04
5.2	-0.4	0.16
4.9	-0.7	0.49
5.1	-0.5	0.25
5.3	-0.3	0.09
6.1	0.5	0.25
5.9	0.3	0.09
6.5	0.9	0.81
44.8		2.18

$$s = \sqrt{\frac{2.18}{8 - 1}} = \sqrt{0.311429} \approx 0.558$$

Lower boundary: $5.6 - 1.895\left(\dfrac{0.558}{\sqrt{8}}\right) = 5.226$

Upper boundary: $5.6 + 1.895\left(\dfrac{0.558}{\sqrt{8}}\right) = 5.974$

90% confidence interval: Between 5.226 and 5.974

8. Lower boundary: $6.1 - 1.761\left(\dfrac{1.3}{\sqrt{15}}\right) = 5.51$

Upper boundary: $6.1 + 1.761\left(\dfrac{1.3}{\sqrt{15}}\right) = 6.69$

90% confidence interval: Between 5.51 and 6.69

9. Lower boundary: $26.8 - 2.201\left(\dfrac{2.31}{\sqrt{12}}\right) = 25.33$

Upper boundary: $26.8 + 2.201\left(\dfrac{2.31}{\sqrt{12}}\right) = 28.27$

95% confidence interval: Between 25.33 and 28.27

10. We must first find $\overline{x}$ and s. We have $\overline{x} = \dfrac{28.2}{10} = 2.82$

x	$x - \overline{x}$	$(x - \overline{x})^2$
3.3	0.48	0.2304
2.2	-0.62	0.3844
3.1	0.28	0.0784
2.8	-0.02	0.0004
2.6	-0.22	0.0484
2.9	0.08	0.0064
3.0	0.18	0.0324
2.4	-0.42	0.1764
2.7	-0.12	0.0144
3.2	0.38	0.1444
28.2		1.1160

$$s = \sqrt{\frac{1.1160}{10 - 1}} = \sqrt{0.124} \approx 0.352$$

Lower boundary: $2.82 - 2.262\left(\dfrac{0.352}{\sqrt{10}}\right) = 2.57$

Upper boundary: $2.82 + 2.262\left(\dfrac{0.352}{\sqrt{10}}\right) = 3.07$

95% confidence interval: Between 2.57 and 3.07

11. Lower boundary: $18 - 2.447\left(\dfrac{3.2}{\sqrt{7}}\right) = 15.0404$

Upper boundary: $18 + 2.447\left(\dfrac{3.2}{\sqrt{7}}\right) = 20.9596$

95% confidence interval: Between 15.0404 and 20.9596

ANSWERS TO EXERCISES FOR SECTION 9.6 – (PAGES 458 – 459)

1. Lower boundary: $\dfrac{2.68}{1 + \dfrac{1.96}{\sqrt{2(125)}}} = 2.38$

Upper boundary: $\dfrac{2.68}{1 - \dfrac{1.96}{\sqrt{2(125)}}} = 3.06$

95% confidence interval for σ: Between 2.38 and 3.06

2. Lower boundary: $\dfrac{1.23}{1 + \dfrac{1.96}{\sqrt{2(36)}}} = 0.999$

Upper boundary: $\dfrac{1.23}{1 - \dfrac{1.96}{\sqrt{2(36)}}} = 1.599$

95% confidence interval for σ: Between 0.999 and 1.599

3. Lower boundary: $\dfrac{8.23}{1 + \dfrac{2.58}{\sqrt{2(75)}}} = 6.80$

Upper boundary: $\dfrac{8.23}{1 - \dfrac{2.58}{\sqrt{2(75)}}} = 10.43$

99% confidence interval for σ: Between \$6.80 and \$10.43

4. Lower boundary: $\dfrac{8.41}{1 + \dfrac{1.645}{\sqrt{2(50)}}} = 7.22$

Upper boundary: $\dfrac{8.41}{1 - \dfrac{1.645}{\sqrt{2(50)}}} = 10.07$

90% confidence interval for σ: Between \$7.22 and \$10.07

5. $n = \left(\dfrac{1.96(1.49)}{0.85}\right)^2 = 11.80$ Sample size = 12

6. $n = \left(\dfrac{1.96(5.93)}{3}\right)^2 = 15$ Sample size = 15

7. $n = \left(\dfrac{1.96(3.98)}{0.85}\right)^2 = 84.22$ Sample size = 85

8. $n = \left(\dfrac{1.96(4.76)}{1.86}\right)^2 = 25.16$ Sample size = 26

9. $n = \left(\dfrac{1.96(8.29)}{5}\right)^2 = 10.56$ Sample size = 11

10. $n = \left(\dfrac{1.96(29.95)}{15}\right)^2 = 15.32$ Sample size = 16

1. a)

Lower Boundary	Upper boundary
$= 0.3 - 1.96\sqrt{\dfrac{0.3(1 - 0.3)}{1000}}$	$= 0.3 + 1.96\sqrt{\dfrac{0.3(1 - 0.3)}{1000}}$
$= 0.3 - 1.96\sqrt{0.00021}$	$= 0.3 + 1.96\sqrt{0.00021}$
$= 0.3 - 1.96(0.01449)$	$= 0.3 + 1.96(0.01449)$
$= 0.3 - 0.028$	$= 0.3 + 0.028$
$= 0.272$	$= 0.328$

95% confidence interval: Between 0.272 and 0.328

b)

Lower Boundary	Upper Boundary
$= 0.08 - 1.96\sqrt{\dfrac{0.08(1 - 0.08)}{5000}}$	$= 0.08 + 1.96\sqrt{\dfrac{0.08(1 - 0.08)}{5000}}$
$= 0.08 - 0.0075$	$= 0.08 + 0.0075$
$= 0.0725$	$= 0.0875$

95% confidence interval: Between 0.0725 and 0.0875

2. $\hat{p} = \dfrac{369}{450} = 0.82$

Lower Boundary	Upper Boundary
$= 0.82 - 1.96\sqrt{\dfrac{0.82(1 - 0.82)}{450}}$	$= 0.82 + 1.96\sqrt{\dfrac{0.82(1 - 0.82)}{450}}$
$= 0.82 - 0.035$	$= 0.82 + 0.035$
$= 0.785$	$= 0.855$

95% confidence interval: Between 0.785 and 0.855

3. $\hat{p} = \dfrac{312}{688} = 0.4535$

Lower Boundary	Upper Boundary
$= 0.4535 - 1.96\sqrt{\dfrac{0.45(1 - 0.45)}{688}}$	$= 0.4535 + 1.96\sqrt{\dfrac{0.45(1 - 0.45)}{688}}$
$= 0.4535 - 0.037$	$= 0.4535 + 0.037$
$= 0.4165$	$= 0.4905$

95% confidence interval: Between 0.4165 and 0.4905

4. $\sigma_{\hat{p}} = \sqrt{\dfrac{0.40(1 - 0.40)}{200}} = 0.03464$

$$\begin{array}{r} 0.5000 \\ - \ 0.4251 \\ \hline 0.0749 \end{array}$$

$z = \dfrac{0.45 - 0.40}{0.03464} = 1.44$

5. $\sigma_{\hat{p}} = \sqrt{\dfrac{0.80(1 - 0.80)}{60}} = 0.05164$

$$\begin{array}{r} 0.5000 \\ -\ 0.3340 \\ \hline 0.1660 \end{array}$$

$z = \dfrac{0.75 - 0.80}{0.052} = -0.97$

6. $\hat{p} = \dfrac{260}{390} = 0.6667$

Lower Boundary	Upper Boundary
$= 0.6667 - 1.645\sqrt{\dfrac{0.67(1 - 0.67)}{390}}$	$= 0.6667 + 1.645\sqrt{\dfrac{0.67(1 - 0.67)}{390}}$
$= 0.6667 - 0.0392$	$= 0.6667 + 0.0392$
$= 0.6275$	$= 0.7059$

90% confidence interval: Between 62.8% and 70.6%

7. $\hat{p} = \dfrac{330}{700} = 0.4714$

$\sigma_{\hat{p}} = \sqrt{\dfrac{0.45(1 - 0.45)}{700}}$

$z = \dfrac{0.4714 - 0.45}{0.0188} = 1.14$

$= 0.0188$

$$\begin{array}{r} 0.5000 \\ -\ 0.3729 \\ \hline 0.1271 \end{array}$$

8. $\sigma_{\hat{p}} = \sqrt{\dfrac{0.96(1 - 0.96)}{85}} = 0.02125$

$$\begin{array}{r} 0.5000 \\ -\ 0.3264 \\ \hline 0.1736 \end{array}$$

$z = \dfrac{0.93 - 0.95}{0.02125} = -0.94$

9. $\hat{p} = \frac{175}{220} = 0.795$

Lower Boundary	Upper Boundary
$= 0.795 - 1.645\sqrt{\dfrac{(0.795)(1 - 0.795)}{220}}$	$= 0.795 + 1.645\sqrt{\dfrac{0.795(1 - 0.795)}{220}}$
$= 0.795 - 0.045$	$= 0.795 + 0.045$
$= 0.75$	$= 0.84$

90% confidence interval: Between 0.75 and 0.84

10. $\sigma_{\hat{p}} = \sqrt{\dfrac{(0.46)(1 - 0.46)}{100}} = 0.05$

$$z = \frac{0.45 - 0.46}{0.05} = -0.2$$

$$\begin{array}{r} 0.5000 \\ - \ 0.0793 \\ \hline 0.4207 \end{array}$$

11. $\sigma_{\hat{p}} = \sqrt{\dfrac{(0.04)(1 - 0.04)}{500}} = 0.0088$

$$z = \frac{0.02 - 0.04}{0.0088} = -2.27$$

$$z = \frac{0.07 - 0.04}{0.0088} = 3.41$$

$$\begin{array}{r} 0.4884 \\ + \ 0.4997 \\ \hline 0.9881 \end{array}$$

12. $\hat{p} = \frac{145}{500} = 0.29$

Lower Boundary	Upper Boundary
$= 0.29 - 1.96\sqrt{\dfrac{(0.29)(1 - 0.29)}{500}}$	$= 0.29 + 1.96\sqrt{\dfrac{(0.29)(1 - 0.29)}{500}}$
$= 0.29 - 0.0398$	$= 0.29 + 0.0398$
$= 0.2502$	$= 0.3298$

95% confidence interval: Between 25.02% and 32.98%

13. $\hat{p} = \dfrac{102}{525} = 0.194285714$

$$\sigma_{\hat{p}} = \sqrt{\dfrac{(0.23)(1 - 0.23)}{525}}$$

$$= 0.0183667$$

$$z = \dfrac{0.194285714 - 0.23}{0.0183667} = -1.94$$

$$\begin{array}{r} 0.5000 \\ + \; 0.4738 \\ \hline 0.9738 \end{array}$$

ANSWERS TO TESTING YOUR UNDERSTANDING OF THIS CHAPTER'S CONCEPTS -
(PAGES 468 - 469)

1. True. To double accuracy, we cut e in half and formula indicates that we need to quadruple the sample size.

2. Choice (c)

3. We must first find $\overline{x}$ and s. We have $\overline{x} = \dfrac{\Sigma x}{n} = \dfrac{133}{7} = 19$

x	$x - \overline{x}$	$(x - \overline{x})^2$
$18.00	-1	1.00
15.00	-4	16.00
22.00	3	9.00
19.50	0.50	0.25
17.00	-2	4.00
21.50	2.50	6.25
20.00	1	1.00
133.00		37.50

$$s = \sqrt{\dfrac{37.50}{7 - 1}} = \sqrt{6.25} = 2.5$$

Lower boundary: $19 - 1.943\left(\dfrac{2.5}{\sqrt{7}}\right) = 17.164$

Upper boundary: $19 + 1.943\left(\dfrac{2.5}{\sqrt{7}}\right) = 20.836$

90% confidence interval: Between $17.16 and $20.84

4. $\quad \sigma_{\hat{p}} = \sqrt{\dfrac{(0.60)(1 - 0.60)}{450}} = 0.023$

$$\begin{array}{r} 0.5000 \\ -\ 0.4850 \\ \hline 0.0150 \end{array}$$

$\quad z = \dfrac{0.65 - 0.60}{0.023} = 2.17$

5. Lower boundary: $5.28 - 1.761\left(\dfrac{1.06}{\sqrt{15}}\right) = 4.798$

Upper boundary: $5.28 + 1.761\left(\dfrac{1.06}{\sqrt{15}}\right) = 5.762$

90% confidence interval: Between 4.798 minutes and 5.762 minutes.
We are assuming that the population sampled is normally distributed.

ANSWERS TO THINKING CRITICALLY -(PAGES 469 - 470)

1. a) $\hat{p} = \dfrac{650}{1500} = 0.4333$ $\qquad \sigma_{\hat{p}} = \sqrt{\dfrac{(0.4333)(1 - 0.4333)}{1500}} = 0.0128$

Lower boundary: $0.4333 - 1.645\sqrt{\dfrac{(0.4333)(1 - 0.4333)}{1500}} = 0.4333$

$\qquad\qquad\qquad - 0.021 = 0.412$

Upper boundary: $0.4333 + 1.645\sqrt{\dfrac{(0.4333)(1 - 0.4333)}{1500}} = 0.4333$

$\qquad\qquad\qquad + 0.021 = 0.454$

90% confidence interval: Between 41.2% and 45.4%

b) Solving $e = 1.96\sqrt{\dfrac{\hat{p}(1-\hat{p})}{n}}$ for n, we obtain

$$n = \left(\dfrac{1.96}{e}\right)^2 \hat{p}(1 - \hat{p}) = \left(\dfrac{1.96}{0.001}\right)^2 \left(\dfrac{650}{1500}\right)\left(\dfrac{850}{1500}\right)$$

$$= 943,326.22$$

Sample size = 943,327

2. $$\sigma_{\hat{p}} = \sqrt{\frac{(0.80)(1 - 0.80)}{800}} = 0.014$$

We will use z = 2.96 (we could also use z = 2.97)
Lower boundary: 0.80 - 2.96(0.014) = 0.7586
Upper boundary: 0.80 + 2.96(0.014) = 0.8414
99.7% confidence interval: Between 75.86% and 84.14%

3. We must first find $\overline{x}$ and s. We have

$$\overline{x} = \frac{\sum x}{n} = \frac{3800}{300} = 12.667 \text{ and } s = \sqrt{\frac{n(\sum x^2) - (\sum x)^2}{n(n - 1)}}$$

$$= \sqrt{\frac{300(140,000) - 3800^2}{300(300 - 1)}} \approx 17.5284$$

Lower boundary: $12.667 - 1.96\left(\dfrac{17.5284}{\sqrt{300}}\right) = 10.683$

Upper boundary: $12.667 + 1.96\left(\dfrac{17.5284}{\sqrt{300}}\right) = 14.651$

95% confidence interval: Between 10.683 and 14.651

4. Large sample size

5. df = n - 1 = 9 - 1 = 8

$$y^2 = \left[1.645\left(\frac{8\cdot 8 + 3}{8\cdot 8 + 1}\right)\right]^2 = \qquad\qquad t = \sqrt{8\cdot\left(2.718^{\frac{2.8751}{8}} - 1\right)}$$
$$= 2.8751 \qquad\qquad\qquad\qquad\qquad = 1.860$$

The $t_{0.05}$ value with 8 degrees of freedom is also 1.860

270

1. $\hat{p} = \dfrac{164}{190} = 0.863$ $\sigma_{\hat{p}} = \sqrt{\dfrac{(0.863)(1 - 0.863)}{190}} = 0.0249$

Lower Boundary	Upper Boundary
$= 0.863 - 1.96(0.0249)$	$= 0.863 + 1.96(0.0249)$
$= 0.863 - 0.0488$	$= 0.863 + 0.0488$
$= 0.8142$	$= 0.912$

95% confidence interval: Between 81.42% and 91.2%

2. $\sigma_{\hat{p}} = \sqrt{\dfrac{(0.32)(1 - 0.32)}{520}} = 0.020456$

$$\begin{array}{r} 0.3365 \\ + \ 0.4292 \\ \hline 0.7657 \end{array}$$

$z = \dfrac{0.30 - 0.32}{0.020456} = -0.98$

$z = \dfrac{0.35 - 0.32}{0.020456} = 1.47$

3. Lower boundary: $\dfrac{17}{1 + \dfrac{2.58}{\sqrt{2(45)}}} = 13.37$

Upper boundary: $\dfrac{17}{1 - \dfrac{2.58}{\sqrt{2(45)}}} = 23.35$

99% confidence interval: Between \$13.37 and \$23.35

4. $\sigma_{\hat{p}} = \sqrt{\dfrac{(0.96)(1 - 0.96)}{71}} = 0.023256$

$$\begin{array}{r} 0.5000 \\ - \ 0.4573 \\ \hline 0.0427 \end{array}$$

$z = \dfrac{0.92 - 0.96}{0.023256} = -1.72$

5. $n = \left[\dfrac{(1.96)(1.93)}{0.74}\right]^2 = 26.13$ Sample size = 27

6. We must first find $\bar{x}$ and s. We have $\bar{x} = \dfrac{\Sigma x}{n} = \dfrac{63}{9} = 7$

x	x − $\bar{x}$	(x − $\bar{x}$)^2
10	3	9
4	−3	9
11	4	16
3	−4	16
7	0	0
8	1	1
6	−1	1
9	2	4
5	−2	4
63		60

$$s = \sqrt{\frac{60}{9-1}} = \sqrt{7.5} \approx 2.7386$$

Lower boundary: $7 - 2.306\left(\dfrac{2.7386}{\sqrt{9}}\right) = 4.895$

Upper boundary: $7 + 2.306\left(\dfrac{2.7386}{\sqrt{9}}\right) = 9.105$

95% confidence interval: Between 4.895 and 9.105

7. $\hat{p} = \dfrac{295}{425} = 0.694$ $\sigma_{\hat{p}} = \sqrt{\dfrac{(0.694)(1 - 0.694)}{425}} = 0.02235$

Lower Boundary	Upper Boundary
= 0.694 - 1.96(0.02235)	= 0.694 + 1.96(0.02235)
= 0.694 - 0.044	= 0.694 + 0.044
= 0.650	= 0.738

   95% confidence interval: Between 0.650 and 0.738

8. Lower boundary: $29 - 1.96\left(\dfrac{4.3}{\sqrt{100}}\right) = 28.157$

   Upper boundary: $29 + 1.96\left(\dfrac{4.3}{\sqrt{100}}\right) = 29.843$

   95% confidence interval: Between 28.157 and 29.843

9. $\hat{p} = \dfrac{285}{425} = 0.671$ $\sigma_{\hat{p}} = \sqrt{\dfrac{(0.671)(1 - 0.671)}{425}} = 0.02279$

Lower Boundary	Upper Boundary
= 0.671 - 1.96(0.02279)	= 0.671 + 1.96(0.02279)
= 0.671 - 0.0447	= 0.671 + 0.0447
= 0.6263	= 0.7157

   95% confidence interval: Between 62.6% and 71.6%

10. We must first find $\overline{x}$ and s. We have $\overline{x} = \dfrac{\Sigma x}{n} = \dfrac{184}{8} = 23$

x	x – $\overline{x}$	(x – $\overline{x}$)^2
21	-2	4
17	-6	36
32	9	81
19	-4	16
18	-5	25
23	0	0
25	2	4
29	6	36
184		202

$$s = \sqrt{\frac{202}{8-1}} \approx 5.3719$$

$$t_{0.025} = 2.365$$

Lower boundary: $23 - 2.365\left(\dfrac{5.3719}{\sqrt{8}}\right) = 18.508$

Upper boundary: $23 + 2.365\left(\dfrac{5.3719}{\sqrt{8}}\right) = 27.492$

95% confidence interval: Between 18.508 and 27.492

1. $\hat{p} = \dfrac{165}{270} = 0.611$

$\sigma_{\hat{p}} = \sqrt{\dfrac{(0.70)(1 - 0.70)}{270}} = 0.028$

$z = \dfrac{0.611 - 0.70}{0.028} = -3.18$

$$\begin{array}{r} 0.5000 \\ -\ 0.4993 \\ \hline 0.0007 \end{array}$$

2. $\hat{p} = \dfrac{429}{600} = 0.715$

$\sigma_{\hat{p}} = \sqrt{\dfrac{(0.715)(1 - 0.715)}{600}} = 0.0184$

Lower Boundary	Upper Boundary
$= 0.715 - 1.96(0.0184)$	$= 0.715 + 1.96(0.0184)$
$= 0.715 - 0.036$	$= 0.715 + 0.036$
$= 0.679$	$= 0.751$

95% confidence interval: Between 0.679 and 0.751

3. Lower boundary: $1.24 - 2.262\left(\dfrac{0.19}{\sqrt{10}}\right) = 1.10$

Upper boundary: $1.24 + 2.262\left(\dfrac{0.19}{\sqrt{10}}\right) = 1.38$

95% confidence interval: Between \$1.10 and \$1.38

4. Lower boundary: $54.3 - 1.729\left(\dfrac{4.76}{\sqrt{20}}\right) = 52.46$

Upper boundary: $54.3 + 1.729\left(\dfrac{4.76}{\sqrt{20}}\right) = 56.14$

90% confidence interval: Between 52.46 and 56.14

5. $\quad \sigma_{\hat{p}} = \sqrt{\dfrac{0.60(1 - 0.60)}{49}} = 0.07$

$$\begin{array}{r} 0.4236 \\ -\ 0.2157 \\ \hline 0.2079 \end{array}$$

$z = \dfrac{0.50 - 0.60}{0.07} = -1.43$

$z = \dfrac{0.56 - 0.60}{0.07} = -0.57$

6. Lower boundary: $26 - 1.96\left(\dfrac{7.83}{\sqrt{100}}\right) = 24.47$

Upper boundary: $26 + 1.96\left(\dfrac{7.83}{\sqrt{100}}\right) = 27.53$

95% confidence interval: Between 24.47 and 27.53 years.

7. $\quad n = \left[\dfrac{1.96(0.92)}{0.6}\right]^2 = 9.03 \qquad$ Sample size = 10

8. $\quad \hat{p} = \dfrac{9}{75} = 0.12 \qquad \sigma_{\hat{p}} = \sqrt{\dfrac{(0.05)(1 - 0.05)}{75}} = 0.025166$

$z = \dfrac{0.12 - 0.05}{0.025166} = 2.78$

$$\begin{array}{r} 0.5000 \\ -\ 0.4941 \\ \hline 0.0059 \end{array}$$

9. $\quad \hat{p} = \dfrac{475}{800} = 0.59375 \quad \sigma_{\hat{p}} = \sqrt{\dfrac{(0.59375)(1 - 0.59375)}{800}}$

$= 0.01739$

$z = \dfrac{0.55 - 0.59375}{0.01739} = -2.52$

$$\begin{array}{r} 0.5000 \\ +\ 0.4941 \\ \hline 0.9941 \end{array}$$

10.

Lower Boundary	Upper Boundary
$= 35 - 1.833\left(\dfrac{2.98}{\sqrt{10}}\right)$	$= 35 + 1.833\left(\dfrac{2.98}{\sqrt{10}}\right)$
$= 33.27$	$= 36.73$

90% confidence interval: Between 33.27 and 36.73 patients

11. $\hat{p} = \dfrac{390}{600} = 0.65$ $\sigma_{\hat{p}} = \sqrt{\dfrac{(0.65)(1 - 0.65)}{600}} = 0.01947$

$z = \dfrac{0.59 - 0.65}{0.01947} = -3.08$

$$\begin{array}{r} 0.5000 \\ -\ 0.4990 \\ \hline 0.0010 \end{array}$$

12. $n = \left[\dfrac{1.96(1.69)}{0.21}\right]^2 = 248.798$ Sample size = 249

13. $\hat{p} = \dfrac{236}{325} = 0.726$ $\sigma_{\hat{p}} = \sqrt{\dfrac{(0.726)(1 - 0.726)}{325}} = 0.0247$

Lower Boundary	Upper Boundary
$= 0.726 - 1.645(0.0247)$	$= 0.726 + 1.645(0.0247)$
$= 0.685$	$= 0.7666$

90% confidence interval: Between 68.5% and 76.7%

14. Choice (b)

15. Choice (a)

16. Choice (c)

17. Choice (e)

18. Choice (b)

19. Choice (b)

1. The average nightly cost for a similar room at 50 motels was $49.95 with a standard deviation of $1.75. Find a 95% confidence interval for the average nightly cost for a motel room.

   Answer _____

2. A manufacturer wishes to determine the list price for a smoke alarm. A survey of the list price of similar smoke alarms sold by 9 other competing companies showed an average list price of $10.95 with a standard deviation of $1.49. Find a 95% confidence interval for the average list price for a smoke alarm.

   Answer _____

3. Eight plumbers in a city charged an average of $885 for installing baseboard heating. The standard deviation was $45. Find a 90% confidence interval for the average charge for installing baseboard heating in this city.

   Answer _____

4. A sample of 50 elementary school teachers in a city indicated that a teacher spends an average of 15 hours per week preparing lessons. The standard deviation was 1.89 hours. Find a 95% confidence interval for the population standard deviation.

   Answer _____

5. Forty-five orthodontists were asked to indicate their charge for installing braces (no complications). The standard deviation of their charges was computed and found to be $69. Find a 99% confidence interval for the population standard deviation.

   Answer _____

6. An engineer wishes to estimate the tensile strength of a certain material. How large a sample (with a 95% degree of confidence) should the engineer select, if the engineer wishes the estimate to be within 2.2 units of the true value? (Assume that $\sigma = 4.79$ units).

   Answer _____

7. A photographer finds that 7% of all film processed by a certain company will be ruined. Find the probability that a random sample of 81 rolls of film processed by this company will contain at most 5% of the rolls that are ruined.

   Answer _____

8. A bank official claims that 95% of its employees are courteous and efficient. A random sample of 50 of the bank's employees is taken. What is the probability that fewer than 93% of those employees will be found to be courteous and efficient?

Answer _____

9. A random sample of 250 families in Thomsonville indicated that 140 of them had a pet dog or cat at home. Find a 95% confidence interval for the true proportion of all families in Thomsonville who have a pet dog or cat at home.

Answer _____

10. A consumers' group wishes to estimate the average cost of a steel-belted radial tire. How large a sample (with a 95% degree of confidence) should the group take if it wants the estimate to be within $3.50 of the true value? (Assume that σ = $6.95).

Answer _____

279

1. The average charge for a home visit by 75 doctors in a particular city was $35 with a standard deviation of $4. Find a 95% confidence interval for the average charge for a home visit by a doctor in this city.

    Answer _____

2. A manufacturer wishes to determine the list price for a particular type of silverware. A survey of the list price of similar silverware sold by 8 other competing companies showed an average list of $49.95 with a standard deviation of $3.95. Find a 95% confidence interval for the average list price for the silverware.

    Answer _____

3. Nine electricians in a city charged an average of $120 for installing comparable electric meter boxes. The standard deviation was $11. Find a 90% confidence interval for the average charge for installing electric meter boxes in this city.

    Answer _____

4. A sample of 45 sanitation workers in a city disclosed that a sanitation worker spends an average of $425 per year for uniforms. The standard deviation was $39. Find a 95% confidence interval for the population standard deviation.

    Answer _____

5. Forty-five tow truck operators were asked to indicate their charge for towing a special type of vehicle. The standard deviation of their charge was computed and found to be $8. Find a 99% confidence interval for the population standard deviation.

    Answer _____

6. A researcher wishes to estimate the average response time by a rat to certain stimuli. How large a sample (with a 95% degree of confidence) should the researcher take, if it is desired that the estimate be within 0.8 seconds of the true value? (Assume that $\sigma = 2.57$).

    Answer _____

7. A social service official claims that 15% of all applications for welfare payments are fraudulent. Find the probability that a random sample of 100 applications will contain at most 12% of them that are fraudulent.

    Answer _____

8. A government official claims that 40% of all workers in the city commute daily to work. A random sample of 75 of the workers in this city is taken. what is the probability that fewer than 36% of these workers will be found to commute daily to work?

    Answer _____

9. A random sample of 350 people in Vega Valley indicated that 210 of them had a life insurance policy. Find a 95% confidence interval for the true proportion of all families in Vega Valley who have an insurance policy.

    Answer _____

10. A painter wishes to estimate the average drying time of a particular brand of paint under specified conditions. How large a sample (with a 95% degree of confidence) should the painter take, if the painter wants the estimate to be within 12 minutes of the true value? (Assume that σ = 32.37 minutes.)

    Answer _____

1. The average cost for a certain prescription drug at 45 pharmacies was $21.95 with a standard deviation of $2.25. Find a 95% confidence interval for the average cost of this prescription drug.

Answer _____

2. A vendor wishes to determine the price to charge for a shaver. A survey of the prices charged by 8 competing vendors for the same shaver showed an average price of $21.95 with a standard deviation of $1.45. Find a 95% confidence interval for the price charged for the shaver.

Answer _____

3. Seven gardeners in a city charged an average of $85 for pruning a small-sized tree. The standard deviation was $7.95. Find a 90% confidence interval for the average charge for pruning a small-size tree by gardeners in this city.

Answer _____

4. A sample of 50 beauty salons in a city indicated that the beauticians worked an average of 39 hours per week. The standard deviation was 2.84 hours. Find a 95% confidence interval for the population standard deviation.

Answer _____

5. Sixty-five children in an elementary school were asked to indicate how often they visited a library during the school year. The standard deviation of their answers was computed and found to be 8 times. Find a 99% confidence interval for the population standard deviation.

Answer _____

6. A botanist wishes to estimate the time needed for a plant to begin to grow. How large of a sample (with a 95% degree of confidence) should the botanist take, if the botanist wishes the estimate to be within 4 days of the true value? (Assume that $\sigma = 21$ days).

Answer _____

7. A hospital official believes that 95% of all claims submitted to insurance companies are paid promptly. Find the probability that a random sample of 100 claims submitted to insurance companies will result at most 92% of them paid promptly.

Answer _____

8. A receptionist for a doctor claims that 90% of all patients arrive on time for their scheduled appointments. A random survey of 70 patients of this doctor is taken. What is the probability that fewer than 87% of these patients arrive on time for their scheduled appointments?

Answer _____

9. A random sample of 410 doctors in a city indicated that 287 of them accepted consignment as a form of payment for medical services rendered. Find a 95% confidence interval for the true proportion of all doctors in the city who accept consignment as a form of payment for medical services rendered.

Answer _____

10. A researcher wishes to estimate the average family income in a city. How large a sample (with a 95% degree of confidence) should the researcher take if the researcher wishes that the estimate be within $250 if the true value? (Assume that σ = $2000).

Answer _____

Form A

1. Between $49.46 and $50.44   2. Between $9.80 and $12.10
3. Between $854.85 and $915.15   4. Between 1.58 and 2.35
hours   5. Between $54.25 and $94.77   6. 19   7. 0.2389
8. 0.2578   9. Between 49.85% and 62.15%   10. 16

Form B

1. Between $34.09 and $35.91   2. Between $46.65 and $53.25
3. Between $113.18 and $126.82   4. Between $32.32 and $49.16
5. Between $6.29 and $10.99   6. 40   7. 0.2005   8. 0.2389
9. Between 54.87% and 65.13%   10. 28

Form C

1. Between $21.29 and $22.61   2. Between $20.74 and $23.16
3. Between $79.16 and $90.84   4. Between 2.37 and 3.53 hours
5. Between 6.52 and 10.34 times   6. 106   7. 0.0838
8. 0.2005   9. Between 65.56% and 74.44%   10. 246

SECTION 10.4 – (PAGES 493 – 494)

1. $z = \dfrac{30{,}295 - 33{,}000}{1471/\sqrt{49}} = -12.87$ Reject manufacturer's claim.

2. $z = \dfrac{134 - 140}{12.5/\sqrt{45}} = -3.22$ Reject manufacturer's claim.

3. $z = \dfrac{11.88 - 14.00}{1.69/\sqrt{55}} = -9.30$ Reject claim. Ajax pays lower than the average hourly rate.

4. $z = \dfrac{52 - 49}{14.8/\sqrt{40}} = 1.28$ Do not reject claim.

5. $z = \dfrac{11.9 - 9.4}{4.3/\sqrt{45}} = 3.90$ Reject union's claim.

6. $z = \dfrac{36{,}082 - 39{,}104}{3440/\sqrt{42}} = -5.69$ Reject official's claim.

7. $z = \dfrac{90 - 92}{10.83/\sqrt{50}} = -1.31$ Do not reject manager's claim.

8. $z = \dfrac{71 - 68}{13.12/\sqrt{50}} = 1.62$ Do not reject stockbroker's claim.

9. $z = \dfrac{28.3 - 24.2}{3.9/\sqrt{45}} = 7.05$ Reject official's claim.

10. $z = \dfrac{17 - 19}{4/\sqrt{58}} = -3.81$ Reject claim. Average length is less than 19 inches.

11. $z = \dfrac{28 - 35}{9.3/\sqrt{40}} = -4.76$ Reject manufacturer's claim.

ANSWERS TO EXERCISES FOR SECTION 10.5 – (PAGES 497 – 498)

1. $t = \dfrac{5.32 - 7.62}{2.06/\sqrt{10}} = -3.53$ Reject official's claim.

2. $t = \dfrac{1.52 - 1.43}{0.04/\sqrt{18}} = 9.55$ Reject oil company's claim.

3. $t = \dfrac{18 - 25}{4.8/\sqrt{15}} = -5.65$ Reject claim. Service has improved.

4. $t = \dfrac{22.42 - 20.95}{2.88/\sqrt{10}} = 1.61$ Reject industry claim.

5. $t = \dfrac{17,800 - 14,000}{1600/\sqrt{16}} = 9.5$ Reject claim. Average loan is more than $14,000.

6. $t = \dfrac{30 - 28}{6.72/\sqrt{15}} = 1.15$ Do not reject claim. Do not reject mayor's claim.

7. $t = \dfrac{7.1 - 6.8}{0.98/\sqrt{11}} = 1.02$ Do not reject claim. Machine is not significantly overfilling cups.

8. $t = \dfrac{13.17 - 12.71}{2.86/\sqrt{12}} = 0.56$ Do not reject claim.

9. $t = \dfrac{345 - 375}{10.62/\sqrt{16}} = -11.299$ Reject null hypothesis.

10. $t = \dfrac{29 - 25}{4/\sqrt{18}} = 4.24$ Reject null hypothesis.

ANSWERS TO EXERCISES FOR SECTION 10.6 – (PAGES 504 – 507)

1. $z = \dfrac{17 - 15}{\sqrt{\dfrac{5^2}{80} + \dfrac{4^2}{60}}} = 2.63$ Reject null hypothesis. There is a significant difference.

2. $z = \dfrac{222 - 213}{\sqrt{\dfrac{11^2}{38} + \dfrac{15^2}{47}}} = 3.19$ Reject null hypothesis. There is a significant difference.

3. $z = \dfrac{3.4 - 2.98}{\sqrt{\dfrac{(0.69)^2}{45} + \dfrac{(0.97)^2}{62}}}$

$= 2.62$ Reject null hypothesis. There is a significant difference.

4. $z = \dfrac{22{,}000 - 20{,}000}{\sqrt{\dfrac{480^2}{64} + \dfrac{600^2}{52}}} = 19.50$ Reject null hypothesis. There is a significant difference.

5. $z = \dfrac{1.38 - 1.31}{\sqrt{\dfrac{(0.04)^2}{41} + \dfrac{(0.09)^2}{53}}}$

$= 5.05$ Reject null hypothesis. There is a significant difference.

6. $z = \dfrac{41 - 38}{\sqrt{\dfrac{8^2}{36} + \dfrac{7^2}{31}}} = 1.637$ Do not reject null hypothesis. There is no significant difference.

7. $z = \dfrac{27 - 29}{\sqrt{\dfrac{(6.9)^2}{45} + \dfrac{(8.5)^2}{64}}} = -1.35$ Do not reject null hypothesis. There is no significant difference.

ANSWERS TO EXERCISES FOR SECTION 10.6 (CONTINUED) — (PAGES 504 – 507)

8. $z = \dfrac{8 - 9}{\sqrt{\dfrac{(2.96)^2}{60} + \dfrac{(3.32)^2}{75}}}$

$= -1.85$

Do not reject null hypothesis. There is no significant difference.

9. $z = \dfrac{9 - 11.5}{\sqrt{\dfrac{(0.09)^2}{100} + \dfrac{(0.03)^2}{100}}}$

$= -263.52$

Reject null hypothesis. There is a significant difference.

10. $z = \dfrac{23 - 19}{\sqrt{\dfrac{5^2}{80} + \dfrac{8^2}{50}}} = 3.17$

Reject null hypothesis. There is a significant difference.

11. $z = \dfrac{172 - 161}{\sqrt{\dfrac{(11.98)^2}{72} + \dfrac{(14.62)^2}{88}}}$

$= 5.23$

Reject null hypothesis. There is a significant difference.

ANSWERS TO EXERCISES FOR SECTION 10.7 — (PAGES 510 – 512)

1. $s_p = \sqrt{\dfrac{(10 - 1)(8143)^2 + (12 - 1)(9671)^2}{10 + 12 - 2}} \approx 9015.51$

$t = \dfrac{84{,}583 - 88{,}586}{(9015.51)\sqrt{\dfrac{1}{10} + \dfrac{1}{12}}} = -1.04$

Do not reject null hypothesis. There is not enough evidence to indicate a significant difference.

2.
$$s_p = \sqrt{\frac{(15 - 1)(2.61)^2 + (13 - 1)(3.04)^2}{15 + 13 - 2}} \approx 2.817$$

$$t = \frac{21.3 - 25.6}{(2.817)\sqrt{\frac{1}{15} + \frac{1}{13}}} = -4.03$$

Reject null hypothesis. There is evidence to indicate a significant difference.

3.
$$s_p = \sqrt{\frac{(14 - 1)(1.96)^2 + (12 - 1)(2.01)^2}{14 + 12 - 2}} \approx 1.983$$

$$t = \frac{6.2 - 7.1}{(1.983)\sqrt{\frac{1}{14} + \frac{1}{12}}} = -1.15$$

Do not reject null hypothesis. There is not enough evidence to indicate a significant difference.

4.
$$s_p = \sqrt{\frac{(11 - 1)(1220)^2 + (12 - 1)(1410)^2}{11 + 12 - 2}} \approx 1322.93$$

$$t = \frac{24,050 - 23,880}{(1322.93)\sqrt{\frac{1}{11} + \frac{1}{12}}} = 0.31$$

Do not reject null hypothesis. There is not enough information to indicate a significant difference.

5.
$$s_p = \sqrt{\frac{(17 - 1)(2.2)^2 + (13 - 1)(3.2)^2}{17 + 13 - 2}} \approx 2.675$$

$$t = \frac{15 - 11}{(2.675)\sqrt{\frac{1}{17} + \frac{1}{13}}} = 4.06$$

Reject null hypothesis. There is evidence to indicate a significant difference.

6.
$$s_p = \sqrt{\frac{(14-1)(2.26)^2 + (15-1)(3.88)^2}{14+15-2}} \approx 3.204$$

$$t = \frac{18.3 - 24.6}{(3.204)\sqrt{\frac{1}{14} + \frac{1}{15}}} = -5.29$$

Reject null hypothesis. There is evidence to indicate a significant difference.

7.
$$s_p = \sqrt{\frac{(12-1)(1.22)^2 + (14-1)(0.86)^2}{12+14-2}} \approx 1.041$$

$$t = \frac{8 - 6}{(1.041)\sqrt{\frac{1}{12} + \frac{1}{14}}} = 4.88$$

Reject null hypothesis. There is evidence to indicate a significant difference.

8.
$$s_p = \sqrt{\frac{(10-1)(5.63)^2 + (7-1)(4.69)^2}{10+7-2}} \approx 5.274$$

$$t = \frac{41 - 28}{(5.274)\sqrt{\frac{1}{10} + \frac{1}{7}}} = 5.00$$

Reject null hypothesis. There is evidence to indicate a significant difference.

9.
$$s_p = \sqrt{\frac{(13-1)(0.23)^2 + (10-1)(0.12)^2}{13+10-2}} \approx 0.191$$

$$t = \frac{0.997 - 1.013}{(0.191)\sqrt{\frac{1}{13} + \frac{1}{10}}} = -0.199$$

Do not reject null hypothesis. There is not enough evidence to indicate a significant difference.

10. a)

Company A	Company B
$\overline{x} = 12{,}631$	$\overline{x} = 11{,}608$
$s = 1222$	$s = 1973$
$n = 8$	$n = 16$

b)

$$s_p = \sqrt{\frac{(8-1)(1222)^2 + (16-1)(1973)^2}{8 + 16 - 2}} \approx 1768.974$$

$$t = \frac{12{,}631 - 11{,}608}{(1768.974)\sqrt{\frac{1}{8} + \frac{1}{16}}} = 1.34$$

Do not reject null hypothesis. There is not enough evidence to indicate a significant difference.

c) Management can purchase the machines from either company.

1. $\hat{p} = \dfrac{45}{83} = 0.54$

$$z = \frac{0.54 - 0.68}{\sqrt{\dfrac{0.68(1 - 0.68)}{83}}}$$

$$= -2.73$$

Reject null hypothesis. Do not accept manufacturer's claim.

2. $\hat{p} = \dfrac{40}{65} = 0.61538$

$$z = \frac{0.61538 - 0.70}{\sqrt{\dfrac{0.70(1 - 0.70)}{65}}}$$

$$= -1.488$$

Do not reject null hypothesis and the claim.

3. $\hat{p} = \dfrac{44}{90} = 0.4889$

        $z = \dfrac{0.4889 - 0.40}{\sqrt{\dfrac{0.40(1 - 0.40)}{90}}}$

        $= 1.72$

        Do not reject null hypothesis and environmentalist's claim.

4. $\hat{p} = \dfrac{31}{68} = 0.45588$

        $z = \dfrac{0.45588 - 0.23}{\sqrt{\dfrac{0.23(1 - 0.23)}{68}}}$

        $= 4.43$

        Reject null hypothesis. Do not accept Census Bureau's claim.

5. $\hat{p} = \dfrac{33}{84} = 0.392857$

        $z = \dfrac{0.392857 - 0.38}{\sqrt{\dfrac{0.38(1 - 0.38)}{84}}}$

        $= 0.24$

        Do not reject null hypothesis. We cannot reject university's claim.

6. $\hat{p} = \dfrac{35}{90} = 0.38889$

        $z = \dfrac{0.38889 - 0.44}{\sqrt{\dfrac{0.44(1 - 0.44)}{90}}}$

        $= -0.98$

        Do not reject null hypothesis. We cannot reject political scientist's claim.

7. $\hat{p} = \dfrac{42}{48} = 0.875$

        $z = \dfrac{0.875 - 0.90}{\sqrt{\dfrac{0.90(1 - 0.90)}{48}}}$

        $= -0.58$

        Do not reject null hypothesis. We cannot reject dermatologist's claim.

8.　　$\hat{p} = \dfrac{95}{400} = 0.2375$

　　　$z = \dfrac{0.2375 - 0.22}{\sqrt{\dfrac{0.22(1 - 0.22)}{400}}}$

　　　$= 0.84$

Do not reject null hypothesis. We cannot reject Motor Vehicle Bureau's claim.

9.　　$\hat{p} = \dfrac{11}{40} = 0.275$

　　　$z = \dfrac{0.275 - 0.20}{\sqrt{\dfrac{0.20(1 - 0.20)}{40}}}$

　　　$= 1.19$

Do not reject null hypothesis. We cannot reject the housing manager's claim.

10.　　$\hat{p} = \dfrac{28}{39} = 0.7179$

　　　$z = \dfrac{0.7179 - 0.65}{\sqrt{\dfrac{0.65(1 - 0.65)}{39}}}$

　　　$= 0.89$

Do not reject null hypothesis. We cannot reject the driving school's claim.

11.　　$\hat{p} = \dfrac{380}{4823} = 0.0788$

　　　$z = \dfrac{0.0788 - 0.08}{\sqrt{\dfrac{0.08(1 - 0.08)}{4823}}}$

　　　$= -0.31$

Do not reject null hypothesis. Do not reject the travel agency's claim.

1. No. When the null hypothesis is rejected, either a type I error is made or a correct decision is made. When the null hypothesis is not rejected, either a type II error or a correct decision is made. Since it is not possible to simultaneously reject and accept the null hypothesis, it is not possible to make both errors at the same time.

2. **a)** Not for any reasonable level of significance ($\alpha < 0.50$). The rejection region for such a level involves positive values of the test statistic; the given sample mean and hypothesized value for the mean yield a negative value for the test statistic. Therefore, the null hypothesis would not be rejected.

   b) Possibly a Type-II error if H_o is false.

3. If both sample sizes n_1 and n_2 are equal call them both n. Then

   $$s_p = \sqrt{\frac{(n-1)s_1^2 + (n-1)s_2^2}{n+n-2}}$$

   $$= \sqrt{\frac{(n-1)(s_1^2 + s_2^2)}{2n-2}}$$

   $$= \sqrt{\frac{(n-1)(s_1^2 + s_2^2)}{2(n-1)}}$$

   $$= \sqrt{\frac{s_1^2 + s_2^2}{2}}$$

   Thus s_p^2 is just the mean of s_1^2 and s_2^2

4. p(Type II error) could be 1.

ANSWERS TO THINKING CRITICALLY - (PAGES 524 - 525)

1. $s_p = \sqrt{\dfrac{(12-1)(2.1)^2 + (14-1)(1.98)^2}{12+14-2}} \approx 2.03588$

    The endpoints of the confidence interval for $\mu_1 - \mu_2$ are

    $(\overline{x}_1 - \overline{x}_2) \pm t_{\frac{\alpha}{2}} \cdot s_p \sqrt{\dfrac{1}{n} + \dfrac{1}{n_2}}$ 　　 $df = n_1 + n_2 - 2$

    　　　　　　　　　　　　　　　　$= 12 + 14 - 2 = 24$

    Lower boundary $= (15 - 11) - (1.711)(2.0359)\sqrt{\dfrac{1}{12} + \dfrac{1}{14}}$

    　　　　　　$= 2.63$

    Upper boundary $= (15 - 11) + (1.711)(2.0359)\sqrt{\dfrac{1}{12} + \dfrac{1}{14}}$

    　　　　　　$= 5.37$

    90% confidence interval: Between 2.63 cents and 5.37 cents.

2. **a)**

    Jonathan Williams Houses　　　　**Martin Luther King Houses**

    Mean $= \overline{x} = 15{,}691$ 　　　　 Mean $= \overline{x} = 15{,}025$
    Standard deviation $= s = 1631$ 　　 Standard deviation $= s = 1910$
    $n = 10$ 　　　　　　　　　　　 $n = 12$

    b) 　　 $s_p = \sqrt{\dfrac{(10-1)(1631)^2 + (12-1)(1910)^2}{10+12-2}} \approx 1789.84$

    The endpoints of the confidence interval for $\mu_1 - \mu_2$ are

    $(\overline{x}_1 - \overline{x}_2) \pm t_{\frac{\alpha}{2}} \cdot s_p \sqrt{\dfrac{1}{n_1} + \dfrac{1}{n_2}}$ 　　 $df = n_1 + n_2 - 2$

    　　　　　　　　　　　　　　　　$= 10 + 12 - 2 = 20$

    Lower Boundary $= (15{,}691 - 15{,}025)$

    　　　　$- (2.086)(1789.84)\sqrt{\dfrac{1}{10} + \dfrac{1}{12}} = -932.63$

    Upper Boundary $= (15{,}691 - 15{,}025)$

    　　　　$+ (2.086)(1789.84)\sqrt{\dfrac{1}{10} + \dfrac{1}{12}} = 2264.63$

    95% confidence interval: Between $-932.63 and $2264.63

2. (Continued)

c) $t = \dfrac{15{,}691 - 15{,}025}{1789.84\sqrt{\dfrac{1}{10} + \dfrac{1}{12}}} = 0.869$

Do not reject null hypothesis. The mean family incomes are not significantly different.

ANSWERS TO REVIEW EXERCISES FOR CHAPTER 10 - (PAGES 525 - 527)

1. $z = \dfrac{21.4 - 19.2}{\sqrt{\dfrac{(4.9)^2}{45} + \dfrac{(6.9)^2}{45}}}$

$= 1.74$

Do not reject null hypothesis. There is not enough evidence to suggest that the difference is significant.

2. $z = \dfrac{16{,}400 - 18{,}000}{1600/\sqrt{200}}$

$= -14.14$

Reject null hypothesis. Do not accept company's claim.

3. $z = \dfrac{7.9 - 7}{3.02/\sqrt{64}} = 2.38$

Reject null hypothesis. Do not accept company's claim.

4. $\hat{p} = \dfrac{34}{90} = 0.3778$

$z = \dfrac{0.3778 - 0.25}{0.0456} = 2.80$

$\sigma_{\hat{p}} = \sqrt{\dfrac{(0.25)(1 - 0.25)}{90}}$

$= 0.0456$

Reject null hypothesis. Do not accept the 25% estimate.

5. $z = \dfrac{67.88 - 63.98}{\sqrt{\dfrac{(8.49)^2}{180} + \dfrac{(9.88)^2}{160}}}$

$= 3.88$

Reject null hypothesis. The difference is significant.

6. $\hat{p} = \dfrac{81}{132} = 0.6136$

$z = \dfrac{0.6136 - 0.58}{0.04296} = 0.782$

$\sigma_{\hat{p}} = \sqrt{\dfrac{(0.58)(1 - 0.58)}{132}}$

$= 0.04296$

Do not reject null hypothesis. Do not reject fire department claim.

7. $z = \dfrac{7.1 - 6.3}{\sqrt{\dfrac{(3.8)^2}{100} + \dfrac{(3.2)^2}{100}}}$

$= 1.61$

Do not reject null hypothesis. Do not reject farmer's claim.

8. $z = \dfrac{6.8 - 7.9}{\sqrt{\dfrac{(0.98)^2}{50} + \dfrac{(1.3)^2}{49}}}$

$= -4.75$

Reject null hypothesis. The difference is significant.

9. $\hat{p} = \dfrac{11}{88} = 0.125$

$z = \dfrac{0.125 - 0.11}{0.033} = 0.45$

$\sigma_{\hat{p}} = \sqrt{\dfrac{(0.11)(1 - 0.11)}{88}}$

$= 0.033$

Do not reject null hypothesis. Do not reject inspector's claim.

10. $t = \dfrac{12 - 19}{5/\sqrt{20}} = -6.26$

Reject null hypothesis. Service has improved.

11. $\hat{p} = \dfrac{58}{72} = 0.8056$

$z = \dfrac{0.8056 - 0.70}{0.054006} = 1.95$

$\sigma_{\hat{p}} = \sqrt{\dfrac{(0.70)(1 - 0.70)}{72}}$

$= 0.054006$

Do not reject null hypothesis. Do not reject teacher's claim.

12. $z = \dfrac{6.70 - 6.85}{0.56/\sqrt{85}} = -2.47$

Reject null hypothesis. Bank is paying below average hourly rate.

13. $z = \dfrac{21.3 - 19.1}{\sqrt{\dfrac{(2.6)^2}{38} + \dfrac{(1.9)^2}{45}}}$

$= 4.33$

Reject null hypothesis. The sociologist's claim seems to be accurate.

14. $\hat{p} = \dfrac{38}{80} = 0.475$

$z = \dfrac{0.475 - 0.45}{0.0556} = 0.45$

$\sigma_{\hat{p}} = \sqrt{\dfrac{(0.45)(1 - 0.45)}{80}}$

$= 0.0556$

Do not reject null hypothesis. Do not reject Red Cross claim.

15. $z = \dfrac{66 - 60}{6/\sqrt{43}} = 6.56$

Reject null hypothesis. Reject court official's claim.

16. $\hat{p} = \dfrac{18}{98} = 0.1837$

$z = \dfrac{0.1837 - 0.10}{0.0303} = 2.76$

$\sigma_{\hat{p}} = \sqrt{\dfrac{(0.10)(1 - 0.10)}{98}}$

$= 0.0303$

Reject null hypothesis. Reject Chamber of Commerce claim.

17. $z = \dfrac{38 - 33}{\sqrt{\dfrac{(7.9)^2}{40} + \dfrac{(4.8)^2}{50}}}$

$= 3.52$

Reject null hypothesis. The difference is significant.

1. $\hat{p} = \dfrac{33}{93} = 0.3548$

    $z = \dfrac{0.3548 - 0.40}{0.0508} = -0.89$

    $\sigma_{\hat{p}} = \sqrt{\dfrac{(0.40)(1 - 0.40)}{93}}$

    $= 0.0508$

    Do not reject null hypothesis. We cannot reject sociologist's claim.

2. $\hat{p} = \dfrac{10}{85} = 0.1176$

    $z = \dfrac{0.1176 - 0.07}{0.02767} = 1.72$

    $\sigma_{\hat{p}} = \sqrt{\dfrac{(0.07)(1 - 0.07)}{85}}$

    $= 0.02767$

    Reject null hypothesis. Decision is a correct one.

3. $z = \dfrac{119 - 124}{\sqrt{\dfrac{14^2}{65} + \dfrac{19^2}{48}}} = -1.54$

    Do not reject null hypothesis. We cannot say that there is a significant difference.

4. $z = \dfrac{22 - 27}{\sqrt{\dfrac{(2.8)^2}{47} + \dfrac{(7.8)^2}{34}}}$

    $= -3.57$

    Reject null hypothesis. Difference between weight loss is significant.

5. If the coin is fair, the expected number of heads is

    $8\left(\dfrac{1}{2}\right) = 4$ and standard deviation s $= \sqrt{8\left(\dfrac{1}{2}\right)\left(\dfrac{1}{2}\right)} = 1.414$

    $t = \dfrac{1 - 4}{1.414} = -2.12$

    Do not reject null hypothesis. Coin does appear to be fair. Actually more tosses are needed before arriving at this conclusion.

6. Choice (b)

7. $t = \dfrac{10.7 - 14}{1.83/\sqrt{20}} = -8.06$

Reject null hypothesis. Reject manufacturer's claim.

8. $z = \dfrac{9 - 10}{\sqrt{\dfrac{(1.2)^2}{40} + \dfrac{(0.91)^2}{36}}}$

$= -4.12$

Reject null hypothesis. Difference is significant.

9. $\hat{p} = \dfrac{77}{123} = 0.626$

$z = \dfrac{0.626 - 0.68}{0.042} = -1.29$

$\sigma_{\hat{p}} = \sqrt{\dfrac{(0.68)(1 - 0.68)}{123}}$

$= 0.042$

Do not reject null hypothesis. Do not reject representative's claim.

10. $\hat{p} = \dfrac{164}{311} = 0.5273$

$z = \dfrac{0.5273 - 0.65}{0.027} = -4.54$

$\sigma_{\hat{p}} = \sqrt{\dfrac{(0.65)(1 - 0.65)}{311}}$

$= 0.027$

Reject null hypothesis. Reject claim.

11. $z = \dfrac{66 - 75}{5.8/\sqrt{40}} = -9.8$

Reject null hypothesis. Viewing the film reduces connection time significantly.

12. $t = \dfrac{8.25 - 7.00}{0.96/\sqrt{15}} = 5.04$

Reject null hypothesis. Reject banking official's claim.

300

13. <u>Group Exposed to Grow Lite</u>   <u>Group Not Exposed to Grow Lite</u>

$\overline{x} = 16.857$ $\overline{x} = 15.571$

$s = 2.4103$ $s = 2.0702$

$n = 7$ $n = 7$

$$s_p = \sqrt{\frac{(7-1)(2.4103)^2 + (7-1)(2.07)^2}{7+7-2}} \approx 2.247$$

$$t = \frac{16.857 - 15.571}{(2.247)\sqrt{\frac{1}{7} + \frac{1}{7}}} = 1.07$$

Do not reject null hypothesis. There is not enough evidence to indicate a significant difference.

14. <u>Poorer Neighborhoods</u>   <u>Middle-Class Neighborhoods</u>

$\overline{x} = 62.88$ cents $\overline{x} = 60.667$ cents

$s = 3.18$ cents $s = 2.121$ cents

$n = 8$ $n = 9$

$$s_p = \sqrt{\frac{(8-1)(3.18)^2 + (9-1)(2.121)^2}{8+9-2}} \approx 2.668$$

$$t = \frac{62.88 - 60.667}{(2.668)\sqrt{\frac{1}{8} + \frac{1}{9}}} = 1.707$$

Do not reject null hypothesis. There is not enough evidence to indicate a significant difference.

15. Choice (a)

16. Choice (a)

17. Choice (b)

18. Choice (b)

19. Choice (a)

CHAPTER 10 - HYPOTHESIS TESTING
SUPPLEMENTARY TEST FORM A

1. The average weekly salary of a technician in a certain city is $495 with a standard deviation of $47. One large company, which employs 86 technicians, pays its technicians an average weekly salary of $475. Can this company be accused of paying lower wages than the average rate? (Use a 5% level of significance.)

Answer _____

2. From past experience, the traffic department of a certain city has found that the yellow traffic lane markings on the highways remain visible for an average of 185 days with a standard deviation of 12.8 days. This year, highway markings at 46 different locations remained visible for an average of 182 days. Does this indicate that we should reject the traffic department's past average of 185 days? (Use 5% level of significance.)

Answer _____

3. Educators believe that the average time needed to complete a certain reading test by youngsters is 78 minutes. Eight students have received some special tutoring for the exam. Their average time needed to complete the exam (after the tutoring) is found to be 71 minutes with a standard deviation of 6.86 minutes. Using a 1% level of significance, does the tutoring significantly affect the average time needed to complete the reading test?

Answer _____

4. The average weight of a deer in a certain national park is 125 pounds with a standard deviation of 6.8 pounds. A game warden caught 10 dear in the park and determined that their average weight was 130 pounds. At the 5% level of significance, can we reject the game warden's claim that the average weight of a deer in the park is 125 pounds?

Answer _____

5. Two workers are being compared. One worker needed an average of 25 days to complete 80 units of threading. The standard deviation was 2.7 days. A second worker needed 36 days to complete 111 units of threading. The standard deviation was 3.9 days. At the 5% level of significance, is the difference between the average completion time by the two workers significant?

Answer _____

6. A random survey of 50 patients in the emergency room at Harden Hospital indicated that they waited an average of 33 minutes before receiving medical attention. The standard deviation was 3.76 minutes. A similar survey of 45 patients at Lincoln Hospital indicated that they waited an average of 39 minutes before receiving medical attention. The standard deviation was 5.34 minutes. Is the difference between the average waiting time in the emergency rooms at these two hospitals significant? (Use a 5% level of significance.)

Answer _____

7. A college has two campuses at which students can register for next semester's courses. Eight randomly selected students at campus I needed an average of 84 minutes to complete the registration process. The standard deviation was 5.83 minutes. Eleven randomly selected students at campus II needed an average of 78 minutes to complete the registration process. The standard deviation was 6.93 minutes. Using a 5% level of significance, is there any significant difference between the average amount of time needed by students to complete the registration process at both campuses?

Answer _____

8. A mayor claims that 88% of all people in the city are in favor of increasing real estate taxes so as to balance the budget. In a random survey of 70 people in the city, it was found that 50 of them were in favor of increasing the real estate taxes. At the 5% level of significance, should we reject the mayor's claim?

Answer _____

9. An agricultural chemist claims to have developed a new pesticide that is 85% effective in eliminating a certain insect. To test this claim, 58 randomly selected parcels of land are sprayed with this chemical and the chemical successfully eliminates the insect from only 38 of the parcels. At the 5% level of significance, should we reject the chemist's claim?

Answer _____

10. The twelve workers in the production department of a publishing company spend an average of 18 minutes on their morning coffee break. The standard deviation is 2.37 minutes. The eleven workers in the advertising department of the company spend an average of 19.7 minutes on their coffee break. The standard deviation is 1.88 minutes. Is it true that the average number of minutes spent by the workers in the advertising department is significantly more than the average number of minutes spent by the workers in the production department? (Use a 5% level of significance.)

303

Answer _____

CHAPTER 10 – HYPOTHESIS TESTING
SUPPLEMENTARY TEST FORM B

1. The average daily room charge for a semi-private hospital room in a certain state during 1985 was $227. The standard deviation was $13. In the same year, a random sample of nine hospitals in a city within the state showed an average charge of $232. At the 5% level of significance, can we conclude that the average daily charge at these hospitals significantly exceeds the state average?

    Answer _____

2. The average age of a prisoner in a state's jail is 28.76 years with a standard deviation of 2.17 years. One jail in the state has a prisoner average age of 26.89 years for its 117 inmates. At the 5% level of significance, can we conclude that the average age of the prisoners at this jail is significantly lower than the average age of the prisoners at all of the state's jails?

    Answer _____

3. Research indicates that the average life of a transmission on a city police car is 34,000 miles. Eight police cars have a special mechanism added to the transmission. It is found that the average life of the transmission of 8 police cars is 36,000 miles with a standard deviation of 2200 miles. Using a 1% level of significance, does this special mechanism significantly affect the average life of a transmission in a police car?

    Answer _____

4. Police department officials claim that the average height of a police officer in Buscane is 69 inches with a standard deviation of 1.89 inches. A newspaper reporter randomly selected 10 police officers in Buscane and found that their average height was 67.1 inches. At the 1% level of significance, can we conclude that the average height of a police officer in Buscane is significantly less than 69 inches.

    Answer _____

5. Two groups of children are being compared. Group I, which consisted of 40 children, required an average of 57 minutes to complete a task. The standard deviation was 4.62 minutes. Group II, which consisted of 55 children, required an average of 53 minutes to complete the task. The standard deviation was 5.13 minutes. At the 5% level of significance, is the

difference between the average time for both groups significant?

Answer _____

6. A group of 40 baseball fans consumed an average of 96 cans of beer at a baseball game. The standard deviation was 7.1 cans. A second group of 75 baseball fans consumed an average of 111 cans of beer at the same game. The standard deviation was 9.12 cans. Is the difference between the average number of cans of beer consumed by these two groups significant? (Use a 5% level of significance.)

Answer _____

7. Seven lakes in a state had an average of 58 units of coliform bacteria. The standard deviation was 4.69 units. Nine lakes in an adjoining state had an average of 63 units of coliform bacteria. The standard deviation was 6.13 units. Using a 5% level of significance, is there any significant difference between the average amount of coliform bacteria in both states?

Answer _____

8. The nine dolphins in a particular park needed an average of 28 practice days before mastering a dangerous act. The standard deviation was 3.76 days. The twelve dolphins in a different park needed an average of 32 practice days before mastering the same act. The standard deviation was 5.38 days. Is it true that the average number of practice days required by the dolphins in the first park is significantly less than the average number of days required by the dolphins in the second park? (Use a 5% level of significance.)

Answer _____

9. A researcher claims that 88% of all the residents of a city are opposed to any further tax abatements. A random survey of 80 residents of this city disclosed that 69 of them were opposed to any further tax abatements. Should we reject the researcher's claim? (Use a 5% level of significance.)

Answer _____

10. A researcher claims that as a result of many anti-smoking campaigns, only about 53% of the staff at a school still smokes. To test this, a random survey of 168 staff members at this school is taken. It is found that only 70 of them still smoke. At the 5% level of significance, should we reject the researcher's claim?

Answer _____

1. An official of a particular company claims that the typical company employee retires after an average of 21.7 years on the job. The standard deviation is 3.14 years. A survey of 49 randomly selected company retirees indicates that these employees retired after 24.7 years of service. Should we reject the company official's claim? (Use a 5% level of significance.)

    Answer _____

2. A manufacturer of a certain foreign car sold in the United States claims that it will average 34 miles per gallon of gas (highway driving). To test this claim, a consumer's group randomly selects 40 of these cars and drives them under normal driving conditions (highway driving). These cars average 29.7 miles per gallon with a standard deviation of 3.79. Should we reject the manufacturer's claim? (Use a 5% level of significance.)

    Answer _____

3. A bank official claims that the average new home mortgage loan is for $90,000. A survey of 10 randomly selected new home mortgage loans disclosed an average of $94,000 with a standard deviation of $6500. Using a 5% level of significance, should we reject the bank official's claim?

    Answer _____

4. According to the manufacturer, the average length of a ruler produced by a certain company is 12.01 inches. The average length of 11 randomly selected rulers produced by this company was 11.96 inches with a standard deviation of 0.41 inches. At the 5% level of significance, should we reject the manufacturer's claim?

    Answer _____

5. The average annual salary of 50 statistical typists in one city during 1987 was $19,000 with a standard deviation of $548. The average annual salary of 40 statistical typists in another city during 1987 was $18,600 with a standard deviation of $622. At the 5% level of significance, is the difference between the average annual salaries of both groups of statistical typists significant?

    Answer _____

6. Fifty-five traffic lights painted with Brand A rust inhibitor paint lasted an average of 7.1 years before repainting was necessary. The standard deviation was 1.48 years. Sixty-five traffic lights painted with Brand B rust inhibitor paint lasted an average of 6.8 years before repainting was necessary. The standard deviation was 1.96 years. At the 5% level of significance, is the difference between the average lasting time of these 2 brands of rust inhibitor paints statistically significant?

Answer _____

7. Seven randomly selected assistant professors at Sierra University had an average annual salary of $34,500 during 1987. The standard deviation was $689. Ten randomly selected assistant professors at Gorg College had an annual salary of $36,100. The standard deviation was $941. Using 5% level of significance, is the difference between the average annual salaries of the assistant professors at these 2 schools significant?

Answer _____

8. A consumer's group purchased the same dose of a particular prescription drug at 10 different pharmacies in Baltimore and 12 different pharmacies in Chicago. The following results were obtained:

	Baltimore Pharmacies	Chicago Pharmacies
Average price	$5.43	$5.86
Standard deviation	0.39	0.62

Is it true that the average price charged by pharmacies in Baltimore is significantly less than the average price charged by pharmacies in Chicago? (Use a 5% level of significance.)

Answer _____

9. A fast-food store owner claims that 90% of her customers order a soft drink when ordering french-fried potatoes. In a random survey of 80 customers ordering french-fried potatoes, it was found that 68 of them ordered a soft drink also. At the 5% level of significance should we reject the store owner's claim.

Answer _____

10. A politicians claims that 70% of all voters in her district are in favor of building the proposed super highway through the city. If a random survey of 300 voters shows that 200 of them are in favor of the proposed new super highway, should we reject the politician's claim? (Use a 5% level of

307

significance.)

Answer _____

ANSWER TO SUPPLEMENTARY TESTS
CHAPTER 10 - HYPOTHESIS TESTING

Form A	Form B	Form C
1. Yes	1. No	1. Yes
2. No	2. Yes	2. Yes
3. No	3. No	3. No
4. Yes	4. Yes	4. No
5. Yes	5. Yes	5. Yes
6. Yes	6. Yes	6. No
7. No	7. No	7. Yes
8. Yes	8. Yes	8. Yes
9. Yes	9. No	9. No
10. Yes	10. Yes	10. No

SECTION 11.3 - (PAGES 545 - 549)

1. **a)** Positive correlation
    b) Probably zero correlation. Some people may disagree.
    c) Positive correlation
    d) Negative correlation
    e) Negative correlation
    f) Zero correlation
    g) Probably zero correlation
    h) Positive correlation
    i) Positive correlation

2.

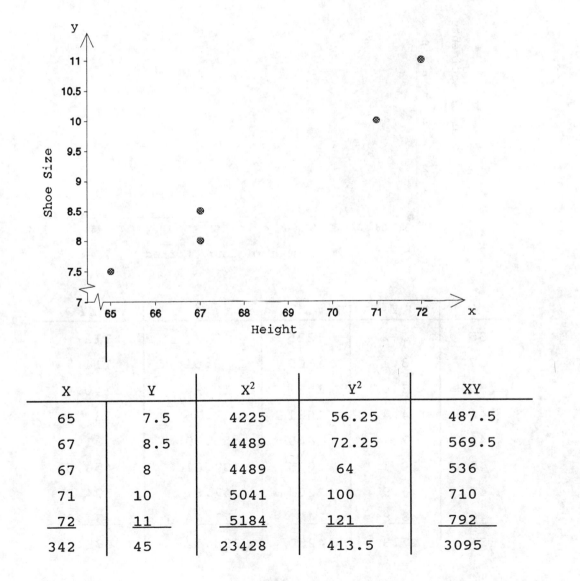

X	Y	X^2	Y^2	XY
65	7.5	4225	56.25	487.5
67	8.5	4489	72.25	569.5
67	8	4489	64	536
71	10	5041	100	710
72	11	5184	121	792
342	45	23428	413.5	3095

309

2. (Continued)

$$r = \frac{5(3095) - (342)(45)}{\sqrt{5(23428) - 342^2}\ \sqrt{5(413.5) - 45^2}}$$

$$= \frac{85}{\sqrt{176}\ \sqrt{42.5}} = 0.9828$$

3. a)

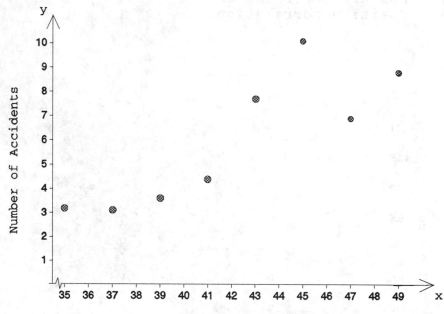

Number of Hours Worked

X	Y	X²	Y²	XY
35	3.2	1225	10.24	112
37	3.1	1369	9.61	114.7
39	3.6	1521	12.96	140.4
41	4.4	1681	19.36	180.4
43	7.7	1849	59.29	331.1
45	10.1	2025	102.01	454.5
47	6.9	2209	47.61	324.3
49	8.8	2401	77.44	431.2
336	47.8	14280	338.52	2088.6

310

3. (Continued)

$$r = \frac{8(2088) - (336)(47.8)}{\sqrt{8(14280) - 336^2} \ \sqrt{8(338.52) - (47.8)^2}}$$

$$= \frac{648}{\sqrt{1344} \ \sqrt{423.32}} = 0.8591$$

b) Yes

4.

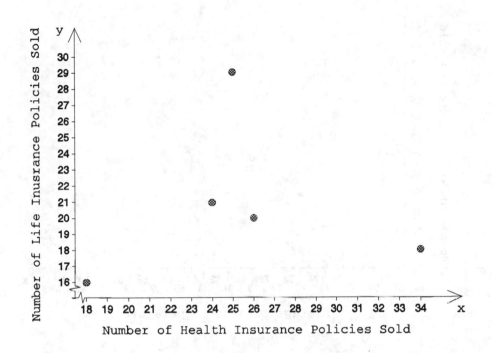

Number of Health Insurance Policies Sold

X	Y	X^2	Y^2	XY
26	20	676	400	520
34	18	1156	324	612
25	29	625	841	725
18	16	324	256	288
24	21	576	441	504
127	104	3357	2262	2649

311

4. (Continued)

$$r = \frac{5(2649) - (127)(104)}{\sqrt{5(3357) - 127^2}\ \sqrt{5(2262) - 104^2}}$$

$$= \frac{37}{\sqrt{656}\ \sqrt{494}} = 0.0650$$

5. a)

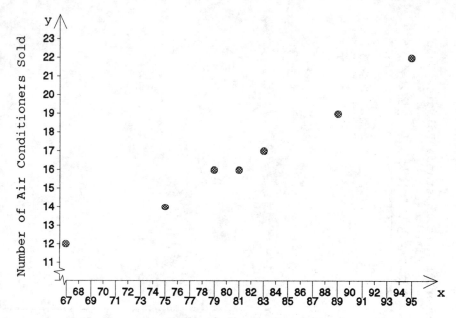

Average Outside Temperature

X	Y	X²	Y²	XY
75	14	5625	196	1050
83	17	6889	289	1411
67	12	4489	144	804
89	19	7921	361	1691
95	22	9025	484	2090
79	16	6241	256	1264
81	16	6561	256	1296
569	116	46751	1986	9606

312

5. (Continued)

$$r = \frac{7(9606) - (569)(116)}{\sqrt{7(46751) - 569^2} \ \sqrt{7(1986) - 116^2}}$$

$$= \frac{1238}{\sqrt{3496} \ \sqrt{446}} = 0.9914$$

b)   Yes

6. **a)**

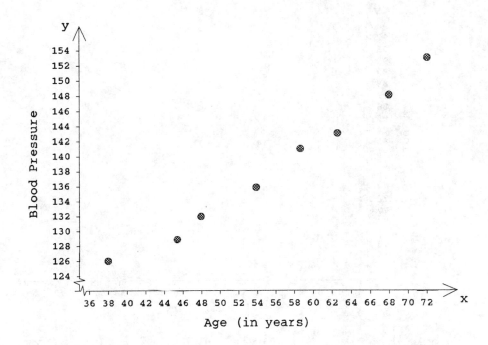

Age (in years)

X	Y	X²	Y²	XY
38	126	1444	15876	4788
45	129	2025	16641	5805
48	132	2304	17424	6336
54	136	2916	18496	7344
59	141	3481	19881	8319
63	143	3969	20449	9009
68	148	4624	21904	10064
72	153	5184	23409	11016
447	1108	25947	154080	62681

6. (Continued)

$$r = \frac{8(62681) - (447)(1108)}{\sqrt{8(25947) - 447^2}\ \sqrt{8(154080) - 1108^2}}$$

$$= \frac{6172}{\sqrt{7767}\ \sqrt{4976}} = 0.9928$$

b) Yes

7. a)

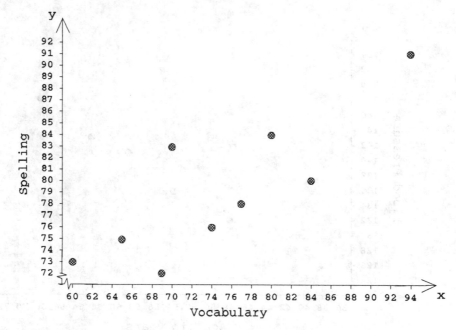

X	Y	X²	Y²	XY
77	78	5929	6084	6006
94	91	8836	8281	8554
65	75	4225	5625	4875
84	80	7056	6400	6720
69	72	4761	5184	4968
60	73	3600	5329	4380
74	76	5476	5776	5624
70	83	4900	6889	5810
80	84	6400	7056	6720
673	712	51183	56624	53657

314

7. (Continued)

$$r = \frac{9(53657) - (673)(712)}{\sqrt{9(51183) - 673^2}\ \sqrt{9(56624) - 712^2}}$$

$$= \frac{3737}{\sqrt{7718}\ \sqrt{2672}} = 0.8229$$

b) Most likely

8. **a)**

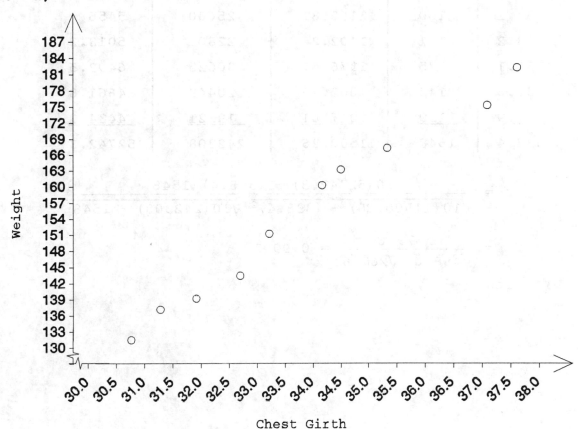

8. (Continued)

X	Y	X^2	Y^2	XY
37.6	182	1413.76	33124	6843.2
34.5	163	1190.25	26569	5623.5
35.3	167	1246.09	27889	5895.1
30.8	131	948.64	17161	4034.8
31.3	137	979.69	18769	4288.1
34.1	160	1162.81	25600	5456
33.2	151	1102.24	22801	5013.2
37.1	175	1376.41	30625	6492.5
32.6	143	1062.76	20449	4661.8
31.9	139	1017.61	19321	4434.1
338.4	1548	11500.26	242308	52742.3

$$r = \frac{10(52742.3) - (338.4)(1548)}{\sqrt{10(11500.26) - (338.4)^2}\ \sqrt{10(242308) - 1548^2}}$$

$$= \frac{3579.8}{\sqrt{488.04}\ \sqrt{26776}} = 0.9903$$

b) Yes

316

9.

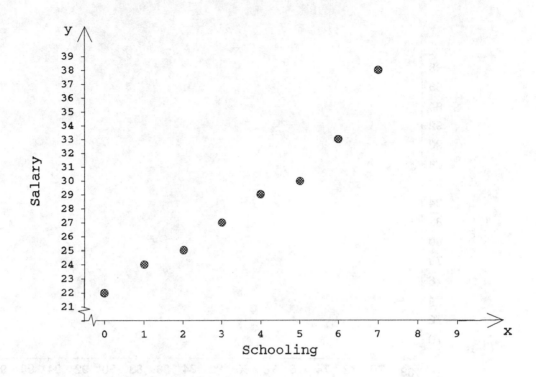

X	Y	X^2	Y^2	XY
2	25	4	625	50
3	27	9	729	81
5	30	25	900	150
1	24	1	576	24
0	22	0	484	0
7	38	49	1444	266
6	33	36	1089	198
4	29	16	841	116
28	228	140	6688	885

$$r = \frac{8(885) - (28)(228)}{\sqrt{8(140) - 28^2} \; \sqrt{8(6688) - 228^2}}$$

$$= \frac{696}{\sqrt{336} \; \sqrt{1520}} = 0.9739$$

b) Yes

10.

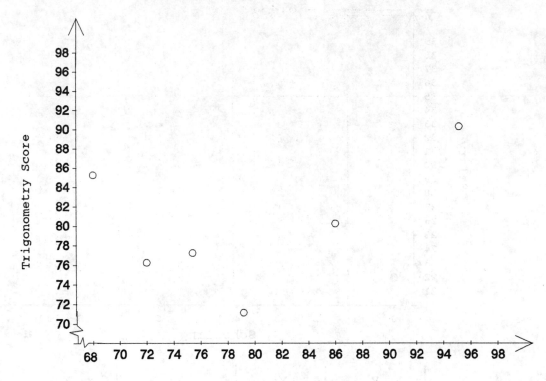

Algebra Score

X	Y	X^2	Y^2	XY
86	80	7396	6400	6880
79	71	6241	5041	5609
68	85	4624	7225	5780
95	90	9025	8100	8550
72	76	5184	5776	5472
75	77	5625	5929	5775
475	479	38095	38471	38066

$$r = \frac{6(38066) - (475)(479)}{\sqrt{6(38095) - 475^2} \ \sqrt{6(38471) - 479^2}}$$

318

10. (Continued)

$$= \frac{871}{\sqrt{2945}\ \sqrt{1385}} = 0.4313$$

11. a)

X	Y	X²	Y²	XY
182	90	33124	8100	16380
169	81	28561	6561	13689
171	84	29241	7056	14364
193	92	37249	8464	17756
185	88	34225	7744	16280
152	79	23104	6241	12008
141	78	19881	6084	10998
199	90	39601	8100	17910
220	97	48400	9409	21340
1612	779	293386	67759	140725

$$r = \frac{9(140725) - (1612)(779)}{\sqrt{9(293386) - 1612^2}\ \sqrt{9(67759) - 779^2}}$$

$$= \frac{10777}{\sqrt{41930}\ \sqrt{2990}} = 0.9625$$

319

11. (Continued)
    b) Yes

12. **a)**

X	Y	X^2	Y^2	XY
7	56	49	3136	392
9	63	81	3969	567
12	79	144	6241	948
8	60	64	3600	480
6	49	36	2401	294
4	45	16	2025	180
9	51	81	2601	459
11	68	121	4624	748
10	53	100	2809	530
14	85	196	7225	1190
90	609	888	38631	5788

$$r = \frac{10(5788) - (90)(609)}{\sqrt{10(888) - 90^2}\ \sqrt{10(38631) - 609^2}}$$

$$= \frac{3070}{\sqrt{780}\ \sqrt{15429}} = 0.8850$$

b) Yes

EXERCISES FOR SECTION 11.4 – (PAGES 551)

1. Significant

2. Significant

3. Not Significant

4. Significant

5. Significant

6. Significant

7. Significant

8. Significant

9. Not Significant

10. Significant

11. Significant

ANSWERS TO EXERCISES FOR SECTION 11.6 - (PAGES 561 - 566)

1.

X	Y	X^2	XY
63	64	3969	4032
64	66	4096	4224
72	74	5184	5328
73	75	5329	5475
74	74	5476	5476
69	71	4761	4899
66	69	4356	4554
72	75	5184	5400
75	76	5625	5700
64	67	4096	4288
692	711	48076	49376

$$b_1 = \frac{10(49376) - (692)(711)}{10(48076) - (692)^2} = \frac{1748}{1896} = 0.9219$$

$$b_0 = \frac{1}{10} [711 - (0.9219)(692)] = 7.3045$$

a) Least-squares prediction equation: $\hat{y} = 7.3045 + 0.9219x$

b) $\hat{y} = 7.3045 + (0.9219)76 = 77.3689$ inches

2.

X	Y	X^2	XY
0.5	80	0.25	40
1.0	93	1.00	93
1.5	101	2.25	151.5
2.0	112	4.00	224
2.4	118	5.76	283.2
2.9	124	8.41	359.6
3.3	139	10.89	458.7
3.9	145	15.21	565.5
17.5	912	47.77	2175.5

$$b_1 = \frac{8(2175.5) - (17.5)(912)}{8(47.77) - (17.5)^2} = \frac{1444}{75.91} = 19.0225$$

$$b_0 = \frac{1}{8}[912 - (19.0225)(17.5)] = 72.3883$$

a)   Least-squares prediction equation: $\hat{y} = 72.3883 + 19.0225x$

b) $\hat{y} = 72.3883 + (19.0225)(2.2)$
     $= 114.2378$ millions of gallons

3.

X	Y	X^2	XY
46	496	2116	22816
54	499	2916	26946
43	500	1849	21500
59	506	3481	29854
63	513	3969	32319
25	479	625	11975
75	520	5625	39000
51	500	2601	25500
416	4013	23182	209910

3. (Continued)

$$b_1 = \frac{8(209910) - (416)(4013)}{8(23182) - 416^2} = \frac{9872}{12400} = 0.7961$$

$$b_0 = \frac{1}{8} [4013 - (0.7961)(416)] = 460.2278$$

a) Least-squares prediction equation: $\hat{y} = 460.2278 + 0.7961x$

b) $\hat{y} = 460.2278 + (0.7961)(70) = 515.9548$

4.

X	Y	X^2	XY
4	326	16	1304
8	197	64	1576
7	409	49	2863
6	400	36	2400
10	628	100	6280
15	709	225	10635
22	978	484	21516
9	680	81	6120
81	4327	1055	52694

$$b_1 = \frac{8(52694) - (81)(4327)}{8(1055) - 81^2} = \frac{71065}{1879} = 37.8206$$

$$b_0 = \frac{1}{8} [4327 - (37.8206)(81)] = 157.9414$$

a) Least-squares prediction equation:
$\hat{y} = 157.9414 + (37.8206)x$

b) $\hat{y} = 157.9414 + (37.8206)11 = 573.968$ parking tickets

323

5.

X	Y	X^2	XY
62	66	3844	4092
67	67	4489	4489
61	65	3721	3965
64	66	4096	4224
63	67	3969	4221
63	69	3969	4347
65	67	4225	4355
66	68	4356	4488
68	72	4624	4896
71	74	5041	5254
60	62	3600	3720
64	66	4096	4224
774	809	50030	52275

$$b_1 = \frac{12(52275) - (774)(809)}{12(50030) - 774^2} = \frac{1134}{1284} = 0.8832$$

$$b_0 = \frac{1}{12} [809 - (0.8832)(774)] = 10.4503$$

a)   Least-squares prediction equation: $\hat{y} = 10.4503 + 0.8832x$

b) $\hat{y} = 10.4503 + 0.8832(70) = 72.2743$

6.

X	Y	X^2	XY
9	9	81	81
6	7	36	42
4	5	16	20
3	4	9	12
5	5	25	25
7	7	49	49
2	2	4	4
36	39	220	233

6. (Continued)

$$b_1 = \frac{7(233) - (36)(39)}{7(220) - 36^2} = \frac{227}{244} = 0.9303$$

$$b_0 = \frac{1}{7}[39 - (0.9303)36] = 0.787$$

a) Least-squares prediction equation: $\hat{y} = 0.787 + 0.9303x$

b) $\hat{y} = 0.787 + 0.9303(8) = 8.2294$ centimeters

7.

X	Y	X^2	XY
7	115	49	805
4	96	16	384
3	90	9	270
6	109	36	654
2	81	4	162
1	72	1	72
5	100	25	500
9	122	81	1098
37	785	221	3945

$$b_1 = \frac{8(3945) - (37)(785)}{8(221) - 37^2} = \frac{2515}{399} = 6.3033$$

$$b_0 = \frac{1}{8}[785 - (6.3033)37] = 68.9722$$

a) Least-squares prediction equation: $\hat{y} = 68.9722 + 6.3033x$

b) $\hat{y} = 68.9722 + 6.3033(8) = 119.3986$ heartbeats

8.

X	Y	X^2	XY
25	2	625	50
31	8	961	248
38	7	1444	266
23	1	529	23
29	6	841	174
47	9	2209	423
193	33	6609	1184

$$b_1 = \frac{6(1184) - (193)(33)}{6(6609) - 193^2} = \frac{735}{2405} = 0.3056$$

$$b_0 = \frac{1}{6} [33 - (0.3056)(193)] = -4.3301$$

a)   Least-squares prediction: $\hat{y} = -4.3301 + 0.3056x$

b) $\hat{y} = -4.3301 + (0.3056)(33) = 5.7547$

9.

X	Y	X^2	XY
20,000	220	400,000,000	4,400,000
24,000	290	576,000,000	6,960,000
29,000	400	841,000,000	11,600,000
25,000	470	625,000,000	11,750,000
40,000	550	1,600,000,000	22,000,000
50,000	650	2,500,000,000	32,500,000
188,000	2580	6,542,000,000	89,210,000

$$b_1 = \frac{6(89,210,000) - (188,000)(2580)}{6(6,542,000,000) - 188,000^2} = \frac{50,220,000}{3,908,000,000}$$

$$= 0.0128505$$

$$b_0 = \frac{1}{6} [2580 - (0.0128505)(188,000)] = 27.349$$

a)   Least-squares prediction equation: $\hat{y} = 27.349 + 0.01285x$

b) $\hat{y} = 27.349 + 0.01285(33,000) = 451.399$

10.

X (in thousands)	Y	X^2	XY
670	0.290	448,900	194.3
662	0.281	438,244	186.022
698	0.299	487,204	208.702
825	0.302	680,625	249.15
900	0.309	810,000	278.1
1400	0.345	1,960,000	483
800	0.304	640,000	243.2
850	0.306	722,500	260.1
685	0.295	469,225	202.075
1300	0.320	1,690,000	416
8790	3.051	8,346,698	2720.649

$$b_1 = \frac{10(2720.649) - (8790)(3.051)}{10(8346698) - 8790^2} = \frac{388.2}{6202880} = 0.00006$$

$$b_0 = \frac{1}{10} [3.051 - (0.00006)8790] = 0.2524$$

a) Least-squares prediction equation: $\hat{y} = 0.2524 + 0.00006x$

b) $\hat{y} = 0.2524 + 0.00006(175) = 0.2629$

Actually \$175,000 is outside the range of the sampled independent variable and a prediction should not be made for this value

327

11.

X (in thousands)	Y (in thousands)	X^2	XY
100	800	10000	80000
200	1000	40000	200000
500	1300	250000	650000
700	1600	490000	1120000
900	2000	810000	1800000
1100	2400	1210000	2640000
1500	3200	2250000	4800000
5,000	12,300	5,060,000	11,290,000

$$b_1 = \frac{7(11,290,000) - (5000)(12300)}{7(5060000) - 5000^2} = \frac{17530000}{10420000} = 1.6823$$

$$b_0 = \frac{1}{7}[12300 - (1.6823)5000] = 555.5$$

a) Least-squares prediction equation: $\hat{y} = 555.5 + 1.6823x$

b) $\hat{y} = 555.5 + 1.6823(600)$
   $= \$1564.88$ thousands or $\$1,564,800$

ANSWERS TO EXERCISES FOR SECTION 11.7 – (PAGES 572)

1. $\Sigma y^2 = 50721$

$$s_e = \sqrt{\frac{50721 - (7.3045)(711) - (0.9219)49376}{10 - 2}}$$

$$= \sqrt{\frac{7.7611}{8}} \approx 0.9853$$

2. $\Sigma y^2 = 107,440$

$$s_e = \sqrt{\frac{107440 - (72.3883)(912) - (19.0225)(2175.5)}{8 - 2}}$$

$$= \sqrt{6.4036} \approx 2.5305$$

3. $\Sigma y^2 = 2,014,063$

$$s_e = \sqrt{\frac{2014063 - (460.2278)(4013) - (0.7961)(209910)}{8 - 2}}$$

$$= \sqrt{9.9146} \approx 3.1487$$

4. $\Sigma y^2 = 2,788,315$

$$s_e = \sqrt{\frac{2788315 - (157.9414)(4327) - (37.8206)(52694)}{8 - 2}}$$

$$= \sqrt{18663.9776} \approx 136.6162$$

5. $\Sigma y^2 = 54649$

$$s_e = \sqrt{\frac{54649 - (10.4503)(809) - (0.8832)(52275)}{12 - 2}}$$

$$= \sqrt{2.54273} \approx 1.5946$$

6. $\Sigma y^2 = 249$

$$s_e = \sqrt{\frac{249 - (0.787)(39) - (0.9303)(233)}{7 - 2}}$$

$$= \sqrt{0.30942} \approx 0.5563$$

7. $\Sigma y^2 = 79051$

$$s_e = \sqrt{\frac{79051 - (68.9722)(785) - (6.3033)(3945)}{8 - 2}}$$

$$= \sqrt{6.88408} \approx 2.6238$$

8. $\Sigma y^2 = 235$

$$s_e = \sqrt{\frac{235 - (-4.3301)(33) - (0.3056)(1184)}{6 - 2}}$$

$$= \sqrt{4.015725} \approx 2.0039$$

329

9. $\Sigma y^2 = 1,238,400$

$$s_e = \sqrt{\frac{1238400 - (25.8)(2580) - (0.0129)(89,210,000)}{6 - 2}}$$

$$= \sqrt{5256.75} \approx 72.5034$$

10. $\Sigma y^2 = 0.933649$

$$s_e = \sqrt{\frac{0.933649 - (0.2524)(3.051) - (0.00006)(2720.649)}{10 - 2}}$$

$$= \sqrt{0.000042} \approx 0.0065$$

11. $\Sigma y^2 = 25,890,000$

$$s_e = \sqrt{\frac{25890000 - (555.5)(12300) - (1.6823)11290000}{7 - 2}}$$

$$= \sqrt{12836.6} \approx 113.2987$$

ANSWERS TO EXERCISES FOR SECTION 11.8 - (PAGES 578)

1. $$t = \frac{0.9219}{0.9853 \bigg/ \sqrt{48076 - \dfrac{692^2}{10}}} \qquad\qquad t_{0.025} = 2.306$$

$= 12.8835$ Do not accept $H_0 : \beta_1 = 0$

When $x_p = 76$, $\hat{y}_p = 77.3689$

Also $s_e = 0.9853$ and $\bar{x} = \dfrac{692}{10} = 69.2$

Lower boundary

$$= \hat{y}_p - t_{\frac{\alpha}{2}} \cdot s_e \cdot \sqrt{1 + \frac{1}{n} + \frac{n\left(x_p - \bar{x}\right)^2}{n\left(\Sigma x^2\right) - (\Sigma x)^2}}$$

$$= 77.3689 - (2.306)(0.9853) \sqrt{1 + \frac{1}{10} + \frac{10(76 - 69.2)^2}{10(48076) - 692^2}}$$

$$= 77.3689 - (2.306)(0.9853) \sqrt{1 + 0.1 + 0.243882}$$

$$= 77.3689 - (2.306)(0.9853)(1.15926)$$

1.   (Continued)
            $= 77.3689 - 2.633956 = 73.7349$

Upper boundary

$$= \hat{y} + t_{\frac{\alpha}{2}} \cdot s_e \cdot \sqrt{1 + \frac{1}{n} + \frac{n\left(x_p - \bar{x}\right)^2}{n(\Sigma x^2) - (\Sigma x)^2}}$$

$$= 77.3689 + (2.633956)(0.9853) \sqrt{1 + 0.1 + 0.243882}$$
$$= 77.3689 + 2.4093 = 80.0029$$

95% prediction interval: 74.7349 to 80.0029

2. $t = \dfrac{19.0225}{2.5305 \Big/ \sqrt{47.77 - \dfrac{17.5^2}{8}}}$ $t_{0.025} = 2.447$

            $= 23.1561$ Do not accept $H_0 : \beta_1 = 0$

When $x_p = 2.2$, $\hat{Y}_p = 114.2378$

Also $s_e = 2.5305$ and $\bar{x} = \dfrac{17.5}{8} = 2.1875$

Lower boundary

$$= 114.2378 - (2.447)(2.5305)\sqrt{1 + \frac{1}{8} + \frac{8(2.2 - 2.1875)^2}{8(47.77) - 17.5^2}}$$

$$= 114.2378 - (2.447)(2.5305)(1.0607)$$
$$= 114.2378 - 6.5680 = 107.6698$$

Upper boundary

$$= 114.2378 + (2.447)(2.5305)\sqrt{1 + \frac{1}{8} + \frac{8(2.2 - 2.1875)^2}{8(47.77) - 17.5^2}}$$

$$= 114.2378 + (2.447)(2.5305)(1.0607)$$
$$= 114.2378 + 6.5680 = 120.8058$$

95% prediction interval: 107.6698 to 120.8058

3. $t = \dfrac{0.7961}{3.1487 \Big/ \sqrt{23182 - \dfrac{416^2}{8}}}$ $t_{0.025} = 2.306$

   $= 9.9541$ Do not accept H_0 : $\beta_1 = 0$

When $x_p = 70$, $\hat{y}_p = 515.9548$

Also $s_e = 3.1487$ and $\bar{x} = \dfrac{416}{8} = 52$

Lower boundary

   $= 515.9548 - (2.306)(3.1487)\sqrt{1 + \dfrac{1}{8} + \dfrac{8(70 - 52)^2}{8(23182) - 416^2}}$

   $= 515.9548 - (2.306)(3.1487)(1.1550)$
   $= 515.9548 - 8.3863 = 507.5685$

Upper boundary
   $= 515.9548 + (2.306)(3.1487)(1.1550)$
   $= 515.9548 + 8.3863 = 524.3411$

95% prediction interval: 507.5685 to 524.3411

4. $t = \dfrac{37.8206}{136.6162 \Big/ \sqrt{1055 - \dfrac{81^2}{8}}}$ $t_{0.25} = 2.447$

   $= 4.2427$ Do not accept H_0: $\beta_1 = 0$

When $x_p = 11$, $\hat{y} = 573.968$

Also $s_e = 136.6162$ and $\bar{x} = \dfrac{81}{8} = 10.125$

Lower boundary

   $= 573.968 - (2.447)(136.6162)\sqrt{1 + \dfrac{1}{8} + \dfrac{8(11 - 10.125)^2}{8(1055) - 81^2}}$

   $= 573.968 - (2.447)(136.6162)(1.0622)$
   $= 573.968 - 355.0933 = 218.8747$

Upper boundary
   $= 573.968 + (2.447)(136.6162)(1.0622)$
   $= 573.968 + 355.0933 = 929.0613$

95% prediction interval: 218.8747 to 929.0613

5.

$$t = \frac{0.8832}{1.5946 \bigg/ \sqrt{50030 - \frac{774^2}{12}}} \qquad t_{0.025} = 2.228$$

$$= 5.7293 \qquad \text{Do not accept } H_0 : \beta_1 = 0$$

When $x_p = 70$, $\hat{y} = 72.2743$

Also $s_e = 1.5946$ and $\bar{x} = \frac{774}{12} = 64.5$

Lower boundary

$$= 72.2743 - (2.228)(1.5946)\sqrt{1 + \frac{1}{12} + \frac{12(70 - 64.5)^2}{12(50030) - 774^2}}$$

$$= 72.2743 - (2.228)(1.5946)(1.1688)$$
$$= 72.2743 - 4.1525 = 68.1218$$

Upper boundary
$$= 72.2743 + (2.228)(1.5946)(1.1688)$$
$$= 72.2743 + 4.1525 = 76.4268$$

95% prediction interval: 68.1218 to 76.4268

6.

$$t = \frac{0.9303}{0.5563 \bigg/ \sqrt{220 - \frac{36^2}{7}}} \qquad t_{0.025} = 2.571$$

$$= 9.8732 \qquad \text{Do not accept } H_0 : \beta_1 = 0$$

When $x_p = 8$, $\hat{y} = 8.2294$

Also $s_e = 0.5563$ and $\bar{x} = \frac{36}{7} = 5.1429$

Lower boundary

$$= 8.2294 - (2.571)(0.5563)\sqrt{1 + \frac{1}{7} + \frac{7(8 - 5.1429)^2}{7(220) - 36^2}}$$

$$= 8.2294 - (2.571)(0.5563)(1.1735)$$
$$= 8.2294 - 1.6784 = 6.551$$

Upper boundary
$$= 8.2294 + (2.571)(0.5563)(1.1735)$$
$$= 8.2294 + 1.6784 = 9.9078$$

95% prediction interval: 6.551 to 9.9078

7. $t = \dfrac{6.3033}{2.6238\Big/\sqrt{221 - \dfrac{37^2}{8}}}$ $t_{0.025} = 2.447$

$= 16.96597$ Do not accept $H_0 : \beta_1 = 0$

When $x_p = 8$, $\hat{y} = 119.3986$

Also $s_e = 2.6238$ and $\bar{x} = \dfrac{37}{8} = 4.625$

Lower boundary

$= 119.3986 - (2.447)(2.6238)\sqrt{1 + \dfrac{1}{8} + \dfrac{8(8 - 4.625)^2}{8(221) - 37^2}}$

$= 119.3986 - (2.447)(2.6238)(1.1634)$
$= 119.3986 - 7.4695$
$= 111.9291$

Upper boundary
$= 119.3986 + (2.447)(2.6238) + (1.1634)$
$= 119.3986 + 7.4695$
$= 126.8681$

95% prediction interval: 111.9291 to 126.8681

8. $t = \dfrac{0.3056}{2.0039\Big/\sqrt{6609 - \dfrac{193^2}{6}}}$ $t_{0.025} = 2.776$

$= 3.0532$ Do not accept $H_0 : \beta_1 = 0$

When $x_p = 33$, $\hat{y} = 5.7547$

Also $s_e = 2.0039$ and $\bar{x} = \dfrac{193}{6} = 32.1667$

Lower boundary

$= 5.7547 - (2.776)(2.0039)\sqrt{1 + \dfrac{1}{6} + \dfrac{6(33 - 32.1667)^2}{6(6609) - 193^2}}$

$= 5.7547 - (2.776)(2.0039)(1.0809)$
$= 5.7547 - 6.01285$
$= -0.2582$ Note: we use 0 as the lower boundary.

Upper boundary
$= 5.7547 + (2.776)(2.0039)(1.0809)$
$= 5.7547 + 6.01285$
$= 11.76755$

95% prediction interval: 0 to 11.76755

9. $t = \dfrac{0.0129}{72.5034 \Big/ \sqrt{6542000000 - \dfrac{188,000^2}{6}}}$ $t_{0.025} = 2.776$

$= 4.5408$ Do not accept $H_0 : \beta_1 = 0$

When $x_p = 33,000$, $\hat{y} = 451.5$

Also $s_e = 72.5034$ and $\bar{x} = \dfrac{188,000}{6} = 31333.33$

Lower boundary

$= 451.5 - (2.776)(72.5034)\sqrt{1 + \dfrac{1}{6} + \dfrac{6\,(33000 - 31333.33)^2}{6\,(6542000000) - 188000^2}}$

$= 451.5 - (2.776)(72.5034)(1.082)$
$= 451.5 - 217.7735$
$= 233.7265$

Upper boundary
$= 451.5 + (2.776)(72.5034)(1.082)$
$= 451.5 + 217.7735$
$= 669.2735$

95% prediction interval: 233.7265 to 669.2735

10. $t = \dfrac{0.00006}{0.0065 \Big/ \sqrt{8346698 - \dfrac{8790^2}{10}}}$ $t_{0.025} = 2.306$

$= 7.27$ Do not accept $H_0 : \beta_1 = 0$

When $x_p = 175$, $\hat{y} = 0.2629$

Also $s_e = 0.0065$ and $\bar{x} = \dfrac{8790}{10} = 879$

Lower boundary
$= 0.2629 - (2.306)(0.0065)\sqrt{1 + \dfrac{1}{10} + \dfrac{10\,(175 - 879)^2}{10\,(8346698) - 8790^2}}$

$= 0.2629 - (2.306)(0.0065)(1.3780)$
$= 0.2629 - 0.0207 = 0.2422$

Upper boundary
$= 0.2629 + (2.306)(0.0065)(1.3780)$
$= 0.2629 + 0.0207 = 0.2836$

95% prediction interval: 0.2422 to 0.2836

11. $$t = \frac{1.6823}{113.2987 \bigg/ \sqrt{5060000 - \dfrac{5000^2}{7}}}$$ $t_{0.025} = 2.571$

$= 18.116$ Do not accept $H_0 : \beta_1 = 0$

When $x_p = 600$, $\hat{y} = 1564.88$

Also $s_e = 113.2987$ and $\bar{x} = \dfrac{5000}{7} = 714.2857$

Lower boundary

$$= 1564.88 - (2.571)(113.2987)\sqrt{1 + \frac{1}{7} + \frac{7(600 - 714.2857)^2}{7(5060000) - 5000^2}}$$

$= 1564.88 - (2.571)(113.2987)(1.0731)$
$= 1564.88 - 312.5843 = 1252.2257$

Upper boundary
$= 1564.88 + (2.571)(113.2987)(1.0731)$
$= 1564.88 + 312.5846 = 1877.4646$

95% prediction interval: 1252.2257 to 1877.4646

ANSWERS TO EXERCISES FOR SECTION 11.10 - (PAGES 581 - 582)

1. a)

X_1	X_2	Y	$X_1 Y$	$X_2 Y$	X_1^2	$X_1 X_2$	X_2^2
1.6	5.1	98	156.8	499.8	2.56	8.16	26.01
2.1	2.1	92	193.2	193.2	4.41	4.41	4.41
1.6	4.1	97	155.2	397.7	2.56	6.56	16.81
2.6	2.6	93	241.8	241.8	6.76	6.76	6.76
3.4	3.1	97	329.8	300.7	11.56	10.54	9.61
2.4	3.6	96	230.4	345.6	5.76	8.64	12.96
4.3	2.6	95	408.5	247.0	18.49	11.18	6.76
18	23.2	668	1715.7	2225.8	52.10	56.25	83.32

$668 = 7b_0 + 18b_1 + 23.2b_2$
$1715.7 = 18b_0 + 52.1b_1 + 56.25b_2$
$225.8 = 23.2b_0 + 56.25b_1 + 83.32b_2$

Solving simultaneously
gives $b_0 = 84.705$,
$b_1 = 1.0652$,
$b_2 = 2.4090$

1.   **a)**   (Continued)
Least-squares prediction equation:
$$\hat{y} = 84.705 + 1.0652x_1 + 2.409x_2$$

   b) $\hat{y} = 84.705 + 1.0652(1.8) + 2.409(2.8) = 93.36756$

2.   **a)**

X_1	X_2	Y	X_1Y	X_2Y	X_1^2	X_1X_2	X_2^2
22	22	48	1056	1056	484	484	484
17	24	40	680	960	298	408	576
18	8	29	522	232	324	144	64
15	10	35	525	350	225	150	100
20	12	37	740	444	400	240	144
19	46	52	988	2392	361	874	2116
24	13	56	1344	728	576	312	169
135	135	297	5855	6162	2659	2612	3653

$$\left. \begin{array}{l} 297 = 7b_0 + 135b_1 + 135b_2 \\ 5855 = 135b_0 + 2659b_1 + 2612b_2 \\ 6162 = 135b_0 + 2612b_1 + 3653b_2 \end{array} \right\}$$

Solving simultaneously gives $b_0 = -8.28$, $b_1 = 2.2336$, $b_2 = 0.3958$

Least-squares prediction equation is
$$\hat{y} = -8.28 + 2.2336x_1 + 0.3958x_2$$

   b) $\hat{y} = -8.28 + 2.2336(21) + 0.3958(17) = 45.3542$

3.   **a)**

X_1	X_2	Y	X_1Y	X_2Y	X_1^2	X_1X_2	X_2^2
1	14,000	8,800	8,800	123,200,000	1	14,000	196,000,000
2	23,000	8,000	16,000	184,000,000	4	46,000	529,000,000
3	30,000	7,100	21,300	213,000,000	9	90,000	900,000,000
4	40,000	6,100	24,400	244,000,000	16	160,000	1,600,000,000
5	55,000	4,900	24,500	269,500,000	25	275,000	3,025,000,000
6	68,000	3,700	22,200	251,600,000	36	408,000	4,624,000,000
21	230,000	38,600	117,200	1,285,300,000	91	993,000	10,874,000,000

337

3.   a)   (Continued)

$$38600 = 6b_0 + 21b_1 + 230,000b_2$$
$$117200 = 21b_0 + 91b_1 + 993,000b_2$$
$$1,285,300,000 = 230,000b_0 + 993,000b_1 + 10,874,000,000b_2$$

Solving simultaneously gives $b_0 = 10053.6$, $b_1 = -432.8$, $b_2 = -0.054929$

Least-squares prediction equation is
$$\hat{y} = 10053.6 - 432.8x_1 - 0.054929x_2$$

b) $\hat{y} = 10053.6 - 432.8(2.5) - 0.054929(45000) = \$6499.80$

ANSWERS TO TESTING YOUR UNDERSTANDING OF THIS CHAPTER'S CONCEPTS - (PAGES 587 - 588)

1.   Choice (d)

2.   Choice (b)

3.   Yes

4.   a)   0

     b)   A very large number

ANSWERS TO THINKING CRITICALLY - (PAGES 588)

1.   Start with the formula for b_1 in 11.2. Divide numerator and denominator by n-1. Using the fact that $s_x^2 = \dfrac{n \sum x^2 - (\sum x)^2}{n(n-1)}$ we get the equation for b_1 given in Formula 11.3. Also the formulas for b_0 are equivalent since $\dfrac{1}{n} \sum x = \bar{x}$ and $\dfrac{1}{n} \sum y = \bar{y}$

2. $s_x = \sqrt{\dfrac{n \Sigma x^2 - (\Sigma x)^2}{n(n-1)}}$ and $s_y = \sqrt{\dfrac{n \Sigma y^2 - (\Sigma y)}{n(n-1)}}$.

Also $s_{xy} = \dfrac{\Sigma (x-\overline{x})(y-\overline{y})}{n-1}$

Thus $\dfrac{\Sigma (x-\overline{x})(y-\overline{y})/n-1}{\sqrt{\dfrac{n \Sigma x^2 - (\Sigma x)^2}{n(n-1)}} \sqrt{\dfrac{n \Sigma y^2 - (\Sigma y)^2}{n(n-1)}}} = \dfrac{s_{xy}}{s_x s_y}$

$= \dfrac{n (\Sigma xy) - (\Sigma x)(\Sigma y)}{\sqrt{n \Sigma x^2 - (\Sigma x)^2} \sqrt{n \Sigma y^2 - (\Sigma y)^2}}$

This is the formula for r. Thus $r = \dfrac{s_{xy}}{s_x s_y}$

3. Correlation analysis determines a correlation coefficient for measuring the strength of a relationship between the variables. Regression analysis involves finding an equation connecting the variables. One determines a regression equation once we know that there is a significant correlation between the variables.

1. **a)**

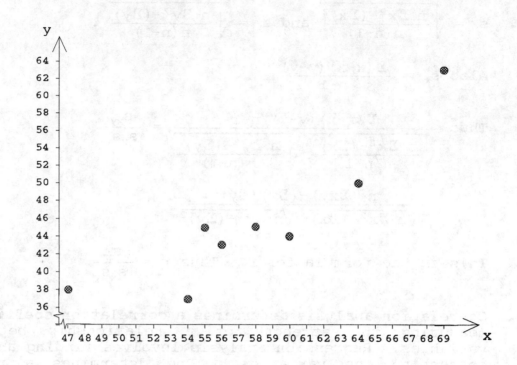

b)

X	Y	X^2	Y^2	XY
58	45	3364	2025	2610
54	37	2916	1369	1998
47	38	2209	1444	1786
60	44	3600	1936	2640
56	43	3136	1849	2408
55	45	3025	2025	2475
64	50	4096	2500	3200
69	63	4761	3969	4347
463	365	27107	17117	21464

$$r = \frac{8(21464) - (463)(365)}{\sqrt{8(27107) - 463^2}\ \sqrt{8(17117) - 365^2}}$$

$$= \frac{2717}{\sqrt{2487}\ \sqrt{3711}} = 0.8943$$

340

2.

X	Y	X^2	XY
10	98	100	980
12	111	144	1332
13	128	169	1664
15	175	225	2625
16	221	256	3536
17	281	289	4777
83	1014	1183	14914

$$b_1 = \frac{6(14914) - (83)(1014)}{6(1183) - 83^2} = \frac{5322}{209} = 25.4641$$

$$b_0 = \frac{1}{6}\,[1014 - (25.4641)83] = -183.2534$$

a) Least-squares prediction equation:
$$\hat{y} = -183.2534 + 25.4641x$$

b) $\hat{y} = -183.2534 + 25.4641(14) = 173.244$

3. $\Sigma y^2 = 196736$ $t_{0.025} = 2.776$ $\bar{x} = \frac{83}{6} = 13.8333$

$$s_e = \sqrt{\frac{196736 - (-183.2534)(1014) - (25.4641)(14914)}{6 - 2}}$$

$$= \sqrt{\frac{2783.3602}{4}} \approx 26.3788$$

Lower boundary
$$= 173.244 - (2.776)(26.3788)\sqrt{1 + \frac{1}{6} + \frac{6(14 - 13.8333)^2}{6(1183) - 83^2}}$$

$$= 173.244 - (2.776)(26.3788)(1.0805)$$
$$= 173.244 - 79.1224 = 94.1216$$

Upper boundary
$$= 173.244 + (2.776)(26.3788)(1.0805)$$
$$= 173.244 + 79.1224 = 252.3664$$

95% prediction interval: From 94.1216 to 252.3664

4.

X	Y	X^2	XY
110	12	12100	1320
105	14	11025	1470
115	18	13225	2070
121	8	14641	968
100	16	10000	1600
90	20	8100	1800
641	88	69091	9228

$$b_1 = \frac{6(9228) - (641)(88)}{6(69091) - 641^2} = \frac{-1040}{3665} = -0.2838$$

$$b_0 = \frac{1}{6}[88 - (-0.2838)(641)] = 44.986$$

Least-square prediction equation: $\hat{y} = 44.986 - 0.2838x$

5.

X	Y	X^2	XY
30	7	900	210
25	9	625	225
20	12	400	240
15	16	225	240
10	20	100	200
5	24	25	120
0	30	0	0
105	118	2275	1235

$$b_1 = \frac{7(1235) - (105)(118)}{7(2275) - 105^2} = \frac{-3745}{4900} = -0.7643$$

$$b_0 = \frac{1}{7}[118 - (-0.7643)(105)] = 28.3216$$

Least-squares prediction equation: $\hat{y} = 28.3216 - 0.7643x$

6.

X	Y	X^2	XY
30	24	900	720
50	23	2500	1150
80	21	6400	1680
110	19	12100	2090
120	17	14400	2040
140	15	19600	2100
530	119	55900	9780

$$b_1 = \frac{6(9780) - (530)(119)}{6(55900) - 530^2} = \frac{-4390}{54500} = -0.0806$$

$$b_2 = \frac{1}{6}[119 - (-0.0806)(530)] = 26.953$$

Least-squares prediction equation: $\hat{y} = 26.953 - 0.0806x$

7.

X_1	X_2	Y	X_1Y	X_2Y	X_1^2	X_1X_2	X_2^2
120	20	84	10080	1680	14400	2400	400
130	19	88	11440	1672	16900	2470	361
118	17	81	9558	1377	13924	2006	289
142	21	92	13064	1932	20164	2982	441
116	12	78	9048	936	13456	1392	144
626	89	423	53190	7597	78844	11250	1635

$$423 = 5b_0 + 626b_1 + 89b_2$$
$$53190 = 626b_0 + 78844b_1 + 11250b_2$$
$$7597 = 89b_0 + 11250b_1 + 1635b_2$$

Solving simultaneously gives $b_0 = 29.213$, $b_1 = 0.36172$, $b_2 = 0.5674$

Least-squares prediction equation:
$$\hat{y} = 29.213 + 0.36172x_1 + 0.5674x_2$$

b) $\hat{y} = 29.213 + (0.36172)(128) + (0.5674)(18) = 85.726$

8. Choice (a)

9.

X_1	X_2	X^2	Y^2	X_2Y
40	33	1600	1089	1320
35	37	1225	1369	1295
30	40	900	1600	1200
25	44	625	1936	1100
20	56	400	3136	1120
15	60	225	3600	900
10	61	100	3721	610
5	71	25	5041	355
180	402	5100	21492	7900

$$r = \frac{8(7900) - (180)(402)}{\sqrt{8(5100) - 180^2}\ \sqrt{8(21492) - 402^2}}$$

$$= \frac{-9160}{\sqrt{8400}\ \sqrt{10332}} = -0.9832$$

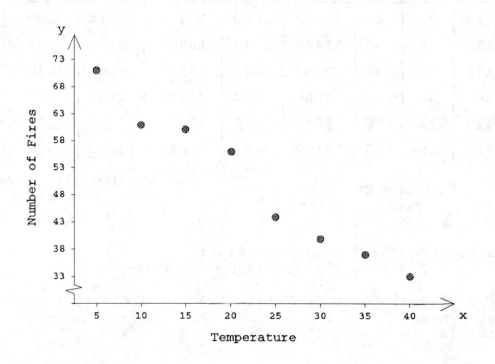

344

9. **b)** Yes

10.

X	Y	X^2	XY
0.5	12,000	0.25	6,000
1	9,500	1.00	9,500
1.5	9,100	2.25	13,650
2	8,500	4.00	17,000
2.5	8,100	6.25	20,250
3	7,500	9.00	22,500
4	7,000	16.00	28,000
5	6,000	25.00	30,000
19.5	67,700	63.75	146,900

$$b_1 = \frac{8(146,900) - (19.5)(67700)}{8(63.75) - (19.5)^2} = \frac{-144950}{129.75} = -1117.1484$$

$$b_0 = \frac{1}{8}[67700 - (-1117.1484)(19.5)] = 11185.5492$$

Least-squares prediction equation: $\hat{y} = 11185.5492 - 1117.1484x$

b) $\hat{y} = 11185.5492 - 1117.1484(3.5) = \$7275.53$

ANSWERS TO CHAPTER TEST – (PAGES 592 – 595)

1.

X	Y	X^2	XY
8	5	64	40
10	7	100	70
12	10	144	120
14	14	196	196
16	18	256	288
18	22	324	396
78	76	1084	1110

1. (Continued)

$$b_1 = \frac{6(1110) - (78)(76)}{6(1084) - 78^2} = \frac{732}{420} = 1.7429$$

$$b_0 = \frac{1}{6} [76 - (1.7429)(78)] = -9.991$$

a) Least-squares prediction equation: $\hat{y} = -9.991 + 1.7429x$

b) $\hat{y} = -9.991 + 1.7429(15) = 16.1525$

2.

X	Y	X^2	Y^2	XY
30	15	900	225	450
34	19	1156	361	646
35	20	1225	400	700
38	22	1444	484	836
39	24	1521	576	936
42	28	1764	784	1176
218	128	8010	2830	4744

$$r = \frac{6(4744) - (218)(128)}{\sqrt{6(8010) - 218^2} \ \sqrt{6(2830) - 128^2}}$$

$$= \frac{560}{\sqrt{536} \ \sqrt{596}} = 0.9908$$

3.

X	Y	X^2	XY
18	2	324	36
19	3	361	57
20	1	400	20
21	1	441	21
22	0	484	0
23	2	529	46
24	1	576	24
25	2	625	50
26	0	676	0
27	1	729	27
225	13	5145	281

$$b_1 = \frac{10(281) - (225)(13)}{10(5145) - 225^2} = \frac{-115}{825} = -0.1394$$

$$b_0 = \frac{1}{10} [13 - (-0.1394)(225)] = 4.4365$$

a) Least-squares prediction equation: $\hat{y} = 4.4365 - 0.1394x$

b) $\hat{y} = 4.4365 - (0.1394)(21.5) = 1.4394$

347

4.

X	Y	X^2	Y^2	XY
5	54	25	2916	270
6	57	36	3249	342
7	61	49	3721	427
8	63	64	3969	504
9	70	81	4900	630
10	76	100	5776	760
11	84	121	7056	924
12	91	144	8281	1092
13	104	169	10816	1352
14	121	196	14641	1694
95	781	985	65325	7995

a) $r = \dfrac{10(7995) - (95)(781)}{\sqrt{10(985) - 95^2}\ \sqrt{10(65325) - 781^2}}$

$= \dfrac{5755}{\sqrt{825}\ \sqrt{43289}} = 0.9630$

b) $b_1 = \dfrac{10(7995) - (95)(781)}{10(985) - 95^2} = \dfrac{5755}{825} = 6.9758$

$b_0 = \dfrac{1}{10}\ [781 - (6.9758)(95)] = 11.8299$

Least-squares prediction equation: $\hat{y} = 11.8299 + 6.9758x$

c) $s_e = \dfrac{\sqrt{65325 - (11.8299)(781) - (6.9758)(7995)}}{10 - 2}$

$\approx \sqrt{39.2909} \approx 6.2682$

d) $\hat{y} = 11.8299 + 6.9758(10.5) = 85.0758$ pounds

5.

X	Y	X^2	XY
9	29	81	261
7	25	49	175
5	20	25	100
10	33	100	330
9	28	81	252
8	27	64	216
48	162	400	1334

$$b_1 = \frac{6(1334) - (48)(162)}{6(400) - 48^2} = \frac{228}{96} = 2.375$$

$$b_0 = \frac{1}{6} [162 - (2.375)(48)] = 8$$

Least-squares prediction equation: $\hat{y} = 8 + 2.375x$

6.

X	Y	X^2	XY
4	25	16	100
9	46	81	414
6	34	36	204
8	41	64	328
12	58	144	696
11	50	121	550
3	20	9	60
53	274	471	2352

$$b_1 = \frac{7(2352) - (53)(274)}{7(471) - 53^2} = \frac{1942}{488} = 3.9795$$

$$b_0 = \frac{1}{7} [274 - (3.9795)(53)] = 9.0124$$

a) Least-squares prediction equation: $\hat{y} = 9.0124 + 3.9795x$

b) $\hat{y} = 9.0124 + 3.9795(10) = 48.8074$

349

7. $\Sigma y^2 = 11842$ $\qquad$ $t_{0.025} = 2.571$ $\qquad$ $\bar{x} = \dfrac{53}{7} = 7.5714$

$$s_e = \dfrac{\sqrt{11842 - (9.0124)(274) - (3.9795)(2352)}}{7 - 2}$$

$$= \sqrt{2.56368} \approx 1.6011$$

Lower boundary

$$= 48.8074 - (2.571)(1.6011)\sqrt{1 = \dfrac{1}{7} + \dfrac{7(10 - 5714)^2}{7(471) - 53^2}}$$

$$= 48.8074 - (2.571)(1.6011)(1.1079)$$
$$= 48.8074 - 4.5606 = 44.2468$$

Upper boundary $= 48.8074 + (2.571)(1.6011)(1.1079)$
$\qquad\qquad\qquad = 48.8074 + 4.5606 = 53.368$

95% prediction interval: From 44.2468 to 53.368

8.

X	Y	X^2	XY
30	39	900	1170
25	44	625	1100
20	65	400	1300
15	73	225	1095
10	80	100	800
5	89	25	445
0	101	0	0
105	491	2275	5910

$$b_1 = \dfrac{7(5910) - (105)(491)}{7(2275) - 105^2} = \dfrac{-10185}{4900} = -2.0786$$

$$b_0 = \dfrac{1}{7}[491 - (-2.0786)(105)] = 101.3219$$

a) Least-squares prediction equation: $\hat{y} = 101.3219 - 2.0786x$

b) $\hat{y} = 101.3219 - 2.0786(12) = 76.3787$

9.

X	Y	X^2	XY
7	20,000	49	140,000
8	17,500	64	140,000
9	16,000	81	144,000
10	14,500	100	145,000
12	13,000	144	156,000
15	12,000	225	180,000
61	93,000	663	905 000

$$b_1 = \frac{6(905,000) - (61)(93000)}{6(663) - 61^2} = \frac{-243000}{257} = -945.5253$$

$$b_0 = \frac{1}{6}[93000 - (-945.5253)61] = 25112.8401$$

a) Least-squares prediction equation:
$$\hat{y} = 25112.8401 - 945.5253x$$

b) $\hat{y} = 25112.8401 - 945.5253(13) = 12821.0112$

10.

X_1	X_2	Y	X_1Y	X_2Y	X_1^2	X_1X_2	X_2^2
2.5	4	28	70.0	112	6.25	10.0	16
4.2	6	19	79.8	114	17.64	25.2	36
4.4	8	21	92.4	168	19.36	35.2	64
1.6	4	31	49.6	124	2.56	6.4	16
5.8	8	19	110.2	152	33.64	46.4	64
3.8	6	23	87.4	138	14.44	22.8	36
5.0	8	21	105.0	168	25.00	40.0	64
27.3	44	162	594.4	976	118.89	186.0	296

$162 = 7b_0 + 27.3b_1 + 44b_2$
$594.4 = 27.3b_0 + 118.89b_1 + 186b_2$
$976 = 44b_0 + 186b_1 + 296b_2$

Solving simultaneously for b_1, b_2, and b_3 gives
$b_0 = 34.192$,
$b_1 = -3.468$
$b_2 = 0.394$

Least-squares prediction equation:
$$\hat{y} = 34.192 - 3.468x_1 + 0.394x_2$$

351

11. $\hat{y} = 34.192 - 3.468(2.3) + (0.394)(4) = 27.7916$

12. Choice (c)

13. Choice (a)

14. Choice (b)

15. Choice (c)

16. Choice (d)

17. Choice (a)

18. Choice (a)

CHAPTER 11 - LINEAR CORRELATION AND REGRESSION
SUPPLEMENTARY TEST FORM A

For question 1 - 7, use the following: A used car dealer has been analyzing the prices of used cars and has determined the following information concerning the age of a particular model used car and its price.

Age of car in years, x	0	1	2	4	5	6
Price of used car, y	$16,000	$11,000	$9000	$5000	$4000	$2500

1. Compute the coefficient of correlation for the data.

   a) -0.973   b) -0.895   c) -0.991   d) -0.937
   e) none of these

   Answer _____

2. Determine whether r is significant.

   a) yes   b) no   c) not enough information
   d) none of these

   Answer _____

3. Find the least-squares prediction equation.

   a) y = -14184.52 + 2089.286x   b) y = 14184.52 - 2089.286x
   c) y = -2089.286 + 14184.52x   d) y = 14184.52 + 2089.286x
   e) none of these

   Answer _____

4. If a car is 3 years old, what is its predicted price?

   a) $8147.79   b) $7844.78   c) $7916.66   d) $8217.69
   e) none of these

   Answer _____

5. What is the value of the standard error of the estimate?

   a) 1179.45   b) 1397.576   c) 1278.628   d) 1321.469
   e) none of these

   Answer _____

6. What is the value of the coefficient of determination for the data?

   a) 0.917 b) 0.927   c) 0.946 d) 0.964 e) none of these

   Answer _____

7. At the 5% level of significance, does the data indicate that the age of a car can be used as a predictor of its price as a used car?

   a) yes   b) no   c) not enough information given
   e) none of these

   Answer _____

8. What type of correlation would you think exists between high blood pressure and the incidence of obesity (overweight)?

   a) positive correlation   b) negative correlation
   c) zero correlation   d) not enough information given
   e) none of these

   Answer _____

9. A correlation coefficient of +0.96

   a) is impossible
   b) indicates a weak positive correlation
   c) indicates a strong positive correlation
   d) is insignificant
   e) none of these

   Answer _____

10. When determining the values of b_0, b_1, and b_2 which are used in the multiple regression formula, what does $b_0(\Sigma x_1) + b_1(\Sigma x_1^2) + b_2(\Sigma x_1 x_2)$ equal?

   a) Σy b) $\Sigma x_1 y$ c) $\Sigma x_2 y$ d) $\Sigma(x_1 x_2)$ e) none of these

   Answer _____

For question 1 - 7, use the following: A magazine publisher has determined that the monthly circulation of the magazine depends upon the price charged per issue as shown below:

Price per issue, x	1.00	1.25	1.50	1.75	2.00	2.50
Circulation (in thousands), y	55	49	43	39	37	30

1. Compute the coefficient of correlation for the data.

   a) -0.927   b) -0.976   c) -0.984   d) -0.948
   e) none of these

   Answer _____

2. Determine whether r is significant.

   a) yes   b) no   c) not enough information
   d) none of these

   Answer _____

3. Find the least-squares prediction equation.

   a) y = -16.229 + 69.21x   b) y = 69.21 - 16.229x
   c) y = 69.21 + 16.229x   d) y = -69.21 + 16.229x
   e) none of these

   Answer _____

4. If the magazine is priced to sell at $2.25, what is its predicted circulation?

   a) 33.182   b) 35.186   c) 34.169   d) 32.695
   e) none of these

   Answer _____

5. What is the value of the standard error of the estimate?

   a) 1.937   b) 1.876   c) 1.786   d) 1.678   e) none of these

   Answer _____

6. What is the value of the coefficient of determination for the data?

   a) 0.986   b) 0.968   c) 0.948   d) 0.984   e) none of these

   Answer _____

7. At the 5% level of significance, does the data indicate that the price charged per issue can be used as a predictor of its circulation?

    a) yes   b) no   c) not enough information given
    e) none of these

                                    Answer _____

8. What type of correlation would you think exists between near-sightedness and high blood pressure?

    a) positive correlation
    b) negative correlation
    c) very little correlation
    d) not enough information given
    e) none of these

                                    Answer _____

9. A correlation coefficient of -0.02

    a) is impossible
    b) indicates a weak negative correlation
    c) indicates a strong negative correlation
    d) is insignificant
    e) none of these

                                    Answer _____

10. When determining the values of b_0, b_1, and b_2 which are used in the multiple regression formula, what does $b_0(\Sigma x_2)$

    $+ b_1(\Sigma x_1 x_2) + b_2(\Sigma x_2^2)$ equal?

    a) Σy b) $\Sigma x_1 y$ c) $\Sigma x_2 y$ d) $\Sigma x_1 x_2$ e) none of these

                                    Answer _____

CHAPTER 11 - LINEAR CORRELATION AND REGRESSION
SUPPLEMENTARY TEST FORM C

For question 1 - 7, use the following: A state judicial system judge believes that the number of cases adjudicated daily is dependent upon the number of judges working on that particular day as shown below:

Number of judges working, x	3	5	8	9	10	13
Number of cases adjudicated, y	27	34	41	53	76	98

1. Compute the coefficient of correlation for the data.

   a) 0.902   b) 0.957   c) 0.939   d) 0.993
   e) none of these

   Answer _____

2. Determine whether r is significant.

   a) yes   b) no   c) not enough information
   d) none of these

   Answer _____

3. Find the least-squares prediction equation.

   a) y = 7.156 + 2.42x   b) y = -2.42 + 7.156x
   c) y = 7.156 - 2.42x   d) y = 2.42 + 7.156x
   e) none of these

   Answer _____

4. If 11 judges are working on a particular day , what is its predicted number of cases to be adjudicated?

   a) 82.076   b) 81.583   c) 78.413   d) 76.296
   e) none of these

   Answer _____

5. What is the value of the standard error of the estimate?

   a) 10.861   b) 9.869   c) 10.456   d) 11.158
   e) none of these

   Answer _____

6. What is the value of the coefficient of determination for the data?

    a) 0.939   b) 0.916   c) 0.828   d) 0.882   e) none of these

    Answer _____

7. At the 5% level of significance, does the data indicate that the number of judges working can be used as a predictor of the number of cases to be adjudicated?

    a) yes   b) no   c) not enough information given
    e) none of these

    Answer _____

8. What type of correlation would you think exists between alcohol consumption and ability to see clearly?

    a) positive correlation   b) negative correlation
    c) zero correlation   d) not enough information given
    e) none of these

    Answer _____

9. A correlation coefficient of +0.12

    a) is impossible
    b) indicates a weak correlation
    c) indicates a strong positive correlation
    d) is insignificant
    e) none of these

    Answer _____

10. When making predictions, $\Sigma(y - \hat{y})^2$ is called

    a) error sum of squares, SSE
    b) total sum of squares, SST
    c) mean square, MS
    d) coefficient of nondetermination
    e) none of these

    Answer _____

Form A	Form B	Form C
1. Choice (a)	1. Choice (c)	1. Choice (c)
2. Choice (a)	2. Choice (a)	2. Choice (a)
3. Choice (b)	3. Choice (b)	3. Choice (b)
4. Choice (c)	4. Choice (d)	4. Choice (d)
5. Choice (d)	5. Choice (c)	5. Choice (c)
6. Choice (c)	6. Choice (b)	6. Choice (d)
7. Choice (a)	7. Choice (a)	7. Choice (a)
8. Choice (a)	8. Choice (c)	8. Choice (b)
9. Choice (c)	9. Choice (b)	9. Choice (b)
10. Choice (b)	10. Choice (c)	10. Choice (a)

ANSWERS TO EXERCISES FOR CHAPTER 12

SECTION 12.2 - (PAGES 605 - 610)

Note: Although expected frequencies will usually be given to two decimal places and the chi-square subtotals to three decimal places, the calculations will usually be done using full calculator accuracy.

1.

	Age 20 to 29	Age 30 to 39	Age 40 to 49	Age over 50
Yes	82 (75.02)	67 (63.86)	25 (30.69)	12 (16.43)
No	160 (166.98)	139 (142.14)	74 (68.31)	41 (36.57)
	242	206	99	53

$$p = \frac{82 + 67 + 25 + 12}{242 + 206 + 99 + 53} = \frac{186}{600} = 0.31$$

$$\chi^2_{0.05} = 7.815$$

$$\chi^2 = \frac{(82 - 75.02)^2}{75.02} + \frac{(67 - 63.86)^2}{63.86} + \frac{(25 - 30.69)^2}{30.69}$$

$$+ \frac{(12 - 16.43)^2}{16.43} + \frac{(160 - 166.98)^2}{166.98} + \frac{(139 - 142.14)^2}{142.14}$$

$$+ \frac{(74 - 68.31)^2}{68.31} + \frac{(41 - 36.57)^2}{36.57} = 0.649 + 0.154 + 1.055$$

$$+ 1.194 + 0.292 + 0.069 + 0.474 + 0.537 = 4.425$$

Do not reject null hypothesis that there is no significant difference between the corresponding proportion of men in the various age groups who drink alcoholic beverages.

2.

Pesticide

	A	B	C
Yes	51 (50.66)	63 (56.2475)	35 (42.0925)
No	85 (85.34)	88 (94.7525)	78 (70.9075)
	136	151	113

$$p = \frac{51 + 63 + 35}{136 + 151 + 113} = \frac{149}{400} = 0.3725$$

$$\chi^2_{0.01} = 9.210$$

$$\chi^2 = \frac{(51 - 50.66)^2}{50.66} + \frac{(63 - 56.2475)^2}{56.2475} + \frac{(35 - 42.0925)^2}{42.0925}$$

$$+ \frac{(85 - 85.34)^2}{85.34} + \frac{(88 - 94.7525)^2}{94.7525} + \frac{(78 - 70.9075)^2}{70.9075}$$

$$= 0.002 + 0.811 + 1.195 + 0.001 + 0.481 + 0.709 = 3.200$$

Do not reject null hypothesis that there is a significant difference between the proportion of dead fish with each of the different pesticides in their bodies.

3.

	Male	Female
Yes	41 (43.45)	25 (22.55)
No	117 (114.55)	57 (59.45)
	158	82

$$p = \frac{41 + 25}{158 + 82} = \frac{66}{240} = 0.275$$

$$\chi^2_{0.05} = 3.841$$

3. (Continued)

$$\chi^2 = \frac{(41 - 43.45)^2}{43.45} + \frac{(25 - 22.55)^2}{22.55} + \frac{(117 - 114.55)^2}{114.55}$$

$$+ \frac{(57 - 59.45)^2}{59.45}$$

$$= 0.138 + 0.266 + 0.052 + 0.101 = 0.558$$

Do not reject null hypothesis that there is a significant difference between the proportion of male and female passengers who rent headphones.

4.

	A	B	C	D	E
Yes	9 (11.22)	11 (10.608)	16 (8.874)	6 (10.2)	9 (10.098)
No	101 (98.78)	93 (93.392)	71 (78.126)	94 (89.8)	90 (88.902)
	110	104	87	100	99

$$p = \frac{9 + 11 + 16 + 6 + 9}{110 + 104 + 87 + 100 + 99} = \frac{51}{500} = 0.102$$

$$\chi^2_{0.01} = 13.277$$

4. (Continued)

$$\chi^2 = \frac{(9 - 11.22)^2}{11.22} + \frac{(11 - 10.608)^2}{10.608} + \frac{(16 - 8.874)^2}{8.874}$$

$$+ \frac{(6 - 10.2)^2}{10.2} + \frac{(9 - 10.098)^2}{10.098} + \frac{(101 - 98.78)^2}{98.78}$$

$$+ \frac{(93 - 93.392)^2}{93.392} + \frac{(71 - 78.126)^2}{78.126} + \frac{(94 - 89.8)^2}{89.8}$$

$$+ \frac{(90 - 88.902)^2}{88.902}$$

$$= 0.439 + 0.014 + 5.722 + 1.729 + 0.119 + 0.050 + 0.002$$
$$+ 0.650 + 0.196 + 0.014 = 8.936$$

Do not reject null hypothesis that there is a significant difference between the proportion of refrigerators from all suppliers with defective thermostats.

5.

	New Jersey	Texas	Illinois
Yes	160 (166.29)	135 (137.37)	240 (231.36)
No	70 (63.71)	55 (52.63)	80 (88.64)
	230	190	320

$$p = \frac{160 + 135 + 240}{230 + 190 + 320} = \frac{535}{740} = 0.723$$

$$\chi^2_{0.05} = 5.991$$

5. (Continued)

$$\chi^2 = \frac{(160 - 166.29)^2}{166.29} + \frac{(135 - 137.37)^2}{137.37} + \frac{(240 - 231.36)^2}{231.36}$$

$$+ \frac{(70 - 63.71)^2}{63.71} + \frac{(55 - 52.63)^2}{52.63} + \frac{(80 - 88.64)^2}{88.64}$$

$$= 0.237 + 0.041 + 0.323 + 0.620 + 0.106 + 0.844 = 2.171$$

Do not reject null hypothesis that there is a significant difference between the families in all three states that own a VCR.

6.

	North	South	East	West
Yes	139 (150.984)	147 (144.18)	154 (150.984)	168 (161.676)
No	327 (315.016)	298 (300.82)	312 (315.016)	331 (337.324)
	466	445	466	499

$$p = \frac{139 + 147 + 154 + 168}{466 + 445 + 466 + 499} = \frac{608}{1876} = 0.324$$

$$\chi^2_{0.05} = 7.815$$

364

6. (Continued)

$$\chi^2 = \frac{(139 - 150.984)^2}{150.984} + \frac{(147 - 144.18)^2}{144.18} + \frac{(154 - 150.984)^2}{150.984}$$

$$+ \frac{(168 - 161.676)^2}{161.676} + \frac{(327 - 315.016)^2}{315.016} + \frac{(298 - 300.82)^2}{300.82}$$

$$+ \frac{(312 - 315.016)^2}{315.016} + \frac{(331 - 337.324)^2}{337.324}$$

$$= 0.958 + 0.054 + 0.058 + 0.244 + 0.459 + 0.026 + 0.028$$
$$+ 0.117 = 1.943$$

Do not reject null hypothesis that there is a significant difference in the proportion of motorists in each of the geographic areas mentioned that favor raising the gasoline tax.

7.

	Ave N	Riggs Blvd	Bailey Drive	Lashly Place	Hew Ave	7th Street
Yes	14 (13.376)	18 (13.376)	6 (14.08)	16 (11.968)	12 (15.84)	20 (17.6)
No	62 (62.624)	58 (62.624)	74 (65.92)	52 (56.032)	78 (74.16)	80 (82.4)
	76	76	80	68	90	100

$$p = \frac{14 + 18 + 6 + 16 + 12 + 20}{76 + 76 + 80 + 68 + 90 + 100} = \frac{86}{490} = 0.176$$

$$\chi^2_{0.01} = 15.086$$

7. (Continued)

$$\chi^2 = \frac{(14 - 13.376)^2}{13.376} + \frac{(18 - 13.376)^2}{13.376} + \frac{(6 - 14.08)^2}{14.08}$$

$$+ \frac{(16 - 11.968)^2}{11.968} + \frac{(12 - 15.84)^2}{15.84} + \frac{(20 - 17.6)^2}{17.6}$$

$$+ \frac{(62 - 62.624)^2}{62.624} + \frac{(58 - 62.624)^2}{62.624} + \frac{(74 - 65.92)^2}{65.92}$$

$$+ \frac{(52 - 56.032)^2}{56.032} + \frac{(78 - 74.16)^2}{74.16} + \frac{(80 - 82.4)^2}{82.4}$$

$$= 0.033 + 1.629 + 4.605 + 1.385 + 0.912 + 0.342 + 0.007$$
$$+ 0.347 + 0.980 + 0.295 + 0.194 + 0.073 = 10.801$$

Do not reject null hypothesis that there is a significant difference between the percentage of homes on all the streets containing excessive levels of radon gas.

8.

	A	B	C	D	E
Yes	193 (206.30)	203 (225.97	128 (158.60)	309 (435.47)	512 (318.67)
No	646 (632.70)	716 (693.03)	517 (486.40)	1462 (1335.53)	784 (977.33)
	839	919	645	1771	1296

$$p = \frac{193 + 203 + 128 + 309 + 512}{839 + 919 + 645 + 1771 + 1296} = \frac{1345}{5470} = 0.2459$$

$$\chi^2_{0.01} = 13.277$$

8. (Continued)

$$\chi^2 = \frac{(193 - 206.30)^2}{206.30} + \frac{(203 - 225.97)^2}{225.97} + \frac{(128 - 158.60)^2}{158.60}$$

$$+ \frac{(309 - 435.47)^2}{435.47} + \frac{(512 - 318.67)^2}{318.67} + \frac{(646 - 632.70)^2}{632.70}$$

$$+ \frac{(716 - 693.03)^2}{693.03} + \frac{(517 - 486.40)^2}{486.40} + \frac{(1462 - 1335.53)^2}{1335.53}$$

$$+ \frac{(784 - 977.33)^2}{977.33}$$

$$= 0.857 + 2.335 + 5.903 + 36.727 + 117.290 + 0.280 + 0.761$$
$$+ 1.925 + 11.975 + 38.244 = 216.297$$

Reject null hypothesis that the percentage of college students receiving state tuition assistance and working part-time is essentially the same at these colleges.

9.

	1987	1988	1989	1990	
Yes	469 (407.391)	582 (565.129)	731 (782.76)	646 (672.462)	$p = \frac{2428}{4094} = 0.593$
No	218 (279.609)	371 (387.871)	589 (537.24)	488 (461.538)	$\chi^2_{0.05} = 7.815$
	687	953	1320	1134	

$$\chi^2 = \frac{(469 - 407.391)^2}{407.391} + \frac{(582 - 565.129)^2}{565.129} + \frac{(731 - 782.76)^2}{782.76}$$

$$+ \frac{(646 - 672.462)^2}{672.462} + \frac{(218 - 279.609)^2}{279.609} + \frac{(371 - 387.871)^2}{387.871}$$

$$+ \frac{(589 - 537.24)^2}{537.24} + \frac{(488 - 461.538)^2}{461.538}$$

$$= 9.303 + 0.500 + 3.433 + 1.047 + 13.558 + 0.729 + 5.004$$
$$+ 1.526 = 35.009$$

Reject null hypothesis that the percentage of former graduates who contributed money for scholarships is the same in the different graduating classes.

10.

	Upper	Upper-Middle	Middle-Lower	Lower
Yes	27 (23.484)	69 (62.418)	84 (84.666)	98 (107.532)
No	11 (14.516)	32 (38.582)	53 (52.334)	76 (66.468)
	38	101	137	174

$p = \dfrac{278}{450} = 0.618$

$\chi^2_{0.05} = 7.815$

$$\chi^2 = \frac{(27 - 23.484)^2}{23.484} + \frac{(69 - 62.418)^2}{62.418} + \frac{(84 - 84.666)^2}{84.666}$$

$$+ \frac{(98 - 107.532)^2}{107.532} + \frac{(11 - 14.516)^2}{14.516} + \frac{(32 - 38.582)^2}{38.582}$$

$$+ \frac{(53 - 52.334)^2}{52.334} + \frac{(76 - 66.468)^2}{66.468}$$

$$= 0.529 + 0.699 + 0.005 + 0.838 + 0.855 + 1.130 + 0.008$$
$$+ 1.355 = 5.419$$

Do not reject null hypothesis that the percentage of people in the various social classes who are willing to give blood is the same.

11.

	Statistics	Algebra or Trigonometry	Geometry	Calculus	Advanced Books
Yes	13 (13.944)	19 (19.92)	10 (9.296)	15 (14.608	22 (21.248)
No	8 (7.056)	11 (10.08)	4 (4.704)	7 (7.392)	10 (10.752)
	21	30	14	22	32

$p = \dfrac{79}{119} = 0.664$

$\chi^2_{0.05} = 9.488$

11. (Continued)

$$\chi^2 = \frac{(13 - 13.944)^2}{13.944} + \frac{(19 - 19.92)^2}{19.92} + \frac{(10 - 9.296)^2}{9.296}$$

$$+ \frac{(15 - 14.608)^2}{14.608} + \frac{(22 - 21.248)^2}{21.248} + \frac{(8 - 7.056)^2}{7.056}$$

$$+ \frac{(11 - 10.08)^2}{10.08} + \frac{(4 - 4.704)^2}{4.704} + \frac{(7 - 7.392)^2}{7.392}$$

$$+ \frac{(10 - 10.752)^2}{10.752}$$

$$= 0.064 + 0.042 + 0.054 + 0.011 + 0.027 + 0.125 + 0.083$$
$$+ 0.106 + 0.021 + 0.053 = 0.586$$

Do not reject null hypothesis that the percentage of books or periodicals added to the library's holdings is the same for all types of math-related books or periodicals. Actually there is one cell whose expected count is less than 5.0.

12.

	Broadway	Main Street	Driggs Ave	Boynton Blvd	Forest Mall
Yes	312 (305.01)	414 (427.02)	375 (374.73)	280 (284.32)	253 (242.92)
No	248 (254.99)	370 (356.98)	313 (313.27)	242 (237.68)	193 (203.08)
	560	784	688	522	446

$$p = \frac{1634}{3000} = 0.544$$

$$\chi^2_{0.05} = 9.488$$

12. (Continued)

$$\chi^2 = \frac{(312 - 305.01)^2}{305.01} + \frac{(414 - 427.02)^2}{427.02} + \frac{(375 - 374.73)^2}{374.73}$$

$$+ \frac{(280 - 284.32)^2}{284.32} + \frac{(253 - 242.92)^2}{242.92} + \frac{(248 - 254.99)^2}{254.99}$$

$$+ \frac{(370 - 356.98)^2}{356.98} + \frac{(313 - 313.27)^2}{313.27} + \frac{(242 - 237.68)^2}{237.68}$$

$$+ \frac{(193 - 203.08)^2}{203.08}$$

$$= 0.160 + 0.397 + 0.000 + 0.066 + 0.418 + 0.191 + 0.475$$
$$+ 0.000 + 0.078 + 0.500 = 2.286$$

Do not reject null hypothesis that the level of satisfaction is the same at all of the bank branches.

13.

	East	Midwest	West	South	
Yes	90 (92.862)	70 (74.772)	102 (104.118)	140 (130.248)	$p = \frac{402}{1000} = 0.402$
No	141 (138.138)	116 (111.228)	157 (154.882)	184 (193.752)	$\chi^2_{0.01} = 11.345$
	231	186	259	324	

$$\chi^2 = \frac{(90 - 92.862)^2}{92.862} + \frac{(70 - 74.772)^2}{74.772} + \frac{(102 - 104.118)^2}{104.118}$$

$$+ \frac{(140 - 130.248)^2}{130.248} + \frac{(141 - 138.138)^2}{231} + \frac{(116 - 111.228)^2}{111.228}$$

$$+ \frac{(157 - 154.882)^2}{259} + \frac{(184 - 193.752)^2}{193.752}$$

$$= 0.088 + 0.305 + 0.043 + 0.730 + 0.059 + 0.205 + 0.029$$
$$+ 0.491 = 1.950$$

Do not reject null hypothesis that the proportion of people in the different geographic areas who believe that the defense budget should be cut is the same.

1.

Observed	28	32	12	13	21	14
Expected	20	20	20	20	20	20

Expected $= \dfrac{120}{6} = 6$

$\chi^2_{0.05} = 11.070$

$$\chi^2 = \frac{(28-20)^2}{20} + \frac{(32-20)^2}{20} + \frac{(12-20)^2}{20} + \frac{(13-20)^2}{20}$$

$$+ \frac{(21-20)^2}{20} + \frac{(14-20)^2}{20}$$

$$= 17.9$$

Reject null hypothesis. Die is not fair.

2.

Observed	130	194	196	106	174
Expected	160	160	160	160	160

Expected $= \dfrac{800}{5} = 160$

$\chi^2_{0.05} = 9.488$

$$\chi^2 = \frac{(130-160)^2}{160} + \frac{(194-160)^2}{160} + \frac{(196-160)^2}{160} + \frac{(106-160)^2}{160}$$

$$+ \frac{(174-160)^2}{160}$$

$$= 40.4$$

Reject null hypothesis. All toll booths are not used with same frequency.

3.

Observed	54	38	44	40	24
Expected	40	40	40	40	40

Expected $= \dfrac{200}{5} = 40$

$\chi^2_{0.05} = 9.488$

$$\chi^2 = \frac{(54-40)^2}{40} + \frac{(38-40)^2}{40} + \frac{(44-40)^2}{40} + \frac{(40-40)^2}{40}$$

$$+ \frac{(24-40)^2}{40}$$

$$= 11.8$$

Reject null hypothesis. Absences do not occur with equal frequency.

4. $8x + 4x + 3x + 2x = 17x = 148 + 84 + 61 + 47$

$$17x = 340$$
$$x = 20$$

$8x = 160$
$4x = 80$
$3x = 60$
$2x = 40$

Observed	148	84	61	47
Expected	160	80	60	40

$\chi^2_{0.05} = 7.815$

$$\chi^2 = \frac{(148 - 160)^2}{160} + \frac{(84 - 80)^2}{80} + \frac{(61 - 60)^2}{60} + \frac{(47 - 40)^2}{40}$$

$$= 2.3417$$

Do not reject null hypothesis that the frequencies of the types of peas mentioned are in the specified ratio.

5. $9x + 7x + 4x + 3x = 261 + 213 + 111 + 105$

$$23x = 690$$
$$x = 30$$

$9x = 270$
$7x = 210$
$4x = 120$
$3x = 90$

Observed	261	213	111	105
Expected	270	210	120	90

$\chi^2_{0.01} = 11.345$

$$\chi^2 = \frac{(261 - 270)^2}{270} + \frac{(213 - 210)^2}{210} + \frac{(111 - 120)^2}{120} + \frac{(105 - 90)^2}{90}$$

$$= 3.5179$$

Do not reject null hypothesis that the frequencies of the types of characteristics obtained by gene-splicing are in the specified ratio.

6.

Observed	276	212	198	246	253
Expected	237	237	237	237	237

Expected $= \dfrac{1185}{5} = 237$

$\chi^2_{0.05} = 9.488$

6. (Continued)

$$\chi^2 = \frac{(276 - 237)^2}{237} + \frac{(212 - 237)^2}{237} + \frac{(198 - 237)^2}{237}$$

$$+ \frac{(246 - 237)^2}{237} + \frac{(253 - 237)^2}{237}$$

$$= 16.8945$$

Reject null hypothesis. Number of calls received is <u>not</u> independent of the day of the week.

7. $7x + 3x + 4x + 2x + 5x = 21x = 163 + 51 + 78 + 44 + 84$

$$21x = 420$$
$$x = 20$$

$7x = 140$
$3x = 60$
$4x = 80$
$2x = 40$
$5x = 100$

Observed	163	51	78	44	84
Expected	140	60	80	40	100

$$\chi^2_{0.05} = 9.488$$

$$\chi^2 = 3.7786 + 1.3500 + 0.0500 + 0.4000 + 2.5600 = 8.1386$$

Do not reject null hypothesis. The manager's claim seems to be correct.

8.

Observed	1329	876	1021	946	820
Expected	1000	1000	1000	1000	1000

$$\text{Expected} = \frac{5000}{5} = 1000$$

$$\chi^2_{0.05} = 9.488$$

8. (Continued)

$$\chi^2 = \frac{(1329 - 1000)^2}{1000} + \frac{(876 - 1000)^2}{1000} + \frac{(1021 - 1000)^2}{1000}$$

$$+ \frac{(946 - 1000)^2}{1000} + \frac{(820 - 1000)^2}{1000}$$

$$= 108.241 + 15.376 + 0.441 + 2.916 + 32.4 = 159.374$$

Reject null hypothesis. All candidates do not share the same popularity.

9.

Observed	241	288	263	208
Expected	250	250	250	250

Expected $= \dfrac{1000}{4} = 250$

$\chi^2_{0.05} = 7.815$

$$\chi^2 = \frac{(241 - 250)^2}{250} + \frac{(288 - 250)^2}{250} + \frac{(263 - 250)^2}{250} + \frac{(208 - 250)^2}{250}$$

$$= 0.324 + 5.776 + 0.676 + 7.056 = 13.832$$

Reject null hypothesis. All TV stations <u>do not</u> have equal shares of the viewing audience.

10.

Observed	48	32	66	38	45	44	42
Expected	45	45	45	45	45	45	45

Expected $= \dfrac{315}{7} = 45$

$\chi^2_{0.05} = 12.592$

$$\chi^2 = \frac{(48 - 45)^2}{45} + \frac{(32 - 45)^2}{45} + \frac{(66 - 45)^2}{45} + \frac{(38 - 45)^2}{45}$$

$$+ \frac{(45 - 45)^2}{45} + \frac{(44 - 45)^2}{45} + \frac{(42 - 45)^2}{45}$$

$$= 0.2 + 3.7556 + 9.8 + 1.0889 + 0 + 0.0222 + 0.2 = 15.0667$$

Reject null hypothesis. Number of calls is not independent of the day of the week.

1.

	Defective	Good	Total
Morning	21 (23.21)	347 (344.79)	368
Afternoon	19 (19.37)	288 (287.63)	307
Night	28 (25.42)	375 (377.58)	403
Total	68	1010	1078

$\chi^2_{0.05} = 5.991$

$df = (2 - 1)(3 - 1) = 2$

$$\chi^2 = \frac{(21 - 23.21)^2}{23.21} + \frac{(347 - 344.79)^2}{344.79} + \frac{(19 - 19.37)^2}{19.37}$$

$$+ \frac{(288 - 287.63)^2}{287.63} + \frac{(28 - 25.42)^2}{25.42} + \frac{(375 - 377.58)^2}{377.58}$$

$$= 0.211 + 0.014 + 0.007 + 0.000 + 0.262 + 0.018 = 0.512$$

Do not reject null hypothesis that the number of defective calculators produced is independent of the production work shift.

2.

	Excellent	Poor	Fair	Good	Total
Required	12 (12.15)	16 (14.85)	11 (14.85)	24 (21.15)	63
Elective	15 (14.85)	17 (18.15)	22 (18.15)	23 (25.85)	77
Total	27	33	33	47	140

$\chi^2_{0.05} = 7.815$

$df = (4 - 1)(2 - 1) = 3$

2. (Continued)

$$\chi^2 = \frac{(12 - 12.15)^2}{12.15} + \frac{(16 - 14.85)^2}{14.85} + \frac{(11 - 14.85)^2}{14.85}$$

$$+ \frac{(24 - 21.15)^2}{21.15} + \frac{(15 - 14.85)^2}{14.85} + \frac{(17 - 18.15)^2}{18.15}$$

$$+ \frac{(22 - 18.15)^2}{18.15} + \frac{(23 - 25.85)^2}{25.85}$$

$$= 0.002 + 0.089 + 0.998 + 0.384 + 0.002 + 0.073 + 0.817$$
$$+ 0.314 = 2.678$$

Do not reject null hypothesis that the rating of the course is independent of the reason for taking the course.

3.

	None	Social only	Heavy drinker	Total
None	61 (46.32)	38 (46.80)	21 (26.88)	120
Light	57 (47.48)	41 (47.97)	25 (27.55)	123
Moderate	46 (49.41)	55 (49.92)	27 (28.67)	128
Heavy	29 (49.79)	61 (50.31)	39 (28.90)	129
Total	193	195	112	500

$$\chi^2_{0.05} = 12.592$$

$$df = (3 - 1)(4 - 1) = 6$$

3. (Continued)

$$\chi^2 = \frac{(61 - 46.32)^2}{46.32} + \frac{(38 - 46.80)^2}{46.80} + \frac{(21 - 26.88)^2}{26.88}$$

$$+ \frac{(57 - 47.48)^2}{47.48} + \frac{(41 - 47.97)^2}{47.97} + \frac{(25 - 27.55)^2}{27.55}$$

$$+ \frac{(46 - 49.41)^2}{49.41} + \frac{(55 - 49.92)^2}{49.92} + \frac{(27 - 28.67)^2}{28.67}$$

$$+ \frac{(29 - 49.79)^2}{49.79} + \frac{(61 - 50.31)^2}{50.31} + \frac{(39 - 28.90)^2}{28.90}$$

$$= 4.652 + 1.655 + 1.286 + 1.910 + 1.013 + 0.236 + 0.235$$
$$+ 0.517 + 0.098 + 8.684 + 2.271 + 3.533$$
$$= 26.090$$

Reject null hypothesis that smoking and drinking are independent.

4.

	Poor	Average	Good	Total
Below $30,000	18 (14.57)	25 (26.42)	36 (38.02)	79
$30,000 – $70,000	19 (23.78)	49 (43.13)	61 (62.08)	129
Above $70,000	22 (20.65)	33 (37.45)	57 (53.90)	112
Total	59	107	154	320

$$\chi^2_{0.05} = 9.488$$

$$df = (3 - 1)(3 - 1) = 4$$

4. (Continued)

$$\chi^2 = \frac{(18 - 14.57)^2}{14.57} + \frac{(25 - 26.42)^2}{26.42} + \frac{(36 - 38.02)^2}{38.02}$$

$$+ \frac{(19 - 23.78)^2}{23.78} + \frac{(49 - 43.13)^2}{43.13} + \frac{(61 - 62.08)^2}{62.08}$$

$$+ \frac{(22 - 20.65)^2}{20.65} + \frac{(33 - 37.45)^2}{37.45} + \frac{(57 - 53.90)^2}{53.90}$$

$$= 0.810 + 0.076 + 0.107 + 0.962 + 0.798 + 0.019 + 0.088$$
$$+ 0.529 + 0.178$$
$$= 3.567$$

Do not reject null hypothesis that the broker's rating is independent of the customer's annual income.

5.

	Pregnant	Not Pregnant	Total
Positive	368 (259.29)	29 (137.71)	397
Negative	18 (126.71)	176 (67.29)	194
Total	386	205	591

$\chi^2_{0.05} = 3.841$

$df = (2 - 1)(2 - 1) = 1$

$$\chi^2 = \frac{(368 - 259.29)^2}{259.29} + \frac{(29 - 137.71)^2}{137.71} + \frac{(18 - 126.71)^2}{126.71}$$

$$+ \frac{(176 - 67.29)^2}{67.29}$$

$$= 45.575 + 85.814 + 93.264 + 175.610$$
$$= 400.264$$

Reject null hypothesis that the pregnancy test kit results are independent of the clinical test results.

6.

	Master Card	Visa	American Express	Discover Card	Store Card	Total
Under $25	78 (85.56)	82 (79.28)	32 (29.49)	53 (47.37)	46 (49.31)	291
Between $25 and $75	62 (58.22)	53 (53.94)	18 (20.06)	28 (32.23)	37 (33.55)	198
Over $75	37 (33.22)	29 (30.78)	11 (11.45)	17 (18.40)	19 (19.15)	113
Total	177	164	61	98	102	602

$$\chi^2_{0.05} = 15.507$$

$$df = (5 - 1)(3 - 1) = 8$$

$$\chi^2 = \frac{(78 - 85.56)^2}{85.56} + \frac{(82 - 79.28)^2}{79.82} + \frac{(32 - 29.49)^2}{29.49}$$

$$+ \frac{(53 - 47.37)^2}{47.37} + \frac{(46 - 49.31)^2}{49.31} + \frac{(62 - 58.22)^2}{58.22}$$

$$+ \frac{(53 - 53.94)^2}{53.94} + \frac{(18 - 20.06)^2}{20.06} + \frac{(28 - 32.23)^2}{32.23}$$

$$+ \frac{(37 - 33.55)^2}{33.55} + \frac{(37 - 33.22)^2}{33.22} + \frac{(29 - 30.78)^2}{30.78}$$

$$+ \frac{(11 - 11.45)^2}{11.45} + \frac{(17 - 18.40)^2}{18.40} + \frac{(19 - 19.15)^2}{19.15}$$

$$= 0.668 + 0.094 + 0.214 + 0.669 + 0.222 + 0.246 + 0.016$$
$$+ 0.212 + 0.556 + 0.355 + 0.429 + 0.103 + 0.018 + 0.106$$
$$+ 0.001 = 3.909$$

Do not reject null hypothesis that the type of credit card
used is independent of the amount of purchase.

379

7.

	In favor of proposal	Against proposal	Had no opinion	Total
East	164 (125.54)	204 (249.71)	21 (13.75)	389
Midwest	110 (156.53)	358 (311.34)	17 (17.14)	485
South	128 (133.29)	276 (265.12)	9 (14.59)	413
Farwest	146 (132.64)	252 (263.83)	13 (14.52)	411
Total	548	1090	60	1698

$$\chi^2_{0.05} = 12.592$$

$$df = (3 - 1)(4 - 1) = 6$$

$$\chi^2 = \frac{(164 - 125.54)^2}{125.54} + \frac{(204 - 249.71)^2}{249.71} + \frac{(21 - 13.75)^2}{13.75}$$

$$+ \frac{(110 - 156.53)^2}{156.53} + \frac{(358 - 311.34)^2}{311.34} + \frac{(17 - 17.14)^2}{17.14}$$

$$+ \frac{(128 - 133.29)^2}{133.29} + \frac{(276 - 265.12)^2}{265.12} + \frac{(9 - 14.59)^2}{14.59}$$

$$+ \frac{(146 - 132.64)^2}{132.64} + \frac{(252 - 263.83)^2}{263.83} + \frac{(13 - 14.52)^2}{14.52}$$

$$= 11.780 + 8.368 + 3.829 + 13.829 + 6.994 + 0.001 + 0.210$$
$$+ 0.447 + 2.144 + 1.345 + 0.531 + 0.160 = 49.637$$

Reject null hypothesis that the region in which a person lives is independent of the person's opinion about the proposal.

8.

	A	B	C	D	Total
Male	256 (266.90)	262 (262.11)	236 (241.38)	203 (186.62)	957
Female	246 (235.10)	231 (230.89)	218 (212.62)	148 (164.38)	843
Total	502	493	454	351	1800

$$\chi^2_{0.05} = 7.815$$

$$df = (4 - 1)(2 - 1) = 3$$

$$\chi^2 = \frac{(256 - 266.90)^2}{266.90} + \frac{(262 - 262.11)^2}{262.11} + \frac{(236 - 241.38)^2}{241.38}$$

$$+ \frac{(203 - 186.62)^2}{186.82} + \frac{(246 - 235.10)^2}{235.10} + \frac{(231 - 230.89)^2}{230.89}$$

$$+ \frac{(218 - 212.62)^2}{212.62} + \frac{(148 - 164.38)^2}{164.38}$$

$$= 0.445 + 0.000 + 0.120 + 1.439 + 0.505 + 0.000 + 0.136$$
$$+ 1.633 = 4.278$$

Do not reject null hypothesis that the sex of the consumer is independent of the brand preferred.

9.

	Supports Enthusiastically	Supports Moderately	Opposed	Total
Male Frequent	43 (47.80)	67 (63.80)	21 (19.40)	131
Male Infrequent	79 (76.63)	99 (102.27)	32 (31.10)	210
Female Frequent	48 (44.88)	58 (59.90)	17 (18.22)	123
Female Infrequent	69 (69.69)	95 (93.02)	27 (28.29)	191
Total	239	319	97	655

381

9. (Continued)
$$\chi^2_{0.05} = 12.592$$

$$df = (3 - 1)(4 - 1) = 6$$

$$\chi^2 = \frac{(43 - 47.80)^2}{47.80} + \frac{(67 - 63.80)^2}{63.80} + \frac{(21 - 19.40)^2}{19.40}$$

$$+ \frac{(79 - 76.63)^2}{76.63} + \frac{(99 - 102.27)^2}{102.27} + \frac{(32 - 31.10)^2}{31.10}$$

$$+ \frac{(48 - 44.88)^2}{44.88} + \frac{(58 - 59.90)^2}{59.90} + \frac{(17 - 18.22)^2}{18.22}$$

$$+ \frac{(69 - 69.69)^2}{69.69} + \frac{(95 - 93.02)^2}{93.02} + \frac{(27 - 28.29)^2}{28.29}$$

$$= 0.482 + 0.161 + 0.132 + 0.074 + 0.105 + 0.026 + 0.217$$
$$+ 0.061 + 0.081 + 0.007 + 0.042 + 0.058$$
$$= 1.445$$

Do not reject null hypothesis that the type of traveler is independent of the degree of satisfaction.

10.

	Caplet	Capsule	Tablet	Total
Between 20 and 30	75 (78.44)	78 (90.17)	84 (68.39)	237
Between 30 and 50	109 (107.57)	127 (123.65)	89 (93.79)	325
Over 50	97 (94.99)	118 (109.19)	72 (82.82	287
Total	281	323	245	849

$$\chi^2_{0.01} = 13.277$$

$$df = (3 - 1)(3 - 1) = 4$$

10. (Continued)

$$\chi^2 = \frac{(75 - 78.44)^2}{78.44} + \frac{(78 - 90.17)^2}{90.17} + \frac{(84 - 68.39)^2}{68.39}$$

$$+ \frac{(109 - 107.57)^2}{107.57} + \frac{(127 - 123.65)^2}{123.65} + \frac{(89 - 93.79)^2}{93.79}$$

$$+ \frac{(97 - 94.99)^2}{94.99} + \frac{(118 - 109.19)^2}{109.19} + \frac{(72 - 82.82)^2}{82.82}$$

$$= 0.151 + 1.642 + 3.562 + 0.019 + 0.091 + 0.244 + 0.043$$
$$+ 0.711 + 1.414 = 7.876$$

Do not reject null hypothesis that the preference in medicine form is the same for all age groups.

11.

	Energy Conservation	Water Pollution	Air Pollution	Nuclear Energy	Total
Under 25 years	187 (209.22)	123 (153.38)	199 (298.92)	432 (279.48)	941
25 to 40 years	168 (218.55)	221 (160.23)	117 (312.27)	277 (291.95)	983
Over 40 years	112 (239.23)	145 (175.39)	637 (341.81)	182 (319.57)	1076
Total	667	489	953	891	3000

$$\chi^2_{0.05} = 12.592$$

$$df = (4 - 1)(3 - 1) = 6$$

11. (Continued)

$$\chi^2 = \frac{(187 - 209.22)^2}{209.22} + \frac{(123 - 153.38)^2}{153.38} + \frac{(199 - 298.92)^2}{298.92}$$

$$+ \frac{(432 - 279.48)^2}{279.48} + \frac{(168 - 218.55)^2}{218.55} + \frac{(221 - 160.23)^2}{160.23}$$

$$+ \frac{(117 - 312.27)^2}{312.27} + \frac{(277 - 291.95)^2}{291.95} + \frac{(112 - 239.23)^2}{239.23}$$

$$+ \frac{(145 - 175.39)^2}{175.39} + \frac{(637 - 341.81)^2}{341.81} + \frac{(182 - 319.57)^2}{319.57}$$

$$= 2.359 + 6.018 + 33.403 + 83.239 + 102.191 + 23.049$$
$$+ 122.104 + 0.766 + 67.665 + 5.265 + 254.930 + 59.223$$
$$= 760.212$$

Reject null hypothesis that age is independent of the environmental problem that most concerns an individual.

12.

	Under $20,000	$20,000 - $35,000	Over $35,000	Total
2.00 - 2.59	17 (19.31)	53 (50.51)	47 (47.17)	117
2.60 - 2.99	19 (21.96)	58 (57.42)	56 (53.62)	133
3.00 - 3.59	30 (27.90)	71 (72.97)	68 (68.14)	169
3.60 - 4.00	38 (34.83)	90 (91.10)	83 (85.07)	211
Total	104	272	254	630

$$\chi^2_{0.01} = 16.812$$

$$df = (3 - 1)(4 - 1) = 6$$

12. (Continued)

$$\chi^2 = \frac{(17 - 19.31)^2}{19.31} + \frac{(53 - 50.51)^2}{50.51} + \frac{(47 - 47.17)^2}{47.17}$$

$$+ \frac{(19 - 21.96)^2}{21.96} + \frac{(58 - 57.42)^2}{57.42} + \frac{(56 - 53.62)^2}{53.62}$$

$$+ \frac{(30 - 27.90)^2}{27.90} + \frac{(71 - 72.97)^2}{72.97} + \frac{(68 - 68.14)^2}{68.14}$$

$$+ \frac{(38 - 34.83)^2}{34.83} + \frac{(90 - 91.10)^2}{91.10} + \frac{(83 - 85.07)^2}{85.07}$$

$$= 0.277 + 0.122 + 0.001 + 0.398 + 0.006 + 0.105 + 0.158$$
$$+ 0.053 + 0.000 + 0.288 + 0.013 + 0.050 = 1.473$$

Do not reject null hypothesis that the grade-point average of a graduate and the starting salary of the graduate are independent.

**ANSWERS TO TESTING YOUR UNDERSTANDING OF THIS CHAPTER'S CONCEPTS -
(PAGES 628 - 629)**

1. Since the null hypothesis is rejected only when the value of the test statistic is too large, the rejection is always on the right i.e. it is always right-tailed.

2. No

3. **b)** Since this is a contingency table and not a simple chi-square problem, the value of p will be different for each cell.

1.

	Ignition Shut-off	Steering Wheel Lock	Burglar Alarm	Total
Compact	8 (8.35)	7 (8.84)	13 (10.81)	28
Intermediate	2 (4.18)	9 (4.42)	3 (5.40)	14
Large	7 (4.47)	2 (4.74)	6 (5.79)	15
Total	17	18	22	57

$\chi^2_{0.05} = 9.488$

$df = (3 - 1)(3 - 1) = 4$

$$\chi^2 = \frac{(8 - 8.35)^2}{8.35} + \frac{(7 - 8.84)^2}{8.84} + \frac{(13 - 10.81)^2}{10.81} + \frac{(2 - 4.18)^2}{4.18}$$

$$+ \frac{(9 - 4.42)^2}{4.42} + \frac{(3 - 5.40)^2}{5.40} + \frac{(7 - 4.47)^2}{4.47} + \frac{(2 - 4.74)^2}{4.74}$$

$$+ \frac{(6 - 5.79)^2}{5.79}$$

$= 0.015 + 0.384 + 0.445 + 1.133 + 4.742 + 1.069 + 1.427$
$+ 1.581 + 0.008 = 10.804$

Reject null hypothesis that the type of antitheft device used is independent of the size of the car.

2.

	Ignition Shut-off	Steering Wheel Lock	Burglar Alarm	Total
Compact	8 (8.35)	7 (8.84)	13 (10.81)	28
Intermediate or Large	9 (8.65)	11 (9.16)	9 (11.19)	29
	17	18	22	57

$\chi^2_{0.05} = 5.991$

$df = (3 - 1)(2 - 1) = 2$

2. (Continued)

$$\chi^2 = \frac{(8 - 8.35)^2}{8.35} + \frac{(7 - 8.84)^2}{8.84} + \frac{(13 - 10.81)^2}{10.81} + \frac{(9 - 8.65)^2}{8.65}$$

$$+ \frac{(11 - 9.16)^2}{9.16} + \frac{(9 - 11.19)^2}{11.19}$$

$$= 0.015 + 0.384 + 0.445 + 0.014 + 0.371 + 0.430 = 1.658$$

When the cells are combined, we would not reject the null hypothesis. By combining cells, we arrive at a different conclusion than when we did not combine any cells. Actually, some statisticians believe that the requirement that all expected frequencies should be at least 5 is too restrictive.

3.

		Age (in years)				
		11 - 20	21 - 30	31 - 40	41 - 50	51 - 60
Afraid of	Yes	121 (89.4)	93 (89.4)	88 (89.4)	76 (89.4)	69 (89.4)
Heights?	No	79 (110.6)	107 (110.6)	112 (110.6)	124 (110.6)	131 (110.6)
		200	200	200	200	200

$$p = \frac{121 + 93 + 88 + 76 + 69}{1000} = \frac{447}{1000} = 0.447$$

$$\chi^2 = \frac{(121 - 89.4)^2}{89.4} + \frac{(93 - 89.4)^2}{89.4} + \frac{(88 - 89.4)^2}{89.4}$$

$$+ \frac{(76 - 89.4)^2}{89.4} + \frac{(69 - 89.4)^2}{89.4} + \frac{(79 - 110.6)^2}{110.6}$$

$$+ \frac{(107 - 110.6)^2}{110.6} + \frac{(112 - 110.6)^2}{110.6} + \frac{(124 - 110.6)^2}{110.6}$$

$$+ \frac{(131 - 110.6)^2}{110.6}$$

$$= 11.170 + 0.145 + 0.022 + 2.009 + 4.655 + 9.029 + 0.117$$
$$+ 0.018 + 1.624 + 3.763 = 32.550$$

Reject null hypothesis that the proportion of people in each age group who fear heights is the same.

$\chi^2_{0.05} = 9.488$
df = 4

4.

	1	2	Total
1	a	b	a + b
2	c	d	c + d
Total	a + c	b + d	a + b + c + d

Column one, row 1 expected value: $\dfrac{(a + b)(a + c)}{a + b + c + d}$

Column two, row 1 expected value: $\dfrac{(a + b)(b + d)}{a + b + c + d}$

Column one, row 2 expected value: $\dfrac{(a + c)(c + d)}{a + b + c + d}$

Column two, row 2 expected value: $\dfrac{(c + d)(b + d)}{a + b + c + d}$

$$\chi^2 = \frac{\left[a - \dfrac{(a + b)(a + c)}{a + b + c + d}\right]^2}{\dfrac{(a + b)(a + c)}{a + b + c + d}} + \frac{\left[b - \dfrac{(a + b)(b + d)}{a + b + c + d}\right]^2}{\dfrac{(a + b)(b + d)}{a + b + c + d}}$$

$$+ \frac{\left[c - \dfrac{(a + c)(c + d)}{a + b + c + d}\right]^2}{\dfrac{(a + c)(c + d)}{a + b + c + d}} + \frac{\left[d - \dfrac{(c + d)(b + d)}{a + b + c + d}\right]^2}{\dfrac{(c + d)(b + d)}{a + b + c + d}}$$

This simplifies to $\chi^2 = \dfrac{(a + b + c + d)(ad - bc)^2}{(a + b)(c + d)(b + d)(a + c)}$.

388

1.

Total

$\dfrac{(25)(15)}{75} = 5$	$\dfrac{(25)(15)}{75} = 5$	$\dfrac{(25)(15)}{75} = 5$	15
$\dfrac{(25)(20)}{75} = 6.67$	$\dfrac{(25)(20)}{75} = 6.67$	$\dfrac{(25)(20)}{75} = 6.67$	20
$\dfrac{(25)(25)}{75} = 8.33$	$\dfrac{(25)(25)}{75} = 8.33$	$\dfrac{(25)(25)}{75} = 8.33$	25
$\dfrac{(25)(15)}{75} = 5$	$\dfrac{(25)(15)}{75} = 5$	$\dfrac{(25)(15)}{75} = 5$	15

The expected frequency for all the cells in row 1 is 5

The expected frequency for all the cells in row 2 is 6.67

The expected frequency for all the cells in row 3 is 8.33

The expected frequency for all the cells in row 4 is 5

Total   25   25   25   75

2. $\quad p = \dfrac{30 + 10 + 22}{30 + 10 + 22 + 18 + 20 + 25} = \dfrac{62}{125} = 0.496$

3.

	I	II	III
Yes	30 (23.81)	10 (14.88)	22 (23.31)
No	18 (24.19)	20 (15.12)	25 (23.69)
	48	30	47

df = 2

$$\chi^2 = \frac{(30 - 23.81)^2}{23.81} + \frac{(10 - 14.88)^2}{14.88} + \frac{(22 - 23.31)^2}{23.31}$$

$$+ \frac{(18 - 24.19)^2}{24.19} + \frac{(20 - 15.12)^2}{15.12} + \frac{(25 - 23.69)^2}{23.69}$$

$$= 1.610 + 1.600 + 0.074 + 1.585 + 1.575 + 0.073 = 6.517$$

389

4.

	Below Average	Average	Above Average	Total
Male	47 (49.20)	27 (25.06)	8 (7.74)	82
Female	61 (58.80)	28 (29.94)	9 (9.26)	98
Total	108	55	17	180

$\chi^2_{0.05} = 5.991$

$df = (3 - 1)(2 - 1) = 2$

$$\chi^2 = \frac{(47 - 49.20)^2}{49.20} + \frac{(27 - 25.06)^2}{25.06} + \frac{(8 - 7.74)^2}{7.74}$$

$$+ \frac{(61 - 58.80)^2}{58.80} + \frac{(28 - 29.94)^2}{29.94} + \frac{(9 - 9.26)^2}{9.26}$$

$$= 0.098 + 0.151 + 0.008 + 0.082 + 0.126 + 0.007 = 0.473$$

Do not reject hypothesis that the rating of the meal is independent of the sex of the flier.

5.

	Drug user	Non drug user	Total
Harmful	198 (402.38)	712 (507.62)	910
Not Harmful	452 (247.62)	108 (312.38)	560
Total	650	820	1470

$\chi^2_{0.05} = 3.841$

$df = (2 - 1)(2 - 1) = 1$

Expected number of drug users who believe that drug use is

harmful $= \dfrac{(650)(910)}{1470} = 402.38$ or 402.4 Choice (a)

6.

Observed	46	54	76	62
Expected	59.5	59.5	59.5	59.5

Expected $= \dfrac{46 + 54 + 76 + 62}{4} = 59.5$

$df = 3$ $\chi^2_{0.05} = 7.815$

6. (Continued)

$$\chi^2 = \frac{(46 - 59.5)^2}{59.5} + \frac{(54 - 59.5)^2}{59.5} + \frac{(76 - 59.5)^2}{59.5} + \frac{(62 - 59.5)^2}{59.5}$$

$$= 3.063 + 0.508 + 4.576 + 0.105 = 8.252$$

Reject null hypothesis that the proportion of police officers who are not working because of job-related disabilities is the same for all categories.

7.

	Sent to jail	Not sent to jail	Total
Guilty	403 (431.60)	69 (40.40)	472
Not guilty	612 (583.40)	26 (54.60)	638
Total	1015	95	1110

$$\chi^2_{0.05} = 3.841$$

$$df = (2 - 1)(2 - 1) = 1$$

$$\chi^2 = \frac{(403 - 431.60)^2}{431.60} + \frac{(69 - 40.40)^2}{40.40} + \frac{(612 - 583.40)^2}{583.40}$$

$$+ \frac{(26 - 54.60)^2}{54.60}$$

$$= 1.896 + 20.253 + 1.402 + 14.984 = 38.535$$

Reject null hypothesis that the plea entered is independent of the jail sentence.

8.

	Car theft	Murder	Robbery	Burglary	Rape	Total
I	68 (62.83)	14 (21.14)	37 (42.08)	57 (50.61)	28 (27.34)	204
II	46 (57.29)	19 (19.27)	39 (38.37)	61 (46.15)	21 (24.93)	186
III	103 (81.62)	28 (27.46)	48 (54.66)	54 (65.75)	32 (35.52)	265
IV	49 (61.90)	17 (20.83)	62 (41.46)	40 (49.87)	33 (26.94)	201
V	58 (60.37)	31 (20.31)	31 (40.43)	49 (48.63)	27 (26.27)	196
Total	324	109	217	261	141	1052

$$\chi^2_{0.05} = 26.296$$

$$df = (5 - 1)(5 - 1) = 16$$

$$\chi^2 = \frac{(68 - 62.83)^2}{62.83} + \frac{(14 - 21.14)^2}{21.14} + \frac{(37 - 42.08)^2}{42.08}$$

$$+ \frac{(57 - 50.61)^2}{50.61} + \frac{(28 - 27.34)^2}{27.34} + \frac{(46 - 57.29)^2}{57.29}$$

$$+ \frac{(19 - 19.27)^2}{19.27} + \frac{(39 - 38.37)^2}{38.37} + \frac{(61 - 46.15)^2}{46.15}$$

$$+ \frac{(21 - 24.93)^2}{24.93} + \frac{(103 - 81.62)^2}{81.62} + \frac{(28 - 27.46)^2}{27.46}$$

$$+ \frac{(48 - 54.66)^2}{54.66} + \frac{(54 - 65.75)^2}{65.75} + \frac{(32 - 35.52)^2}{35.52}$$

$$+ \frac{(49 - 61.90)^2}{61.90} + \frac{(17 - 20.83)^2}{20.83} + \frac{(62 - 41.46)^2}{41.46}$$

$$+ \frac{(40 - 49.87)^2}{49.87} + \frac{(33 - 26.94)^2}{26.94} + \frac{(58 - 60.37)^2}{60.37}$$

8. (Continued)

$$+ \frac{(31 - 20.31)^2}{20.31} + \frac{(31 - 40.43)^2}{40.43} + \frac{(49 - 48.63)^2}{48.63}$$

$$+ \frac{(27 - 26.27)^2}{26.27}$$

$$= 0.426 + 2.410 + 0.613 + 0.806 + 0.016 + 2.223 + 0.004$$
$$+ 0.010 + 4.781 + 0.619 + 5.603 + 0.011 + 0.812 + 2.099$$
$$+ 0.348 + 2.690 + 0.703 + 10.175 + 1.953 + 1.363 + 0.093$$
$$+ 5.629 + 2.199 + 0.003 + 0.020 = 45.609$$

Reject null hypothesis that the type of crime committed is independent of the precinct where it was committed.

9.

	Liberal	Fair	Vindictive	Total
Male	31 (36.90)	27 (27.80)	35 (28.30)	93
Female	42 (36.10)	28 (27.20)	21 (27.70)	91
Total	73	55	56	184

$$\chi^2_{0.05} = 5.991$$

$$df = (3 - 1)(2 - 1) = 2$$

$$\chi^2 = \frac{(31 - 36.90)^2}{36.90} + \frac{(27 - 27.80)^2}{27.80} + \frac{(35 - 28.30)^2}{28.30}$$

$$+ \frac{(42 - 36.10)^2}{36.10} + \frac{(28 - 27.20)^2}{27.20} + \frac{(21 - 27.70)^2}{27.70}$$

$$= 0.942 + 0.023 + 1.584 + 0.963 + 0.023 + 1.619 = 5.155$$

Do not reject null hypothesis that the sex of the juror is independent of his or her tendency to be liberal.

10.

Observed	87	40	38	10	20	73	132
Expected	100	44	36	12	20	76	112

10. (Continued)

$$\chi^2 = \frac{(87 - 100)^2}{100} + \frac{(40 - 44)^2}{44}$$

$$+ \frac{(38 - 36)^2}{36} + \frac{(10 - 12)^2}{12}$$

$$+ \frac{(20 - 20)^2}{20} + \frac{(73 - 76)^2}{76}$$

$$+ \frac{(132 - 112)^2}{112}$$

$$= 1.69 + 0.364 + 0.111 + 0.333$$
$$+ 0.000 + 0.118 + 3.571 = 6.1879$$

$(0.25)(400) = 100$
$(0.11)(400) = 44$
$(0.09)(400) = 36$
$(0.03)(400) = 12$
$(0.05)(400) = 20$
$(0.19)(400) = 76$
$(0.28)(400) = 112$

$df = 6$

$\chi^2_{0.05} = 12.592$

Do not reject null hypothesis that the percentages are correct.

1.

	8:00 AM– 3:59 PM	4:00 PM– 11:59 PM	12:00 AM– 7:59 AM	Total
less than $3.00	62 (61.89)	56 (51.63)	21 (25.48)	139
$3.01–$8.00	72 (61.89)	48 (51.63)	19 (25.48)	139
over $8.00	53 (63.22)	52 (52.74)	37 (26.03)	142
Total	187	156	77	420

$$\chi^2_{0.05} = 9.488$$

$$df = (3 - 1)(3 - 1) = 4$$

1. (Continued)

$$\chi^2 = \frac{(62 - 61.89)^2}{61.89} + \frac{(56 - 51.63)^2}{51.63} + \frac{(21 - 25.48)^2}{25.48}$$

$$+ \frac{(72 - 61.89)^2}{61.89} + \frac{(48 - 51.63)^2}{51.63} + \frac{(19 - 25.48)^2}{25.48}$$

$$+ \frac{(53 - 63.22)^2}{63.22} + \frac{(52 - 52.74)^2}{52.74} + \frac{(37 - 26.03)^2}{26.03}$$

$$= 0.000 + 0.370 + 0.789 + 1.652 + 0.255 + 1.649 + 1.653$$
$$+ 0.010 + 4.260 = 10.999$$

Reject null hypothesis that the amount of any purchase at store is independent of the time that it is purchased.

2.

	Opposed	In Favor	No Opinion	Total
Male	31 (35.50)	71 (64.67)	22 (23.83)	124
Female	42 (37.50)	62 (68.33)	27 (25.17)	131
Total	73	133	49	255

$\chi^2_{0.05} = 5.991$

$df = (3 - 1)(2 - 1) = 2$

$$\chi^2 = \frac{(31 - 35.50)^2}{35.50} + \frac{(71 - 64.67)^2}{64.67} + \frac{(22 - 23.83)^2}{23.83}$$

$$+ \frac{(42 - 37.50)^2}{37.50} + \frac{(62 - 68.33)^2}{68.33} + \frac{(27 - 25.17)^2}{25.17}$$

$$= 0.570 + 0.619 + 0.140 + 0.540 + 0.586 + 0.133 = 2.587$$

Do not reject null hypothesis that the sex of the viewer is independent of the viewer's opinion.

3.

	Teacher	Lawyer	Doctor	Accountant
Yes	21 (24.97)	48 (37.46)	12 (16.50)	18 (20.07)
No	35 (31.03)	36 (46.54)	25 (20.50)	27 (24.93)
	56	84	37	45

$\chi^2_{0.01} = 11.345$

$df = 3$

3. (Continued)

$$\chi^2 = \frac{(21 - 24.97)^2}{24.97} + \frac{(48 - 37.46)^2}{37.46} + \frac{(12 - 16.50)^2}{16.50}$$

$$+ \frac{(18 - 20.07)^2}{20.07} + \frac{(35 - 31.03)^2}{31.03} + \frac{(36 - 46.54)^2}{46.54}$$

$$+ \frac{(25 - 20.50)^2}{20.50} + \frac{(27 - 24.93)^2}{24.93}$$

$$= 0.632 + 2.966 + 1.227 + 0.213 + 0.509 + 2.387 + 0.988$$
$$+ 0.171 = 9.094$$

Do not reject null hypothesis that the proportion of smokers in the different occupations mentioned is the same.

4.

Observed	18	16	14	17	29	27	26
Expected	21	21	21	21	21	21	21

$$\text{Expected} = \frac{18 + 16 + 14 + 17 + 29 + 27 + 26}{7} = \frac{147}{7} = 21$$

$$\chi^2_{0.05} = 12.592 \qquad df = 6$$

$$\chi^2 = \frac{(18 - 21)^2}{21} + \frac{(16 - 21)^2}{21} + \frac{(14 - 21)^2}{21} + \frac{(17 - 21)^2}{21}$$

$$+ \frac{(29 - 21)^2}{21} + \frac{(27 - 21)^2}{21} + \frac{(26 - 21)^2}{21}$$

$$= 0.429 + 1.190 + 2.333 + 0.762 + 3.048 + 1.714 + 1.190$$
$$= 10.666$$

Do not reject null hypothesis that the number of arrests for drunken driving is the same for the different days of the week.

5.

	A	B	C	D	Total
Low	3 (4.46)	14 (10.69)	9 (9.80)	4 (5.05)	30
Moderate	4 (5.05)	12 (12.12)	11 (11.11)	7 (5.72)	34
High	8 (5.50)	10 (13.19)	13 (12.09)	6 (6.23)	37
Total	15	36	33	17	

$$\chi^2_{0.05} = 12.592$$

$$df = (4 - 1)(3 - 1) = 6$$

<u>Note:</u> 1 cell has an expected frequency less than 5.

$$\chi^2 = \frac{(3 - 4.46)^2}{4.46} + \frac{(14 - 10.69)^2}{10.69} + \frac{(9 - 9.80)^2}{9.80} + \frac{(4 - 5.05)^2}{5.05}$$

$$+ \frac{(4 - 5.05)^2}{5.05} + \frac{(12 - 12.12)^2}{12.12} + \frac{(11 - 11.11)^2}{11.11} + \frac{(7 - 5.72)^2}{5.72}$$

$$+ \frac{(8 - 5.50)^2}{5.50} + \frac{(10 - 13.19)^2}{13.19} + \frac{(13 - 12.09)^2}{12.09} + \frac{(6 - 6.23)^2}{6.23}$$

$$= 0.475 + 1.023 + 0.066 + 0.218 + 0.218 + 0.001 + 0.001$$
$$+ 0.285 + 1.142 + 0.771 + 0.069 + 0.008 = 4.277$$

Do not reject null hypothesis that the level of pollution is independent of the river sampled.

6.

Observed	79	59	42	20
Expected	80	50	40	30

$$8x + 5x + 4x + 3x = 200 \qquad 8x = 80$$
$$20x = 200 \qquad 5x = 50$$
$$x = 10 \qquad 4x = 40$$
$$3x = 30$$

$$\chi^2_{0.05} = 7.815$$

$$\chi^2 = \frac{(79 - 80)^2}{80} + \frac{(59 - 50)^2}{50} + \frac{(42 - 40)^2}{40} + \frac{(20 - 30)^2}{30}$$

$$= 0.0125 + 1.620 + 0.100 + 3.333 = 5.0655$$

Do not reject null hypothesis that the sizes of the dresses sold are in the specified ratio.

7.

	Under $30,000	$30,000-$60,000	More than $60,000	Total
Gas	31 (31.03)	41 (40.18)	37 (37.79)	109
Oil	28 (25.34)	34 (32.81)	27 (30.86)	89
Wood/Coal	19 (21.64)	26 (28.01)	31 (26.35)	76
Total	78	101	95	274

$$\chi^2_{0.01} = 13.277 \qquad df = (3 - 1)(3 - 1) = 4$$

<u>Note:</u> 1 cell has an expected frequency less than 5.

$$\chi^2 = \frac{(31 - 31.03)^2}{31.03} + \frac{(41 - 40.18)^2}{40.18} + \frac{(37 - 37.79)^2}{37.79}$$

$$+ \frac{(28 - 25.34)^2}{25.34} + \frac{(34 - 32.81)^2}{32.81} + \frac{(27 - 30.86)^2}{30.86}$$

$$+ \frac{(19 - 21.64)^2}{21.64} + \frac{(26 - 28.01)^2}{28.01} + \frac{(31 - 26.35)^2}{26.35}$$

$$= 0.000 + 0.017 + 0.017 + 0.280 + 0.043 + 0.482 + 0.321$$
$$+ 0.145 + 0.820 = 2.126$$

Do not reject null hypothesis that family income is independent of the method of heating used.

8.

	Los Angeles	New York	Chicago	Detroit	Miami	Total
Yes	56 (57.56)	41 (45.84)	55 (59.60)	48 (51.45)	72 (57.56)	272
No	57 (55.44)	49 (44.16)	62 (57.40)	53 (49.55)	41 (55.44)	262
Total	113	90	117	101	113	534

$$\chi^2_{0.05} = 9.488$$

$$df = 4$$

8. (Continued)

$$\chi^2 = \frac{(56 - 57.56)^2}{57.56} + \frac{(41 - 45.84)^2}{45.84} + \frac{(55 - 59.60)^2}{59.60}$$

$$+ \frac{(48 - 51.45)^2}{51.45} + \frac{(72 - 57.56)^2}{57.56} + \frac{(57 - 55.44)^2}{55.44}$$

$$+ \frac{(49 - 44.16)^2}{44.16} + \frac{(62 - 57.40)^2}{57.40} + \frac{(53 - 49.55)^2}{49.55}$$

$$+ \frac{(41 - 55.44)^2}{55.44}$$

$$= 0.042 + 0.511 + 0.355 + 0.231 + 3.623 + 0.044 + 0.531$$
$$+ 0.369 + 0.240 + 3.761 = 9.707$$

Reject null hypothesis that the proportion of Americans who think that our government is doing enough for the homeless is the same for the cities mentioned.

9.

	Mon	Tues	Wed	Thurs	Fri	Total
Morning	7 (7.69)	6 (5.59)	4 (5.24)	3 (3.14)	9 (7.34)	29
Afternoon	5 (6.63)	8 (4.82)	3 (4.52)	2 (2.71)	7 (6.33)	25
Evening	10 (7.69)	2 (5.59)	8 (5.24)	4 (3.14)	5 (7.34)	29
Total	22	16	15	9	21	83

$$\chi^2_{0.01} = 20.090$$

$$df = (5 - 1)(3 - 1) = 8$$

<u>Note:</u> Since there are 5 cells with expected frequencies less than 5 it might be advisable to combine cells.

9. (Continued)

$$\chi^2 = \frac{(7 - 7.69)^2}{7.69} + \frac{(6 - 5.59)^2}{5.59} + \frac{(4 - 5.24)^2}{5.24} + \frac{(3 - 3.14)^2}{3.14}$$

$$+ \frac{(9 - 7.34)^2}{7.34} + \frac{(5 - 6.63)^2}{6.63} + \frac{(8 - 4.82)^2}{4.82} + \frac{(3 - 4.52)^2}{4.52}$$

$$+ \frac{(2 - 2.71)^2}{2.71} + \frac{(7 - 6.33)^2}{6.33} + \frac{(10 - 7.69)^2}{7.69} + \frac{(2 - 5.59)^2}{5.59}$$

$$+ \frac{(8 - 5.24)^2}{5.24} + \frac{(4 - 3.14)^2}{3.14} + \frac{(5 - 7.34)^2}{7.34}$$

$= 0.061 + 0.030 + 0.294 + 0.007 + 0.377 + 0.399 + 2.099$
$+ 0.510 + 0.186 + 0.072 + 0.696 + 2.306 + 1.452 + 0.233$
$+ 0.745 = 9.467$

Do not reject null hypothesis that the time of day when the accident occurs is independent of the day of the week when the accident occurs.

10.

Observed	325	98	92	65
Expected	315	104	88	73

$\chi^2_{0.05} = 7.815$

$$\chi^2 = \frac{(325 - 315)^2}{315} + \frac{(98 - 104)^2}{104} + \frac{(92 - 88)^2}{88} + \frac{(65 - 73)^2}{73}$$

$= 0.31746 + 0.34615 + 0.18182 + 0.87671$
$= 1.72214$

Do not reject null hypothesis. The data seem to be consistent with the theory.

11. Choice (a)

12. Choice (b)

13. Choice (c)

14. Choice (d)

15. Choice (a)

CHAPTER 12 - THE CHI-SQUARE DISTRIBUTION
SUPPLEMENTARY TEST FORM A

For question 1 - 5 use the following information: 1158 patients in Walker Hospital were asked to indicate whether or not they were satisfied with the nursing service at the hospital. The following results were obtained:

		Satisfied	Not Satisfied	No Opinion
Age of patient	Under 30 years	226	182	123
	30 - 50 years	117	153	89
	Over 50 years	88	112	68

1. What is the expected number of patients over 50 years of age who had no opinion on the nursing service at the hospital?

   a) 99.7   b) 103.5   c) 64.8   d) 86.8   e) none of these

   Answer _____

2. What is the expected number of patients under 30 years of age who were satisfied with the nursing service at the hospital?

   a) 197.6   b) 205   c) 128.4   d) 133.6   e) none of these

   Answer _____

3. The number of degrees of freedom for this problem is

   a) 3   b) 9   c) 4   d) 8   e) none of these

   Answer _____

4. The value of χ^2 for this problem is

   a) 11.183   b) 12.743   c) 13.486   d) 12.147
   e) none of these

   Answer _____

5. Using a 5% level of significance, test the null hypothesis that the age of the patient is independent of the view expressed by the patient.

   a) Do not reject null hypothesis   b) Reject null hypothesis
   c) Not enough information given

   Answer _____

401

6. When a certain plant is crossbred with another plant, the offspring should be red, pink, and yellow in the ratio 2:5:7. Of 280 new plants, 22 were red, 110 were pink and 148 were yellow. At the 5% level of significance, should we reject the null hypothesis that the true proportion is 2:5:7?

   a) Do not reject null hypothesis   b) Reject null hypothesis
   c) Not enough information given

   Answer _____

7. The number of express delivery packages received by a publishing company is shown below:

Mon	Tues	Wed	Thurs	Fri
12	22	18	19	14

   Using a 5% level of significance, test the null hypothesis that the number of express delivery packages received is independent of the day of the week.

   a) Do not reject null hypothesis   b) Reject null hypothesis
   c) Not enough information given

   Answer _____

For questions 8 - 10 use the following information: A survey of 400 residents of a senior citizen home was taken to determine their view on the social activities provided by the senior citizen home. The results of the survey according to the sex of the resident are shown below.

Do you like the social activities?		Male	Female
	Yes	88	127
	No	87	98

8. Find the expected number of males who like the social activities?

   a) 80.9   b) 104.1   c) 94.1   d) 120.9   e) none of these

   Answer _____

9. The number of degrees of freedom for the problem is

   a) 1   b) 2   c) 3   d) 4   e) none of these

   Answer _____

402

10. The value of χ^2 for this problem is

a) 1.493   b) 1.397   c) 1.468   d) 1.502
e) none of these

Answer _____

For question 1 - 5 use the following information: 682 patients in Harley Hospital were asked to indicate whether or not they were satisfied with the bedside manner of the resident doctors at the hospital. The following results were obtained:

		Satisfied	Not Satisfied	No Opinion
Age of patients	Under 30 years	76	39	52
	30 - 50 years	82	68	23
	Over 50 years	42	198	102

1. What is the expected number of patients between 30 and 50 years of age who had no opinion?

   a) 50.7   b) 43.3   c) 44.9   d) 49   e) none of these

   Answer _____

2. What is the expected number of patients over 50 years of age who were satisfied with the bedside manner of the doctors?

   a) 97.4   b) 100.3   c) 152.9   d) 88.8   e) none of these

   Answer _____

3. The number of degrees of freedom for this problem is

   a) 3   b) 9   c) 4   d) 8   e) none of these

   Answer _____

4. The value of χ^2 for this problem is

   a) 94.158   b) 97.692   c) 88.431   d) 113.907
   e) none of these

   Answer _____

5. Using a 5% level of significance, test the null hypothesis that the age of the patient is independent of the view expressed by the patient.

   a) Do not reject null hypothesis   b) Reject null hypothesis
   c) Not enough information given

   Answer _____

6. When a certain plant is crossbred with another plant, the offspring should be green, yellow, and red in the ratio 3:8:4. Of 300 new plants, 68 were green, 179 were yellow, and 53 were red. At the 5% level of significance, should we reject the null hypothesis that the true proportion is 3:8:4?

   a) Do not reject null hypothesis   b) Reject null hypothesis
   c) Not enough information given

                                          Answer _____

7. The type of cars parked in a lot is as follows:

Compact	Subcompact	Intermediate	Large	Station-wagon
98	89	78	83	62

   Using a 5% level of significance, test the null hypothesis that the type of car parked in the lot is independent of its size.

   a) Do not reject null hypothesis   b) Reject null hypothesis
   c) Not enough information given

                                          Answer _____

For questions 8 - 10 use the following information: Two hundred residents in a college dormitory were asked to indicate whether they owned a musical instrument. The results of the survey according to the sex of the resident are shown below:

		Male	Female
Do you own a	Yes	58	61
musical instrument?	No	49	32

8. Find the expected number of males who owned a musical instrument:

   a) 63.7   b) 43.3   c) 37.7   d) 55.3   e) none of these

                                          Answer _____

9. The number of degrees of freedom for the problem is

   a) 1   b) 2   c) 3   d) 4   e) none of these

                                          Answer _____

10. The value of χ^2 for this problem is

a) 2.832   b) 3.014   c) 2.667   d) 2.513   e) none of these

Answer _____

CHAPTER 12 - THE CHI-SQUARE DISTRIBUTION
SUPPLEMENTARY TEST FORM C

For question 1 - 5 use the following information: 539 new car buyers were asked to indicate what influenced them to buy the particular car model purchased. The following results were obtained:

		Style	Economy	Reputation
Age of buyer	Under 30 years	53	47	61
	30 - 50 years	47	39	72
	Over 50 years	66	73	81

1. What is the expected number of buyers under 30 years of age who purchased the car because of its style?

   a) 46.6   b) 49.6   c) 47.5   d) 48.7   e) none of these

   Answer _____

2. What is the expected number of buyers over 50 years of age who purchased the car because of its reputation?

   a) 62.7   b) 67.8   c) 87.3   d) 64.9   e) none of these

   Answer _____

3. The number of degrees of freedom for this problem is

   a) 3   b) 9   c) 4   d) 8   e) none of these

   Answer _____

4. The value of χ^2 for this problem is

   a) 4.56   b) 5.37   c) 3.16   d) 4.89   e) none of these

   Answer _____

5. Using a 5% level of significance, test the null hypothesis that the age of the buyer is independent of the reason why the particular car model was purchased.

   a) Do not reject null hypothesis   b) Reject null hypothesis
   c) Not enough information given

   Answer _____

6. According to one theory, a certain plant is supposed to produce red, yellow, and pink plants in the ratio 8:5:6. In a sample of 380 plants, it was found that 149 were red, 107 were yellow, and 124 were pink. At the 5% level of significance, should we reject the theory?

a) yes   b) no   c) not enough information given
d) none of these

Answer _____

7. The number of marriage licenses in Delton issued during one week is shown below:

Mon	Tues	Wed	Thurs	Fri
58	49	72	68	61

Using a 5% level of significance, test the null hypothesis that the number of marriage licenses issued in Delton is independent of the day of the week.

a) Do not reject null hypothesis   b) Reject null hypothesis
c) Not enough information given

Answer _____

For question 8 - 10 use the following information: A survey of 255 college students was taken to determine their view on instituting a new pass-fail system for certain courses. The results of the survey according to the sex of the student are shown below:

		Male	Female
In favor of new system?	Yes	69	48
	No	76	62

8. Find the expected number of males who are in favor of the new system.

a) 50.5   b) 66.5   c) 78.5   d) 59.5   e) none of these

Answer _____

9. The number of degrees of freedom for the problem is

a) 1   b) 2   c) 3   d) 4   e) none of these

408

10. The value of χ^2 for this problem is

    a) 0.789   b) 0.547   c) 0.876   d) 0.393   e) none of these

Answer _____

ANSWERS TO SUPPLEMENTARY TESTS
CHAPTER 12 - THE CHI-SQUARE DISTRIBUTION

Form A	Form B	Form C
1. Choice (c)	1. Choice (c)	1. Choice (b)
2. Choice (a)	2. Choice (b)	2. Choice (c)
3. Choice (c)	3. Choice (c)	3. Choice (c)
4. Choice (b)	4. Choice (d)	4. Choice (a)
5. Choice (b)	5. Choice (b)	5. Choice (a)
6. Choice (b)	6. Choice (b)	6. Choice (b)
7. Choice (a)	7. Choice (a)	7. Choice (a)
8. Choice (c)	8. Choice (a)	8. Choice (b)
9. Choice (a)	9. Choice (a)	9. Choice (a)
10. Choice (d)	10. Choice (c)	10. Choice (d)

SECTION 13.4 – (PAGES 658 – 664)

1.

				Row Total
101	107	106	103	417
102	105	109	107	423
101	104	111	105	421
102	107	106	104	419
Column Total: 406	423	432	419	Grand Total: 1680

Cell (1): $\dfrac{417^2 + 423^2 + 421^2 + 419^2}{4} - \dfrac{1680^2}{16} = 5.00$

Cell (2): $101^2 + 107^2 + \ldots + 104^2 -$

$\left(\dfrac{417^2 + 423^2 + 421^2 + 419^2}{4} \right) = 117.00$

Cell (3): $101^2 + 107^2 + \ldots + 104^2 - \dfrac{1680^2}{16} = 122.00$

Cell (4): $4 - 1 = 3$
Cell (5): $4(4 - 1) = 12$
Cell (6): $16 - 1 = 15$

Cell (7): $\dfrac{5.00}{3} = 1.67$

Cell (8): $\dfrac{117.00}{12} = 9.75$

Cell (9): $\dfrac{1.67}{9.75} = 0.17$

1. (Continued)

Source of Variation	Sum of Squares	Degrees of Freedom	Mean Square	F-ratio
Stations	(1) 5.00	(4) 3	(7) 1.67	(9) 0.17
Error	(2) 117.00	(5) 12	(8) 9.75	
Total	(3) 122.00	(6) 15		

$F_{12}^{3}(0.05) = 3.49$

Do not reject null hypothesis that there is no significant difference in the average price charged by these gas stations for a gallon of unleaded gas.

2.

					Row Total
27	35	28	41	32	163
26	21	39	47	30	163
29	21	28	32	36	146
26	28	19	47	37	157

Column Total: 108 105 114 167 135 | 629 Grand Total

Cell (1): $\dfrac{163^2 + 163^2 + 146^2 + 157^2}{5} - \dfrac{629^2}{20} = 38.55$

Cell (2): $27^2 + 35^2 + \ldots + 37^2$

$$- \left(\dfrac{163^2 + 163^2 + 146^2 + 157^2}{5} \right) = 1154.4$$

Cell (3): $27^2 + 35^2 + \ldots + 37^2 - \dfrac{629^2}{20} = 1192.95$

Cell (4): $4 - 1 = 3$
Cell (5): $4(5 - 1) = 16$
Cell (6): $20 - 1 = 19$

412

2. (Continued)

Cell (7): $\dfrac{38.5}{3} = 12.8$

Cell (8): $\dfrac{1154.4}{16} = 72.2$

Cell (9): $\dfrac{12.8}{72.2} = 0.18$

Source of Variation	Sum of Squares	Degrees of Freedom	Mean Square	F-ratio
Cities	(1) 38.55	(4) 3	(7) 12.85	(9) 0.18
Error	(2) 1154.4	(5) 16	(8) 72.2	
Total	(3) 1192.95	(6) 19		

$F_{16}^{3}(0.01) = 5.29$

Do not reject null hypothesis that the average number of murders reported over the 5-month period is not significantly different for all four cities.

3.

					Row Total
22	11	17	15	10	75
12	16	18	13	15	74
19	11	14	15	17	76
16	3	9	10	12	50
Column Total 69	41	58	53	54	275 Grand Total

Cell (1): $\dfrac{75^2 + 74^2 + 76^2 + 50^2}{5} - \dfrac{275^2}{20} = 94.2$

Cell (2): $22^2 + 11^2 + \ldots + 12^2$

$\qquad - \left(\dfrac{75^2 + 74^2 + 76^2 + 50^2}{5} \right) = 243.6$

413

3. (Continued)

Cell (3): $22^2 + 11^2 + \ldots + 12^2 - \dfrac{275^2}{20} = 337.8$

Cell (4): $4 - 1 = 3$
Cell (5): $4(5 - 1) = 16$
Cell (6): $20 - 1 = 19$

Cell (7): $\dfrac{94.2}{3} = 31.4$

Cell (8): $\dfrac{243.6}{16} = 15.2$

Cell (9): $\dfrac{31.4}{15.2} = 2.06$

Source of Variation	Sum of Squares	Degrees of Freedom	Mean Square	F-ratio
Blood Pressure Pills	(1) 94.2	(4) 3	(7) 31.4	(9) 2.06
Error	(2) 243.6	(5) 16	(8) 15.2	
Total	(3) 377.8	(6) 19		

$F^3_{16}(0.01) = 5.29$

Do not reject null hypothesis that the average blood pressure loss is not significantly different for the various blood pressure pills.

4.

				Row Total
427	382	502	476	1787
391	402	427	501	1721
517	378	476	409	1780
501	499	404	428	1832
Column Total				Grand Total
1836	1661	1809	1814	7120

ANSWERS TO EXERCISES FOR SECTION 13.4 (CONTINUED) –
(PAGES 658 – 664)

4. (Continued)

Cell (1): $\dfrac{1787^2 + 1721^2 + 1780^2 + 1832^2}{4} - \dfrac{(7120)^2}{16} = 1558.5$

Cell (2): $(427^2 + 382^2 + \ldots + 428^2)$

$-\left(\dfrac{1787^2 + 1721^2 + 1780^2 + 1832^2}{4}\right) = 35121.5$

Cell (3): $(427^2 + 382^2 + \ldots + 428^2) - \dfrac{7120^2}{16} = 36680$

Cell (4): $4 - 1 = 3$
Cell (5): $4(4 - 1) = 12$
Cell (6): $16 - 1 = 15$

Cell (7): $\dfrac{1558.5}{3} = 519.5$

Cell (8): $\dfrac{35121.5}{12} = 2926.79$

Cell (9): $\dfrac{519.5}{2926.79} =$

Source of Variation	Sum of Squares	Degrees of Freedom	Mean Square	F-ratio
Locations	(1) 1558.5	(4) 3	(7) 519.5	(9) 0.18
Error	(2) 35121.5	(5) 12	(8) 2926.79	
Total	(3) 36680	(6) 15		

$F_{12}^{3}(0.05) = 3.49$

Do not accept commissioner's claim that the average daily hospital charge for a routine delivery is significantly different for the various hospitals.

5.

						Row Total
28.0	26.4	25.7	29.6	26.5	28.2	164.4
31.1	27.8	28.6	30.8	27.9	29.0	175.2
26.5	27.8	26.1	22.5	23.6		126.5
24.3	29.2	34.1	30.7	27.6	21.4	167.3

Column Total: 109.9 111.2 114.5 113.6 105.6 78.6 | 633.4 Grand Total

Cell (1): $\left[\dfrac{(164.4)^2 + (175.2)^2 + (167.3)^2}{6} + \dfrac{126.5)^2}{5}\right]$

$-\dfrac{(633.4)^2}{23} = 42.446$

Cell (2): $(28.0^2 + 26.4^2 + \ldots + 21.4^2)$

$-\left[\dfrac{164.4^2 + 175.2^2 + 167.3^2}{6} + \dfrac{126.5^2}{5}\right] = 143.088$

Cell (3): $(28.0^2 + 26.4^2 + \ldots + 21.4^2)$

$-\left[\dfrac{(633.4)^2}{23}\right] \doteq 185.534$

Cell (4): $4 - 1 = 3$
Cell (5): $3(6 - 1) + 1(5 - 1) = 19$
Cell (6): $23 - 1 = 22$

Cell (7): $\dfrac{42.446}{3} = 14.149$

Cell (8): $\dfrac{143.088}{19} = 7.531$

Cell (9): $\dfrac{14.149}{7.531} = 1.879$

5. (Continued)

Source of Variation	Sum of Squares	Degrees of Freedom	Mean Square	F-ratio
Gasolines	(1) 42.446	(4) 3	(7) 14.149	(9) 1.879
Error	(2) 143.088	(5) 19	(8) 7.531	
Total	(3) 185.534	(6) 22		

$F_{19}^{3}(0.05) = 3.13$

Do not accept claim that the differences among the sample means are significant.

6.

						Row Total
88	94	62	86	74	89	493
76	81	74	79	75		385
69	83	95	77	80		404
82	68	70	71			291

Column Total: 315 326 301 313 229 89 | 1573 Grand Total

Cell (1): $\left[\dfrac{493^2}{6} + \dfrac{385^2 + 404^2}{5} + \dfrac{291^2}{4} \right] - \dfrac{1573^2}{20} = 250.167$

Cell (2): $(88^2 + 94^2 + 62^2 + \ldots + 71^2)$

$\qquad - \left[\dfrac{493^2}{6} + \dfrac{385^2 + 404^2}{5} + \dfrac{291^2}{4} \right] = 1222.383$

Cell (3): $(88^2 + 94^2 + 62^2 + \ldots + 71^2) - \dfrac{1573^2}{20} = 1472.55$

Cell (4): $4 - 1 = 3$
Cell (5): $1(6 - 1) + 2(5 - 1) + 1(4 - 1) = 16$
Cell (6): $20 - 1 = 19$

Cell (7): $\dfrac{250.167}{3} = 83.389$

6. (Continued)

Cell (8): $\dfrac{122.383}{16} = 7.649$

Cell (9): $\dfrac{83.389}{7.649} = 10.902$

Source of Variation	Sum of Squares	Degrees of Freedom	Mean Square	F-ratio
Cartons	(1) 250.167	(4) 3	(7) 83.389	(9) 1.09
Error	(2) 1222.383	(5) 16	(8) 76.4	
Total	(3) 1472.55	(6) 19		

$F_{16}^{3}(0.05) = 3.24$

Do not reject null hypothesis. The data do not indicate that the average breaking strength of the cartons produced by the different companies is significantly different.

7.

			Row Total
1.21	1.25	1.33	3.79
1.19	1.23	1.29	3.71
1.23	1.27	1.27	3.77
1.18	1.21	1.28	3.67
1.25	1.27	1.22	3.74

Column Total: 6.06   6.23   6.39   18.68 Grand Total

Cell (1): $\left(\dfrac{3.79^2 + 3.71^2 + 3.77^2 + 3.67^2 + 3.74^2}{3} \right) - \dfrac{18.68^2}{15}$

$= 0.003$

Cell (2): $\left(\dfrac{6.06^2 + 6.23^2 + 6.39^2}{5} \right) - \dfrac{18.68^2}{15} = 0.011$

7. (Continued)

Cell (3): $(1.21^2 + 1.25^2 + 1.33^2 + \ldots + 1.22^2)$

$$- \left(\frac{3.79^2 + 3.71^2 + 3.77^2 + 3.67^2 + 3.74^2}{3} \right)$$

$$- \left(\frac{6.06^2 + 6.23^2 + 6.39^2}{5} \right) + \frac{18.68^2}{15} = 0.009$$

Cell (4): $(1.21^2 + 1.25^2 + 1.33^2 + \ldots + 1.22^2)$

$$- \frac{18.68^2}{15} = 0.023$$

Cell (5): $5 - 1 = 4$
Cell (6): $3 - 1 = 2$
Cell (7): $(5 - 1)(3 - 1) = 8$
Cell (8): $(5)(3) - 1 = 14$

Cell (9): $\dfrac{0.003}{4} = 0.00075$

Cell (10): $\dfrac{0.011}{2} = 0.0055$

Cell (11): $\dfrac{0.009}{8} = 0.001125$

Cell (12): $\dfrac{0.00075}{0.001125} = 0.6667$

Cell (13): $\dfrac{0.0055}{0.001125} = 4.8889$

Source of Variation	Sum of Squares	Degrees of Freedom	Mean Square	F-ratio
Brands	(1) 0.003	(5) 4	(9) 0.00075	(12) 0.6667
Areas	(2) 0.011	(6) 2	(10) 0.0055	(13) 4.8889
Error	(3) 0.009	(7) 8	(11) 0.001125	
Total	(4) 0.023	(8) 14		

$F_8^4(0.05) = 3.84$

7.   (Continued)

$F_8^2(0.05) = 4.46$

We do reject null hypothesis that the average price of gas is
the same for all brands, However, we do reject the null
hypothesis that average price of gas is the same for all
neighborhoods.

8.

			Row Total
36	21	31	88
32	29	32	93
33	31	36	100
19	32	22	73
24	38	27	89

Column Total 144   151   148   443   Grand Total

Cell (1): $\left(\dfrac{88^2 + 93^2 + 100^2 + 73^2 + 89^2}{3}\right) - \dfrac{443^2}{15} = 131.067$

Cell (2): $\left(\dfrac{144^2 + 151^2 + 148^2}{5}\right) - \dfrac{443^2}{15} = 4.934$

Cell (3): $(36^2 + 21^2 + \ldots + 27^2)$

$- \left(\dfrac{88^2 + 93^2 + 100^2 + 73^2 + 89^2}{3}\right)$

$- \left(\dfrac{144^2 + 151^2 + 148^2}{5}\right) + \dfrac{443^2}{15} = 331.733$

Cell (4): $(36^2 + 21^2 + \ldots + 27^2) - \left(\dfrac{443^2}{15}\right) = 467.734$

Cell (5): $5 - 1 = 4$
Cell (6): $3 - 1 = 2$
Cell (7): $(5 - 1)(3 - 1) = 8$
Cell (8): $15 - 1 = 14$

8. (Continued)

Cell (9): $\dfrac{131.067}{4}$ = 32.767

Cell (10): $\dfrac{4.934}{2}$ = 2.467

Cell (11): $\dfrac{331.733}{8}$ = 41.467

Cell (12): $\dfrac{32.767}{41.467}$ = 0.790

Cell (13): $\dfrac{2.467}{41.467}$ = 0.059

Source of Variation	Sum of Squares	Degrees of Freedom	Mean Square	F-ratio
Days	(1) 131.067	(5) 4	(9) 32.767	(12) 0.790
Machines	(2) 4.934	(6) 2	(10) 2.467	(13) 0.059
Error	(3) 331.733	(7) 8	(11) 41.467	
Total	(4) 467.734	(8) 14		

$F_8^4(0.05)$ = 3.84 and $F_8^2(0.05)$ = 4.46

Do not reject null hypothesis. The data do not indicate that there is a significant difference in the average number of defective items produced by these machines.

9.

				Row Total
12	9	23	12	56
14	12	8	18	52
11	15	17	19	62
16	11	9		36
10	8			18
Column Total: 63	55	57	49	224 Grand Total

421

9. (Continued)

Cell (1): $\left[\dfrac{63^2 + 55^2}{5} + \dfrac{57^2}{4} + \dfrac{49^2}{3}\right] - \dfrac{224^2}{17} = 59.8539$

Cell (2): $(12^2 + 9^2 + 23^2 + \ldots + 8^2)$

$\qquad\qquad - \left[\dfrac{63^2 + 55^2}{5} + \dfrac{57^2}{4} + \dfrac{49^2}{3}\right] = 232.6167$

Cell (3): $(12^2 + 9^2 + 23^2 + \ldots + 8^2) - \dfrac{224^2}{17} = 292.4706$

Cell (4): $4 - 1 = 3$
Cell (5): $2(5 - 1) + 1(4 - 1) + 1(3 - 1) = 13$
Cell (6): $17 - 1 = 16$

Cell (7): $\dfrac{59.8539}{3} = 19.9513$

Cell (8): $\dfrac{232.6167}{13} = 17.8936$

Cell (9): $\dfrac{19.9513}{17.8936} = 1.115$

Source of Variation	Sum of Squares	Degrees of Freedom	Mean Square	F-ratio
Banks	(1) 59.8539	(4) 3	(7) 19.9513	(9) 1.115
Error	(2) 232.6167	(5) 13	(8) 17.8936	
Total	(3) 292.4706	(6) 16		

$F_{13}^{3}(0.01) = 5.74$

Do not reject null hypothesis. The data do not indicate that there is a significant difference in the average time required to complete the transaction at these banks.

10.

				Row Total
42	28	45	36	151
29	49	24	40	142
45	31	29	47	152
24	37	32	45	138
37	29	35	36	137

Column Total: 177   174   165   204   720   Grand Total

Cell (1): $\left(\dfrac{151^2 + 142^2 + 152^2 + 138^2 + 137^2}{4}\right) - \dfrac{720^2}{20} = 50.5$

Cell (2): $\left(\dfrac{177^2 + 174^2 + 165^2 + 204^2}{5}\right) - \dfrac{720^2}{20} = 169.2$

Cell (3): $(42^2 + 28^2 + \ldots + 36^2)$

$- \left(\dfrac{151^2 + 142^2 + 152^2 + 138^2 + 137^2}{4}\right)$

$- \left(\dfrac{177^2 + 174^2 + 165^2 + 204^2}{5}\right) + \dfrac{720^2}{20} = 908.3$

Cell (4): $(42^2 + 28^2 + \ldots + 36^2) - \dfrac{720^2}{20} = 1128$

Cell (5): $5 - 1 = 4$
Cell (6): $4 - 1 = 3$
Cell (7): $(5 - 1)(4 - 1) = 12$
Cell (8): $20 - 1 = 19$

Cell (9): $\dfrac{50.5}{4} = 12.625$

Cell (10): $\dfrac{169.2}{3} = 56.4$

Cell (11): $\dfrac{908.3}{12} = 75.6917$

10. (Continued)

Cell (12): $\dfrac{12.625}{75.6917} = 0.167$

Cell (13): $\dfrac{56.4}{75.6917} = 0.745$

Source of Variation	Sum of Squares	Degrees of Freedom	Mean Square	F-ratio
Days	(1) 50.5	(5) 4	(9) 12.625	(12) 0.167
Hospitals	(2) 169.2	(6) 3	(10) 56.4	(13) 0.745
Error	(3) 908.3	(7) 12	(11) 75.6917	
Total	(4) 1128	(8) 19		

$F_{12}^{4}(0.05) = 3.26$ and $F_{12}^{3}(0.05) = 3.49$

Do not reject null hypothesis. The data do not indicate that these is a significant difference between the average number of angiograms performed at these hospitals.

11.

				Row Total
268	280	261	232	1041
211	251	278	280	1020
235	245	255	270	1005
240	253	249	261	1003
Column Total 954	1029	1043	1043	4069 Grand Total

Cell (1): $\left(\dfrac{954^2 + 1029^2 + 1043^2 + 1043^2}{4}\right) - \dfrac{4069^2}{16} = 1366.1875$

Cell (2): $(268^2 + 280^2 + \ldots + 261^2)$

$-\left(\dfrac{954^2 + 1029^2 + 1043^2 + 1043^2}{4}\right) = 4117.0025$

424

11. (Continued)

Cell (3): $(268^2 + 280^2 + \ldots + 261^2) - \dfrac{4069^2}{16} = 5483.19$

Cell (4): $4 - 1 = 3$
Cell (5): $4(4 - 1) = 12$
Cell (6): $16 - 1 = 15$

Cell (7): $\dfrac{1366.1875}{3} = 455.396$

Cell (8): $\dfrac{4117.0025}{12} = 343.0835$

Cell (9): $\dfrac{455.396}{343.0835} = 1.33$

Source of Variation	Sum of Squares	Degrees of Freedom	Mean Square	F-ratio
	(1)	(4)	(7)	(9)
Diets	1366.1875	3	455.396	1.33
	(2)	(5)	(8)	
Error	4117.0025	12	343.0835	
	(3)	(6)		
Total	5483.19	15		

$F_{12}^{3}(0.01) = 5.95$

Do not reject null hypothesis. The data do not indicate that the type of diet used significantly affects average blood serum cholesterol level.

12.

					Row Total
12.8	13.3	12.6	12.9	13.5	65.1
12.1	12.3	12.8	13.7	12.7	63.6
13.8	13.4	13.5	13.1	12.9	66.7
12.8	12.7	13.1	13.2	13.3	65.1
12.8	13.3	12.9	13.0	13.1	65.1

Column Total: 64.3   65.0   64.9   65.9   65.5   325.6   Grand Total

Cell (1):
$$\left(\frac{65.1^2 + 63.6^2 + 66.7^2 + 65.1^2 + 65.1^2}{5}\right) - \left(\frac{325.6^2}{25}\right)$$
$$= 0.9616$$

Cell (2):
$$\left(\frac{64.3^2 + 65.0^2 + 64.9^2 + 65.9^2 + 65.5^2}{5}\right)$$
$$- \left(\frac{325.6^2}{25}\right) = 0.2976$$

Cell (3):
$$(12.8^2 + 13.3^2 + \ldots + 13.1^2)$$
$$- \left(\frac{65.1^2 + 63.6^2 + 66.7^2 + 65.1^2 + 65.1^2}{5}\right)$$
$$- \left(\frac{64.3^2 + 65.0^2 + 64.9^2 + 65.9^2 + 65.5^2}{5}\right)$$
$$+ \frac{325.6^2}{25} = 2.6864$$

Cell (4):
$$(12.8^2 + 13.3^2 + \ldots + 13.1^2) - \frac{325.6^2}{25}$$
$$= 3.9456$$

Cell (5): $5 - 1 = 4$

Cell (6): $5 - 1 = 4$

Cell (7): $(5 - 1)(5 - 1) = 16$

Cell (8): $(5)(5) - 1 = 24$

12. (Continued)

Cell (9): $\dfrac{0.9616}{4} = 0.2404$

Cell (10): $\dfrac{0.2976}{4} = 0.0744$

Cell (11): $\dfrac{2.6864}{16} = 0.1679$

Cell (12): $\dfrac{0.2404}{0.1679} = 1.4318$

Cell (13): $\dfrac{0.0744}{0.1679} = 0.4431$

Source of Variation	Sum of Squares	Degrees of Freedom	Mean Square	F-ratio
Locations	(1) 0.9616	(5) 4	(9) 0.2404	(12) 1.4318
Days	(2) 0.2976	(6) 4	(10) 0.0744	(13) 0.4431
Error	(3) 2.6864	(7) 16	(11) 0.1679	
Total	(4) 3.9456	(8) 24		

$F_{16}^{4}(0.05) = 3.01$

Do not reject null hypothesis. The data do not indicate that the average amount of sulfur oxide pollutants is significantly different at all the bridges and tunnels or on the day of the week.

427

13.

					Row Total
42	38	46	44	43	213
34	37	41	49	58	219
46	37	26	35	41	185
26	29	25	28	27	135
Column Total 148	141	138	156	169	752 Grand Total

Cell (1): $\left(\dfrac{213^2 + 219^2 + 185^2 + 135^2}{5} \right) - \dfrac{752^2}{20} = 880.8$

Cell (2): $\left(\dfrac{148^2 + 141^2 + 138^2 + 156^2 + 169^2}{4} \right)$

$- \dfrac{752^2}{20} = 156.3$

Cell (3): $(42^2 + 38^2 + \ldots + 27^2)$

$- \left(\dfrac{213^2 + 219^2 + 185^2 + 135^2}{5} \right)$

$- \left(\dfrac{148^2 + 141^2 + 138^2 + 156^2 + 169^2}{4} \right) + \dfrac{752^2}{20}$

$= 489.7$

Cell (4): $(42^2 + 38^2 + \ldots + 27^2) - \dfrac{752^2}{20} = 1526.8$

Cell (5): $4 - 1 = 3$
Cell (6): $5 - 1 = 4$
Cell (7): $(4 - 1)(5 - 1) = 12$
Cell (8): $4(5) - 1 = 19$

Cell (9): $\dfrac{880.8}{3} = 293.6$

Cell (10): $\dfrac{156.3}{4} = 39.075$

13. (Continued)

Cell (11): $\dfrac{489.7}{12} = 40.808$

Cell (12): $\dfrac{293.6}{40.808} = 7.195$

Cell (13): $\dfrac{39.075}{40.808} = 0.958$

Source of Variation	Sum of Squares	Degrees of Freedom	Mean Square	F-ratio
Techniques	(1) 880.0	(5) 3	(9) 293.6	(12) 7.195
Regions	(2) 156.3	(6) 4	(10) 39.075	(13) 0.958
Error	(3) 489.7	(7) 12	(11) 40.808	
Total	(4) 1526.8	(8) 19		

$F^3_{12}(0.01) = 5.95$

$F^4_{12}(0.01) = 5.41$

The data do not indicate that the difference in the average oil obtained from the various regions is significant. However, the difference in the average oil obtained by the different conversion techniques is significant.

14.

				Row Total
3	6	1	34	44
2	5	2	36	45
4	7	1	35	47
3	8	2	37	50
Column Total 12	26	6	142	186 Grand Total

429

14. (Continued)

Cell (1): $\left(\dfrac{44^2 + 45^2 + 47^2 + 50^2}{4}\right) - \dfrac{186^2}{16} = 5.25$

Cell (2): $\left(\dfrac{12^2 + 26^2 + 6^2 + 142^2}{4}\right) - \dfrac{186^2}{16} = 3092.75$

Cell (3): $(3^2 + 6^2 + \ldots + 37^2) - \left(\dfrac{44^2 + 45^2 + 47^2 + 50^2}{4}\right)$

$\qquad - \left(\dfrac{12^2 + 26^2 + 6^2 + 142^2}{4}\right) + \dfrac{186^2}{16} = 7.75$

Cell (4): $(3^2 + 6^2 + \ldots + 37^2) - \dfrac{186^2}{16} = 3105.75$

Cell (5): $4 - 1 = 3$
Cell (6): $4 - 1 = 3$
Cell (7): $(4 - 1)(4 - 1) = 9$
Cell (8): $4(4) - 1 = 15$

Cell (9): $\dfrac{5.25}{3} = 1.75$

Cell (10): $\dfrac{3092.75}{3} = 1030.92$

Cell (11): $\dfrac{7.75}{9} = 0.861$

Cell (12): $\dfrac{1.75}{0.861} = 2.033$

Cell (13): $\dfrac{1030.92}{0.861} = 1197.35$

14. (Continued)

Source of Variation	Sum of Squares	Degrees of Freedom	Mean Square	F-ratio
States	(1) 5.25	(5) 3	(9) 1.75	(12) 2.033
Crimes	(2) 3092.75	(6) 3	(10) 1030.92	(13) 1197.35
Error	(3) 7.75	(7) 9	(11) 0.861	
Total	(4) 3105.75	(8) 15		

$F_9^3(0.01) = 6.99$

The data indicate that the average length of a jail term is significantly different for the various crimes mentioned but is not significantly different for the several states.

1. Assumptions for one-way ANOVA
   a) <u>Independent samples</u>: The samples taken from the various populations are independent of one another.
   b) <u>Normal populations</u>: The populations from which the samples are obtained are (approximately) normally distributed.
   c) <u>Equal standard deviations</u>: The populations from which the samples are obtained all have the same (often unknown) variance, σ^2.

2. $F_{10}^{20}(0.01) = 3.3$ so that the probability that $F \leq 3.37$ is approximately 0.99

3. ANOVA Techniques tell us whether the variation among the sample means is too large to be attributed to chance. This, of course, implies that the differences among the sample means is significant.

1. A, B, C, D, and E

2.

Source of Variation	Sum of Squares	Degrees of Freedom	Mean Square	F-ratio
Factor	250	4	62.5	8.27
Error	150	20	7.5	
Total	400	24		

$F_{20}^{4}(0.05) = 2.87$

Reject null hypothesis that the sample means are equal.

3. $\bar{x}_1 = \dfrac{\sum x}{n_1} = \dfrac{84}{6} = 14$ $\qquad \bar{x}_2 = \dfrac{\sum y}{n_2} = \dfrac{89}{6} = 14.833$

MSE = 14.01 $\qquad t_{0.025} = 2.131$ for 15 degrees of freedom.

Lower boundary:

$$14 - 14.833 - 2.131\sqrt{14.01\left(\frac{1}{6} + \frac{1}{6}\right)} = -5.438$$

Upper boundary:

$$14 - 14.833 + 2.131\sqrt{14.01\left(\frac{1}{6} + \frac{1}{6}\right)} = 3.772$$

The 95% confidence interval for the difference between average tar content of Brand X and Brand Y cigarettes is between -5.438 and 3.772.

4. a) $\bar{x}_1 = \dfrac{\sum x}{n_1} = \dfrac{84}{6} = 14$ $\qquad \bar{x}_3 = \dfrac{\sum z}{n_3} = \dfrac{122}{6} = 20.333$

Lower boundary:

$$14 - 20.833 - 2.131\sqrt{1401\left(\frac{1}{6} + \frac{1}{6}\right)} = -11.438$$

Upper boundary:

$$14 - 20.833 + 2.131\sqrt{1401\left(\frac{1}{6} + \frac{1}{6}\right)} = -2.228$$

The 95% confidence interval for the difference between the average tar content of Brand X and Brand Z cigarettes is between -11.438 and -2.228.

4. b) $\bar{x}_2 = \dfrac{\Sigma y}{n_2} = \dfrac{89}{6} = 14.833$ $\qquad\qquad$ $\bar{x}_3 = \dfrac{\Sigma z}{n_3} = \dfrac{122}{6} = 20.333$

Lower boundary:

$$14.833 - 20.833 - 2.131\sqrt{1401\left(\dfrac{1}{6} + \dfrac{1}{6}\right)} = -10.605$$

Upper boundary:

$$14.833 - 20.833 + 2.131\sqrt{1401\left(\dfrac{1}{6} + \dfrac{1}{6}\right)} = -1.395$$

The 95% confidence interval for the difference between the average tar content of Brand Y and Brand Z cigarettes is between -10.605 and -1.395.

ANSWERS TO REVIEW EXERCISES FOR CHAPTER 13 - (PAGES 668 - 671)

				Row Total
29	33	26	27	115
24	27	33	31	115
25	24	33	32	114
78	84	92	90	344

Column Total: 78 84 92 90 $\qquad$ 344 Grand Total

1. Cell (1) entry: $\left(\dfrac{115^2 + 115^2 + 114^2}{4}\right) - \dfrac{344^2}{12} = 0.1667$ or 0.2

2. Cell (2) entry: $(29^2 + 33^2 + \ldots + 32^2) - \left(\dfrac{115^2 + 115^2 + 114^2}{4}\right)$

$\qquad\qquad\qquad\qquad = 142.5$

3. Cell (3) entry: $(29^2 + 33^2 + \ldots + 32^2) - \dfrac{344^2}{12} = 142.7$

4. Cell (4) entry: $3 - 1 = 2$

5. Cell (5) entry: $3(4 - 1) = 9$

6. Cell (6) entry: $12 - 1 = 11$

7. Cell (7) entry: $\dfrac{0.1667}{2}$ = 0.08335 or 0.1

8. Cell (8) entry: $\dfrac{142.5}{9}$ = 15.833

9. Cell (9) entry: $\dfrac{0.08335}{15.833}$ = 0.00526 or 0.01

10. Choice (a) – (Technically speaking choice (b) is also correct
     if we are testing diffences between variances.)

11. Choice (a)

12. Choice (c)

13.

					Row Total
26	42	35	25	45	173
16	19	27	14	22	98
40	34	29	33	37	173
23	14	16	20	12	85
17	14	16	13	18	78

Column Total   122   123   123   105   134   607   Grand Total

Cell (1): $\left(\dfrac{173^2 + 98^2 + 173^2 + 85^2 + 78^2}{5} \right) - \dfrac{607^2}{25}$ = 1816.2

Cell (2): $\left(\dfrac{122^2 + 123^2 + 123^2 + 105^2 + 134^2}{5} \right) - \dfrac{607^2}{25}$ = 86.64

13. (Continued)

Cell (3): $(26^2 + 42^2 + \ldots + 18^2)$

$$- \left(\frac{173^2 + 98^2 + 173^2 + 85^2 + 78^2}{5} \right)$$

$$- \left(\frac{122^2 + 123^2 + 123^2 + 105^2 + 134^2}{5} \right) + \frac{607^2}{25} = 514.16$$

Cell (4): $(26^2 + 42^2 + \ldots + 18^2) - \frac{607^2}{25} = 2417.0$

Cell (5): $5 - 1 = 4$

Cell (6): $5 - 1 = 4$

Cell (7): $(5 - 1)(5 - 1) = 16$

Cell (8): $25 - 1 = 24$

Cell (9): $\frac{1816.2}{4} = 454.05$

Cell (10): $\frac{86.64}{4} = 21.66$

Cell (11): $\frac{514.16}{16} = 32.135$

Cell (12): $\frac{454.05}{32.135} = 14.129$

Cell (13): $\frac{21.66}{32.135} = 0.674$

Source of Variation	Sum of Squares	Degrees of Freedom	Mean Square	F-ratio
Sections	(1) 1816.2	(5) 4	(9) 454.05	(12) 14.129
Days	(2) 86.64	(6) 4	(10) 21.66	(13) 0.674
Error	(3) 514.16	(7) 16	(11) 32.135	
Total	(4) 2417.0	(8) 24		

$F_{16}^{4}(0.01) = 4.77$

13. (Continued)
    Do not accept null hypothesis. There is a significant difference in the average number of false alarms reported in the various section of the city.

14.

				Row Total
49	36	40	44	169
41	38	50	38	167
40	42	40	49	171
46	43	35	57	181

Column Total: 176, 159, 165, 188 | 688 Grand Total

Cell (1): $\left(\dfrac{169^2 + 167^2 + 171^2 + 181^2}{4}\right) - \dfrac{688^2}{16} = 29.0$

Cell (2): $\left(\dfrac{176^2 + 159^2 + 165^2 + 188^2}{4}\right) - \dfrac{688^2}{16} = 122.5$

Cell (3): $(49^2 + 36^2 + \ldots + 57^2)$

$- \left(\dfrac{169^2 + 167^2 + 171^2 + 181^2}{4}\right)$

$- \left(\dfrac{176^2 + 159^2 + 165^2 + 188^2}{4}\right) + \dfrac{688^2}{16} = 370.5$

Cell (4): $(49^2 + 36^2 + \ldots + 57^2) - \dfrac{688^2}{20} = 522.0$

Cell (5): $4 - 1 = 3$
Cell (6): $4 - 1 = 3$
Cell (7): $(4 - 1)(4 - 1) = 9$
Cell (8): $16 - 1 = 15$

Cell (9): $\dfrac{29.0}{3} = 9.667$

Cell (10): $\dfrac{122.5}{3} = 40.833$

436

14. (Continued)

Cell (11): $\dfrac{370.5}{9} = 41.667$

Cell (12): $\dfrac{9.667}{41.667} = 0.232$

Cell (13): $\dfrac{40.833}{41.667} = 0.980$

Source of Variation	Sum of Squares	Degrees of Freedom	Mean Square	F-ratio
Location	(1) 29.0	(5) 3	(9) 9.667	(12) 0.232
Day	(2) 122.5	(6) 3	(10) 40.833	(13) 0.980
Error	(3) 370.5	(7) 9	(11) 41.667	
Total	(4) 522.0	(8) 15		

$F_9^3(0.05) = 3.86$

Do not reject null hypothesis. The data does not indicate that the average number of accidental breakage is significantly different for all the stores.

1.

					Row Total
22	29	19	16	18	104
33	12	17	26	17	105
18	27	19	17	32	113
34	17	19	32	29	131

Column Total   107   85   74   91   96   453   Grand Total

Cell (1): $\left(\dfrac{104^2 + 105^2 + 113^2 + 131^2}{5} \right) - \dfrac{453^2}{15} = 93.8$

Cell (2): $(22^2 + 29^2 + \ldots + 29^2)$

$\qquad - \left(\dfrac{104^2 + 105^2 + 113^2 + 131^2}{5} \right) = 796.8$

Cell (3): $(22^2 + 29^2 + \ldots + 29^2) - \dfrac{453^2}{15} = 890.6$

Cell (4): $4 - 1 = 3$

Cell (5): $4(5 - 1) = 16$

Cell (6): $20 - 1 = 19$

Cell (7): $\dfrac{93.8}{3} = 31.267$

Cell (8): $\dfrac{796.8}{16} = 49.8$

Cell (9): $\dfrac{31.267}{49.8} = 0.628$

Source of Variation	Sum of Squares	Degrees of Freedom	Mean Square	F-ratio
Batteries	(1) 93.8	(4) 3	(7) 31.267	(9) 0.628
Error	(2) 796.8	(5) 16	(8) 49.8	
Total	(3) 890.6	(6) 19		

438

1. (Continued)

$F_{16}^{3}(0.01) = 5.29$

Do not reject null hypothesis. The data does not indicate that these is a significant difference between the average lives of these batteries.

2.

					Row Total
17	14	28	16	11	86
12	19	18	16	24	89
14	13	18	22	19	86

Column Total: 43   46   64   54   54   261   Grand Total

Cell (1): $\left(\dfrac{86^2 + 89^2 + 86^2}{5}\right) - \dfrac{261^2}{15} = 1.2$

Cell (2): $\left(\dfrac{43^2 + 46^2 + 64^2 + 54^2 + 54^2}{3}\right) - \dfrac{261^2}{15} = 89.6$

Cell (3): $(17^2 + 14^2 + \ldots + 19^2) - \left(\dfrac{86^2 + 89^2 + 86^2}{5}\right)$

$\qquad - \left(\dfrac{43^2 + 46^2 + 64^2 + 54^2 + 54^2}{3}\right) + \dfrac{261^2}{15} = 208.8$

Cell (4): $(17^2 + 14^2 + \ldots + 19^2) - \dfrac{261^2}{15} = 299.6$

Cell (5): $3 - 1 = 2$
Cell (6): $5 - 1 = 4$
Cell (7): $(3 - 1)(5 - 1) = 8$
Cell (8): $15 - 1 = 14$

Cell (9): $\dfrac{1.2}{2} = 0.6$

2. (Continued)

Cell (10): $\dfrac{89.6}{4} = 22.4$

Cell (11): $\dfrac{208.8}{8} = 26.1$

Cell (12): $\dfrac{0.6}{26.1} = 0.023$

Cell (13): $\dfrac{22.4}{26.1} = 0.858$

Source of Variation	Sum of Squares	Degrees of Freedom	Mean Square	F-ratio
Workers	(1) 1.2	(5) 2	(9) 0.6	(12) 0.023
Days	(2) 89.6	(6) 4	(10) 22.4	(13) 0.858
Error	(3) 208.8	(7) 8	(11) 26.1	
Total	(4) 299.6	(8) 14		

$F_8^2(0.05) = 4.46$ and $F_8^4(0.05) = 3.84$

Do not reject null hypothesis. The data does not indicate that these is a significant difference in the average production of these employees.

3.

					Row Total
22	17	32	16	19	106
19	36	24	18	31	128
25	29	14	30	26	124
20	33	26	11	17	107
25	17	22	34	27	125
Column Total 111	132	118	109	120	590 Grand Total

3. (Continued)

Cell (1): $\left(\dfrac{106^2 + 128^2 + 124^2 + 107^2 + 125^2}{5}\right) - \dfrac{590^2}{25} = 90.0$

Cell (2): $\left(\dfrac{111^2 + 132^2 + 118^2 + 109^2 + 120^2}{5}\right) - \dfrac{590^2}{25} = 66$

Cell (3): $(22^2 + 17^2 + \ldots + 27^2)$

$\qquad - \left(\dfrac{106^2 + 128^2 + 124^2 + 107^2 + 125^2}{5}\right)$

$\qquad - \left(\dfrac{111^2 + 132^2 + 118^2 + 109^2 + 120^2}{5}\right) + \dfrac{590^2}{25} = 948$

Cell (4): $(22^2 + 17^2 + \ldots + 27^2) - \dfrac{590^2}{25} = 1104.0$

Cell (5): $5 - 1 = 4$
Cell (6): $5 - 1 = 4$
Cell (7): $(5 - 1)(5 - 1) = 16$
Cell (8): $25 - 1 = 24$

Cell (9): $\dfrac{90.0}{4} = 22.5$

Cell (10): $\dfrac{66}{4} = 16.5$

Cell (11): $\dfrac{948}{16} = 59.25$

Cell (12): $\dfrac{22.5}{59.25} = 0.380$

Cell (13): $\dfrac{16.5}{59.25} = 0.278$

441

3.   (Continued)

Source of Variation	Sum of Squares	Degrees of Freedom	Mean Square	F-ratio
Judges	(1) 90	(5) 4	(9) 22.5	(12) 0.380
Day	(2) 66	(6) 4	(10) 16.5	(13) 0.278
Error	(3) 948	(7) 16	(11) 59.25	
Total	(4) 1104.0	(8) 24		

$F_{16}^{4}(0.05) = 3.01$

Do not reject null hypothesis. The data does not indicate that there is a significant difference in the average number of cases handled by these judges.

4.

				Row Total
55	48	49	58	210
42	39	59	50	190
46	32	51	48	177
38	47	54	39	178

Column Total   181   166   213   195 | 755   Grand Total

Cell (1): $\left(\dfrac{210^2 + 190^2 + 177^2 + 178^2}{4} \right) - \dfrac{755^2}{16} = 176.7$

Cell (2): $(55^2 + 48^2 + \ldots + 39^2)$

$- \left(\dfrac{210^2 + 190^2 + 177^2 + 178^2}{4} \right) = 691.8$

Cell (3): $(55^2 + 48^2 + \ldots + 39^2) - \dfrac{755^2}{16} = 868.4$

Cell (4): $4 - 1 = 3$
Cell (5): $4(4 - 1) = 12$
Cell (6): $16 - 1 = 15$

442

4. (Continued)

Cell (7): $\dfrac{176.7}{3} = 58.9$

Cell (8): $\dfrac{691.8}{12} = 57.65$

Cell (9): $\dfrac{58.9}{57.65} = 1.022$

Source of Variation	Sum of Squares	Degrees of Freedom	Mean Square	F-ratio
Methods	(1) 176.7	(4) 3	(7) 58.9	(9) 1.022
Error	(2) 691.8	(5) 12	(8) 57.65	
Total	(3) 868.4	(6) 15		

$F_{12}^{3}(0.05) = 3.49$

Do not reject null hypothesis. The data does not indicate that there is a significant difference in the average time needed by each student to learn to overcome the particular speech defect by the different methods.

5.

				Row Total
10	13	7	9	39
6	14	8	11	39
13	6	8	11	38
10	9	15	13	47
18	7	8	14	47
12	13	8	9	42
Column Total 69	62	54	67	252 Grand Total

Cell (1): $\left(\dfrac{39^2 + 39^2 + 38^2 + 47^2 + 47^2 + 42^2}{4} \right) - \dfrac{252^2}{24} = 21.0$

5. (Continued)

Cell (2): $(10^2 + 13^2 + \ldots + 9^2)$

$$- \left(\frac{39^2 + 39^2 + 38^2 + 47^2 + 47^2 + 42^2}{4} \right) = 205.0$$

Cell (3): $(10^2 + 13^2 + \ldots + 9^2) - \frac{252^2}{24} = 226.0$

Cell (4): $6 - 1 = 5$
Cell (5): $6(4 - 1) = 18$
Cell (6): $24 - 1 = 23$

Cell (7): $\frac{21.0}{5} = 4.2$

Cell (8): $\frac{205.0}{18} = 11.389$

Cell (9): $\frac{4.2}{11.389} = 0.369$

Source of Variation	Sum of Squares	Degrees of Freedom	Mean Square	F-ratio
Chemicals	(1) 21.0	(4) 5	(7) 4.2	(9) 0.369
Error	(2) 205.0	(5) 18	(8) 11.389	
Total	(3) 226.0	(6) 23		

$F_{18}^{5}(0.01) = 4.25$

Do not reject null hypothesis. The data does not indicate that there is a significant difference in the average weight gain of an animal over a fixed length of time as a result of the different chemicals.

6.

			Row Total
84	75	87	246
60	81	78	219
78	60	90	228
90	86		176
61			61

Column Total: 373   302   255   930   Grand Total

Cell (1): $\left(\dfrac{373^2}{5} + \dfrac{302^2}{4} + \dfrac{255^2}{3}\right) - \dfrac{930^2}{12} = 226.8$

Cell (2): $(84^2 + 75^2 + \ldots + 61^2)$

$$- \left(\dfrac{373^2}{5} + \dfrac{302^2}{4} + \dfrac{255^2}{3}\right) = 1194.2$$

Cell (3): $(84^2 + 75^2 + \ldots + 61^2) - \dfrac{930^2}{12} = 1421$

Cell (4): $3 - 1 = 2$

Cell (5): $1(5 - 1) + 1(4 - 1) + 1(3 - 1) = 9$

Cell (6): $12 - 1 = 11$

Cell (7): $\dfrac{226.8}{2} = 113.4$

Cell (8): $\dfrac{1194.2}{9} = 132.69$

Cell (9): $\dfrac{113.4}{132.69} = 0.855$

445

6. (Continued)

Source of Variation	Sum of Squares	Degrees of Freedom	Mean Square	F-ratio
Companies	(1) 226.8	(4) 2	(7) 113.4	(9) 0.855
Error	(2) 1194.2	(5) 9	(8) 132.69	
Total	(3) 1421	(6) 11		

$F_9^2(0.01) = 8.02$

Do not reject null hypothesis. The data does not indicate that there is a significant difference in the average number of errors in the books typeset by each of the companies.

7.

			Row Total
72	67	49	188
66	79	69	214
58	59	92	209
82	88	83	253
91	72	75	238
85	91	71	247
75	69	83	227
Column Total 529	525	522	1576 **Grand Total**

Cell (1): $\left(\dfrac{529^2 + 525^2 + 522^2}{7} \right) - \dfrac{1576^2}{21} = 3.5238$

Cell (2): $(72^2 + 67^2 + \ldots + 83^2)$

$$- \left(\frac{529^2 + 525^2 + 522^2}{7} \right) = 2731.476$$

446

7.   (Continued)

Cell (3): $(72^2 + 67^2 + \ldots + 83^2) - \dfrac{1576^2}{21} = 2735$

Cell (4): $3 - 1 = 2$
Cell (5): $3(7 - 1) = 18$
Cell (6): $21 - 1 = 20$

Cell (7): $\dfrac{3.5238}{2} = 1.7619$

Cell (8): $\dfrac{2731.476}{18} = 151.749$

Cell (9): $\dfrac{1.7619}{151.749} = 0.0116$

Source of Variation	Sum of Squares	Degrees of Freedom	Mean Square	F-ratio
Professors	(1) 3.5238	(4) 2	(7) 1.7619	(9) 0.0116
Error	(2) 2731.476	(5) 18	(8) 151.749	
Total	(3) 2735	(6) 20		

$F^2_{18}(0.05) = 3.55$

Do not reject null hypothesis. The data does not indicate that there is a significant difference in the preparation of the students in each of the teacher's classes.

8.

					Row Total
2.2	1.8	1.1	1.9	1.7	8.7
3.3	3.2	2.7	2.0	2.9	14.1
1.7	1.9	2.8	1.9	1.2	9.5
3.4	1.7	1.6	1.1	2.8	10.6
1.9	3.4	2.6	1.8	3.1	12.8
Column Total 12.5	12.0	10.8	8.7	11.7	55.7 Grand Total

447

8. (Continued)

Cell (1): $\left(\dfrac{12.5^2 + 12.0^2 + 10.8^2 + 8.7^2 + 11.7^2}{5} \right)$

$- \dfrac{55.7^2}{25} = 1.7944$

Cell (2): $(2.2^2 + 1.8^2 + \ldots + 3.1^2)$

$- \left(\dfrac{12.5^2 + 12.0^2 + 10.8^2 + 8.7^2 + 11.7^2}{5} \right) = 10.9556$

Cell (3): $(2.2^2 + 1.8^2 + \ldots + 3.1^2) - \dfrac{55.7^2}{25} = 12.750$

Cell (4): $5 - 1 = 4$
Cell (5): $5(5 - 1) = 20$
Cell (6): $25 - 1 = 24$

Cell (7): $\dfrac{1.7944}{4} = 0.4486$

Cell (8): $\dfrac{10.9556}{20} = 0.5478$

Cell (9): $\dfrac{0.4486}{0.5478} = 0.8189$

Source of Variation	Sum of Squares	Degrees of Freedom	Mean Square	F-ratio
Stimuli	(1) 1.7944	(4) 4	(7) 0.4486	(9) 0.8189
Error	(2) 10.9556	(5) 20	(8) 0.5478	
Total	(3) 12.750	(6) 24		

$F^4_{20}(0.01) = 4.43$

Do not reject null hypothesis. The data does not indicate that the average reaction time to the different stimuli is significantly different.

9.

					Row Total
29	17	13	21	74	154
37	68	41	32	47	225
41	84	79	68	37	309

Column Total: 107   169   133   121   158   688 Grand Total

Cell (1): $\left(\dfrac{154^2 + 225^2 + 309^2}{5}\right) - \dfrac{688^2}{15} = 2408.133$

Cell (2): $\left(\dfrac{107^2 + 169^2 + 133^2 + 121^2 + 158^2}{3}\right) - \dfrac{688^2}{15} = 878.4$

Cell (3): $(29^2 + 17^2 + \ldots + 37^2) - \left(\dfrac{154^2 + 225^2 + 309^2}{5}\right)$

$- \left(\dfrac{107^2 + 169^2 + 133^2 + 121^2 + 158^2}{3}\right) + \dfrac{688^2}{15}$

$= 4251.2$

Cell (4): $(29^2 + 17^2 + \ldots + 37^2) - \left(\dfrac{688^2}{15}\right) = 7537.733$

Cell (5): $3 - 1 = 2$
Cell (6): $5 - 1 = 4$
Cell (7): $(3 - 1)(5 - 1) = 8$
Cell (8): $3(5) - 1 = 14$

Cell (9): $\dfrac{2408.133}{2} = 1204.067$

Cell (10): $\dfrac{878.4}{4} = 219.6$

Cell (11): $\dfrac{4215.2}{8} = 531.4$

Cell (12): $\dfrac{1204.067}{531.4} = 2.266$

449

9.   (Continued)

Cell (13): $\dfrac{219.6}{531.4} = 0.413$

Source of Variation	Sum of Squares	Degrees of Freedom	Mean Square	F-ratio
	(1)	(5)	(9)	(12)
Ages	2408.133	2	1204.067	2.266
	(2)	(6)	(10)	(13)
Reasons	878.4	4	219.6	0.413
	(3)	(7)	(11)	
Error	4251.2	8	531.4	
	(4)	(8)		
Total	7537.733	14		

$F_8^2(0.01) = 8.65$

$F_8^4(0.01) = 7.01$

Do not reject null hypothesis. The data do not indicate that the average age of people hospitalized is significantly different for all the age groups. Also, the data do not indicate that the average age of people hospitalized is significantly different for all reasons for hospitalization.

10.

				Row Total
1225	1240	1175	1205	4845
1420	1395	1105	1295	5215
1095	1600	1245	1265	5205
1525	1305	1420	1150	5400
1240	1310	1290	1430	5270
Column Total 6505	6850	6235	6345	25935 **Grand Total**

10. (Continued)

Cell (1): $\left(\dfrac{4845^2 + 5215^2 + 5205^2 + 5400^2 + 5270^2}{4}\right) - \dfrac{25935^2}{20}$

$= 42582.5$

Cell (2): $\left(\dfrac{6505^2 + 6850^2 + 6235^2 + 6345^2}{5}\right) - \dfrac{25935^2}{20}$

$= 43143.75$

Cell (3): $(1225^2 + 1240^2 + \ldots + 1430^2)$

$\quad - \left(\dfrac{4845^2 + 5215^2 + 5205^2 + 5400^2 + 5270^2}{4}\right)$

$\quad - \left(\dfrac{6505^2 + 6850^2 + 6235^2 + 6345^2}{5}\right) + \dfrac{25935^2}{20}$

$= 253{,}937.5$

Cell (4): $(1225^2 + 1240^2 + \ldots + 1430^2) - \dfrac{25935^2}{20}$

$= 339{,}663.75$

Cell (5): $5 - 1 = 4$
Cell (6): $4 - 1 = 3$
Cell (7): $(5 - 1)(4 - 1) = 12$
Cell (8): $5(4) - 1 = 19$

Cell (9): $\dfrac{42582.5}{4} = 10645.625$

Cell (10): $\dfrac{43143.75}{3} = 14381.25$

Cell (11): $\dfrac{253937.5}{12} = 21161.458$

Cell (12): $\dfrac{10645.625}{21161.458} = 0.503$

Cell (13): $\dfrac{14381.25}{21161.458} = 0.6796$

10. (Continued)

Source of Variation	Sum of Squares	Degrees of Freedom	Mean Square	F-ratio
Examiners	(1) 42582.5	(5) 4	(9) 10645.625	(12) 0.503
Centers	(2) 43143.75	(6) 3	(10) 14381.25	(13) 0.6796
Error	(3) 253937.5	(7) 12	(11) 21161.458	
Total	(4) 339663.75	(8) 19		

$F_{12}^{4}(0.05) = 3.26$

$F_{12}^{3}(0.05) = 3.49$

Do not reject null hypothesis. The data do not indicate that the average amount of money in a settled claim is significantly different for all the drive-in centers or that it is significantly different for all the claims examiners.

11. Choice (a)

12. Choice (b)

13. Choice (c)

14. Choice (c)

15. Choice (c)

16. Choice (b)

For questions 1-10 use the following information: The average math scores for five different years were analyzed for the five high schools in a city. The following results were obtained:

	Calvin	89	84	86	88	83
High	Lincoln	79	82	83	77	78
School	Gates	91	86	84	79	78
	Rogers	76	86	77	75	78
	Paul	73	78	82	81	80

In an effort to determine whether there is a significant difference in the average math scores at the various high schools, the following one-way ANOVA table has been set up:

ANOVA Table

Source of Variation	Sum of Squares	Degrees of Freedom	Mean Square	F-ratio
Different schools	(1)	(4)	(7)	(9)
Error	(2)	(5)	(8)	
Total	(3)	(6)		

1. The appropriate entry for cell (1) is _____

2. The appropriate entry for cell (2) is _____

3. The appropriate entry for cell (3) is _____

4. The appropriate entry for cell (4) is _____

5. The appropriate entry for cell (5) is _____

6. The appropriate entry for cell (6) is _____

7. The appropriate entry for cell (7) is _____

8. The appropriate entry for cell (8) is _____

9. The appropriate entry for cell (9) is _____

10. Do the data indicate that there is a significant difference between the average number of reports process daily at the five different locations? (Use a 5% level of significance.)

a) Yes   b) No   c) not enough information given
d) none of these

Answer _____

For questions 1-10 use the following information: The number of deliveries made by five different trucking companies during a week is as follows:

	A	28	37	47	41	39
Trucking	B	29	33	42	40	37
Company	C	46	41	35	33	39
	D	53	44	29	32	37
	E	28	43	52	37	38

In an effort to determine whether there is a significant difference in the average number of deliveries per week made by these trucking companies, the following one-way ANOVA table has been set up:

ANOVA Table

Source of Variation	Sum of Squares	Degrees of Freedom	Mean Square	F-ratio
Different companies	(1)	(4)	(7)	(9)
Error	(2)	(5)	(8)	
Total	(3)	(6)		

1. The appropriate entry for cell (1) is _____

2. The appropriate entry for cell (2) is _____

3. The appropriate entry for cell (3) is _____

4. The appropriate entry for cell (4) is _____

5. The appropriate entry for cell (5) is _____

6. The appropriate entry for cell (6) is _____

7. The appropriate entry for cell (7) is _____

8. The appropriate entry for cell (8) is _____

9. The appropriate entry for cell (9) is _____

10. Do the data indicate that there is a significant difference in the average number of deliveries per week made by these companies? (Use a 5% level of significance.)

a) Yes   b) No   c) not enough information given
d) none of these

Answer _____

For questions 1-10 use the following information: The number of children reported lost on a daily basis at the five city beaches during a five day July 4th weekend are as follows:

Beach 1	48	39	45	49	42
Beach 2	46	38	36	35	48
Beach 3	40	32	29	40	35
Beach 4	24	59	29	45	42
Beach 5	23	35	40	28	41

In an effort to determine whether there is a significant difference in the average number of children lost on a daily basis at the various beaches, the following one-way ANOVA table has been set up:

ANOVA Table

Source of Variation	Sum of Squares	Degrees of Freedom	Mean Square	F-ratio
Different beaches	(1)	(4)	(7)	(9)
Error	(2)	(5)	(8)	
Total	(3)	(6)		

1. The appropriate entry for cell (1) is _____

2. The appropriate entry for cell (2) is _____

3. The appropriate entry for cell (3) is _____

4. The appropriate entry for cell (4) is _____

5. The appropriate entry for cell (5) is _____

6. The appropriate entry for cell (6) is _____

7. The appropriate entry for cell (7) is _____

8. The appropriate entry for cell (8) is _____

9. The appropriate entry for cell (9) is _____

10. Do the data indicate that there is a significant difference between the average number of reports processed daily at the five different locations? (Use a 5% level of significance.)

a) Yes   b) No   c) not enough information given
d) none of these

Answer _____

ANSWERS TO SUPPLEMENTARY TESTS
CHAPTER 13 - ANALYSIS OF VARIANCE

Form A		Form B		Form C	
1.	221.44	1.	34	1.	399.84
2.	294	2.	1090	2.	1315.2
3.	515.44	3.	1124	3.	1715.04
4.	4	4.	4	4.	4
5.	20	5.	20	5.	20
6.	24	6.	24	6.	24
7.	55.36	7.	8.5	7.	99.96
8.	14.7	8.	54.5	8.	65.76
9.	3.77	9.	0.16	9.	1.52
10.	Choice (a)	10.	Choice (b)	10.	Choice (b)

ANSWERS TO EXERCISES FOR CHAPTER 14

SECTION 14.3 (PAGES 687 - 693)

1. We replace each salary with a plus sign if it is above $27,000 and with a minus sign if it is below $27,000. We neglect those salaries that equal $27,000. We have - - + - + + + - + - + Here n = 11 and the number of minus signs is 5. From Table 14.1 test statistic exceeds the chart value of 1, so we do not reject null hypothesis that the median salary is $27,000.

2. We replace each number with a plus sign if it is above 10 and with a minus sign if it is below 15. We neglect those numbers that equal 10. We have - + + + - - - + + + + - + + Here n = 13 and the number of minus signs is 4. From Table 14.1 test statistic exceeds the chart value of 3, so we do not reject null hypothesis that the median time is 10 days.

3. We replace each number with a plus sign if it is above 19 and with a minus sign if it is below 19. We neglect those numbers that equal 19. We have - + - - + + + + + + - - Here n = 12 and the number of minus signs is 5. From Table 14.1 test statistic exceeds the chart value of 2, so we do not reject null hypothesis that the median age is 19 years.

4.

Before	After	Sign of Difference
7	2	-
4	3	-
8	6	-
5	4	-
9	9	
9	7	-
9	8	-
5	3	-
6	7	+
8	8	
9	8	-
10	9	-

There are 9 minus signs out of a possible 10 sign changes, so

$$\hat{p} = \frac{9}{10} = 0.90$$

$$z = \frac{0.90 - 0.50}{\sqrt{\dfrac{0.50(1 - 0.50)}{10}}}$$

$$= \frac{0.40}{0.158} = 2.53$$

Reject null hypothesis. The number of weekly arrests has decreased.
(One can also use Table 14.1 to obtain the same results. Here n = 10 and the number of plus signs is 1.)

5. We replace each case where the after is greater than the before with a plus sign, each case where the before is greater than the after with a minus sign, and drop any cases of equal before and after amounts and reduce the sample size accordingly. We obtain – – – –
   Here n = 4. Since this is a one-tailed test with an alternative that after is less than before, the test statistic is the number of plus signs. There are no plus signs. Using Table 14.1, we find in the n = 4 row and the $\alpha = 2(0.05) = 0.10$ a blank spot (rather than a numerical value.) This means that, with this sample size and α, the test statistic can not be rejected, regardless of the value of the test statistic. We conclude that there is not enough evidence to show that the new fares have decreased ridership.

6.

Before	After	Sign of Difference
18	24	+
19	16	−
22	25	+
16	19	+
12	15	+
7	7	
8	4	−
9	12	+
18	21	+
19	17	−

There are 6 plus signs out of a possible 9 sign changes, so

$$\hat{p} = \frac{6}{9} = 0.6667$$

$$z = \frac{0.6667 - 0.50}{\sqrt{\dfrac{0.50(1 - 0.50)}{9}}}$$

$$= \frac{0.1667}{0.1667} = 1.00$$

Do not reject null hypothesis. The data do not indicate that the medicine has a significant effect on the number of times that dizziness is reported.

Actually some people might question the use of z as a test statistic in this case since a sample of size 9 is not "large enough" for the test statistics to be used. These people could use Table 14.1 with n = 9 and 4 minus signs. Since the test statistic exceeds the chart value, we do not reject null hypothesis.

7.

Before	After	Sign of Difference
23	17	−
23	21	−
14	10	−
23	29	+
20	20	
21	16	−
28	16	−
29	24	−
27	18	−
37	28	−

There are 8 minus signs out of a possible 9 sign changes, so

$$\hat{p} = \frac{8}{9} = 0.8889$$

$$z = \frac{0.8889 - 0.50}{\sqrt{\dfrac{0.50(1 - 0.50)}{9}}}$$

$$= \frac{0.3889}{0.1667} = 2.33$$

Reject null hypothesis. The number of complaints has decreased.

Some people would prefer to arrive at the same conclusion by using Table 14.1 since the sample size may not be large enough. Thus z cannot be used as a test statistic.

8.

Before	After	Sign of Difference
18	11	−
14	13	−
16	16	
19	20	+
22	16	−
15	18	+
17	17	
11	11	
15	8	−
13	11	−

There are 5 minus signs out of a possible 7 sign changes, so

$$\hat{p} = \frac{5}{7} = 0.7143$$

$$z = \frac{0.7143 - 0.50}{\sqrt{\dfrac{0.50(1 - 0.50)}{7}}}$$

$$= \frac{0.2143}{0.189} = 1.13$$

Do not reject null hypothesis. The data do not indicate that the two-way radios have had a significant effect on the number of robberies of cab drivers.

8. (Continued)
   Some people would prefer to arrive at the same conclusion by using Table 14.1 since the sample size may not be large enough. Thus z cannot be used as a test statistic.

9.

Before	After	Sign of Difference
11	11	
28	18	-
22	17	-
19	5	-
20	10	-
22	20	-
16	17	+
12	12	
8	7	-
9	10	+
18	19	+
16	16	
21	20	-
17	15	-

There are 8 minus signs out of a possible 11 sign changes, so

$$\hat{p} = \frac{8}{11} = 0.7273$$

$$z = \frac{0.7273 - 0.50}{\sqrt{\dfrac{0.50(1 - 0.50)}{11}}}$$

$$= \frac{0.2273}{0.1508} = 1.51$$

Do not reject null hypothesis. The data do not indicate that the new equipment has significantly reduced the number of damaged pieces of mail.

Some people would prefer to arrive at the same conclusion by using Table 14.1 since the sample size may not be large enough. Thus z cannot be used as a test statistic.

10.

Before	After	Sign of Difference
512	512	
642	601	–
397	388	–
760	758	–
490	500	+
601	585	–
454	400	–
768	601	–
491	448	–
587	508	–

There are 8 minus signs out of a possible 9 sign changes, so

$$\hat{p} = \frac{8}{9} = 0.8889$$

$$z = \frac{0.8889 - 0.5000}{\sqrt{\dfrac{0.50(1 - 0.50)}{9}}}$$

$$= \frac{0.3889}{0.1667} = 2.33$$

Reject null hypothesis. The charge affects the number of calls for directory assistance.

Some people would prefer to arrive at the same conclusion by using Table 14.1 since the sample size may not be large enough. Thus z cannot be used as a test statistic.

11.

Before	After	Sign of Difference
12	8	–
6	4	–
10	9	–
8	8	
10	6	–
14	9	–
11	5	–
10	6	–
9	7	–
13	12	–

There are 9 minus signs out of a possible 9 sign changes, so

$$\hat{p} = \frac{9}{9} = 1.000$$

$$z = \frac{1 - 0.50}{\sqrt{\dfrac{0.50(1 - 0.50)}{9}}}$$

$$= \frac{0.50}{0.1667} = 2.999$$

11. (Continued)
    Reject null hypothesis. The number of felony arrests has decreased as a result of the number of police cars in the patrol car.

    Some people would prefer to arrive at the same conclusion by using Table 14.1 since the sample size may not be large enough. Thus z cannot be used as a test statistic.

ANSWERS TO EXERCISES FOR SECTION 14.4 - (PAGES 698 - 700)

1.

Before	After	Difference D	Absolute value of Difference, $\|D\|$	Rank of $\|D\|$	Signed Rank
29	28	1	1	1.5	+1.5
26	23	3	3	4	+4
21	19	2	2	3	+3
25	26	-1	1	1.5	-1.5
26	19	7	7	5	+5
25	25	0	---	---	---
26	18	8	8	6	+6
27	27	0	---	---	---

Positive sign ranks = (1.5) + (+4) + (+3) + (+5) + (+6)
$$= +19.5$$
Negative sign ranks = -1.5
We select -1.5 (the smallest sum). The absolute value is 1.5. Using n = 6 with α = 0.05, the critical value is 0 for a two-tailed test. We do not reject null hypothesis. The new policy does not seem to have an effect on drug use at the schools.

2.

Before	After	Difference, D	Absolute Value, $|D|$	Rank of $|D|$	Signed Rank
112	109	+ 3	3	4.5	+ 4.5
120	121	– 1	1	1.5	– 1.5
139	141	– 2	2	3	– 3
117	116	+ 1	1	1.5	+ 1.5
121	121	0	---	---	---
138	141	– 3	3	4.5	– 4.5
129	137	– 8	8	6	– 6
118	130	–12	12	8.5	– 8.5
121	105	+16	16	10	+10
119	130	–11	11	7	– 7
137	125	+12	12	8.5	+ 8.5
128	150	–22	22	11	–11

Negative sign ranks = (–1.5) + (–3) + (–4.5) + (–6) + (–8.5)
  + (–7) + (–11) = –41.5
Positive sign ranks = (+4.5) + (+1.5) + (+10) + (+8.5) = +24.5
We select –24.5 (the smallest sum). The absolute value is
24.5. Using n = 11 with α = 0.05, the critical value is 10 for
a two-tailed test. We do not reject null hypothesis. The data
do not indicate that there is a significant difference in the
ratings before and after the egg yolks are removed.

3.

Before	After	Difference, D	Absolute Value, $\|D\|$,	Rank of $\|D\|$	Signed Rank
39	35	+ 4	4	5	+5
43	37	+ 6	6	6.5	+6.5
47	44	+ 3	3	3.5	+3.5
45	35	+10	10	9	+9
42	43	- 1	1	1	-1
41	41	0	---	---	---
57	49	+ 8	8	8	+8
51	57	- 6	6	6.5	-6.5
59	57	+ 2	2	2	+2
50	47	+ 3	3	3.5	+3.5

Negative sign ranks = (-1) + (-6.5) = -7.5
Positive sign ranks = (+5) + (+6.5) + (+3.5) + (+9) + (+8)
                    + (+2) + (+3.5) = +37.5

We select -7.5 (the smaller sum). The absolute value is 7.5.
Using n = 9 with α = 0.05, the critical value is 5 for a two-tailed test. We do not reject null hypothesis. The data do not indicate that the new policy has a significant effect on reducing burglaries.

4.

Before	After	Difference, D	Absolute value, |D|	Rank of |D|	Signed Rank
24	28	−4	4	7.5	−7.5
23	27	−4	4	7.5	−7.5
26	25	+1	1	3	+3
25	26	−1	1	3	−3
28	27	+1	1	3	+3
29	28	+1	1	3	+3
31	30	+1	1	3	+3
21	21	0	---	---	---
24	27	−3	3	6	−6
28	33	−5	5	9	−9

Negative sign ranks = (−7.5) + (−7.5) + (−3) + (−6) + (−9)
$\qquad\qquad\qquad$ = −33
Positive sign ranks = (+3) + (+3) + (+3) + (+3) = +12
We select +12 (the smaller sum). The absolute value is 12.
Using n = 9 with α = 0.05, the critical value is 5 for a two-tailed test. We do not reject null hypothesis. We cannot say that the number of campers completing their meals has changed significantly.

468

1.

Results	Group	Rank
30	B	1
37	B	2
38	B	3
40	B	4
41	B	6
41	B	6
41	B	6
42	B	8.5
42	B	8.5
43	B	10.5
43	B	10.5
44	A	12.5
44	B	12.5
45	A	14.5
45	B	14.5
46	B	16
47	A	17
48	A	18
49	A	19
50	A	20
52	B	21
53	A	22
54	A	23
55	A	24
57	A	25
58	A	26

$n_1 = 11, \quad n_2 = 15$

R = sum of ranks for group A
= 12.5 + 14.5 + 17 + 18
+ 19 + 20 + 22 + 23 + 24
+ 25 + 26 = 221

$\mu_R = \dfrac{11(11 + 15 + 1)}{2} = 148.5$

$\sigma_R = \sqrt{\dfrac{11(15)(11 + 15 + 1)}{12}}$

≈ 19.2678

$z = \dfrac{221 - 148.5}{19.2678} = 3.76$

Reject null hypothesis. The mean score for both groups is not the same.

469

2.

Trials	Group	Rank
18	F	1
20	F	2.5
20	M	2.5
21	F	4
22	F	5
24	F	6.5
24	M	6.5
25	F	8.5
25	M	8.5
26	F	10
28	M	11
29	F	12.5
29	M	12.5
30	M	14.5
30	M	14.5
33	F	16
34	M	17
35	M	18
37	M	19

$n_1 = 9, \quad n_1 = 10$

R = sum of ranks for females (F)
$= 1 + 2.5 + 4 + 5 + 6.5$
$\quad + 8.5 + 10 + 12.5 + 16$
$= 66$

$$\mu_R = \frac{9(9 + 10 + 1)}{2} = 90$$

$$\sigma_R = \sqrt{\frac{9(10)(9 + 10 + 1)}{12}}$$

≈ 12.2474

$$z = \frac{66 - 90}{12.2474} = -1.9596$$

Do not reject null hypothesis. We cannot conclude that the number of trials required by a member of each group to complete task is not the same.

470

3.

Number of Patients	Hospital	Rank
3	M	1
13	M	2
32	S	3
46	M	4
49	S	5
53	M	6
55	S	7
57	S	8
60	S	9
61	M	10
69	S	11
70	M	12
72	S	13
82	S	14
83	M	15
88	M	16
95	M	17

$n_1 = 8 \qquad n_2 = 9$

R = sum of ranks for Spovik (S)
$= 3 + 5 + 7 + 8 + 9 + 11$
$\qquad + 13 + 14 = 70$

$\mu_R = \dfrac{8(8 + 9 + 1)}{2} = 72$

$\sigma_R = \sqrt{\dfrac{8(9)(8 + 9 + 1)}{12}}$

≈ 10.3923

$z = \dfrac{70 - 72}{10.3923} = -0.19$

Do not reject null hypothesis. The data do not indicate that the average number of patients treated at both hospitals is the same.

471

4.

Results	Tunnel	Rank
20	1	2
20	1	2
20	2	2
21	1	4.5
21	2	4.5
22	1	7
22	1	7
22	2	7
23	2	9
24	1	10
25	2	11.5
25	2	11.5
26	1	14
26	2	14
26	2	14
27	2	16
28	1	17.5
28	2	17.5
29	1	19.5
29	2	19.5

$n_1 = 8 \quad n_2 = 12$

R = sum of ranks for Tunnel 1
$= 2 + 2 + 4.5 + 7 + 7 + 10 + 14 + 17.5 + 19.5 = 83.5$

$\mu_R = \dfrac{8(8 + 12 + 1)}{2} = 84$

$\sigma_R = \sqrt{\dfrac{8(12)(8 + 12 + 1)}{12}}$

≈ 12.9615

$z = \dfrac{83.5 - 84}{12.9615} = 0.04$

Do not reject null hypothesis. The data do not indicate that the average amount of pollutants in the air at both tunnels is significantly different.

472

5.

Number of loans	Bank	Rank
2	B	1.5
2	B	1.5
3	A	3.5
3	B	3.5
4	A	6.5
4	A	6.5
4	B	6.5
4	B	6.5
5	A	11.5
5	A	11.5
5	A	11.5
5	B	11.5
5	B	11.5
5	B	11.5
6	A	16
6	B	16
6	B	16
7	A	19
7	B	19
7	B	19
8	A	22.5
8	A	22.5
8	B	22.5
8	B	22.5

$n_1 = 10 \qquad n_2 = 14$

R = sum of ranks for bank A
$= 3.5 + 6.5 + 6.5 + 11.5 + 11.5 + 11.5 + 16 + 19 + 22.5 + 22.5 = 131$

$\mu_R = \dfrac{10(10 + 14 + 1)}{2} = 125$

$\sigma_R = \sqrt{\dfrac{10(14)(10 + 14 + 1)}{12}}$

≈ 17.078

$z = \dfrac{131 - 125}{17.078} = 0.351$

Do not reject null hypothesis. The data does not indicate that there is a significant difference in the average number of home equity loans approved by both banks.

6.

Number of Accidents	Expressway	Rank
23	A	1
28	B	2
43	B	3
47	A	4
51	A	5.5
51	B	5.5
54	A	7
57	B	8
59	B	9
61	B	10
63	A	11
65	B	12
68	A	13
69	A	14
71	B	15
75	A	16
76	B	17
86	B	18

$n_1 = 8 \qquad n_2 = 10$

R = sum of ranks for Expressway A
$= 1 + 4 + 5.5 + 7 + 11 + 13 + 14 + 16 = 71.5$

$\mu_R = \dfrac{8(8 + 10 + 1)}{2} = 76$

$\sigma_R = \sqrt{\dfrac{8(10)(8 + 10 + 1)}{12}}$

≈ 11.2546

$z = \dfrac{71.5 - 76}{11.2546} = -0.40$

Do not reject null hypothesis. The data does not indicate that there is a significant difference in the average number of accidents occurring on both highways.

7.

Number of cars	Agency	Rank
20	1	1
31	1	2
32	2	3
40	1	4
42	1	5
43	1	6
44	2	7
47	2	8
48	1	9
49	2	10.5
49	2	10.5
53	2	12
56	1	13
57	1	14
68	1	15
69	2	16
80	1	17
92	2	18

$n_1 = 8$, $n_2 = 10$

R = sum of ranks for Agency 2
$= 3 + 7 + 8 + 10.5 + 10.5 + 12 + 16 + 18 = 85$

$\mu_R = \dfrac{8(8 + 10 + 1)}{2} = 76$

$\sigma_R = \sqrt{\dfrac{8(10)(8 + 10 + 1)}{12}}$

≈ 11.2546

$z = \dfrac{85 - 76}{11.2546} = 0.80$

Do not reject null hypothesis. The data do not indicate that the average number of abandoned cars towed away by the two disposal agencies is significantly different.

1. Let x, y, z, and w represents the rankings of scout 1, 2, 3, and 4 respectively. We then have

x	y	z	w	x-y	$(x-y)^2$	x-z	$(x-z)^2$	y-w	$(y-w)^2$
1	1	5	5	0	0	-4	16	-4	16
2	5	3	2	-3	9	-1	1	3	9
3	4	4	4	-1	1	-1	1	0	0
4	2	2	3	2	4	2	4	-1	1
5	3	1	1	2	4	4	16	2	4
					18		38		30

a) $R = 1 - 6 \dfrac{\Sigma(x-y)^2}{5(5^2-1)} = 1 - \dfrac{6(18)}{5(24)} = 1 - 0.9 = 0.1$

   R = 0.1 is not significant. We cannot conclude that there is a significant correlation between the ratings of scouts 1 and 2.

b) $R = 1 - \dfrac{6(38)}{5(5^2-1)} = 1 - 1.9 = -0.9$

   R = -0.9 is not significant. We cannot conclude that there is a significant correlation between the ratings of scouts 1 and 3.

c) $R = 1 - \dfrac{6(30)}{5(5^2-1)} = 1 - 1.5 = -0.5$

   R = -0.5 is not significant. We cannot conclude that there is a significant correlation between the ratings of scouts 2 and 4.

2.

	x	y	x - y	$(x - y)^2$
Bill	3	5	-2	4
Mary	9	9	0	0
Joe	4	3	1	1
Francine	2	2	0	0
Edward	1	1	0	0
Jason	7	7	0	0
Marilyn	5	8	-3	9
George	10	6	4	16
Bruce	6	10	-4	16
Lisa	8	4	4	16
				62

$$R = 1 - \frac{6(62)}{10(10^2 - 1)}$$

$$= 1 - 0.376 = 0.624$$

Chart value is 0.648

R = 0.624 is not significant. We cannot conclude that there is a significant correlation between the calculus I and calculus II grades.

3.

x	y	x - y	$(x - y)^2$
5	6	-1	1
4	4	0	0
6	5	1	1
3	3	0	0
1	7	-6	36
2	1	1	1
7	2	5	25
			64

$$R = 1 - \frac{6(64)}{7(7^2 - 1)}$$

$$= 1 - 1.1429 = -0.1429$$

Chart value is 0.786

R = -0.1429 is not significant. We cannot conclude that there is a significant correlation between the student's rankings of the teachers.

477

4.

x	y	x - y	$(x - y)^2$
7	8	-1	1
4	3	1	1
5	5	0	0
3	7	-4	16
2	2	0	0
1	1	0	0
6	4	2	4
8	6	2	4
			26

$$R = 1 - \frac{6(26)}{8(8^2 - 1)}$$

$$= 1 = 0.3095 = 0.6905$$

Chart value is 0.738

R = 0.6905 is not significant. We cannot conclude that there is a significant correlation between the two sportscaster's rankings of the teams.

5.

Run	Letters
1	C
2	I
3	CC
4	I
5	CCC
6	II
7	C
8	III
9	CCC
10	I
11	CC
12	I
13	CC
14	I
15	C

There are 15 runs where there are 15 C's and 10 I's.

Here $n_1 = 10$ and $n_2 = 15$

Do not reject null hypothesis of randomness.

6.

Run	Letters
1	M
2	FF
3	M
4	F
5	MM
6	FFF
7	MM
8	F
9	M
10	FFF
11	MMM
12	FFF
13	M

There are 13 runs where there are 11 M's and 13 F's.

Here $n_1 = 11$ and $n_2 = 13$

Do not reject null hypothesis of randomness.

7.

Run	Letters
1	AA
2	NNNN
3	AAAAAAAA
4	NN
5	AAA
6	NN
7	AA
8	N

There are 8 runs where there are 15 A's and 9 N's.

Here $n_1 = 9$ and $n_2 = 15$

Do not reject null hypothesis of randomness.

8.

Run	Letters
1	YYY
2	NNN
3	YY
4	N
5	Y
6	NN
7	YYYY
8	NNN
9	Y
10	N
11	Y
12	N
13	Y
14	N
15	Y

There are 15 runs where there are 14 Y's and 12 N's.

Here $n_1 = 12$ and $n_2 = 14$

Do not reject null hypothesis of randomness.

9. The median of the numbers is 17.5. We then have the following sequence where a = above median and b = below median
b,a,a,a,b,a,a,a,b,b,b,b,b,b,a,a

Run	Letters
1	b
2	aaa
3	b
4	aaa
5	bbbbbb
6	aa

There are 6 runs where we have 8 a's and 8 b's.

Here $n_1 = 8$ and $n_2 = 8$

Do not reject null hypothesis of randomness.

10. The median of the numbers is 73. We then have the following sequence where a = above median and b = below median
b,b,b,b,a,b,b,b,a,b,a,a,b,a,b,a,a,a,a,a

Run	Letters
1	bbbb
2	a
3	bbb
4	a
5	b
6	aa
7	b
8	a
9	b
10	aaaaa

There are 10 runs where we have 10 b's and 10 a's.

Here $n_1 = 10$ and $n_2 = 10$

Do not reject null hypothesis of randomness.

11.

Run	Letters
1	DD
2	R
3	D
4	R
5	DD
6	RRRR
7	D
8	RRR
9	D
10	R
11	D
12	RR
13	D
14	RR
15	DD
16	R
17	D
18	R

There are 18 runs where we have 12 D's and 16 R's.

Here $n_1 = 12$ and $n_2 = 16$

Do not reject null hypothesis of randomness.

12. The median of the numbers is 16. We then have the following
    sequence where a = above median and b = below median.
    b,a,b,a,b,b,b,a,a,a,a,a,a,a,b,b

Run	Letters
1	b
2	a
3	b
4	a
5	bbb
6	aaaaaaa
7	bb

There are 7 runs where we have
7 b's and 9 a's.

Here $n_1 = 7$ and $n_2 = 9$

Do not reject null hypothesis of
randomness.

13. The median of the numbers is 19. We then have the following
    sequence where a = above median and b = below median.
    a,a,a,b,a,b,a,a,b,b,b,a,b

Run	Letters
1	aaa
2	b
3	a
4	b
5	aa
6	bbb
7	a
8	b

There are 8 runs where we have
7 a's and 6 b's.

Here $n_1 = 6$ and $n_2 = 7$

Do not reject null hypothesis of
randomness.

483

14. The median of numbers is 38584. We then have the following
    sequence where a = above median and b = below median.
    a,a,b,a,a,b,b,b,a,b,b,a,a,b,a,a,b,b,b,a,a,b

Run	Letters
1	aa
2	b
3	aa
4	bbb
5	a
6	bb
7	aa
8	b
9	aa
10	bbb
11	aa
12	b

There are 12 runs where we have
11 a's and 11 b's.

Here $n_1 = 11$ and $n_2 = 11$

Do not reject null hypothesis of
randomness.

15.

x	y	z	w	t	x-y	$(x-y)^2$	$(x-z)$	$(x-z)^2$	$(x-w)$	$(x-w)^2$
2	2	4	5	7	0	0	-2	4	-3	9
3	4	6	6	5	-1	1	-3	9	-3	9
7	7	3	4	3	0	0	4	16	3	9
1	5	5	3	4	-4	16	-4	16	-2	4
5	1	7	2	6	4	16	-2	4	3	9
6	3	1	1	1	3	9	5	25	5	25
4	6	2	7	2	-2	<u>4</u>	2	<u>4</u>	-3	<u>9</u>
						46		78		74

(x-t)	$(x-t)^2$	y-z	$(y-z)^2$	y-w	$(y-w)^2$	y-t	$(y-t)^2$
-5	25	-2	4	-3	9	-5	25
-2	4	-2	4	-2	4	-1	1
4	16	4	16	3	9	4	16
-3	9	0	0	2	4	1	1
-1	1	-6	36	-1	1	-5	25
5	25	2	4	2	4	2	4
2	<u>4</u>	4	<u>16</u>	-1	<u>1</u>	4	<u>16</u>
	84		80		32		88

z-w	$(z-w)^2$	z-t	$(z-t)^2$	w-t	$(w-t)^2$
-1	1	-3	9	-2	4
0	0	1	1	1	1
-1	1	0	0	1	1
2	4	1	1	-1	1
5	25	1	1	-4	16
0	0	0	0	0	0
-5	<u>25</u>	0	<u>0</u>	5	<u>25</u>
	56		12		48

15. (Continued)

Between Woman 1 and Woman 2 (x and y) $R = 1 - \dfrac{6(46)}{7(7^2 - 1)}$

$= 1 - 0.82 = 0.18$

Between Woman 1 and Woman 3 (x and z) $R = 1 - \dfrac{6(78)}{7(7^2 - 1)}$

$= 1 - 1.39 = -0.39$

Between Woman 1 and Woman 4 (x and w) $R = 1 - \dfrac{6(74)}{7(7^2 - 1)}$

$= 1 - 1.32 = -0.32$

Between Woman 1 and Woman 5 (x and t) $R = 1 - \dfrac{6(84)}{7(7^2 - 1)}$

$= 1 - 1.5 = -0.50$

Between Woman 2 and Woman 3 (y and z) $R = 1 - \dfrac{6(80)}{7(7^2 - 1)}$

$= 1 - 1.43 = -0.43$

Between Woman 2 and Woman 4 (y and w) $R = 1 - \dfrac{6(32)}{7(7^2 - 1)}$

$= 1 - 0.57 = 0.43$

Between Woman 2 and Woman 5 (y and t) $R = 1 - \dfrac{6(88)}{7(7^2 - 1)}$

$= 1 - 1.57 = -0.57$

Between Woman 3 and Woman 4 (z and w) $R = 1 - \dfrac{6(56)}{7(7^2 - 1)}$

$= 1 - 1 = 0$

Between Woman 3 and Woman 5 (z and t) $R = 1 - \dfrac{6(12)}{7(7^2 - 1)}$

$= 1 - 0.21428 = 0.78571$

Between Woman 4 and Woman 5 $R = 1 - \dfrac{6(48)}{7(7^2 - 1)}$

$= 1 - 0.86 = 0.14$

There is no significant correlation between the ratings of the women.

1.

Time	Person	Rank
45	Sandra	1
47	Bill	2
49	Mary	4
49	Sandra	4
49	Bob	4
51	Sandra	6.5
51	Bill	6.5
53	Mary	8.5
53	Mary	8.5
56	Sue	10
57	Bob	11.5
57	Bob	11.5
58	Bob	14
58	Mary	14
58	Sandra	14
59	Sue	16
61	Bob	17
62	Bill	18.5
62	Mary	18.5
63	Sue	20
64	Bob	21
65	Bill	22.5
65	Sue	22.5
72	Bill	24.5
72	Bob	24.5
81	Bill	26

Sum of rankings for Sandra:
$$R_1 = 1 + 4 + 6.5 + 14 = 25.5$$

Sum of rankings for Bill:
$$R_2 = 2 + 6.5 + 18.5 + 22.5$$
$$+ 24.5 + 26 = 100$$

Sum of rankings for Mary:
$$R_3 = 4 + 8.5 + 8.5 + 14 + 18.5$$
$$= 53.5$$

Sum of rankings for Bob:
$$R_4 = 4 + 11.5 + 11.5 + 14 + 17$$
$$+ 21 + 24.5 = 103.5$$

Sum of rankings for Sue:
$$R_5 = 10 + 16 + 20 + 22.5$$
$$= 68.5$$

1. (Continued)

Test statistic =

$$\frac{12}{26(26 + 1)} \left[\frac{25.5^2}{4} + \frac{100^2}{6} + \frac{53.5^2}{5} + \frac{103.5^2}{7} + \frac{68.5^2}{4} \right] - 3(26 + 1)$$

$$= 6.266$$

χ^2 with 4 degrees of freedom = 13.277. We do not reject null hypothesis. The data do not indicate that there is a significant difference in the average time required to assemble the computer.

2.

Coverage	Brand	Rank
390	A	1
400	A	2
402	A	3
407	A	4
410	A	5.5
410	C	5.5
411	C	7
413	B	8
415	C	9
416	B	10
420	B	11
421	B	12
422	B	13.5
422	C	13.5
425	C	15

Sum of rankings for Brand A:
$R_1 = 1 + 2 + 3 + 4 + 5.5$
   $= 15.5$

Sum of rankings for Brand B:
$R_2 = 8 + 10 + 11 + 12 + 13.5$
   $= 54.5$

Sum of rankings for Brand C:
$R_3 = 5.5 + 7 + 9 + 13.5 + 15$
   $= 50$

2. (Continued)

$$\text{Test statistic} = \frac{12}{15(15+1)}\left[\frac{15.5^2}{5} + \frac{54.5^2}{5} + \frac{50^2}{5}\right] - 3(15+1)$$

$$= 9.105$$

χ^2 with 2 degrees of freedom = 5.991
Reject null hypothesis. There is a significant difference between the average coverage of each of these brands of paint.

3.

Decrease	Brand	Rank
3	C	1
9	C	2
10	B	3.5
10	C	3.5
11	B	5.5
11	D	5.5
12	A	7.5
12	C	7.5
13	A	9
14	D	10
15	A	12
15	B	12
15	D	12
16	A	14.5
16	C	14.5
17	B	16.5
17	D	16.5
18	A	18
19	D	19
22	B	20

Sum of rankings for Brand A:
$R_1 = 7.5 + 9 + 12 + 14.5 + 18$
$ = 61$

Sum of rankings for Brand B:
$R_2 = 3.5 + 5.5 + 12 + 16.5$
$ + 20 = 57.5$

Sum of rankings for Brand C:
$R_3 = 1 + 2 + 3.5 + 7.5 + 14.5$
$ = 28.5$

Sum of rankings for Brand D:
$R_4 = 5.5 + 10 + 12 + 16.5 + 19$
$ = 63$

3. (Continued)

Test statistic =

$$\frac{12}{20(20+1)}\left[\frac{61^2}{5} + \frac{57.5^2}{5} + \frac{28.5^2}{5} + \frac{63^2}{5}\right] - 3(20+1)$$

$$= 4.477$$

χ^2 with 3 degrees of freedom = 11.345
Do not reject null hypothesis. The data do not indicate that there is a significant difference between the average decrease in the blood serum cholesterol levels of people taking each of these types of pills.

4.

Oxygen	Brand	Rank
3.7	4	1
3.8	2	2
3.9	2	3
4.1	1	4
4.2	1	5
4.6	2	6
4.7	1	7
4.8	4	8
5.1	1	9
5.2	3	10
5.3	4	11
5.4	2	12
5.5	3	13
5.6	3	14
5.7	2	15
5.8	3	16
5.9	3	17
6.0	4	18
6.1	2	19
6.2	2	20
6.3	2	21
6.4	1	22
6.5	4	23
6.6	1	24
7.3	3	25

Sum of rankings for Brand 1:
$$R_1 = 4 + 5 + 7 + 9 + 22 + 24 = 71$$

Sum of rankings for Brand 2:
$$R_2 = 2 + 3 + 6 + 12 + 15 + 19 + 20 + 21 = 98$$

Sum of rankings for Brand 3:
$$R_3 = 10 + 13 + 14 + 16 + 17 + 25 = 95$$

Sum of rankings for Brand 4:
$$R_4 = 1 + 8 + 11 + 18 + 23 = 61$$

4. (Continued)

Test statistic =

$$\frac{12}{25(25 + 1)}\left[\frac{71^2}{6} + \frac{98^2}{8} + \frac{95^2}{6} + \frac{61^2}{5}\right] - 3(25 + 1)$$
$$= 1.182$$

χ^2 with 3 degrees of freedom = 11.345
Do not reject null hypothesis. The data do not indicate that there is a significant difference in the average dissolved oxygen content at these four locations.

ANSWERS TO TESTING YOUR UNDERSTANDING OF THIS CHAPTER'S CONCEPTS - (PAGE 729)

1. Yes. In the one-tailed test the alternate hypothesis is that the probability distribution for population A is shifted to the right of that for B. In the two-tailed test the alternate hypothesis is that the probability distribution for population A is shifted to the left or to the right of that for B.

2. The distributions are assumed to be continuous so that the probability of tied measurements is 0, and each measurement can be assigned a unique rank.

3. Yes. Because large values of the test statistic support the alternative hypothesis that the populations have different probability distributions, the rejection region is located in the upper tail of the χ^2 distribution.

4. The lowest value H of the test statistic is 0 and largest value is 12.5 and occurs when the ranks for sample 1 are 1, 2, 3, 4, and 5, the ranks for sample 2 are 6, 7, 8, 9, and 10 and the ranks for sample 3 are 11, 12, 13, 14, and 15.

ANSWERS TO THINKING CRITICALLY - (PAGE 729)

1. $R_a = 12$, $n_a = 13$, $n_b = 12$

$$z = \frac{12 - \left[\frac{2(13)(12)}{13 + 12} + 1\right]}{\sqrt{\frac{2(13)(12)(2 \cdot 13 \cdot 12 - 13 - 12)}{(13 + 12)^2(13 + 12 - 1)}}} = \frac{-1.48}{2.44} = -0.61$$

Do not reject null hypothesis.

3. Yes

ANSWERS TO REVIEW EXERCISES FOR CHAPTER 14 - (PAGES 730 - 734)

1.

Number of minutes	Group	Rank
12	A	1.5
12	B	1.5
14	A	3
15	A	4.5
15	B	4.5
16	A	7
16	B	7
16	B	7
17	A	9.5
17	B	9.5
18	B	11
19	A	13
19	B	13
19	B	13
20	A	15
25	B	16
30	A	17
31	B	18

$n_1 = 8 \qquad n_2 = 10$

R = sum of ranks for group A
$= 1.5 + 3 + 4.5 + 7 + 9.5 + 13 + 15 + 17 = 70.5$

$$\mu_R = \frac{8(8 + 10 + 1)}{2} = 76$$

$$\sigma_R = \sqrt{\frac{8(10)(8 + 10 + 1)}{12}}$$

$$\approx 11.2546$$

$$z = \frac{70.5 - 76}{5.339} = -0.489$$

Do not reject null hypothesis. The data do not indicate that there is a significant difference in the average time needed to run the marathon by both groups.

2.

Run	Letters
1	RR
2	HHH
3	R
4	HH
5	RRRR
6	HHH
7	R
8	H
9	R
10	HH
11	RRRR
12	HH
13	R
14	H

There are 14 runs where there are 14 R's and 14 H's.

Here $n_1 = 14$ and $n_2 = 14$

Do not reject null hypothesis of randomness.

3.

Man	Woman	Sign of Difference
3	2	+
2	1	+
1	1	
2	2	
3	2	+
4	1	+
3	0	+
0	0	
2	5	–
3	2	+
5	4	+
6	6	
8	8	
2	1	+
1	2	–
2	2	
3	3	
5	6	–
6	2	+
3	0	+

There are 10 plus signs out of a possible 13 sign changes, so

$$\hat{p} = \frac{10}{13} = 0.769$$

$$z = \frac{0.769 - 0.50}{\sqrt{\dfrac{0.50(1 - 0.50)}{13}}}$$

$$= \frac{0.269}{0.139} = 1.935$$

Do not reject null hypothesis. The data do not indicate that the men and women differ significantly on the issue.

(One can also use Table 14.1 to obtain the same results.)

4.

	x Week 1	y Week 2	z Week 3	x-y	$(x-y)^2$	(x-z)	$(x-z)^2$	y-z	$(y-z)^2$
Mon	3	2	3	1	1	0	0	-1	1
Tues	2	3	5	-1	1	-3	9	-2	4
Wed	4	1	1	3	9	3	9	0	0
Thurs	5	5	2	0	0	3	9	3	9
Fri	1	4	4	-3	9	-3	9	0	0
					20		36		14

Between x and y: $R = 1 - \dfrac{6(20)}{5(5^2 - 1)} = 1 - 1 = 0$

Between x and z: $R = 1 - \dfrac{6(36)}{5(5^2 - 1)} = 1 - 1.8 = -0.8$

Between y and z: $R = 1 - \dfrac{6(14)}{5(5^2 - 1)} = 1 - 0.7 = 0.3$

We cannot conclude that there is a significant correlation
between the day of the weeks on which transactions took place
and the number of transactions conducted.

5.

Number of miles	Brand	Rank
17	B	1
18	A	2
19	A	3.5
19	B	3.5
21	A	5
22	A	6
23	A	7.5
23	B	7.5
24	A	10
24	B	10
24	B	10
25	A	13
25	A	13
25	B	13
26	B	15
27	A	17.5
27	A	17.5
27	B	17.5
27	B	17.5
28	B	20
29	B	21.5
29	B	21.5

$n_1 = 10 \quad n_2 = 12$

R = sum of ranks for group A
$= 2 + 3.5 + 5 + 6 + 7.5 + 10 + 13 + 13 + 17.5 + 17.5 = 95$

$\mu_R = \dfrac{10(10 + 12 + 1)}{2} = 115$

$\sigma_R = \sqrt{\dfrac{10(12)(10 + 12 + 1)}{12}}$

≈ 15.166

$z = \dfrac{95 - 115}{15.166} = -1.319$

Do not reject null hypothesis. The data do not indicate that the average number of miles per gallon is significantly different for both cars.

6. The median of the numbers is 53. We then have the following
   sequence where a = above median and b = below median.
   a,a,b,a,b,a,b,a,b,a,b,b,b,b,b,a,a,a,b

Run	Letters
1	aa
2	b
3	a
4	b
5	a
6	b
7	a
8	b
9	a
10	bbbbb
11	aaa
12	b

There are 12 runs where we have
9 a's and 10 b's.

Here $n_1 = 9$ and $n_2 = 10$.

Do not reject null hypothesis of
randomness.

7.

x	y	x - y	$(x - y)^2$
2	3	-1	1
3	2	1	1
1	1	0	0
4	4	0	0
6	5	1	1
5	6	-1	1
			4

$$R = 1 - \frac{6(4)}{6(6^2 - 1)} = 1 - 0.1143$$

$$= 0.8857$$

The R value is very close to
chart value of 0.886. Thus, we
may conclude that there is no
significant correlation between
the rankings. Actually, more
data is needed before arriving
at a definitive conclusion.

8.

Before	After	Sign of Difference
58	65	+
61	65	+
79	82	+
63	63	
52	52	
78	70	-
82	81	-
42	45	+
39	41	+
75	77	+
85	88	+

There are 7 plus signs out of a possible 9 sign changes so that

$$\hat{p} = \frac{7}{9} = 0.778$$

$$z = \frac{0.778 - 0.50}{\sqrt{\dfrac{0.50(1 - 0.50)}{9}}}$$

$$= \frac{0.278}{0.167} = 1.665$$

Do not reject null hypothesis. The data do not indicate that the special teaching technique is effective.

Some people would prefer to arrive at the same conclusion by using Table 14.1 since the sample size may not be large enough. Thus z cannot be used as a test statistic.

9.

Not on Drugs	On Drugs	Sign of Difference
92	89	−
70	48	−
85	91	+
91	93	+
55	42	−
55	12	−
70	73	+
90	90	
70	61	−
91	87	−
91	97	+
91	88	−
65	65	
93	92	−
55	20	−

There are 9 minus signs out of a possible 13 sign changes so that $\hat{p} = \dfrac{9}{13} = 0.692$

$$z = \frac{0.692 - 0.50}{\sqrt{\dfrac{0.50(1 - 0.50)}{13}}}$$

$$= \frac{0.192}{0.139} = 1.38$$

Do not reject null hypothesis. The data do not indicate that drugs necessarily have an effect on performance on the anxiety test.

Some people might prefer to arrive at the same conlusion by using Table 14.1.

500

10. The median of the numbers is 12. We then have the following sequence where a = above median and b = below median.
a,b,a,a,a,a,a,b,b,a,b,b,b,b,b,b,b,a,b,b,a,a,a

Run	Letters
1	a
2	b
3	aaaaa
4	bb
5	a
6	bbbbbbb
7	a
8	bb
9	aaa

There are 9 runs where we have 11 a's and 12 b's

Here n_1 = 11 and n_2 = 12.

Do not reject null hypothesis of randomness.

11.

Level	Group	Rank
90	M	1
92	M	2
94	F	3
95	M	4
96	F	5
97	M	6
101	F	7
106	F	8
110	F	9.5
110	M	9.5
111	M	11
112	F	12
113	M	13
115	F	14
116	F	16
116	F	16
116	M	16
117	F	18
125	M	19
129	M	20
130	F	21
134	F	22

$n_1 = 10 \qquad n_2 = 12$

R = sum of ranks for group M
   (males)
  $= 1 + 2 + 4 + 6 + 9.5 + 11$
   $+ 13 + 16 + 19 + 20$
  $= 101.5$

$\mu_R = \dfrac{10(10 + 12 + 1)}{2} = 115$

$\sigma_R = \sqrt{\dfrac{10(12)(10 + 12 + 1)}{12}}$

≈ 15.166

$z = \dfrac{101.5 - 115}{15.166} = -0.89$

Do not reject null hypothesis.
The data do not indicate that
the average tolerance level
differs significantly for
females and males.

12.

Results	Group	Rank
87	A	1.5
87	B	1.5
91	B	3
92	A	4.5
92	B	4.5
93	B	6
99	A	7.5
99	B	7.5
100	B	9
101	B	10
103	A	11
105	A	12
106	B	13
110	A	14
112	A	15.5
112	B	15.5
114	A	17.5
114	A	17.5
115	B	19
116	B	20
119	A	21
121	B	22

$n_1 = 10 \qquad n_2 = 12$

R = sum of ranks for group A
(25 year old people)
$= 1.5 + 4.5 + 7.5 + 11 + 12 + 14 + 15.5 + 17.5 + 17.5 + 21 = 122$

$\mu_R = \dfrac{10(10 + 12 + 1)}{2} = 115$

$\sigma_R = \sqrt{\dfrac{10(12)(10 + 12 + 1)}{12}}$

≈ 15.166

$z = \dfrac{122 - 115}{15.166} = +0.462$

Do not reject null hypothesis. The data do not indicate that there is a significant difference in the average results at both ages.

13.

Run	Letters
1	M
2	W
3	MM
4	WW
5	MMMM
6	WWW
7	MM
8	WW
9	M
10	W
11	M
12	WW
13	MMM

There are 13 runs where there are 14 M's and 11 W's.

Here $n_1 = 12$ and $n_2 = 11$

Do not reject null hypothesis of randomness.

14.

Before	After	Sign of Difference
147	153	+
165	160	–
182	175	–
173	168	–
177	170	–
180	175	–
162	158	–
169	161	–
175	171	–
155	150	–

There are 9 minus signs out of a possible 10 sign changes so

$$\hat{p} = \frac{9}{10} = 0.90$$

$$z = \frac{0.90 - 0.50}{\sqrt{\dfrac{0.50(1 - 0.50)}{10}}}$$

$$= \frac{0.40}{0.158} = 2.53$$

Reject null hypothesis. Stopping drinking has an effect on a person's weight.

Some people would prefer arriving at the same conclusion by using Table 14.1 since the sample size may not be large enough.

15. The median of the numbers is 31. We then have the following
sequence where a = above median and b = below median.
b,a,a,a,b,a,b,a,b,a,a,a,b,b,b,a,a,b,b,b

Run	Letters
1	b
2	aaa
3	b
4	a
5	b
6	a
7	b
8	aaa
9	bbb
10	aa
11	bbb

There are 11 runs where we have
10 a's and 10 b's.

Here $n_1 = 10$ and $n_2 = 10$

Do not reject null hypothesis of
randomness.

1.

x	y	x - y	$(x - y)^2$
7	7	0	0
2	2	0	0
9	3	6	36
8	10	-2	4
1	4	-3	9
3	6	-3	9
4	9	-5	25
6	1	5	25
10	5	5	25
5	8	-3	9
			142

$$R = 1 - \frac{6(142)}{10(10^2 - 1)} = 1 - 0.86$$

$$= 0.14$$

There is no significant correlation between the rankings of the male and female reviewers.

2.

Run	Letters
1	F
2	MM
3	FFF
4	MM
5	F
6	M
7	FFF
8	MMM
9	FFFF
10	MM
11	FFFFF

There are 11 runs where we have 17 F's and 10 M's.

Here $n_1 = 10$ and $n_2 = 17$

Do not reject null hypothesis of randomness.

3.

Score	Method	Rank
380	2	1
450	2	2
480	1	3.5
480	3	3.5
485	1	5
490	2	6
500	2	7
510	3	8
520	1	9.5
520	3	9.5
550	2	11
580	1	13
580	2	13
580	3	13
610	3	15
630	1	16
640	1	17.5
640	3	17.5

Sum of ranks for method 1:
$$R_1 = 3.5 + 5 + 9.5 + 13 + 16 + 17.5 = 64.5$$

Sum of ranks for method 2:
$$R_2 = 1 + 2 + 6 + 7 + 11 + 13 = 40$$

Sum of ranks for method 3:
$$R_3 = 3.5 + 8 + 9.5 + 13 + 15 + 17.5 = 66.5$$

Test statistic =

$$\frac{12}{18(18 + 1)}\left[\frac{64.5^2}{6} + \frac{40^2}{6} + \frac{66.5^2}{6}\right] - 3(18 + 1)$$
$$= 2.547$$

χ^2 with 2 degrees of freedom = 5.991
Do not reject null hypothesis. The data do not indicate that there is a significant difference in the scores obtained by students using any of these three programs.

4.

Prices	City	Rank
$438	N	1
444	N	2
446	L	3
451	N	4
456	N	5
459	N	6
468	N	7
469	L	8
470	N	9
476	L	10
479	L	11.5
479	N	11.5
482	N	13
484	L	14.5
484	L	14.5
487	L	16
488	N	18
488	L	18
488	L	18
493	N	20
494	L	21
498	N	22.5
498	L	22.5
499	L	24
501	L	25

$n_1 = 12$ $n_2 = 13$

R = sum of ranks for group N (New York City)

$= 1 + 2 + 4 + 5 + 6 + 7 + 9 + 11.5 + 13 + 18 + 20 + 22.5 = 119$

$\mu_R = \dfrac{12(12 + 13 + 1)}{2} = 156$

$\sigma_R = \sqrt{\dfrac{12(13)(12 + 13 + 1)}{12}}$

≈ 18.385

$z = \dfrac{119 - 156}{18.385} = -2.01$

Reject null hypothesis. The average price for the computer printer is different in both cities.

5.

Before	After	Sign of Difference
20	15	-
17	15	-
27	27	
13	16	+
14	12	-
8	6	-
12	14	+
11	9	-
17	13	-
15	11	-

There are 7 minus signs out of a possible 9 sign changes so

$$\hat{p} = \frac{7}{9} = 0.778$$

$$z = \frac{0.778 - 0.50}{\sqrt{\frac{0.50(1 - 0.50)}{9}}}$$

$$= \frac{0.278}{0.167} = 1.66$$

Do not reject null hypothesis. The data do not indicate that the medication has a significant effect on the number of tasks completed.

Some people would prefer to arrive at the same conclusion by using Table 14.1 since the sample size may not be large enough.

6. The median of the numbers is 32. We then have the following sequence where a = above median and b = below median.
b,a,a,a,a,b,b,b,a,b,b,b,b,b,a,a,a,a,a,a,a,b,b,b,b,b,a

Run	Letters
1	b
2	aaaa
3	bbb
4	a
5	bbbbb
6	aaaaaaa
7	bbbbb
8	a

There are 8 runs where we have 14 b's and 13 a's.

Here $n_1 = 13$ and $n_2 = 14$

Reject null hypothesis of randomness.

7.

Contestant	Vacation 1	Vacation 2	Sign of Difference
A	$875	$912	–
B	795	725	+
C	999	845	+
D	820	820	
E	795	880	–
F	845	1099	–
G	920	750	+
H	800	900	–
I	700	700	
J	825	865	–

There are 3 plus signs out of a possible 8 sign changes so that

$$\hat{p} = \frac{3}{8} = 0.375$$

$$z = \frac{0.375 - 0.5}{\sqrt{\frac{0.5(1 - 0.5)}{8}}} = \frac{-0.125}{0.177} = -0.706$$

Do not reject null hypothesis. The data do not indicate that there is a significant difference in the contestants estimate of the value of both vacations.

Some people would prefer to arrive at the same conclusion by using Table 14.1 since the sample size may not be large enough.

8.

Time Needed	Pollster	Rank
17	3	1
18	3	2
19	3	3
22	3	4.5
22	2	4.5
25	1	6
27	3	7
28	1	8.5
28	2	8.5
29	3	10
30	2	11
32	2	12.5
32	1	12.5
33	2	14
34	1	15
35	2	16
36	1	17
37	1	18

We use the Kruskal-Wallis H-Test.

Sum of rankings for pollster 1:
$R_1 = 6 + 8.5 + 12.5 + 15 + 17 + 18 = 77$

Sum of rankings for pollster 2:
$R_2 = 4.5 + 8.5 + 11 + 12.5 + 14 + 16 = 66.5$

Sum for rankings for pollster 3:
$R_3 = 1 + 2 + 3 + 4.5 + 7 + 10 = 27.5$

Test statistic =

$$\frac{12}{18(18 + 1)}\left[\frac{77^2}{6} + \frac{66.5^2}{6} + \frac{27.5^2}{6}\right] - 3(18 + 1)$$
$$= 7.956$$

χ^2 with 2 degrees of freedom = 5.991
Reject null hypothesis. The data do indicate that there is a significant difference in the average time needed to complete the questionnaire depending on which pollster gives the instructions.

511

9.

x	y	x - y	$(x - y)^2$
2	4	-2	4
6	3	3	9
3	6	-3	9
5	2	3	9
1	1	0	0
4	5	-1	1
			32

$$R = 1 - \frac{6(32)}{6(6^2 - 1)} = 1 - 0.914$$

$$= 0.086$$

There is no significant correlation between the rankings.

10.

Performance	Location	Rank
39	D	2
39	M	2
39	U	2
40	M	4
42	M	5
46	D	6
47	M	7.5
47	U	7.5
48	D	9
50	D	10
51	U	11
53	M	13
53	U	13
53	D	13
59	U	15
60	D	16
61	U	17
62	D	18.5
62	M	18.5
68	M	20
78	U	21

Sum of rankings for downtown D:
$R_1 = 2 + 6 + 9 + 10 + 13 + 16$
$+ 18.5 = 74.5$

Sum of rankings for midtown M:
$R_2 = 2 + 4 + 5 + 7.5 + 13$
$+ 18.5 + 20 = 70$

Sum of rankings for uptown U:
$R_3 = 2 + 7.5 + 11 + 13 + 15$
$+ 17 + 21 = 86.5$

Test statistics =

$$\frac{12}{21(21 + 1)}\left[\frac{74.5^2}{7} + \frac{70^2}{7} + \frac{86.5^2}{7}\right] - 3(21 + 1)$$
$$= 0.540$$

Do not reject null hypothesis. We cannot say that there is a significant difference in the performance evaluations.

11.

Number of Pushups	Class	Rank
21	B	1
23	A	2
26	B	3
35	A	4
38	B	5
39	A	6
40	B	7
43	B	8
45	B	9
46	A	10
47	A	11
49	A	12.5
49	B	12.5
51	B	14
52	A	15
53	A	16.5
53	B	16.5
54	B	18
58	A	19
59	B	20

$n_A = 9 \qquad n_B = 11$

R = sum of ranks for group A (Prof. Brier's class)
$= 2 + 4 + 6 + 10 + 11 + 12.5 + 15 + 16.5 + 19$
$= 96$

$\mu_R = \dfrac{9(9 + 11 + 1)}{2} = 94.5$

$\sigma_R = \sqrt{\dfrac{9(11)(9 + 11 + 1)}{12}}$

≈ 13.162

$z = \dfrac{96 - 94.5}{13.162} = 0.11$

Do not reject null hypothesis. The data do not indicate that there is a significant difference in the average number of push-ups performed by students in both classes.

12. Choice (a)

13. Choice (a)

14. Choice (b)

15. Choice (a)

16. Choice (a)

1. The ages of the 18 people applying for unemployment insurance benefits on a particular day in a city (in the order in which they applied) are as follows: 19, 23, 32, 27, 35, 26, 31, 44, 57, 48, 53, 32, 24, 29, 34, 52, 19 and 25. Test for randomness.

Answer _____

2. There are 25 people waiting in line to board an airplane. The order in which they are lined up (where M = male and F = female) is as follows:

F F F F M M F F M F M M M M F M F F M M M F M F F

Test for randomness.

Answer _____

3. Eleven male students and twelve female students were asked to assemble a puzzle. The number of minutes needed by each student to assemble the puzzle is as follows:

Female	38	44	29	57	41	36	53	42	40	54	50	
Male	43	37	55	45	48	59	34	39	51	49	56	58

Using the rank-sum test, test the null hypothesis (at the 5% level of significance) that the mean number of minutes needed by both groups is not significantly different.

Answer _____

4. A circus performer trained two different groups of animals to perform a particular act. The performer used different teaching techniques. The following chart indicates the number of practice sessions needed by each of the animals to learn the act:

Group A	36	28	19	25	42	33	21	40	35	30	
Group B	27	29	31	26	39	34	32	43	18	37	38

Using the rank-sum test, test the null hypothesis (at the 5% level of significance) that the mean number of practice sessions is not significantly different for both groups.

Answer _____

5. A certain weight-reducing technique produced the following results for 10 people.

Weight before	132	147	153	179	182	158	147	180	193	175
Weight after	128	146	154	179	169	150	149	175	185	170

Using the sign test, test the null hypothesis (at the 5% level of significance) that there is no significant difference in weight changes as a result of this weight-reducing technique.

Answer _____

6. The blood serum cholesterol level of ten men both before and after taking an experimental drug was as follows:

Before taking drug	280	275	291	338	261	240	223	257	298	302
After taking drug	263	260	273	281	263	251	247	257	276	295

Using the sign test, test the null hypothesis (at the 5% level of significance) that the experimental drug does not significantly affect the blood serum cholesterol level of an individual.

Answer _____

7. Three movie reviewers were asked to rate six different movies that they had seen during the year. Their ratings are as follows:

	Reviewer 1	Reviewer 2	Reviewer 3
Movie A	1	3	5
Movie B	4	4	1
Movie C	3	1	6
Movie D	6	5	2
Movie E	2	6	4
Movie F	5	2	3

Using a 5% level of significance, test the null hypothesis that there is no significant correlation between the ratings of Reviewer 1 and Reviewer 2.

Answer _____

8. Refer back to the previous question. Test the null hypothesis (at the 5% level of significance) that there is no significant correlation between the ratings of Reviewer 1 and Reviewer 3.

Answer _____

9. Refer back to question 7. Test the null hypothesis (at the 5% level of significance) that there is no significant correlation between the ratings of Reviewer 2 and Reviewer 3.

Answer _____

10. The number of patients treated (on a daily basis) in the emergency room of Beaver Hospital during February was as follows:
38, 27, 29, 17, 39, 47, 53, 23, 32, 38, 51, 46, 25, 41, 37, 40, 29, 28, 19, 33, 40, 44, 50, 30, 18, 24, 29, 32.
Test for randomness.

Answer _____

1. The ages of the first 25 people registering their car at Motor Vehicle Bureau on January 25, 1988 (in the order in which they registered) are as follows: 31, 23, 27, 41, 33, 59, 47, 35, 46, 40, 19, 21, 22, 30, 29, 18, 24, 36, 38, 29, 28, 25, 32, 24, 37.
Test for randomness.

Answer _____

2. Refer back to the previous question. The sex of the 25 people registering their car was as follows (where M = male and F = female):

F F F M F M F F F F M M M M M F M M M F M M F F M

Test for randomness.

Answer _____

3. The following data are available on the number of delayed flights (on a monthly basis) for two airlines. For airline A, data are available for 11 months only.

Airline A	26	30	31	35	27	28	38	24	32	37	39
Airline B	34	23	14	21	33	16	25	29	36	22	19	20

Using the rank-sum test, test the null hypothesis (at the 5% level of significance) that the mean number of delayed flights is not significantly different for both airlines.

Answer _____

4. Two groups of mechanics where trained by the manufacturer using different teaching techniques on how to satisfactorily service a particular auto part. The number of minutes needed by each mechanic (after training) to service the part satisfactorily is as follows:

Group A	56	50	42	39	53	54	47	38	48	43
Group B	35	55	51	57	41	46	52	59	44	49	40	45

Using the rank-sum test, test the null hypothesis (at the 5% level of significance) that the mean number of minutes needed to service the part satisfactorily is not significantly different for both groups.

Answer _____

5. An experimental triglyceride-reducing pill was given to 10 people. The following triglyceride levels were obtained:

Triglyceride level before	132	147	120	131	99	84	103	109	123	148
Triglyceride level after	130	140	123	139	99	81	104	100	110	128

Using the sign test, test the null hypothesis (at the 5% level of significance) that there is no significant difference in the triglyceride level of a person as a result of using this pill.

Answer _____

6. The pulse rate of 10 people both before and after seeing a particularly gruesome scene was as follows:

Before	74	68	71	75	70	79	76	73	81	80
After	76	62	62	68	70	72	71	70	70	81

Using the sign test, test the null hypothesis (at the 5% level of significance) that the gruesome scene does not significantly affect the person's pulse rate.

Answer _____

7. Six candidates (Bob, Paul, Sue, Kim, Dave, and Dale) at a college are being ranked by the President, Vice President and Dean for promotion opportunities. Their rankings are as follows:

President	Vice President	Dean
Bob	Dave	Dale
Sue	Kim	Kim
Kim	Sue	Sue
Dale	Paul	Paul
Paul	Bob	Dave
Dave	Dale	Bob

Using a 5% level of significance, test the null hypothesis that there is no significant correlation between the President's and the Vice President's rankings.

Answer _____

519

8. Refer to the previous question. Test the null hypothesis (at the 5% level of significance) that there is no significant correlation between the President's and the Dean's rankings.

Answer _____

9. Refer back to question 7. Test the null hypothesis (at the 5% level of significance) that there is no significant correlation between the Vice President's and the Dean's rankings.

Answer _____

10. The number of daily calls for emergency road assistance to a local AAA club during February was as follows:
    21 26 60 65 44 41 33 30 24 65 45 39 55 34 29 20
    32 34 48 50 23 51 46 49 31 39 40 33
    Test for randomness.

Answer _____

1. The ages of the first 20 workers to enter a Wall Street brokerage office (in the order in which they entered) are as follows: 22, 26, 34, 29, 38, 21, 47, 59, 49, 57, 50, 40, 53, 39, 44, 51, 62, 27, 20, 49.
   Test for randomness.

   Answer _____

2. Refer back to the previous question. The sex of these workers was as follows (where M = male and F = female):
   F F F M F F M M M M M F M F M F F M M F
   Test for randomness.

   Answer _____

3. The following data are available on the number of canceled appointments (on a monthly basis) for 2 dentists. For Dr. Kok, data are available for 11 months only.

Dr. Kok	20	18	21	30	23	28	34	24	29	37	31	
Dr. Blau	26	16	40	35	22	19	17	25	33	39	36	38

   Using the rank-sum test, test the null hypothesis (at the 5% level of significance) that the mean number of canceled appointments is not significantly different for both dentists.

   Answer _____

4. Two groups of dogs were trained by two different trainers to perform a difficult task. The following chart indicates the number of practice sessions needed by each of the dogs before mastering the task.

Group A	31	40	27	19	21	30	38	25	20	34	41	
Group B	35	28	39	32	33	42	26	24	29	36	37	43

   Using the rank-sum test, test the null hypothesis (at the 5% level of significance) that the mean number of practice sessions is not significantly different for both groups.

   Answer _____

5. A certain muscle-building technique produced the following results (on a particular scale) for 10 people:

Before	73	64	82	69	71	75	78	68	75	81
After	70	71	82	75	77	78	79	69	76	84

Using the sign test, test the null hypothesis (at the 5% level of significance) that there is no significant difference in the muscle strength of an individual as a result of using this technique.

Answer _____

6. The blood pressure of 11 people both before and after viewing a particular horror movie was as follows:

Before	130	140	132	128	156	129	132	137	120	127	128
After	137	141	132	124	148	135	134	139	125	135	142

Using the sign test, test the null hypothesis (at the 5% level of significance) that seeing the horror movie does not affect the person's blood pressure.

Answer _____

7. Six candidates (Pete, Debbie, Jane, Sherry, Jean, and Roy) in a bank are being ranked by the President, Vice President and Treasurer for possible advancement. Their rankings are as follows:

President	Vice President	Treasurer
Debbie	Sherry	Jean
Jane	Jane	Roy
Jean	Jean	Debbie
Roy	Pete	Jane
Pete	Debbie	Pete
Sherry	Roy	Sherry

Using a 5% level of significance, test the null hypothesis that there is no significant correlation between the President's and Vice President's rankings.

Answer _____

8. Refer back to the previous question. Test the null hypothesis (at the 5% level of significance) that is no significant correlation between the President's and the Treasurer's rankings.

9. Refer back to question 7. Test the null hypothesis (at the 5% level of significance) that is no significant correlation between the Vice President's and the Treasurer's rankings.

10. The number of credit card sales (on a daily basis) at Rochelle's Department store during February was as follows: 68, 39, 53, 47, 69, 57, 61, 29, 30, 38, 31, 35, 46, 52, 28, 56, 49, 37, 71, 64, 62, 26, 25, 32, 33, 48, 44, 36. Test for randomness.

ANSWERS TO SUPPLEMENTARY TESTS
CHAPTER 14 - NONPARAMETRIC STATISTICS

Form A

1. Random   2. Random   3. Do not reject null hypothesis 4. Do not reject null hypothesis   5. Do not reject null hypothesis   6. Do not reject null hypothesis   7. No significant correlation 8. No significant correlation 9. No significant correlation 10. Random

Form B

1. Random   2. Random   3. Reject null hypothesis   4. Do not reject null hypothesis   5. Do not reject null hypothesis 6. Do not reject null hypothesis   7. No significant correlation 8. No significant correlation 9. No significant correlation 10. Random

Form C

1. Random   2. Random   3. Do not reject null hypothesis   4. Do not reject null hypothesis   5. Reject null hypothesis 6. Do not reject null hypothesis   7. No significant correlation 8. No significant correlation 9. No significant correlation 10. Random